Selected Papers on the
History of Psychology

R. I. Watson's Selected Papers on the History of Psychology

Edited by

Josef Brožek and Rand B. Evans

Published by the University of New Hampshire
Distributed by the University Press of New England
Hanover, New Hampshire 1977

Copyright © 1977 by Trustees of the University of New Hampshire

All rights reserved

Library of Congress Catalogue Card Number 76-11675
International Standard Book Number 0-87451-130-5
Printed in the United States of America

Permission for republication of journal articles has been granted by *Isis, Journal of the History of the Behavioral Sciences,* and *Neuropsychiatry,* and by Reidel, of Holland.

Frontispiece photograph courtesy of University of New Hampshire Media Services.

Contents

Introduction by Josef Brožek and Rand B. Evans   vii
Autobiography   3

Part I. Organizational Development of American Historiography of Psychology
1. The History of Psychology: A Neglected Area   25
2. The Role and Use of History in the Psychology Curriculum   34
3. A Note on the History of Psychology as a Specialization   43
4. The Birth of a Journal   46
5. Editorial Policy and Its Implementation   49
6. Recent Developments in the Historiography of American Psychology   51
7. The History of Psychology as a Specialty: A Personal View of Its First Fifteen Years   61
8. The Organization and Preservation of Personal Papers   74

Part II. Multidimensional Framework of the History of Psychology
9. The Historical Background for National Trends in Psychology: The United States   83
10. Psychology: A Prescriptive Science   95
11. Prescriptions as Operative in the History of Psychology   113
12. Prescriptive Theory and the Social Sciences   130
13. A Prescriptive Analysis of Descartes' Psychological Views   156

Part III. Fields and Selected Aspects of Psychology
14. A Brief History of Clinical Psychology   195
15. Progress in Orthopsychiatry: Psychology   230
16. Historical Review of Objective Personality Testing: The Search for Objectivity   254

17. Historical Perspectives on the Relationship of Psychologists to Medical Research   276
18. The Experimental Tradition and Clinical Psychology   284
19. The Individual, Social-Educational, Economic, and Political Conditions for the Original Practices of Detection and Utilization of Individual Aptitude Differences   308

Part IV. Eminent Psychologists

20. Important Psychologists, 1600–1967   327
21. Characteristics of Individuals Eminent in Psychology in Temporal Perspective   338
22. Classification of Eminent Contributors to Psychology, 1600–1967, According to Nationality, Field, Date of Birth, and Eminence Score   352

Bibliography of the Writings of Robert I. Watson   368
Index of Names   375
Index of Subjects   387

Introduction by Josef Brožek and Rand B. Evans

In the development of the historiography of psychology in the United States, R. I. Watson occupies a place of distinction as organizer, teacher, editor, and author.

When the editors of *Contemporary Psychology* were introducing Watson as coeditor of a volume of selected papers by E. G. Boring (Carmichael, 1964), they wrote: "Watson holds a Ph.D. from Columbia, has had an active career in clinical psychology, is well known for his contributions to personality theory and the history of psychology and is now at Northwestern." This vignette needs two addenda: (1) in the 1960s and 1970s Watson focused his attention on the history of psychology; (2) in 1967 he moved to the University of New Hampshire, with history of psychology as his primary area of responsibility.

The purpose of the present volume is to make available, between two covers, Watson's journal articles devoted to this area. They are preceded by the author's autobiography.

The materials are arranged in five sections:
I. Autobiography;
II. Organizational Development of American Historiography of Psychology;
III. Multidimensional Framework of the History of Psychology;
IV. Fields and Selected Aspects of Psychology;
V. Eminent Psychologists.

At Watson's suggestion, we left out notes and some other minor publications. Economy of space dictated the omission of a joint report on the first Summer Institute on the History of Psychology for College Teachers (Brožek, Watson, and Ross, 1969, 1970).

EMERGENCE OF HISTORIOGRAPHY OF PSYCHOLOGY AS A SPECIALTY

Hermann Ebbinghaus once said that psychology has had a long past but only a short history. That statement applies not only to psychology as a discipline but to the historiography of psychology as well. Writings on the history of psychology go back to Aristotle. In the twentieth century, Klemm's *Geschichte der Psychologie* appeared in 1911, Brett's *A History of Psychology* in the 1920's, Murphy's *Historical Introduction to Modern Psychology* in 1929, and Heidbreder's *Seven Psychologies* in 1932. The most erudite and influential volume on the history of psychology, produced during the 1920's, was E. G. Boring's *A History of Experimental Psychology*, which first appeared in 1929. Many authors shared the attitude that their involvement in the history of psychology was only a passing phase in their careers. Boring was one of the first to break away from this view, although he was unable to free himself from it entirely. At first, he tells us, he was surprised to find that so many people would buy a book on the history of psychology. Later, however, he came to think of himself more and more as a historian of psychology. In some ways Boring stands in relationship to American historiography of psychology as Fechner did to the founding of experimental psychology. He demonstrated that the thing could be done, that it was worth the effort, and that certain conceptual tools could be applied to the task. At the same time, he looked on the history of psychology as the work of "elder statesmen," subscribing to E. B. Titchener's axiom that scientists as they age turn either toward application or to the history and philosophy of their field. The history of psychology needed someone to fill the organizational role. Robert I. Watson made important contributions to the field in this capacity.

Watson tells us in his autobiography how he was influenced by public response to some of his early historical articles to move away from his career in clinical psychology toward the neglected field of history of psychology. He discovered that others were working in the field, isolated from each other and often finding their work unappreciated by academic administrators. In 1960, Watson, along with a few others, began to take steps that would lead to legitimizing the concern with history of psychology as a specialization within academic psychology. The first step was to point out how little had been done in the field and, by implication, how much needed to be done. This he accomplished with an article, "The History of Psychology: A Neglected Area," published in the widely read *American Psychologist*. Later articles, "The Role and Use of History in the Psychology Curriculum" and "A Note on the History of Psychology as a Specialization," further emphasized and consolidated that position.

Two other events in 1960 were of particular significance to the institutionalization of the history of psychology. The History of Psychology Interest Group, established at the American Psychological Association meeting in St. Louis, was transformed five years later into Division 26 (History of Psychology) of the APA. The other important event, spearheaded by Watson in 1960, was the establishment of a newsletter concerned with current work in the history of psychology. It was the predecessor of the *Journal of the History of the Behavioral Sciences*, founded in 1965. These organizational efforts contributed substantially to the vitality and success of the study of the history of psychology in the United States.

In 1967 Watson established, at the University of New Hampshire, a doctoral program in the history of psychology. The program has been the primary source of Ph.D.-level specialists in the history of psychology. Watson's imprint can be seen clearly in the work of his students. He had an important share in laying the foundation on which scholars of the future can build.

Among the other organizational and professional contributions made by Watson one cannot neglect his cooperation with Joseph Brožek in the first National Science Foundation Summer Institute, held in Durham, New Hampshire, in 1968. Personal and professional interaction at that Institute has had a profound impact on the development of this field. It was here that the idea was born to organize an International Society for the History of the Behavioral and Social Sciences, known as the Cheiron Society. More interdisciplinary than APA's Division 26, Cheiron has had a broadening influence on historians of psychology.

HISTORIOGRAPHY'S MULTIDIMENSIONAL CONCEPTUAL FRAMEWORK

The approach commonly called prescriptive theory has two major functions: as an analytical tool, to describe the way scientists have looked at their field; and as a theoretical model, to explain the attitudinal basis of scientific work.

The concept of prescriptions was developed by Watson in response to T. S. Kuhn's views, formulated in *Structure of Scientific Revolutions*, on the nature of scientific paradigms. Kuhn held that social sciences, including psychology, had no paradigm, no "contentual model, universally accepted by practitioners of a science at a particular temporal period in its development." Watson agreed that psychology was preparadigmatic but wondered how one is able to describe and understand the operation of concepts which, although not universally accepted, guide a significant part of the field over a relatively long period of time. "What seems to be required," he argued, "is some form of trends or themes, numerous enough to deal with the complexity of psychology yet not so numerous as to render each of them only narrowly meaningful." Toward this end, Watson proposed 18 opposing conceptual dimensions as the framework of historiography.

There are several similarities between prescriptions and *Zeitgeist* as used by Boring; but prescriptions are explicit, while *Zeitgeist* is often vague. Prescriptions facilitate detailed analysis of schools of psychology, individual theoretical or methodological positions, and the scientific climate of a given time or country. They constitute a new analytical tool, reasonably objective and quantifiable, which allows the historian to describe and compare conceptual positions. Watson first mentioned prescriptions in "The Historical Background for National Trends in Psychology: United States," delivered before the XVIIth International Congress of Psychology in 1963. Here he used prescriptions almost entirely as a descriptive device in an attempt to analyze the salient characteristics of American psychology. In "Psychology: A Prescriptive Science," published in 1967, Watson still presents prescriptions in their primarily descriptive aspect but he also introduces a "directive-orientative function": these prescriptions "were and are part of the intellectual equipment of psychologists." As such they act as sets or habits of thought, and determine how a particular scientist goes about his work—what he rejects and what he accepts. Watson's projected history of psychology, based on prescriptive principles, will be a testing stone for evaluating the role of prescriptive analysis in historiography.

MAJOR WORKS

The entries in the present volume are limited to shorter contributions. Any attempt to assess Watson's writings on the history of psychology, however, must give due consideration to his book-length publications.

It happens that all of Watson's books in this area are tied, although in very different ways, to Harvard's E. G. Boring (1886–1968). *The Great Psychologists*, first published in 1963, is dedicated "To E. G. B. my teacher, under whom I have never studied." The second volume contains a collection of Boring's papers, edited jointly with D. T. Campbell (Watson and Campbell 1963). The *Eminent Contributors of Psychology* (1974, Vol. 1) grew out of Watson's collaboration with Boring.

The Great Psychologists. It is not surprising that the author of *The Clinical Method of Psychology* would choose to approach the history of science in terms of *persons* (cf. Brožek, 1965). A chronological sequence of the lives and works of "great men" provides a built-in organizational structure that is easy to follow both for the writer and for the reader.

Portraits of the history of psychology differ importantly depending on the way one defines psychology. Watson's scope is broad. He writes a history of the science of human experience and of behavior, not of experimental psychology alone. The span of time covered in the book stretches from the Greek thinkers to psychoanalysis. Furthermore, Watson welcomes into the fold such great "psychologists by adoption" as Darwin, Helmholtz, Galton, and Pavlov.

The epilogue, entitled "Just Yesterday" and dealing with recent developments, shifts from men to trends (behaviorism and operationism, gestalt influence, psychoanalysis) and geographical areas (United States, Europe).

The second edition (1968) adds a separate chapter on "Psychology until 1945." The epilogue "Just Yesterday" is retained, but it has been largely rewritten and contains sections on national trends (Continental Europe, Great Britain, Soviet Union, Japan, United States), international enterprises, theoretical currents (including the humanistic strain, the existential approach, the phenomenological method and theory, and neo-behaviorism), and on research in different fields of psychology (physiological, engineering, social, child, animal), and specific topics (sensory processes, perception, learning, maturation, intelligence, cognition, thinking and communication, personality). The third edition is a paperback reprint of the second revised and enlarged edition.

A Collection of Boring's Papers. Historians of psychology and psychologists in general owe a debt of thanks to R. I. Watson and D. T. Campbell (1963) for bringing out E. G. Boring's *History, Psychology, and Science: Selected Papers.* The volume contains the Editors' Foreword and informative introductions to each of the five sections into which the volume was divided: (1) The Zeitgeist and the Psychology of Science; (2) The History of Psychology; (3) The Scientific Method; (4) The Mind-Body Problem; (5) The Psychology of Communicating Science.

Eminent Contributors of Psychology. The aim of this work was to provide selected primary references to the publications of some 500 eminent contributors to psychology living between 1600 and 1967. The actual number of individuals is 538. Of these, 228 are identified primarily with psychology; the remaining 310 were identified with biomedical sciences (103), philosophy (92), psychiatry and psychoanalysis (55), anthropology and sociology (20), and other fields (40). In terms of language or geography, 178 individuals were identified as German-speaking (or at least German-writing), 163 as American, 86 British (English, Scottish), 79 French-speaking, and 32 other.

The initial list of potential candidates, prepared by E. G. Boring and R. I. Watson, included 1040 names. They were rated by a panel of nine prominent psychologists on a 4-point rating scale (0 = not known to the rater, 1 = recognized, 2 = person's contribution could be identified, 3 = person's contribution to psychology was considered important). The sum of the scores assigned by the panelists constituted each individual's overall score. The top 538 individuals attained or exceeded a score of 11.

Criteria for selecting the works cited are described and the actual process of collecting and verifying the references is indicated. In about 70 percent of the cases it was feasible to obtain the bibliographical data by examining the publications directly. References to publications not examined directly were verified using a variety of sources of information.

The editor sought and received advice on the publications of 349 eminent contributors from 239 specialists. Over the years of work on this project, valuable help was provided by the graduate and undergraduate students at the University of New Hampshire.

Inescapably, occasional details will require correction, and some references will need to be added while others may be deleted. Nevertheless, the volume constitutes a reference work of lasting merit, selective in nature and covering the whole period of modern psychology. We have had numerous opportunities to confirm Watson's hope that the book would make work in the history of behavioral sciences "a shade more convenient to do" (p. x).

In preparation is the second volume of the bibliography containing references to the literature about the authors whose selected works are listed in Volume I.

On the horizon is a systematic history of psychology based on Watson's concept of "prescriptions."

Joseph Brožek
June 1977
Rand B. Evans

REFERENCES

Brožek, J., R. I. Watson, and Barbara Ross. A Summer Institute on the History of Psychology, Parts I and II. *Journal of the History of the Behavioral Sciences*, 1969, *5*, 307-319, 1970, *6*, 25-35.

Brožek, J. Review of R. I. Watson's "The Great Psychologists: From Aristotle to Freud," *Journal of the History of the Behavioral Sciences*, 1965, *1*, 292-294.

Carmichael, L. Review of E. G. Boring's *History, Psychology, and Science: Selected Papers*, ed. R. I. Watson and D. T. Campbell. *Contemporary Psychology*, 1964, *9*, 305-306.

Kuhn, T. S. *The Structure of Scientific Revolutions*. Chicago, University of Chicago Press, 1962.

Watson, R. I. *The Great Psychologists from Aristotle to Freud*. Philadelphia: Lippincott, 1963; 2nd ed., 1968; 3rd (paperback) ed., 1971.

Watson, R. I. *Eminent Contributors to Psychology. Vol. 1. A Bibliography of Primary References*. New York: Singer Publishing Company, 1974.

Watson, R. I., and D. T. Campbell (Eds.). E.G. Boring, *History, Psychology, and Science: Selected Papers*. New York: Wiley, 1963.

Selected Papers on the History of Psychology

Autobiography

Methodological Note. After I had given in to my vanity and agreed to write an autobiography, several months elapsed before I saw clearly how to proceed. During this period of groping I found myself again remembering a variety of past experiences—recurrent memories that were already part of my subjective life. I decided that I might take advantage of this "spontaneous" recall.

This was all the more congenial because of my particular, and what to many would be atrocious, work habits. All of my books and most of my articles were written by a "scrap method." That is to say, I have long followed the habit of jotting down whatever occurred to me in connection with whatever I was working on whether this resulted in a sentence, a paragraph, or a page, then classifying it, by major category, and filing it away in one of many folders, the classification for which emerged as the work proceeded. More often than not, to my still recurring surprise, the "stuff" seemed to fit together at least for a first draft.

Why not, I reasoned, use precisely this technique for an autobiography? I resolved to record these recurrent memories that must in one way or another be significant even though my interpretation of them might be riddled with rationalization and self-deception. Further, after getting them down on paper, I resolved to try as best I could to see that I did not later polish to deceive.

When I was fifteen I decided to become a bridge-tender. I was already a high-school dropout, so any occupation at a higher level seemed to be out of the question. As I saw it, the work consisted of a few minutes' furious activity followed by much longer periods of inactivity. The "guided reading" of high school and college was not for me except for a half-day a week in continuation school required of each individual under sixteen having so-called "working papers" so he would not slip back into illiteracy.

Fifteen is the age when reading is obsessive and all literature new. As I saw it, I could use these blessed periods of freedom for reading—reading anything and everything. To this very day, I cannot but feel that the one sure sign of the progress of civilization is that we have libraries from which books may be borrowed free. One habit was established at this age—keeping lists and evaluative notes on what I read. My isolation from sources of guidance other than my own may have instigated this habit, but, as Allport has said, habits become autonomous, and my current predilection for drawing up various lists of references was launched.

I never did get to be a bridge-tender. My first job was as mail boy with a large manufacturer of cotton thread located in one of the industrial towns of northeastern New Jersey. When reaching sixteen, however, I escaped to the beginning of a white-collar career, although at first still functioning as a mail boy. This was with one of the nation's largest insurance corporations in Newark, New Jersey, where after six months I became a very junior clerk, a position I held for about four more years. Although the pay was meager, the hours were relatively short and I managed to indulge my interest in reading and in music via the radio and a few precious records.

A high-school diploma was out of the question but there was an alternative. By a semester or two of cram courses at night I managed to pass enough of the New Jersey regents course examinations to secure the "equivalent" of a high-school diploma. Naturally, I selected the examinations each easiest to master by reading a book. English, history, and something called economic geography were prominent. Three weaknesses thereby began. I was deficient then and now in mathematics and in the natural sciences and I have only partially overcome a weakness in foreign languages.

A minor miracle then occurred. In its wisdom, the state of New Jersey decided that at least two years of college would be necessary before one could attend a law school within its boundaries. It so happened that New Jersey Law School, located in Newark, was the very profitable private property of an individual. So as not to interfere with the flow of new students, the owner decided to inaugurate a program of two years of college study under the severely pedestrian name of New Jersey Law School Pre-legal Department. Since by now we were in the first year of the Depression, the night courses were quite popular. I entered the second class accepted at this fledgling institution and took courses for two years. Despite its somewhat grimy location in a converted brewery, the student body and faculty created a very intellectually stimulating environment.

The faculty was young and enthusiastic. Although they maintained a cynical façade it was not too hard to see that many of them saw it as a bold venture with glorious possibilities. True, there were more than the expected share of "flawed" individuals, those fired from other jobs, restless academic wanderers, and A B D's aplenty, but for a while at least they worked together.

The academic program was severely limited at first. Of the sciences only geology was taught. There were no courses in languages or mathematics, so the social sciences and English dominated the curriculum. Fortunately for me, psychology was offered in the first year. Up to this time the only book that I had read on the subject was a very very dull volume by Henry J. Watt in some English self-improvement series. My first teacher was Frederick J. Gaudet, who some years later transferred to Stevens Institute of Technology in Hoboken, from which he has recently retired. Brilliant, suave, and the epitome of a sophisticated academician, he made a deep impression on me and I decided, then and there, that I would make psychology my career. I had not come to the Pre-legal Department with a firm conviction that I wanted to be a lawyer—I had merely seen it as the only way to a professional career of any sort. Perhaps prophetic of what later happened, the subject which I found next most interesting was history. The second member of the Psychology Department, Charles Webster St. John, had taken his degree at Clark University. Through his help, I secured a scholarship to go to Worcester for my junior year. This was the Clark that still had in its department Walter Hunter and Carl Murchison. However, most undergraduate courses were taught by Vernon Jones and John Paul Nafe, one of Titchener's last Ph.D.'s. During that year I took French, German, experimental psychology, and modern history which, by then, was my official minor. The course in experimental involved our moving through Titchener's qualitative manual. Years later, this experience would become important, because when I came to Washington University to help found their clinical psychology training program, Professor Nafe, then chairman at Washington, was more receptive to my appearance than he would have been to another because, as he put it, "any clinical psychologist who went through Titchener's manual could not be entirely lost to psychology."

The summer after my Clark year I joined a group of graduate students from Clark who were working in what is now Marlboro State Hospital in Marlboro, New Jersey. With no guidance and little rationale, except a vague feeling that personal attention was essential, each of us worked 'round the clock with small groups of deteriorated schizophrenics. Since this was in the mid-thirties, this must have been one of the pioneer attempts at intensive reaching out to these patients. But nothing came of it.

Since I have not saved enough money, I could not return to Clark that fall even with a Jonas G. Clark scholarship and instead stayed on for a year at the hospital as an attendant. By then New Jersey Pre-legal Department had metamorphosed into Dana College and offered a four-year college degree. I returned home therefore and went to school for my senior year at Dana and graduated in its first class. Our Commencement speaker was Norman Thomas, and I, as salutatorian, also spoke. As I remember it, my talk was the more pessimistic of the two.

During my senior year Professor St. John had become ill and I began to teach his classes. Since he did not return, what was meant to be a week or two stretched on over five years. Only a year or two older than my students I did the only thing I could think of to increase my age and dignity—I grew a mustache.

Fortunately for me, Columbia University's laissez-faire policy concerning its graduate students extended to the point that practically anyone with minimum qualifications would be allowed to enter. My problem, of course, was that I did not even meet those qualifications since I came from the first graduating class of an unaccredited institution. As it was, I was first accepted only as a special student.

The focal point of the first-year graduate program was the course by Robert Woodworth in systematic psychology. For convenience's sake it was taught in the evening and consequently all first-year graduate students took this course at this time. About fifty graduate students were in this course. Five of us finished with a Ph.D., although in varying years. I went through the usual offerings —Poffenberger for physiological, Garrett for statistics, Landis for abnormal, Murphy for social, Warden for comparative. I also did some work in anthropology, studying with Franz Boas and Ruth Benedict.

I did venture across that "widest street in the world" to Teachers College to take Rudolf Pintner's course in intelligence testing, only to have academic credit refused on the grounds that it was inappropriate to my degree.

The staff-student research seminars were a tremendous source of stimulation to graduate students. Here it was Professor Woodworth who made the deepest impression. It was the catholicity of his knowledge which then seemed to us to cover all of psychology, his reasoned judgments, expressed firmly and yet gently, that awed us.

Many of the professors were relatively unapproachable. This was not the case with Carl J. Warden who, during the years with which I am familiar at Columbia, attracted a large and profoundly heterogeneous group of students—ostensibly to work in comparative psychology—which actually included such individuals (in the years just ahead of me) as Meredith Crawford, Bob Thorndike, and Ted Reiss. In general, the atmosphere of the department bred heterogeneity that might be further illustrated by the fact that my best friends as students were Saul Sells and Joe Stone. All of us have gone on to quite different careers.

My dissertation was based on material obtained from my teaching at what by then was the University of Newark. It involved retesting undergraduates for their knowledge of elementary psychology with groups extending over a five-year period. Since I was teaching full time, it took me five years to complete the Ph.D., which was achieved in June 1938. Before then I had begun looking for a job.

A more unpleasant facet of Columbia's laissez-faire policy now came into prominence. Almost to a man, when old grads of Columbia of those years gather they revert to what surely is their major complaint about their graduate school days—the casual disinterest on the part of the faculty in our placement. Our favorite illustration of how it should have been done was the Yale Department of Psychology, whose members were seen as working hard at strategic placement of their graduates.

As any provincial New Yorker would, I concentrated on finding an appointment within the city limits or, at the worst, within commuting distance. I was interviewed at such diverse places as Bard College and Brooklyn College, but the worst happened and I was a failure the day I received my degree because the only job I could find was at the University of Idaho, Southern Branch, in Pocatello.

In many ways my two and a half years in Idaho were interesting and rewarding, although the outdoor aspects of life there—the hiking, hunting, and fishing—were completely ignored. The nearest city of any importance was Salt Lake City, some 185 miles away. Boise, the capital, was over two hundred miles away and the main campus of the university in Moscow (whose name produced the usual jokes about from whom one was taking orders) was over five hundred miles and relatively inaccessible to boot. The social geography created a situation that led me into a variety of clinical activities for which I was not prepared. For example, Mooseheart, the home for orphaned children of members of the Order of the Moose, requires intelligence testing before a child is accepted—and I was to carry out the testing. Although I had taken Pintner's course in intelligence testing, I had had no practical experience. It came down to this: at least I was no worse prepared than anyone else in a neighborhood of two hundred square miles. So, quite unexpectedly I had to teach myself something about clinical procedures and to begin a small therapeutic practice. Although it probably resulted in considerable misinformation, I remember slaving over the Rorschach manual then available only in German! Of course, most of my time was taken with the more customary activities of teaching introductory, abnormal, and experimental psychology. One of my earlier publications was a laboratory manual for use in this last course; it was called quite deliberately *Manual of Standard Experiments in Psychology* and was designed so as to use the least expensive equipment obtainable.

My experiences in Idaho were important for other reasons. I met and collaborated with Vivian E. Fisher, a pioneer psychologist-psychotherapist. It was through him that I arranged to spend a summer as research associate at Idaho State Hospital in Blackfoot. Out of this relationship came a series of articles concerned with the meaning and measurement of so-called "affective tolerance." We collaborated on two papers and in publishing the inventory, and I continued this work for a series of three or four more papers that appeared during the years thereafter.

When the opportunity came in February 1941 to accept appointment in the Student Counseling Bureau of the College of the City of New York, I seized it quickly. Not only did I increase my salary almost 50 percent (from $2200 to $3000) but I was still enough of a city person to think that I was returning to civilization.

In December 1941 I applied for a commission in the United States Naval Reserve. I went on active duty in May 1942 and started immediately to evaluate would-be naval aviation cadets. Except for the longer hours and wearing a uniform, there was no immediate change in my style of life. I simply took the same train from the New Jersey suburbs and then the Hoboken ferry, but downtown instead of uptown. I had not a single moment of indoctrination, then or later. For this small favor I am grateful, although possibly it did leave me more readily thinking as a civilian in uniform. Although on active duty for three years, eleven months, and twenty days, I marched in formation only once and I never took the obligatory weekly physical exercises. A certain amount of small shrewdness and petty adroit maneuvering must be acknowledged.

During the first two years on active duty I was concerned with aviation cadet selection. By then, psychologists were being more and more used in connection with many other aspects of Navy life. I heard unofficially I was being sent to "Siberia," an outlying field of Corpus Christi Naval Air Station located on the vastness of the King Ranch. (Why I was to land there is irrelevant to the story.) I carried out some unofficial negotiations and arranged to transfer to the neuropsychiatric service, which resulted in a billet at the Bainbridge Naval Training Center, Bainbridge, Maryland. Here my primary task was on the receiving line, where I gave a one-minute psychiatric–psychological examination consisting of three or four key questions and an immediate decision to investigate further or to let events take their course. The remainder of my time was taken with some in-depth examinations of an hour or two, and sitting on boards which decided whether a recruit would go on to service or return to civilian life.

For the first time since going on active duty I had some leisure that could be devoted to more general psychological activity. The only reading resource, however, was a substantial run of issues of the *Psychological Abstracts*. Since I had to make do with what I had, I decided that I would begin to compile a bibliography preparatory to what proved to be my first two books in clinical psychology. Another officer attached at that time to Bainbridge was Chauncey M. Louttit, who generously encouraged me in this endeavor. I say "generously" because at the time his was the only available book in the field and therefore I was a potential competitor.

As the end of the war approached, my thoughts naturally turned to finding a civilian occupation again. After two or three leaves in order to investigate possibilities I accepted appointment as director of the Bureau of Measurement and Guidance and an assistant professorship in the Department of Psychology of Carnegie Institute of Technology, Pittsburgh. This opening came about because Laurance Shaffer had decided to go to Teachers College, Columbia. As anyone who knows Shaffer will understand, I found the bureau a thoroughly organized and efficient activity. I continued working in counseling activities and teaching the usual array of undergraduate courses appropriate to my interest and experience.

One day early in 1947 I received an unexpected visitor in the person of Edwin F. Gildae, head of the Department of Neuropsychiatry of Washington University School of Medicine, St. Louis. He dropped in to inquire if I would be interested in appointment in his department as a psychologist responsible for the Division of Medical Psychology and to work in the dean's office, replacing Carylye Jacobson. I spent the next five years as assistant dean of the medical school and associate professor of medical psychology.

My duties as assistant dean can be put very succinctly—I selected medical students and then, once they were enrolled, served as their adviser and, of course, in the process, defended my judgment of them. For the freshmen students I was charged with the responsibility of offering a course in medical psychology. I cannot say that I was very happy with the results, although perhaps part of my sense of frustration came about because in the scheme of things this course was allotted twelve out of approximately twelve hundred class hours, leaving a rather overwhelming majority of the hours devoted to somatic considerations. Most of my teaching was on the main campus, where, with Philip Du Bois, I helped to direct the newly founded clinical psychology program of the university. We were later joined on the committee by Saul Rosenzweig, who accepted a dual appointment at the medical school and in the Department of Psychology.

For the first time I had graduate students and interns in psychology. The Division of Medical Psychology, of which I was a part, became a rather closely knit, harmonious group of staff, graduate students, and interns. This was a new and stimulating experience for me since I had been something of a loner before that time. The first doctoral dissertation I directed was in the field of gerontological psychology, carried out by Bettye M. Caldwell. Besides Bettye, who at the time was also on the staff of the medical school, Ivan Mensh joined the staff in medical psychology the year after I arrived, and Samuel Granick and James Palmer a year or so later. Joe Matarazzo was our first intern. He remained on for another year as the first and, so far as I know, the only man to take a year's Ph.D. "minor" in medicine. He then joined the staff. Interns, of course, came and went but I must mention two for whom I developed a special fondness, Evelyn Mason and Benjamin Pope. Associated with the division in a more peripheral manner as consultants were two young statisticians, Goldine Gleser and Jane Loevinger. In view of the brilliance of their later work, is it any wonder that relationship with them increased my conviction that I was a statistical dolt!

I continued to work on the two books whose bibliographies had been prepared in part during the war years, and in 1949 *Readings in the Clinical Methods in Psychology* and in 1952 *The Clinical Method in Psychology* made their appearance. *Psychology as a Profession* (1954) was also largely written while I was still at the medical school. I also began to work on *Psychology of the Child*, but its publication was delayed until 1959, some years after I had arrived at Northwestern. In the meantime I continued the usual variety of research articles, chapters in books, and a series of methodological studies on psychotherapy in collaboration with Ivan Mensh and Edwin F. Gildae.

Interest in the topic and awareness of the need for a particular volume, of course, motivates the would-be author. But I suspect many authors have deeper, less obvious reasons for writing a book. Certainly I had in almost every instance a "private" reason for proceeding with a particular book that had nothing to do with its feasibility, its sales value, my professional advancement, or any other mundane consideration. What I wanted from each book was an answer to a question or questions that writing the book might help to provide. Moreover, as might have been inferred already, the amassing of knowledge is a salient, defensive maneuver on my part and all writing helps to meet this need.

In working on books in clinical psychology this appeared most baldly since I was also trying to see if knowing what I thus learned verbally about clinical methodology would translate into more sensitive and adroit clinical interaction on my part. It didn't.

In my writing *Psychology of the Child* (1959) I had from the very beginning the goal of satisfying myself whether the literature on "academic" child psychology could be reconciled with psychoanalytic contentions. My limited answer to myself would be that the two streams of evidence at least are not incompatible and that many research findings from academic psychology can be integrated under psychoanalytic rubrics. To a somewhat lesser degree, the second edition some years later helped me to answer how integration with the Piagetian literature could be related to the main stream of child psychology.

When I was first appointed assistant dean there was a possibility that I was the youngest assistant dean of a medical school in the United States. It took me five years to realize—the situation being what it was—that if I lived long enough, I would die the oldest associate dean of a medical school in the country! In a medical school a hierarchy is a very real and living thing. In certain respects my status among 750 full-time and clinical faculty members was that of number three man—below the dean and another assistant dean. And yet, in another sense, for many day-to-day decisions I was not even on the hierarchy since I lacked the M.D. degree. I must confess sometimes mentally comparing the situation to that of a poker game in which the other players were allowed to use the joker and I was not.

This problem was by no means the decisive factor that brought about my move to Northwestern University in 1953. Although I had found time to write the books and articles I have already mentioned, I had to do most of the work after ten o'clock at night and on weekends. Illustrating the sheer intensity of the tempo was that events had conspired to give me time for a total of but three weeks' vacation in the five years. I wanted that form of leisure which is freedom to work on what one wishes. The final incident which hardened my resolve to make the move came when a young ophthalmologist with whom I was to collaborate in studies of squint died of a heart attack certainly exacerbated by overwork.

At Northwestern I found a relatively small department. The person I had known best before arriving was William A. Hunt, since we had been in the Navy together. Among other senior members of the department were Benton J. Underwood and Carl Duncan and, a year or two later, Donald Campbell. Essentially there were three graduate programs, with Carl and Ben in general charge of the experimental program, Don in charge of the social program, and I with the responsibility for the clinical program, although naturally Bill Hunt maintained his interest in this last field. A stalwart in the clinical program was Janet Taylor, who supervised perhaps more Ph.D. dissertations than any other member of the department during these years.

The publication most decisive for my future work was "A Brief History of Clinical Psychology," which had appeared in 1953. Research articles of mine, although presumably respectable enough, caused no great response on the part of others. There had been the usual requests for reprints, incidental mention in related literature, and so on, but there was really no great impact. This particular article, however, seemed to strike a responsive chord. It has since been reprinted a half-dozen times and I had more requests for reprints than I had had for all my other articles combined. While still very much actively engaged in clinical teaching, research, and practice, I began to wonder in the early years at Northwestern if my strengths did not lie in the area associated with this particular publication. Increasingly thereafter my publications were to take a historical turn. My teaching responsibilities in the general field of personality made it quite possible to stress historical aspects and I proceeded to do so.

It was in about 1959 that I decided explicitly to become a historian of psychology in the sense that I resolved thereafter this would be my major area of research and publication. But there were many obstacles. For one thing, there seemed to be little in the way of company and hardly any precedent. Heretofore psychologists had turned to history for a text, article, or monograph and then gone back to other, more absorbing interests. The only ones who had been consistent in their interest were aging psychologists who confused an interest in their extended present with an interest in the past. And yet I knew that scattered around the country there had to be a handful of individuals with similar interests.

In 1960 I attempted to stimulate interest in the field by publishing a paper that was meant to serve as a challenge, "The History of Psychology: A Neglected Area." To show how much could be done I emphasized how little had been done. For example, among other findings I reported that approximately 60 psychologists out of 16,000 consider the history of psychology among their several interests. No one could argue that this was an impressive number.

Another step also taken in 1960 was the result of a meeting in Evanston involving David Bakan, John C. Burnham, the historian, and me. We decided to take advantage of a provision in APA convention programing that allows individuals to publish an announcement that at the annual meeting a "special interest group" is to meet. In September 1960, fifteen or so individuals showed up! In subsequent years, however, the number increased to about fifty. In my more pessimistic moments I said our purpose was to huddle together for warmth. Actually, the meetings were quite stimulating and gradually those interested in history came to know one another.

A newsletter containing news and notes about meetings, publications, and courses taught was first published by the group in October 1960. This also tended to bring individuals working in history a bit closer together. Quite deliberately the group was without officers, dues, or even an official name. Many of us found this state of affairs congenial. When the possibility of a formal division within the APA was first broached, I demurred. The argument that convinced me such a step was necessary was the comment of one young psychologist to the effect that a division of the history of psychology would give a stamp of authenticity to work in this area—that it would help bring recognition that the history of psychology is a form of specialization. We decided at our meeting in 1964 to proceed with a petition for divisional status. In September 1965 the governing body of the APA approved the formation of the Division of the History of Psychology with a charter membership of 211. This has grown, so that today there are approximately 400 members.

The next development in which I participated came about in part because of an affiliation I have with a publishing enterprise in clinical psychology. I had been on the Editorial Board of the *Journal of Clinical Psychology* since 1951. At our meeting in 1962, Frederick C. Thorne, editor and chief stockholder of the journal, proposed to us that we consider founding some additional journals. As a first venture in this area, he suggested organization of what eventuated as *Psychology in the Schools.*

The next year or so I spent thinking through and organizing a prospectus for a historical journal. In 1963 a plan was presented to the group and their financial backing was secured. The following year was devoted to soliciting articles and arranging for a multidisciplinary board of editors drawn from psychology, anthropology, sociology, neurophysiology, neurology, psychiatry and psychoanalysis, and history itself. In January 1965 the first issue of the *Journal of the History of the Behavioral Sciences* appeared.

Certain expectations turned out to be all too true. The first few years were touch and go financially. Numerous suspiciously yellowed-page manuscripts came in, along with a horde of papers on the genre that could be epitomized by the title "My Three Hours with Freud." However, with the steadfast cooperation of the Editorial Board, a gradual stability and a certain standing in the field emerged.

During the sixties Edwin G. Boring had an important influence on me. My relationship is epitomized in the dedication of *The Great Psychologists* (1963a)—"To E.G.B. my teacher, under whom I never studied." His erudition, his helpfulness, even his narrowness expressed in the grand manner, were important to me. The latter can be illustrated by our first interaction in 1956. The occasion allows me to deliver a story that has never appeared in print and, since it appeared on a postcard, would not be in his carefully preserved letter correspondence. It was on the occasion of his requesting that I prepare for the *American Journal of Psychology* an obituary for Lightner Witmer. After making the request he seemed to feel that he must justify his not doing it himself. So he went on to explain, "After all, I knew his work until 1896 but then he went into clinical psychology and naturally I lost track of him." I might add that in 1896 Professor Boring was ten years old.

Some years later, Boring agreed to read critically the next-to-last draft of my *The Great Psychologists* (1963a). Anyone who knew him would have guessed correctly that his comments were often longer than the material on which he was commenting. In many ways he did much for the burgeoning specialty of the history of psychology. He lent his support to the history of psychology group, the Division of the History of Psychology, and to the *Journal of the History of the Behavioral Sciences*, the last both by joining the Editorial Board and by submitting an article for the first issue. Just for fun Donald Campbell and I embarked on editing his papers. In this endeavor we were ably abetted by the late Gordon Ierardi of John Wiley & Sons, our mentor on publishing matters. In this connection, let me tell a part of a story that is new. When the idea was broached to Boring in Cambridge by Ierardi that we edit a collection of his papers, he supported the venture with the statement that "only modesty would have prevented me from suggesting it myself," as we have already reported in the Preface to the volume (1963b), but we did not go on to report that under his breath he was heard to mutter "and Tolman had to collect them himself."

At Northwestern I had continued to work in the general clinical area, directed my share of dissertations, and carried out the numerous administrative duties that fall to a director of clinical training. Increasing administrative responsibility is part of that almost inevitable development of a clinician who remains in an institutional setting. Attracted to clinical activities he discovers that his reward for service and for skill consists of inexorably moving in the direction of less and less clinical contact. For the clinical facilities with which I was affiliated I ended up as the consultant to the director of training, who saw the staff psychologist, who saw the psychological trainee, who saw the patient!

Acceptance of an appointment as professor of psychology at the University of New Hampshire beginning in 1967 was influenced by several considerations. I was already familiar to some extent with their plans for the Ph.D. program that they were in the process of installing because, along with Fillmore Sanford, I had made a consultant visit two or three years before to meet with the graduate council, the department, and the administration concerning their plans. Although many individuals contributed to these plans it was Eugene Mills, now president and then chairman of the department, and Raymond Erickson, recently retired as chairman, who offered the leadership. They impressed me tremendously and events have served only to increase my admiration and friendship.

What they were seeking was a classic department involving general experimental psychology, with degrees in physiological, cognitive and perceptual psychology, social psychology and personality, and the one that was particularly intriguing to me, history and theory of psychology. If I were to move to Durham it would give me the opportunity to establish the pioneer Ph.D. program in this field. Evanston was changing as Chicago kept creeping northward and I found a multi-university somewhat less to my liking than it had been in the past. But it was the opportunity to work full time in the history of psychology that was so much of an inducement that I could not but accept the appointment.

Another step toward professionalization of the emerging specialization of the historian of psychology was taken when funds were secured by Josef Brozek and me from the National Science Foundation for the Summer Institute on the History of Psychology (1969, 1970). This institute was held in June 1968 at the University of New Hampshire the summer after I arrived. The thirty participants, twenty-five post-doctoral and five pre-doctoral, seemed to find it stimulating. So too did the five or six instructors whose services we had arranged. We were careful to include among their number both a historian of science and a psychiatrist so as to signalize the fact that our specialization had relation to other areas as well.

One direct outgrowth, instigated by Julian Jaynes, one of the instructors, was an interdisciplinary society, Cheiron: The International Society for the History of the Behavioral and Social Sciences. It held its fourth annual meeting in June 1971. Although the international aspect is still more of a hope than it is an accomplishment, *Cheiron* has proved to be interdisciplinary in scope.

We in the Department of Psychology spent the next years getting organized in a preliminary fashion. One major development was the selection of the department by the administration to apply for a departmental development grant from the National Science Foundation. After some years of assiduous planning this grant was received. It began in 1970.

To go back to history as a field, a point of view that I developed in clinical psychology was to have its counterpart in work in history years later. I had coined (or unconsciously plagiarized) an aphorism, "Clinical enrichment is research contamination." It expressed my awareness of the necessity of attempting on the one hand to do justice to the sheer idiographic subtleties of the psychological functioning in a person that is a patient and on the other hand to conduct research with due attention to the demands for rigorous quantification and careful delimitation of the research variables. The line that I tried to walk was that of a balance of the two in which I saw the clinical psychologist as being as rigorous as the qualitative data permitted —but no more. A similar point of view is being expressed in my work in history through my determination to use quantification as a tool in the study of history but not to the extent that it excludes the qualitative material that is essential to the historian. The goal again is rigor, but not rigor that distorts.

In their doctoral dissertations several current graduate students have found or will find use for quantifying devices—for example, content analysis and statistical manipulation. On the other hand, I support enthusiastically other dissertation topics unequivocally not quantitative in nature.

It is my position that the psychologist has something positive to contribute not only to the study of history of psychology but also to the study of history in general. He is perhaps better equipped with certain skills than the typical historian. His expertise in quantitative methods, his knowledge of social and dynamic psychology, and his familiarity with personality research and theory may well serve in the future to give new breadth and depth to other aspects of history.

The first of the history of psychology Ph.D. dissertations at the University of New Hampshire was completed in 1970 by Barbara Ross. It was entitled "Psychological Thought Within the Context of the Scientific Revolution: 1665–1700." Dr. Ross applied content analysis categories, cast in prescriptive variables terms, to the relevant articles in the *Philosophical Transactions* for this temporal period. When her quantitative findings were combined with the usual narrative approach, she demonstrated, prescriptively speaking, that the basic attitudes and modes of conception of the seventeenth-century scientist included a behavioral view of man, thus tending to cast doubt on the more conventional view that psychology as a science was a product of the nineteenth century.

The Great Psychologists (1963a) followed a predominantly biographical approach. Returning to my theme of having a private reason for writing, I wanted to see how far I could go using the individual as the vehicle of history. Although the book seems pedagogically successful in that it meets an educational need, i.e. it sells rather well, I was not fully satisfied. I had become convinced during the writing that the Great Man approach cannot be *the* framework for historical writing and research, important though it may be as a subsidiary tool. I was also convinced that the Zeitgeist or climate-of-opinion approach was so empty of meaning as to be no more than a subsidiary approach in the same sense as the biographical. This made me restless. I wanted another framework.

Thomas Kuhn's work on the paradigmatic sciences gave me an important clue. He argued that mature sciences are guided by paradigms. In one of his meanings, a paradigm is a universally accepted model that serves for an appreciable time as a framework of that science. He considered all sciences once and some sciences now to be pre-paradigmatic, i.e. to lack this guidance. In view of psychologists' quarrels about what is basic in psychology and our national provincialisms I readily agreed with his position that psychology was pre-paradigmatic. If not paradigmatic, what served in its place as guiding themes? At the outset I assumed a plurality because if the guidance function was monolithic then it would be paradigmatic in the sense just defined. What seemed necessary were trends numerous enough to deal with at least some of the complexity of psychology and yet not so numerous as to make them so specific as to be relatively meaningless. After some years of cutting and filling, I came up with a list of themes that I call "prescriptions." Since it is impossible to go into detail let me say crudely that thirty-six prescriptions emerged, sometimes arranged in terms of eighteen contrasting pairs. To quote a more formal statement about their nature:

> A prescription is an attitude taken by a psychologist toward one or another aspect of his psychological concerns. By conceiving prescriptions in attitudinal terms, in effect, I am opening up the possibility of placing them in the setting of social psychology. The major function of prescriptions is conceived to be orientative or attitudinal in that it tells the psychologist how he should behave. A quantitative prescription is manifested by a psychologist when, faced by a psychological problem, he forthwith starts to ask how he might quantify it without necessarily first inquiring whether the problem is suitable for quantification. Moreover, in order to be of historical value, the prescriptions isolated for study must have existed over some appreciable period of time. The rational and empirical prescriptions have served a guidance function for centuries while more specific manifestations such as logical empiricism have been of historical moment for much shorter temporal periods. Empiricism and rationalism then are the prescriptions; logical empiricism a manifestation of them (1971b).

Prescriptive attitudes may show a variety of interrelationships in a particular formulation and differ according to the particular temporal and national setting. Locke espoused an empirical view of human nature in an England that was overwhelmingly rationalistic in outlook. Rationalism was then dominant, empiricism barely counter-dominant. "Contrast," "dominance," "polarity," "gradation," "integration," "implicitness," "contentual," and "methodological" express in capsule form some of the ways in which temporal changes in prescriptions may be expressed.

A program of research on prescriptive theory has begun to emerge. First there was a paper that was an account of the then current status of psychology in the United States (1965) in a symposium in which others offered papers on the French, English, and German psychology. This symposium took place at the International Congress of Psychology in Washington in 1963. In my paper, some, but not all, prescriptive trends were utilized but merely as aspects of an implicit framework. My own thinking was not at all clear on many issues. For example, I treated "manifestations" and "prescriptions," as I later called them, as equivalent. So far as prescriptive theory is concerned, the paper gave me confidence that, using the beginnings of prescriptive theory as a basis, I, at least, could make sense out of the current scene in psychology in the United States.

Then the opportunity arose for me to give a rather lengthy

paper as a formal address. This paper, "Psychology: A Prescriptive Science" (1967), meant to establish my theoretical position along with an account of whatever scraps of evidence I had at that time. It was a prolegomenon of further work, not a summarization of past accomplishments. In the meantime I was working on a book in the history of modern psychology, which naturally opens with the seventeenth century. Since prescriptive theory was the means of organization, it helped me to answer the question whether it would work for the seventeenth century as it seemed to do for the twentieth. In order to get something in print about it a few years later I "lifted" from this manuscript a paper on Descartes (1971a).

In the meantime students and others were writing dissertations and carrying out factor analytic studies using prescriptive theory, which produced further evidence interpreted as positive in nature. Then the time arrived not only to state a further "refined" view but also to compare the approach with other ways of interpreting the history of psychology. The paper being published as I write this is the result (1971b).

All of this is a far cry from a textbook account of a formal programatic design. It more resembles prospecting by drilling test holes here and there in a terrain that we have some reason to believe will have positive results.

Another project on which I am now engaged originated in a sort of gossipy game that Garry Boring and I had played. The context was of our common editorial interest in necrologies (my territory, I gathered, was to be the sociotropes while he reserved the biotropes for himself). In 1966 I wrote a letter mentioning by name some of the psychologists who I thought would be remembered a century from now. He responded with an almost entirely different list. After a certain amount of argument back and forth we decided we just couldn't agree on living psychologists. So at some point we switched to psychologists of the past and found that there was much more agreement. If we could agree why not submit a list in more formal fashion to a larger panel? So we pooled our files for individuals who contributed to psychology from the seventeenth century coming onward with over a thousand names resulting, submitted the names to individuals we considered knowledgeable, and asked for their evaluation. The study of eminence was published in 1968.

After the study was finished, Garry wrote me that the five hundred or so psychologists who topped the panel ratings would make a rather neat basis for a book of short biographies which he proposed to write. This stirred me to think about what further I might do with our findings. *Eminent Psychologists: Primary and Secondary References* with approximately 12,000 primary and 36,000 secondary references to appear in a year or so is to be the result. The references to be reported are, of course, selective, but include indications about the more complete locations of individual bibliographies. The other secondary references include biographies, past and current critical studies in both books and journals, citations in encyclopedias, handbooks, and so on.

This volume, of course somewhat pedestrian in nature, is my present low-key work. I have found that I function best when I work simultaneously on two (or more) problems each at a different level of complexity and involvement. The demanding problem gets me worked up to a certain level of excitement that cannot be maintained indefinitely—the less-demanding is the laborious but lazy-going activity of my other hours.

What else? Well, historians of psychology still lack a monographic outlet and several of us are working on this problem. A book in the history of personality theory is under way, and I shall return to work on my book on early modern psychology. Two other books have a few scraps in my folders. And then . . .

REFERENCES

References in the clinical method in psychology. (Ed.) New York: Harper, 1949.

The clinical method in psychology. New York: Harper, 1952. (Paperback reprint, Wiley, 1963)

A brief history of clinical psychology. *Psychological Bulletin,* 1953, *50,* 321-46.

Psychology as a profession. New York: Doubleday, 1954.

Psychology of the child. New York: Wiley, 1959. (Second, Oriental, and Spanish editions in later years)

The history of psychology: A neglected area. *American Psychologist,* 1960, *15,* 251-55.

The great psychologists: From Aristotle to Freud. Philadelphia: Lippincott, 1963a. (2nd ed., 1968; 3rd ed., 1971)

With Donald T. Campbell (Eds.). *History, psychology and science: The collected papers of Edwin G. Boring.* New York: Wiley, 1963b.

The historical background for national trends in psychology: United States. *Journal of the History of the Behavioral Sciences,* 1965, *1,* 130-37.

Psychology: A prescriptive science. *American Psychologist,* 1967, *22,* 435-43.

With Edith L. Annin and Edwin G. Boring (Eds.). Important psychologists, 1600-1967. *Journal of the History of the Behavioral Sciences,* 1968, *4,* 303-15.

With Josef Brozek and Barbara Ross. A Summer institute on the history of psychology: I, II. *Journal of the History of the Behavioral Sciences*, 1969, 5, 307-19; 1970, 6, 25-35.

A prescriptive analysis of Descartes' psychological views. *Journal of the History of the Behavioral Sciences*, 1971a, 7, 223-48.

Prescriptions as operative in the history of psychology. *Journal of the History of the Behavioral Sciences*, 1971b, 7, 311-22.

I. Organizational Development of American Historiography of Psychology

1. The History of Psychology: A Neglected Area

In the United States psychology is provincial, both geographically and temporally. While almost any European psychologist whom we meet surprises us by his knowledge of our work, we fall far short of equivalent familiarity with psychological activities in his country. Our relative ignorance of current psychological activities outside the United States is so well known and seemingly so complacently accepted as hardly to need exposition. It is not my intent to discuss our geographical provincialism except to point out that it seems to be similar to our historical provincialism, suggesting the possibility of common causal factors. Instead, I propose to document the extent of the current neglect of the history of our field, to suggest some of the factors which help to bring about this neglect, to answer certain possible criticisms of devoting one's time to advancing knowledge of our history, and to try to show some positive values to be found by research in our history. I shall close with a few comments about the preparation for work in the history of psychology.

A variety of sources of evidence shows our neglect of the history of psychology. Some evidence may be found by examining the number of historical articles in our journals, by establishing the extent of expressions of interest in history by APA members, and by finding the number of psychologists who are members of the leading history of science society in the United States.

Three journals publish most of the historically oriented publication of psychologists in the United States: the *American Journal of Psychology*, the *Journal of General Psychology*, and the *Psychological Bulletin*. The contents of each of these journals for the last 20 years (1938–1957) were examined. Articles, excluding program descriptions, accounts of meetings, and obituaries, were classified as historical or nonhistorical. To be classified as historical the major theme of the article had to be placed in a historical perspective. Reviews, for example, which acknowledged they covered the work of 10, or 20, or some identified number of years, were not considered historical if they treated the research they discussed as more or less equally contemporaneous. In the *American Journal of Psychology* 12 out of 1,207 articles were historical in nature in this 20-year period. In the *Journal of General Psychology* only 13 historical articles appeared from a total of 937 articles. In the *Psychological Bulletin* 682 articles were published during this period, of which 13 were historical in nature. It seems evident that psychologists publish only a handful of historical articles: 38 were primarily historical out of more than 2,800 articles over a 20-year period in the three journals examined.

An obvious source for the expression of interests by psychologists is the statement of their interests given by APA members in the *Directory*. Every tenth page of the 1958 *Directory* was searched for mention of interest in the history of psychology. In this way the stated interests of 1,638 psychologists were examined. Those mentioning an interest in history numbered 6. Extrapolating from the sample to the total membership of 16,644 gives only about 60 psychologists who consider the history of psychology among their interests, irrespective of whether or not they publish.

The History of Science Society is probably the leading organization in its field in the United States. We have some information about its membership. Using the 1951 APA *Directory* as the source, Daniel and Louttit (1953) listed the professional organizations to which a 12 percent sample of APA members belonged. They stopped listing by name of organization when they reached societies with five or less APA members. The History of Science Society was not listed. Moreover, not a single psychologist was found by a name-by-name check of about 5 percent of the organization's membership list.

On the basis of number of publications, expressed interest in the field, and membership in a specialty society, it seems appropriate to conclude that the history of psychology receives relatively little attention from psychologists in the United States at the present time.

Neglect of our history is an indication of a value judgment on the part of psychologists. Almost all psychologists simply have not been interested in it enough to be curious about it, let alone to work and to publish in this area. Probably there is a general distaste for historical matters among scientists in the United States, including psychologists. If this be true, psychologists as social beings share in a characteristic aberration of our times: a relative lack of curiosity about our past. Moreover, we have reached an age of specialization in psychology. The age of encyclopedists, if it ever existed, is certainly past. We must reconcile ourselves to limitation within our field. In short, we are specialists, not generalists.

It is one of the dubious fruits of specialization that one makes a sharp distinction between the historical development of his subject and the additive process by which he, himself, is developing it. The contemporary general lack of interest concerning the past and the age of specialism is shared by psychologists with other scientists. It is my impression that this neglect is even greater in psychology than in neighboring fields such as biology, medicine, and sociology. In these fields even a cursory acquaintance shows signs of considerably greater historical activity.

Specific to psychology, two related factors may accentuate our temporal provincialism, both stemming from psychology's relatively recent emergence as a science in its own right. First, we may be a bit ashamed of our past. The *nouveau riche* does not search his family tree. Second, self-conscious, as we are, of our recent hard-won victory of full-fledged scientific status, we may regard our heritage, as well as much European psychology, as somehow not quite respectable fields of interest simply because they smack of the unscientific. Interest in history is, save the mark, even scholarly!

In a somewhat more encouraging vein, still another reason for our relatively greater neglect of history is our sheer exuberance and what we have before us in the way of what appear to be limitless opportunities for research and service. Making history, we do not study what others have done in the past. There can be little question that our advances apparently are rapid, our expansion in numbers amazing.

The tremendous advances in scientific knowledge in our own and other fields lead to a feeling of exhilaration and satisfaction that should not be decried. The last 50 years has perhaps seen more scientific industry directed toward psychological problems than has all time before it. In the perspective of the future this optimistic judgment concerning the present half century may be shared by our successors, despite the doubt derived from the curious similarity of this remark to that made by many, many others concerning their own particular age. Be that as it may, I suspect many psychologists are influenced by some such unspoken opinion to the detriment of interest in the history of their field.

These speculations about the neglect of the history of psychology just presented may or may not be correct. Whatever their objective status as truth, they do not deal with the crucial question. One may still ask: "Assuming what you have said is correct, of what contemporary interest is the psychology of the past?" To put it baldly, why should serious attention and respect be given the history of psychology? It is necessary to inquire whether or not this lack of attention is precisely what the history of our field deserves. The question may be made more specific by asking whether this lack of attention to history does or does not reflect lack of significant material or lack of relevance of the material even if available.

It might be argued that the neglect of history that has been demonstrated is simply a reflection of the lack of significant material. Within the compass of this paper illustrations from only one temporal period may be given. The most unlikely period of all—the Middle Ages—is chosen for this purpose. Serious attention to the medieval period in our history has not been given since Brett published his *History of Psychology* nearly 50 years ago. In the meanwhile, as I propose to demonstrate, new sources have become available, and the number of workers in the general field of the history of science, who incidentally have touched upon matters of psychological interest, has increased considerably.

The basic source of my illustrations is to be found in the monumental *Introduction to the History of Science* by George Sarton. In connection with the medieval period he prepared a synopsis of about 2,000 pages in length. In these pages he made reference to what I consider to be psychological work on the part of 49 men. These references were to work either said to be psychological by Sarton or to psychological topics such as sensation and oneirology. For records of their accomplishments to appear in this survey of Sarton, they must have been preserved through the centuries of the medieval period and the 500 years since. One would expect that in view of this form of eminence the odds would favor their being known at least vaguely to psychologists. Selecting every fifth name from the list of 49 gives the following: Ibn Sirin, Al-Mas-Udi, Ibn Hibat Allah, Ibn

Al-Jausi, Bahya Ben Joseph, Ibn Sabin, Peter of Spain, Thomas of York, and Witelo. I rather suspect that very, very few would be known to most psychologists.

It is relevant to compare the list of names of men found by reading Sarton to have worked in areas of psychology during the 900 years of the medieval period with those considered in Brett's history 50 years ago. Only 15 of the 49 are considered by Brett. A great majority of the Muslims and Jews found in Sarton were not mentioned at all by him. It would be a mistake to infer that Brett considered the workers he did not discuss as irrelevant because of lack of contact with Western intellectual development. Scholars in the Muslim world, including the Jewish workers among them, are acknowledged to be the intellectual leaders of the later centuries of the medieval period. Most of their works were translated into Latin in their own time or in the centuries that followed. Western commentaries on these works also appeared. Only at the end of the medieval period did their influence wane. It is quite plausible to believe that they were neglected by Brett because knowledge about them was either relatively inaccessible or even unknown at the time he was working.

It is difficult to classify medieval scholars into the neat categories demarcating the fields of knowledge of today. In any age the greater the man the more apt he is to range beyond the boundaries of one particular field. Yet it is possible by study of their contributions to classify them roughly into one or another field of knowledge. Sarton's description of the activities of these 49 medieval scholars was used as the basis of classification.

Contrary to expectation, less than one-half (21) were primarily philosophers and/or theologians. Nearly one-third (14) were physicians. The rest were scattered in a variety of other fields, none including more than two representatives. These fields were those of the chronologist, philologist, oneirologist, folklorist, traveler, physicist, astronomer, mathematician, historian, jurist, and oculist. Only one man, Isaac of Stella, was identified by Sarton as primarily a psychologist. In a broader sense he was a philosopher and was so classified by me. It will be remembered that 15 of these 49 workers were utilized by Brett in his history. Over half (8) of those to whom Brett referred were theologians and philosophers, while of those remaining 6 were physicians and physicists. It is evident that only one of the 14 representatives of the other more peripheral fields, identified in Sarton, was utilized by him. Moreover, 10 philosophers and 10 physicians were found in Sarton that were not touched upon by Brett at all.

Two of the medieval psychologists are chosen for slightly more detailed exposition. One has been already mentioned—Peter of Spain, later John XXI. He had been trained as a physician (and in the classification was so placed) and had wide medical, zoological, logical, philosophical, and psychological interests. In psychology he wrote a volume on psychology, *De Anima*, which included an account of the historical development of psychological ideas found in Greek and Muslim works covering a *thousand years* of the history of psychology. Lest this work be dismissed as "mere" philosophy, it should be added that, according to Sarton, it stresses physiological and medical aspects! Elevated to the pontificate in 1276, he died in an accident eight months later. That there was a psychologist pope is probably not even known among most Catholic psychologists.

One of the greatest minds of the Middle Ages will serve as the second illustration—Moses Maimonides. He is best known for his *Guide for the Perplexed*, a monument of Jewish theology. Other than one relatively obscure reference, it never has been called to the attention of psychologists that this work contains material of psychological significance. For example, memory is discussed in Chapters 33-36 of Part I, and mind in Chapters 31-32 of Part I and Chapter 37 of Part II. Maimonides also wrote on medical matters, including descriptions of prophetic visions as psychological experiences; on the rules of psychotherapy; and various other psychological-medical matters. There is a strong probability that careful study of his works would reveal a theory of personality of some significance for us today.

These two men—Peter of Spain and Moses Maimonides—should have a special appeal to psychologists whose background of Catholic or Jewish scholarship makes them especially well prepared to evaluate their significance.

In general, there appears to be evidence that the 900 years from the sixth to the fifteenth centuries were not without their share of psychological speculation and observation. Scholars have examined this material in a philosophical perspective, but there has been an almost complete neglect of the psychological aspects.

It was following the medieval period that the revival of learning at the beginning of the modern period took place. This was the rebirth of Greek, particularly Aristotelian, ways of thinking in the twelfth and the thirteenth centuries, which gave us the origin of the empirical, especially experimental, ways of approaching nature. Out of the work of Renaissance man comes what we know about the origins of our present knowledge.

That greatest of modern historians of science, George Sarton, has shown that the "Dark Ages" transmitted the science of the Greek and the Hellenistic worlds. Transmission is, in itself, just as important as discovery and is sufficient reason to study the Middle Ages. But even more important, as Sarton puts it, medieval progress occurred not because of, but in spite of, its presumed crowning achievement of scholastic philosophy. Medievalists, he claimed, have stressed the scholastic aspects to the detriment of the real scientific advance, especially in the Muslim world. In spite of scholastic and obscurantist tendencies which repel the modern mind, examination of the contributions of these men of the Middle Ages to psychology as psychology, separated from philosophical and theological preoccupation, would seem to be a worthwhile venture.

For the Middle Ages, and presumably even more cogently for other ages, we do not lack new material, and there would appear to be at least some contemporary relevance for its study. A more general statement of the values of historical study in psychology seems indicated.

It would be a serious mistake to consider the history of psychology to be limited to a mere chronology of events or biographical chitchat. It is a study of long-time cultural trends over time. Psychological contributions are embedded in the social context from which they emerge. Psychology has always responded in part to its social environment, but it also has been guided by an internal logic of its own. We cannot emphasize one of these trends at the expense of the other. Psychology neither reflects culture with passive compliance nor does it exist in a social vacuum. External and internal circumstances are present, and there is a constant interplay between them.

It is a truism of one approach to history that each generation rewrites the history in terms of its own values and attitudes. As yet, we have not looked back on the past from the perspective of today finding values for the present from the past. Old material is still to be seen in a new perspective. In the past writing of our history, material either ignored as irrelevant or simply not known at that time now can be utilized. The material from the Middle Ages commented upon earlier would illustrate the new material available. The presence of newly relevant material needs further comment. The field of psychology has expanded enormously in recent years. That it has re-extended beyond the limits of experimental psychology is a statement of fact on which there can be no disagreement. Consider the influence of the rapidly burgeoning fields of application, such as clinical psychology, and remember that the moment we expand our present concerns in psychology to that extent we have broadened and changed our past. The moment we embrace, even in the smallest degree, the traditions of others as, for example, we have done for some aspects of medicine, we have embraced some aspects of their past as well. Consider the importance in psychology today of personality theories and other influences of quasi- or nonexperimental nature. The history of experimental psychology is the solid core of our history, presumably less changed in this re-examination; but other aspects of its history do exist. In recent years no one has examined all major aspects of our history in the light of these changes.

An even more serious consequence of the neglect of history needs comment. To modify somewhat a statement from Croce via Beard: when we ignore history in the sense of the grand tradition of that field, narrowness and class, provincial and regional prejudices come in their stead to dominate or distort one's views without any necessary awareness of their influence. If psychologists are determined to remain ignorant of our history, are we not, at best, determined to have some of our labors take the form of discoveries which are truisms found independently and, at worst, to repeat the errors of the past? To embody a past of which they are ignorant is, at best, to be subject passively to it, at worst, to be distorted by a false conception of it. Ignorance does not necessarily mean lack of influence upon human conduct, including the human conduct of psychologists. Ignoring the study of the history of one's field through formal sources and published accounts does not result in lack of opinions about the past. Like the traditional man in the street who, too, refuses to read history, such psychologists inevitably have a picture of the past, by and large one which deprecates its importance. This inevitably influences their views just as does any other aspect of the "unverbalized." However little their ahistorical view of the past may correspond to reality, it still helps to determine their views of the present. To neglect history does not mean to escape its influence.

This has been a plea for greater attention on the part of psychologists to their history. With assumption of some knowledge and experience in contemporary psychology, the first stage of development of attention to history would be an interest in it and a conviction that it is a worthwhile field of endeavor. But knowledge, interest, and conviction are not enough for competence. It is not merely a matter of deciding to work in historical aspects of our field. With justice, professional historians have been indignant about the bland assumption, all too often made by scientists, that, because one knows something about a scientific field, the essential equipment for historical research automatically is available. Historical work does not consist of finding a few old books and copying this and that. Trained as he is in his own exacting techniques, the psychologist does not always realize that the technique of establishing the truth or the maximum probability of past events, in other words historical research, has its own complicated rules and methods.

There is a variety of areas with which more than a passing acquaintance is necessary if historical study is planned. Knowledge of the methodology of history—historiography—is essential for more than anecdotal familiarity with any area capable of being approached historically. Knowledge of the philosophy of history is also needed by the psychological historian as a defense against errors of procedure and of content. In psychology, as in similar disciplines, acquaintance with the history of science in general is demanded. Moreover, some appreciation of the influence of social and cultural factors in history is important if the findings are to be seen in broad context. I, for one, think it would be worth the trouble and time to secure this background in order to carry on the task of understanding and interpreting our past in the perspective of today.

REFERENCE

Daniel, R. S., and Loutitt, C. M. *Professional problems in psychology.* New York: Prentice-Hall, 1953.

2. The Role and Use of History in the Psychology Curriculum

Lord Acton (1), the eminent British historian, has indicated that there are two ways in which a science may be studied—through its own particular methods, and through an examination of its history. The method of historical study adds a dimension to the science of psychology. As Collingwood (4) reminds us, history, as such, is concerned with human experiences and, to be more specific, with human thoughts. To an even greater extent than is the case in any of the physical sciences, psychology is in a position to profit from the study of history, since psychology in itself is still another view of human behavior and experience. Both history and psychology are concerned with human behavior and experiences, but in characteristically different ways. Consequently, an appeal to history for understanding of human nature becomes all the more desirable.

Before presenting specific arguments on the role and use of history, the sheer inescapability of historical influences must be made evident. None of us can escape history. Each individual holds some attitude toward history, irrespective of whether or not his view is based on adequate knowledge. Our picture of the past influences our present decisions. History cannot be denied; the choice is between making it a conscious determinant of our behavior as psychologists, or allowing it to influence us unawares. There is no other alternative.

Denying history has stultifying consequences. An unarticulated view of the past results in being passively subject to it. Narrow pro-

---

This paper was presented at the Annual Meeting of the American Psychological Association, St. Louis, Missouri, September 1962, at a symposium entitled "Strategies in the Teaching of Psychology."

vincial, class, and regional prejudices then substitute for a historically founded background. As psychologists, of all people, should realize, failure to take a verbalized position means subjugation to influences of which one is unaware. We have before us an example of the clinical psychologist or psychiatrist who endeavors to make his patient aware of unconscious influences upon his patterns of behavior so that he may be able to face them. Exploration of origins, that is to say, learning the history, before suggesting remedies, is a commonplace of clinical practice. Similarly, the historian by analyzing historical materials often tries to reveal unconscious social trends so that by facing them he may improve conditions through intelligent action (11). The desirability of vigilance in the uncovering of unverbalized sources of bias is further enhanced when it is recognized that history may aid us in that psychological problem of seeing the process by which an investigator comes to the conclusions that he does (2).

All of our classroom teaching is historical in that everything we say concerns the past in the strict sense of the term. Even though its historical character may be unperceived, since it is very recent past with which we are dealing, we find it impossible to teach research conclusions without discussing how they have been reached. A similar situation exists in our research endeavors. In most of our scientific papers there are references to previous papers. These cited papers, in turn, contain references to still earlier literature. Foreshortened though the historical setting of a particular paper may be, it is implicitly the whole history of its particular subject. However, since our present style of presenting research evidence calls for the barest mention of past work, it is quite possible for a researcher to be ignorant of the previous work except that on which his own immediately rests.

It has been remarked with invidious intent that the older the psychologist, the more he seems interested in history. I suspect that sometimes this is not so much a matter of interest in history *per se* as it is a matter of his widening his span of contemporaneity as the years roll on. For example, I must confess to a sense of shock to discover that the beginnings of clinical psychology after World War II, from the point of view of our present graduate students, all too often are "old stuff," and of no real interest. The older the psychologist, the longer the period which appears to him to be contemporaneous. To younger colleagues his particular span is not part of the contemporary scene, but history.

It is relevant to the theme to identify two points of view toward history. One may be interested in the past for its own sake or one may insist that history is of value only to the extent that it throws light on the present. One can expect that many scientists adopt the position of Croce that all history is contemporary history with all the rest being nothing more than chronicle. Croce's position is one which allows history to be a positive force in scientific advance; it admits we cannot escape history, for history is seen as surrounding us in the present. Principles and hypotheses are drawn from our knowledge of the past for use in the present. Historians advance arguments against adoption of this position that are relevant in other contexts, but those who disagree with Croce must admit that the position of insisting on seeing contemporary value is one which is reasonable for non-historians to take. This insistence on contemporaneity does not deny that others may approach history for its own sake. Indeed a historian, as historian, may be as truly following his vocation in trying to see his particular material from the perspective of its time and place as when he does so from the view of his own day. Nevertheless, demand for contemporaneity still allows a legitimate place for the history of psychology.

The history of a science has a characteristic which distinguishes it from all other history, artistic or military-political. The history of a science is cumulative. Indeed the outstanding difference between the arts and the sciences is that the latter are progressive while the former are not. Whether the history of political or military events show progressive or cumulative historical development is a matter of controversy among historians, some insisting that they do, others arguing that they do not. It follows that scientists alone, of all scholars, may be in the exhilarating position of starting from the heights their predecessors have so laboriously climbed.

Ironically enough, this tremendous advantage of the history of a science can be turned into an argument against its study. Since science is cumulative, some scientists hold all that is of value from the past is to be found already available in the present state of knowledge of the field. They take the position that new achievements supersede previous ones and error drops away. One, they go on, can trust that which is of present scientific concern to supply all relevant scientific content. Bakan (2) refers to this view as the Darwinian theory of the evolution of ideas—natural selection among ideas occurs and those that work tend to survive.

Despite the cumulative character of the history of psychology, the view that all that is potentially valuable survives into the present is false on several counts. Errors committed in the past may drop out but this does not prevent their repetition. A remark of Santayana (9) becomes apposite—those who ignore the past repeat its errors. Moreover, a science is constantly developing, with new points of view introduced every day; a point neglected in the immediate past context may become important in the present. As new ideas are introduced, a heretofore neglected, isolated point, not part of the contemporary picture, may need to be rescued from oblivion. A fact, not part of the present pattern, may take on new significance when seen in the context of a new theory (10). We cannot know of these points without historical knowledge.

To return to the analogy with Darwinian theory, it is true that a species, once extinct, cannot be resurrected. With ideas we are more fortunate; we can play Nature and revive an idea at will, and give it a second chance. Moreover, scrutiny of our history shows that there are recurring themes, although often couched under a different terminology. Their similarity or identity may not be recognized until time has passed, making it necessary for its historically based recovery. As an illustration, we are so enamored of the term personality that we forget there were theories of personality long before we began to call certain psychological phenomena by that particular catch word. From Homer onward, we have available records in every form from epics to funeral orations awaiting study to tease out the implicit theories of personality which they contain.

History is ever becoming; it is never finished. This creates a need for contemporary specialists in the history of psychology. Make no mistake, there is plenty of work for them. Several reasons may be given. If the history of psychology is to be rewritten in the light of contemporary interests, then in each age there must be those who sift the material again to bring out its value for that particular age. The selectivity of our interests demands this rewriting with every generation. Moreover, workers in history, both those within psychology and those in other areas, are unearthing material not known to earlier historians in psychology. In writing his monumental history of psychology over fifty years ago, Brett had to work without the aid of Jaeger's later careful work on Aristotle. Consequently, Brett knew nothing of Jaeger's findings on Aristotle's intellectual development, showing a progression away from Plato's teaching in the direction of a much greater naturalism in the mature Aristotle. Nor did Brett know that certain works of physiognomy on which he leaned would later be demonstrated to be Pseudo-Aristotle. In preparing a survey of the great psychologists, a certain number of relatively unknown findings come to light. An illustration of how knowledge of history deepens appreciation of the significance of events on which I wish to dwell is to be found in the work of Robert Harper published in 1949 and 1950.

There is no fragment of history on which there is more agreement among psychologists than that we can date the beginning of the experimental period of our science from the founding in 1879 of the laboratory of the University of Leipzig by Wilhelm Wundt. This date is as well known to us as, say, 1492, for the discovery of America. These two dates have something in common—they are both wrong! Actually, as Harper demonstrates, *two* laboratories were established in 1875, not one in 1879.

It has been customary to consider 1879 as the founding year for the first experimental laboratory in the world on the mistaken belief that it was in this year that Wundt's Leipzig Laboratory was given formal recognition by university authorities. According to Harper, formal recognition to a course in "experimental psychology" did not come from the University until the winter of 1883, while the laboratory, the "Institute for Experimental Psychology," was not listed by University authorities until 1894. So far as we can tell, 1879 is notable only for the appearance of the first student who was to do publishable psychological research under Wundt. Actually, before Wundt's arrival in Leipzig in October 1875, the Royal Ministry formally had set aside a room to be used by him for his experimental work and for demonstrations connected with his *Psychologische Ubungen* or Psychological Practicum. It is on this basis that 1875 is considered the founding year.

It was also in 1875, the same year as Wundt, that William James established at Harvard University the other of the first two psychological laboratories in the world. One especially compelling item Harper cited is the report of the Harvard Treasurer for 1875 which showed an appropriation to James of $300 for use in physiology. Other evidence, including knowledge of the nature of his 1875 course, shows that it was equipment for teaching physiological psychology. In retrospect, James himself was not sure whether it was 1874, 1875, or 1876. Parenthetically, I might mention this is not an entirely uncommon instance of historical research, leading to more accurate conclusions concerning a given point than was allowed an actual participant in the event in question.

Thus, 1875, not 1879, is the year most deserving of being honored by psychologists. Aside from a handful probably concentrated in this room, almost all other psychologists seem blithely unaware of this instance of the influence of later research upon past historical findings.

Time does not permit dwelling on other illustrations, but I cannot forbear throwing out two teasers—that, historically, the first recorded experiment was psychological in nature, and, that, except for someone's mistake, we might more properly have been called thymotologists, not psychologists.

The study of the history of psychology may incite in us new ideas about human nature. We bring to history certain conceptions about human nature; we also revise our notions in the course of our historical readings (13). We start with certain criteria by which to judge behavior and experience; we may be induced to change these criteria when new possibilities are exposed to us. The case of history parallels that of literature—seeing a play or reading a novel teaches us about psychology even though we bring to the play or novel already pre-existing beliefs.

Our knowledge of human nature, after all, does not rest on experience. Revision of our knowledge by extra-laboratory experience is going on whether we wish it or not. Should it not occur on the basis of knowledge of our history as well?

One may question the utility of knowledge of history as a stimulus for current research by remarking that research data reports contain little, if any, mention of its inciting value. The reason is not far to seek: our contentions for reporting research to our colleagues give no place to our sources of inspiration. What happened *after* the problem occurred to us is all that we present. We report the psychology of the discovered with hardly any attention to that of the psychology of discovery.

Two closely related claims sometimes advanced for the utility of history will *not* be made. The study of the history of science does not seem to make a psychologist a better research man. Conant (5), who is not alone in expressing the view that study of the past is insignificant for an investigator *qua* investigator beyond the immediate background of his particular problem, sees the matter as follows: "The scientific investigator develops his skill as an investigator by a method closely akin to that by which masters of a craft trained apprentices in the past or the painters of the Renaissance developed in the studio of a great master. Continuous experience with experimentation from the advanced laboratory courses to the first independent work has kept the embryo research man in contact with the reality of his business. As compared with what he is learning and has learned in his laboratory, the chemist, physicist, or experimental biologist finds the past has little or nothing to tell him about the methods of research."

Nor does the cumulative character of psychological advance make history a predictive device. "A knowledge of history is not a crystal ball," as Boring (3) tersely put it. The antecedents of a psychological event are too numerous and too interrelated for correct specific prediction to be more than happenstance. Although theoretically demanded when one subscribes to causal determinism, in psychology we always seem to know too little about the present to predict the future and I see no reason to hope for an improvement in our ability to predict in the immediate future. So the study of history is not an aid in prediction.

To return to the positive uses of the history of psychology, it may serve to bring psychology to the laymen. According to Sarton (10), as well as many others, the historical approach is the ideal way to present science to unprepared individuals, this is to say, laymen, and to make it understandable.

Let us examine the state of laymanship with an eye to the various levels of unpreparedness. It is a truism that division of labor has entered every field of psychological research. A direct consequence of the subdivision is that the specialist in one branch of psychology becomes a layman in psychology in the other branches of the field, although at a relatively high level of sophistication. At the next level are the scientists in other fields who are therefore laymen so far as psychology is concerned. They are not as well prepared as the psychological specialists, but presumably many of them have some degree of preparation. At a still lower level there are the numbers of the general public who are even less conversant with the field.

The history of psychology may serve as the common meeting ground for individuals at these various levels. The utility of the history of psychology for colleagues in other fields will be singled out for more detailed comment. Through the medium of history we may be able to begin to progress with a task in which up to the present we can hardly be considered to have been conspicuously successful—that of supplying a view of human nature of use as an underpinning to other sciences concerned with human nature, e.g. Walsh (13). From before Adam Smith to beyond Sigmund Freud our colleagues have complained that they have had to build a view of psychology on their own for use in their specialities. We share the method of history with these other fields with which they, too, are conversant. What would be more natural and fitting than that a serious effort be made to aid in this cross-field task through a historical approach?

At all levels of laymanship, among psychologists as well as others, if one does not introduce the historical approach, a survey often forces one to adopt the untenable position that a particular segment is, in fact, separated from the rest of the field. Experimental psychology divorced from abnormal psychology, child psychology isolated from physiological psychology and the even more narrow areas in which a research man works, have existence only of convenience and of specialization of the researcher-teacher. They are artificially separated segments. So, too, psychology itself may serve a separated-out patch from the fabric of science. This is not a plea to give up specialization in research in favor of a more generalized approach, which is quite a different matter. Rather, this is a plea that, in addition to research specialization, there be a cultivation of the historical method to help to supply that more generalized knowledge of psychology which we all need. Nor does acceptance of this argument require a conviction about the ultimate unity of the sciences. It merely requires that one go so far as to admit it is worthwhile to work toward seeing if a unity exists.

Knowledge of history can be part of our wider frame of reference. For each of us history could be a way of escaping the artificial partitioning of a science that specialization brings. To grasp the relative import of one's own work, to place it in perspective, a knowledge of history is invaluable. History demonstrates to us that the science of psychology is part of the human enterprise. There is a liberating influence to history (6). Bound by the realities of this life and hemmed in by circumstances as we are, through knowledge of history we can deepen and broaden our experience. To realize the richness of our inheritance, to know our kinship with times and places past, to see our own time and place as part of a grand progression, are a part of the role and use of history. The history of psychology is a means by which our knowledge of the field may be related to the main stream of our civilization by specification of points of contact between psychology and literature, the arts, philosophy and the other sciences.

I have addressed myself, not to the undergraduate or graduate student, as the title of my paper might seem to call for, but to you, the trained psychologist. This has been a deliberate strategic maneuver. If you are not convinced of the value of history for yourself, you will not be convinced of its value for your students. Freedom from the unverbalized, the realization of the progression of scientific research, appreciation of the cumulative character of psychology, recovery of material from the past relevant to the present, the possibilities and implication to be followed up, the bringing of knowledge of psychology to our majors, to our students from related sciences and the remainder of our students, and the creation of an integrated frame of reference are possible values of the history in the psychology curriculum.

REFERENCES

1. Acton, J. Cited in H. Butterfield (Ed.) *Man and his past: the study of the history of historical scholarship.* New York: Cambridge University Press, 1955.
2. Bakan, D. *A standpoint for the study of the history of psychology.* Unpublished paper.
3. Boring, E. G. Science and the meaning of its history. *Key Reporter,* 1959, 20, No. 4, 2-3.
4. Collingwood, R. G. *The idea of history.* New York: Oxford University Press, 1946.
5. Conant, J. B. History in the education of scientists. *Harvard Libr. Bull.,* 1960, 14, 315-333.
6. Dilthey, W. The understanding of other persons and their life-expressions. In P. Gardiner (Ed.) *Theories of History.* Glencoe, Ill.: Free Press, 1959, 213-225.
7. Harper, R. S. The laboratory of William James. *Harv. Alum. Bull.,* 1949, 52, 169-173.
8. Harper, R. S. The first psychological laboratory. *Isis,* 1950, 41, 158-161.
9. Santayana, G. *Interpretations of poetry and religion.* New York: Scribners, 1900.
10. Sarton, G. *The life of science: essays in the history of civilization.* Bloomington, Ind.: Indiana University Press, 1960.
11. Sigerist, H. *Medicine and human welfare.* New Haven, Conn.: Yale University Press, 1941.
12. Singer, C. *The story of living things.* New York: Harper, 1931.
13. Walsh, W. H. *Philosophy of history: an introduction.* New York: Harper, 1962.

3. A Note on the History of Psychology as a Specialization

A series of developments during the last two or three years seem to indicate that the history of psychology is beginning to be accepted as a separate field of specialization. In a paper given at the Ohio Academy of Science this past spring, Robert C. Davis quite cogently and correctly stressed that the specialization in the history of psychology has been in the tradition of the amateur with no specific training expected before professing that field. This note is an attempt to indicate how psychologists may be escaping from this state of affairs in the direction of greater professionalization. Presumably, our experiences would have some relevance to workers in the other behavioral sciences.

Two contributing factors that are not discussed are the availability of the present *Journal* and the organization of the Archives of the History of American Psychology at the University of Akron discussed in an earlier issue of the *Journal* by John Popplestone and Milton L. Kult.

There is no question that the major step toward emergence of professional specialization in the study of our history came about through the establishment of Division 26, the Division of the History of Psychology of the American Psychological Association. Petitions from members of the APA resulted in the formal approval of the Division at the Chicago meeting in September 1965. The records show that 211 members validated their petition signatures by paying divisional dues and some 75 applications have been received by our

This is a shortened, more formal, and updated version of a paper given at the American Psychological Association Annual Meeting, September 1966, New York.

Membership Committee since then. Interest, then, in the field of the history of psychology is a viable one at the present time. The existence of the Division serves to help make authentic study and work in the specialization.

A Ph.D. degree in the history of psychology (and biology) has already been granted at Cambridge University to Robert M. Young, then and now of Kings College. His was an individual program worked out under the direction of Professor Oliver Zangwill, Director of the Cambridge Psychology Laboratory, and was in no sense part of a continuing program. However, the possibility of other students following a substantially similar curriculum has been materially increased.

Schools of Education in the United States have permitted dissertations based on historical research for some time. Until recently this procedure has been resisted by departments of psychology because of their insistence that dissertations should involve data collection in the narrower sense of the term. A historic step was taken during 1966 at Loyola University, Chicago, when a student in the Department of Psychology was awarded his Ph.D. degree for a thesis on Brentano. This student, Antos Rancurello, Professor of Psychology at the University of Dayton, has also made the first completed English translation of Brentano's *Psychology from an Empirical Standpoint*.

It is now possible to take a graduate degree in history and systems of psychology at Cornell University under the direction of Professor Robert MacLeod. This arrangement differs from Loyola in that it extends beyond the dissertation, as such, to include a specialized program of training in history. Professor Guerlac of the History of Science program is collaborating in the program. The writer of this note has just accepted an appointment to the Department of Psychology, University of New Hampshire, beginning in the fall of 1967. A concentration in the history of psychology is being organized within the departmental offering. Ph.D. dissertations based on library research are an integral part of the program.

Another route toward specialization in the history of psychology was that chosen by one undergraduate major in psychology at Northwestern University. She is enrolled in the history of science graduate program at the University of Chicago with one of her fields that of the history of psychology. She intends to do her dissertation within this field as well. It is quite possible that this offering in the history of psychology is available in other history of science programs around the country. It is also possible that this is a pioneer step of what may be in some small fashion an increasing trend.

Still another route toward specialization is that of the postdoctoral training after a conventional Ph.D. program. This was the course followed by David L. Krantz, a Northwestern Ph.D. now at Lake Forest College. Dr. Krantz spent the last academic year at Princeton University in the department of the History of Science working with Thomas S. Kuhn, Charles Gillespie, and Carl Hempel. In the years to come this might often be used as a means of fostering specialization.

A logical fourth possibility, as yet not implemented so far as is known, would be to take postdoctoral training in the history of psychology as such. Presumably this will be an almost inevitable future development.

Aside from training directed toward the specialization, several other recent innovations deserve mention. On April 30 of last year, the History of Life Sciences Study Section of the Public Health Service held a planning conference on the history of the behavioral sciences. It would appear that the gist of their discussion centered around "*the need for adequate teaching and graduate training: planning a workshop*" as a first step toward meeting the need. Discussion brought out the need for not one but a variety of developmental workshops.

From the perspective of our colleagues in the field of history, ours is an aspect of intellectual history. Interest, although hardly very keen, is not entirely lacking. Professor John C. Burnham, of the Department of History of the Ohio State University, a graduate of Stanford's Department of History, specializes in the history of psychoanalysis.

One of the hallmarks of a specialization nowadays is the presence of grant sources which foster research in that field. In this area, the History of the Life Sciences Study Section of the United States Public Health Service has taken the lead. A variety of grants have been made as, for example, those reported in the July 1965 issue of the *Journal*. Similar grants are also made by the Division of Social Sciences of the National Science Foundation.

Such, then, are some recent events that foster in a modest way the development of the field of the history of psychology as a specialization.

4. The Birth of a Journal

The very appearance of a journal of the history of the behavioral sciences becomes a part of history. An account of how this came about is an appropriate subject for its first editorial.

Early in the 1950s it became popular to speak of the behavioral sciences. The unquestionable upsurge of interest in man's behavior gave renewed strength to old disciplines, and new techniques of research produced new directions. As behavioral science research is not the province of any one discipline, those who consider themselves behavioral scientists have devoted considerable effort to defining their many-faceted field of research. Concomitantly they have shown increasing interest in the heritage of the behavioral sciences, a concern which has found reflection in a growing number of historical studies. Something of a grass-roots phenomenon, this historical specialty has been characterized by researchers who are scattered both geographically and in different disciplines—working simultaneously but often unaware of one another. Such was the case in the development of the *Journal of the History of the Behavioral Sciences*, for unknown to each other Drs. Eric T. Carlson and Robert I. Watson began independently to explore ways in which those interested in this area could meet and communicate. Carlson had discussed the idea of founding a newsletter with the Committee on the History of Psychiatry of the American Psychiatric Association in the winter of 1958-1959. As the project seemed worthy of exploration in the opinion of the Committee, a prospectus was mailed to nearly one hundred people in May 1959. The replies were highly encouraging,

---

A statement prepared by Eric T. Carlson and amplified by Robert I. Watson.

and so, with the backing of Dr. Oskar Diethelm and the support of the Department of Psychiatry of the New York Hospital (Payne Whitney Psychiatric Clinic) – Cornell University Medical College, the *History of the Behavioral Sciences Newsletter* was first issued in July 1960.

The introduction to that first issue stated:

> The *Newsletter* is directed toward all those interested in the history of any of the behavioral sciences, whether they are engaged in specific research, bibliophile activities, or general study. It includes anthropologists, psychiatrists, psychologists, sociologists, and any others who are working in this area, such as biologists, neurologists, and historians.
>
> The *Newsletter* has three principal purposes: to make people working in this historical field aware of each other's existence and special interests; to provide a means by which these separate individuals may communicate with one another (e.g., to request specialized information and bibliographical aids or to make any appropriate announcements of meetings and of actual or potential research grants); to explore bibliographical possibilities by listing new books and co-operative surveys of developments with pertinence to this area. The *Newsletter* will not cover all the work done in the behavioral sciences; it will deal only with historical material.

At the same time Watson, along with David Bakan and John C. Burnham, issued a call for a meeting of members of the American Psychological Association who were interested in advancing the study of the history of their specialty. The group first met on September 3, 1960, in Chicago at the Annual Meeting of the Association. These meetings have continued annually since that time. In October 1960, but three months after its predecessor, the first *Newsletter* of the History of Psychology Group made its appearance. The close collaboration between these two newsletters was strengthened when Watson became Consulting Editor in Psychology to the *History of the Behavioral Sciences Newsletter* in January 1961.

Neither newsletter said anything about aspirations to become a journal, but this certainly was an unspoken hope of both Carlson and Watson. It was Watson, however, who was to make this wish become an actuality. As a founder and stockholder of Psychology Press, a press devoted to the publication of scholarly journals, he proposed that they consider publishing a journal devoted to the history of the behavioral sciences.

They agreed to consider doing so. Watson informed Carlson of this possibility in the fall of 1962, and they met in Evanston in November of that year to review the proposal. After a careful discussion and consultation with pertinent individuals, they decided that such a project was desirable and feasible. Watson asked Carlson to serve as Co-Editor; the latter was enthusiastic about the new journal but decided after considerable deliberation that his research commitments would make it inadvisable. Watson proceeded to write his recommendation for the new journal, presenting it to the Psychology Press in the spring of 1963. At their meeting on Sunday, September 1, 1963, they voted to accept financial sponsorship of the *Journal of the History of the Behavioral Sciences.* Watson immediately set about developing an editorial board, drawing heavily upon individuals associated with the two *Newsletters*, and taking the other steps necessary for launching this, the first issue.

5. Editorial Policy and Its Implementation

The appearance of a new journal makes desirable a general statement of policy and an account of its implementation. This *Journal* has four basic objectives:
1. To advance the study of the history of the various behavioral sciences by providing a publication source.
2. To inform readers about current developments in the historical aspects of these disciplines.
3. To develop more competent historically oriented scholars in these fields.
4. To foster a sense of unity among specialists in the behavioral sciences, while still recognizing that there are differences of emphasis and subject matter.

All of these objectives will be the subject of future, more specific editorials. The interdisciplinary nature of the *Journal* and provisions for implementation will receive some consideration at this time.

The behavioral sciences are not a single ordered body of fact and theory and law. They do not operate through a uniform methodology. Notwithstanding a few valiant attempts, integration is not particularly noticeable and certainly not successful.

The admonition that Lord Acton offered some years ago becomes pertinent. He reminded us that a science may be studied in either one or two ways—through its own particular methods or through an examination of its history. Use of the historical method, common to the behavioral sciences, is a way to implement interdisciplinary cooperation. Often we write from the point of view of a specific discipline but sometimes in a perspective that cuts across the disciplines. In following either procedure we can make a contribution to an increased integration of the behavioral sciences which can only be salutary.

An author is urged to consider if his topic has implications beyond his specialty, to ask himself whether or not it can be set in a larger perspective. Editorial obligation, however, extends only to making sure that the author is aware of this issue, and failure to draw out behavioral science implications is not a reason for hesitation in acceptance.

In a multi-disciplinary journal no one editor is omniscient enough to evaluate all articles. Implementation is carried out under the direction of the Editorial Board. The interdisciplinary character of the *Journal* is reflected in the nine specializations represented. On the Board are scholars in Anthropology, History, Linguistics, Neurology, Neurophysiology, Psychoanalysis, Psychiatry, Psychology and Sociology. The pages of this *Journal* are also open to Philosophers, Educators, and workers in the other Social Sciences. If papers from these other disciplines make their appearance in sufficient numbers, appropriate Board Members will be added.

Referees are also being asked to read papers. They are nominated for the task of reading specific papers by Board members in areas in which they possess specialized competence.

Acceptance, rejection, and suggestions for modification are entrusted to specialists in the field in question who are either members of the Board or referees. At least one subject matter specialist will read each manuscript. Two or more opinions will be sought whenever there is a reason for doubt.

Papers to be considered for publication may be submitted directly to the Editor or to any member of the Board. In either case manuscripts are read by specialists in the area in which they fall. Their comments, along with the manuscripts, are sent to the Editor, who corresponds with the authors.

A viable journal is one that is useful to its readers. It reflects various points of view, not those with which they all necessarily agree, but, at least, ones they consider pertinent to their interests. Policy needs further implementation, expansion and exploration in depth. Members of the Editorial Board already have been invited to write editorials on policy. Suggestions and criticisms from readers are invited in the form of letters addressed to the Editor.

6. Recent Developments in the Historiography of American Psychology

Developments in the study of the history of psychology may conveniently and appropriately be considered by first examining the period of pre-specialization which extended from the turn of the century to about 1960. The events of the organizational period of the few short years thereafter will then be identified.

Interest expressed in research and in teaching the history of psychology toward the end of the pre-specialization period will serve as an introduction. In 1960 a paper was published which reported on this matter.[1] For that study a sample of 1,600 entries was drawn from the 1958 Directory of the American Psychological Association in which each member lists his particular interests within the field. It was found that expressions of interest in the history of psychology were indicated by six psychologists. Extrapolating to the total membership, then 16,000, gave sixty psychologists who considered the history of the field among their interests. Since this was but one interest among the several they reported, it could have been entirely casual and avocational and did not necessarily imply either teaching or research in the field. So, even this figure is misleadingly high. A neglect of the history of their field seemed to characterize American psychologists at this time and to support the contention that specialization in the study of the history of psychology was yet to come.

Publication of monographs, articles, and textbooks also seemed

---

An extended version of this paper was given at a colloquium for the Department of the History of Science, Harvard University.

1. Robert I. Watson, "The History of Psychology: A Neglected Area," *American Psychologist*, 1960, *15:*251-255.

to indicate only very limited interest. Monographic studies in depth are crucial for serious developments in historical specialties. Only a handful had appeared prior to 1960. George M. Stratton[2] of the University of California, Berkeley, published on Theophrastus in 1917. Howard C. Warren[3] of Princeton University wrote on association psychology in 1921. Joseph Peterson[4] of George Peabody College analyzed the history of theory and research in intelligence in 1925. Franklin Fearing[5] of Northwestern University published on the history of reflex action in 1930. H. M. Gardiner and his associates[6] at Smith College appraised emotion and feeling in historical perspective in 1937. Edwin G. Boring[7] of Harvard University examined the history relating to sensation and perception in 1942. Although an exhaustive search of the literature would perhaps turn up two or three more of comparable quality, these were the majority of monographic studies during the first sixty years of this century.

Articles in the journals were also infrequent. Issues of three psychological journals whose editorial policy permitted inclusion of articles of historical nature were examined for the twenty-year period 1938-1957.[8] From the 2,800 articles that appeared, only thirty-eight were found to be historical. Of course, there were occasionally articles of historical nature in other journals, but these were the three main periodicals where one would expect to find them. Publications on the history of psychology were certainly not numerous.

Textbooks fell into one of three categories—general histories of the modern period, books of readings from original sources, and books on schools or systems of psychology. In the first category

---

2. George M. Stratton, *Theophrastus and the Greek Physiological Psychology* (New York: Macmillan, 1917).

3. Howard C. Warren, *A History of Association Psychology* (New York: Scribners, 1921).

4. Joseph Peterson, *Early Conceptions and Tests of Intelligence* (Yonkers: World, 1925).

5. Franklin Fearing, *Reflex Action: A Study in the History of Physiological Psychology* (Baltimore: Williams & Wilkins, 1930).

6. H. M. Gardiner, Ruth C. Metcalf, John Beebe-Center, *Feeling and Emotion: A History of Theories* (New York: American Book, 1937).

7. Edwin G. Boring, *Sensation and Perception in the History of Experimental Psychology* (New York: Appleton, 1942).

8. Watson, *op. cit.*

were those by Edwin G. Boring[9] of Harvard and Gardner Murphy,[10] then of Columbia, both texts first published in 1929 and both destined to become outstanding among the five or six others that also made their appearance. Since they covered only the modern period, for psychological work from the Greeks through the Renaissance, considerable reliance came to be placed upon the monumental three volumes published between 1912 and 1921 by George Sidney Brett,[11] an Oxford-educated University of Toronto Professor of Philosophy. Since 1953 a one-volume abridgment edited by R. S. Peters[12] of the University of London has also been used for this period in the same fashion.

Benjamin Rand[13] of Harvard in 1912 and Wayne Dennis[14] of Brooklyn College in 1948 published books of readings from primary sources. In 1931 Robert Sessions Woodworth[15] of Columbia and in 1933 Edna Heidbreder,[16] shortly thereafter at Wellesley College, published analyses of the schools of psychology that had been so prominent in the earlier years of the century.

The two volumes edited by Carl Murchison[17] of Clark University entitled *Psychologies of 1925* and *Psychologies of 1930*, although having historical overtones and now being valued as historical documents, were essentially statements of the then-current state of affairs. In some measure the same may be said for the continuing

---

9. Edwin G. Boring, *A History of Experimental Psychology* (New York: Century, 1929).

10. Gardner Murphy, *An Historical Introduction to Modern Psychology* (New York: Harcourt, 1929).

11. George S. Brett, *A History of Psychology*, 3 vols. (London: Allen, 1912-1921).

12. R. S. Peters, ed., Brett's *History of Psychology* (London: Allen and Unwin, 1953).

13. Benjamin Rand, *The Classical Psychologists* (New York: Houghton, 1912).

14. Wayne Dennis, ed., *Readings in the History of Psychology* (New York: Appleton, 1948).

15. Robert S. Woodworth, *Contemporary Schools of Psychology* (New York: Ronald, 1931).

16. Edna Heidbreder, *Seven Psychologies* (New York: Century, 1933).

17. Carl Murchison, ed., *Psychologies of 1925* (Worcester, Mass.: Clark University Press, 1926); *Psychologies of 1930* (Worcester, Mass.: Clark University Press, 1930).

series of autobiographical statements by psychologists also launched by Murchison[18] in 1930.

It is symptomatic of the field during the period until 1960 that more than once in this survey has reference been made to only two individuals and two universities. In other words, work on the history of psychology was not only sparse, it was scattered, with no one university trying to make a coordinated effort. With one exception, the individuals that have been mentioned up to this point were both more productive and more visible for their work in some area other than the history of psychology.

Despite wide-ranging authoritative publications in other fields, and despite active direction of the Psychological Laboratory of Harvard for many years, there has been one pioneer specialist in the history of psychology. Our George Sarton, as it were, was Edwin G. Boring, Professor Emeritus of Psychology at Harvard University. The revised edition of his *History of Experimental Psychology*[19] made its appearance in 1950. There is no question that this is still *the* standard textbook on the history of psychology not only for the United States, but probably for the entire world. Professor Boring has also expressed his interest in the history of psychology through numerous papers, now reprinted.[20]

This, then, was the state of affairs in 1960. Interest was so negligible that in that year I tried to demonstrate this in a paper, "The History of Psychology: A Neglected Area,"[21] published in the *American Psychologist*, our professional journal received by all members of the American Psychological Association. With no claim other than this assertion of neglect, this article seemed to reflect rather aptly a just then emerging, changing climate of opinion. Events pertinent to the organizational period in the historiography of American psychology followed each other at a relatively rapid pace in the few years following.

During 1960, David Bakan, a psychologist, John C. Burnham, a

---

18. Carl Murchison, ed., *A History of Psychology in Autobiography*, Vol. I (Worcester, Mass.: Clark University Press, 1930).

19. Edwin G. Boring, *A History of Experimental Psychology* (2nd ed., New York: Appleton, 1950).

20. Edwin G. Boring, *History, Psychology and Science*, ed. Robert I. Watson and Donald T. Campbell (New York: Wiley, 1963); *Psychologist at Large: An Autobiography and Selected Essays* (New York: Basic Books, 1961).

21. Watson, *op. cit.*

historian, and I met in order to make arrangements for what proved to be the first of a series of "special interest" group meetings held in connection with annual conventions of the American Psychological Association.[22] This organization has as one of its minor functions the arrangement of meetings for those who have some special interest in a particular phase or topic of the field, such as the history of psychology. A meeting was held in 1960 at the time of the annual convention, and the fifteen or so individuals who met decided not only to hold annual meetings thereafter, but to launch a newsletter devoted to the history of psychology.

Meanwhile, in psychiatry, a closely related activity was taking place. Dr. Eric T. Carlson of Payne Whitney Clinic and Cornell University Medical School had urged the founding of a newsletter on the Committee on the History of Psychiatry of the American Psychiatric Association in the winter of 1958-1959. As a result of their agreement, a prospectus was mailed, contributions solicited, and, in July 1960, the *History of the Behavioral Sciences Newsletter* first appeared. As the title meant to convey, it was intended to include work not only in psychology, but also in anthropology, psychiatry, sociology, and other relevant fields.

The two newsletters were brought into contact in January 1961 when I was invited to become the consulting editor in psychology to the *History of the Behavioral Sciences Newsletter*. These newsletters continued for some time until the need was no longer present because of the next development.

Both Carlson and I had recognized the value of organizing a journal in the field, and I wrote a prospectus for such a journal and secured approval for its publication through the Psychology Press, Inc., a press devoted to the publication of scholarly journals. In September 1963 the Press voted to accept sponsorship of the new *Journal of the History of the Behavioral Sciences*. An editorial board, including Dr. Carlson, whose other duties made it impossible for him to serve as co-editor, was organized. It drew heavily upon individuals associated with both newsletters.[23] The year of 1964 was spent in preparation for publication, and in January 1965 the first quarterly

22. [Eric T. Carlson and Robert I. Watson] "Editorial: The Birth of a Journal," *Journal of the History of the Behavioral Sciences*, 1965, *1*:3-4.
23. The intact charter board with three additions is Mary A. Andresen (Bibliography), Paul Bohannan (Anthropology), Edwin G. Boring (Psychology), Mary Brazier (Neurophysiology), Eric T. Carlson (Psychiatry and Psychoanalysis),

number appeared. Now in its fourth year, it seems to have achieved a certain amount of acceptance as a vehicle for historical work in the areas for which it is intended.

Meanwhile, meetings of the History of Psychology Group at the annual conventions of the American Psychological Association continued. As attendance increased to about forty or fifty, there was some discussion as to whether or not the organization should take on a more formal character. This was possible because the American Psychological Association is organized on a divisional structure (that is, upon taking certain steps of application, it is possible for members to petition to organize a formal division). Although the informality of the "group" was a strong feature in its favor, it was decided at the meeting in 1964 to proceed with a divisional organization. One of the major arguments for this step was that a younger person in the field of psychology would feel that this division made his interest and his work in the history of psychology "authentic" and an accepted part of psychology. At its meeting in September 1965 the governing body of the American Psychological Association approved the formation of the Division of the History of Psychology. The charter membership numbered 211. Two years later there were approximately 300 members. At the meetings of 1966 and 1967 formal programs of papers and symposia were arranged by the Division. The charter president was the present writer, and Gardner Murphy of the Menninger Foundation is the president for 1967–1968.

Archival matters also received attention from psychologists. An *ad hoc* Committee on Psychological Archives was set up in September 1961 by the American Psychological Association and charged with making an appraisal of its holdings and recommending on their disposition.[24] This was shortly prior to a move from one headquarters building to another. It was found that in large measure old records had been destroyed on the occasion of a move some fifteen years before. After consultation with professional archivists, the com-

---

Edwin Clarke (Neurology and Neurophysiology), Norman Dain (History and Psychiatry), Oskar Diethelm (Psychiatry and Psychoanalysis), Alvin W. Gouldner (Sociology), Dell H. Hymes (Anthropology and Linguistics), Robert B. MacLeod (Psychology), Robert K. Merton (Sociology), George Mora (Book Reviews), George W. Stocking, Jr. (History and Anthropology).

24. The committee consisted of Robert I. Watson, chairman, then of Northwestern, Leonard Carmichael, then of the Smithsonian Institution, and W. Clark Trow of Michigan.

mittee recommended to the Board of Directors of the American Psychological Association that the small amount of material remaining be deposited with the Library of Congress and that a subvention be allocated for its classification. Since the new building costs put a severe drain on the financial resources of the moment, these recommendations were not followed at that time. Another activity of the committee was the sponsorship of a paper offering advice to individual psychologists on how to arrange and preserve private papers for archival purposes.[25]

In 1967, a subsequent *ad hoc* Committee on Archives, chaired by Max Meenes[26] of Harvard University, arranged for the deposit of the archives of the Association with the Library of Congress. This committee is now working collaboratively with the Library in sorting and selecting materials. Association records and materials of officers and editors of the Association journals are to be the major sources of deposit.

The need for additional archival facilities serving the history of American psychology was recognized by John Popplestone,[27] who early in the 1960s began to explore the possibility of such an organization through the University of Akron, with which he is associated. The services of archivists and psychologists interested in this problem were enlisted. In November 1965 the Board of Directors of the University of Akron officially endorsed its establishment. In close collaboration with the Division of the History of Psychology of the American Psychological Association, a board of advisors was organized.[28] Since then, accession and promises of deposit from both individuals and organizations, such as a regional psychological

---

25. Nathan Reingold and Robert I. Watson, "The Organization and Preservation of Private Papers," *American Psychologist*, 1966, *21*:971-973.

26. Max Meenes, personal communication, 4 January 1968.

27. John A. Popplestone and Milton L. Kult, "The Archives of the History of American Psychology, January 1965–August 1966," *Journal of the History of the Behavioral Sciences*, 1967, *3*:60-63; "Annual Report of the Archives of the History of American Psychology," *Journal of the History of the Behavioral Sciences*, 1968, *4*:186-187.

28. Members of the board of advisors are Robert I. Watson, chairman, David Bakan, Josef M. Brozek, Leonard Carmichael, Robert C. Davis, Wayne Dennis, Solomon Diamond, Leonard W. Ferguson, J. A. Gengerelli, Joseph J. Greenbaum, Ernest R. Hilgard, Robert B. MacLeod, George Mandler, Wallace A. Russell, S. Stansfeld Sargent, H. G. Schrickel, Morton A. Seidenfeld, S. B. Sells, Virginia Staudt Sexton, Marie Skodak, and Michael Wertheimer.

association and a journal, have been most gratifying. Research is under way, particularly in the collection of oral histories. The archives also sponsored and will continue to sponsor exhibits of historical apparatus.

In a survey of graduate training in psychology Ronald Mayer[29] of San Francisco State College reported in 1967 that about two-thirds of the departments of psychology surveyed offered an undergraduate course in the history of psychology. At the graduate level it was found that 105 of the 190 departments returning the questionnaire, or 55 percent, reported that there were graduate courses offered in this field. Among the other questions asked in this survey was one which had to do with whether a thesis primarily historical in nature would be acceptable as meeting the Ph.D. degree requirements. Twenty-nine percent said yes or possibly, 61 percent replied no or probably not, and the remaining 10 percent expressed no opinion.

Until the last two years, specialization in the history of psychology at the graduate level demanded initiative such as that shown by Robert M. Young of King's College, Cambridge, who sought and carried through his own particular program under the direction of Professor Oliver Zangwill, Director of the Cambridge Psychological Laboratory, with the assistance of the History of Science Program of the University. He did this by the simple device of asking that he be allowed to do so. So far as I am aware, his Ph.D. degree in the history of psychology is unique.

During the 1960s other routes to specialized training have been found. The following are known to have been followed: the securing of a postgraduate fellowship in the history of science, enrolling in a history of science program with history of psychology as one of the fields, and writing a thesis on a historical topic without an earlier specialized course program in the field.

From the 1967–1968 guide to graduate study in the history of science and medicine, prepared by Derek J. Price,[30] for a total of twenty-nine institutions, two of the 144 full-time faculty members and four of the ninety associated and visiting faculty are psycholo-

---

29. Ronald W. Mayer, "Current Developments in the History of Psychology," paper delivered at meeting at the American Psychological Association, Washington, D.C., 4 September 1967.

30. Derek J. de Solla Price, "A Guide to Graduate Study and Research in the History of Science and Medicine," *Isis*, 1967, *58:*385–395.

gists. There are at least six others teaching some aspect of the history of the behavioral sciences in these programs.

In the last year or two, formal graduate programs leading to a Ph.D. in the history of psychology have been started at Cornell,[31] Princeton,[32] and New Hampshire. Although these programs show differences, the points of similarity are more important. A dissertation in depth based on library research will be expected.[33] As in most graduate specializations in psychology, the would-be historian is expected to have a thorough grounding in all major aspects of the field, and his first year's program is apt to be taken more or less in common with his fellow graduate students, including, however, some work in history and systematic psychology. Specialization is most prominent in the second and subsequent years of training through seminars, individual tutorials, and work outside of the department of psychology. All three programs are in the process of being worked out, and it would be premature to try to go into details.

Another means of increasing skills in teaching and research is the summer workshop or institute. Under the auspices of the National Science Foundation, one is to be held on the campus of the University of New Hampshire during the summer of 1968. The project director is Josef Brozek, Research Professor of Psychology at Lehigh University, the associate director, Robert I. Watson, and other members of the instructional staff are Henry Guerlac and Robert B. MacLeod of Cornell, Julian Jaynes of Princeton, David Krantz of Lake Forest, and George Mora, M.D., of Yale. Participants are to be twenty-five college teachers of the history of psychology and five graduate students.

The first relatively thorough critique of developments in the history of the behavioral sciences was the subject of a paper from Britain by the aforementioned Robert M. Young,[34] which appeared in the 1966 issue of *History of Science.* In this review, primarily of American work, he was sharply critical of many aspects of the work,

31. Robert B. MacLeod, personal communication, 4 January 1968.
32. Julian Jaynes, personal communication, 4 January 1968.
33. This may sound so trite to most historians as not to need specification, but in the somewhat insecure field of psychology, insistence on a hard data-collection in theses was one of the bulwarks of its scientific respectability. The decision to permit such dissertations is therefore a bold and not easily won step.
34. Robert M. Young, "Scholarship and the History of the Behavioral Sciences," *History of Science*, 1966, 5:1–51.

although he centered primarily on the question of the poor quality of scholarship, rather than on the developments which have just been sketched.

There is no question that we are still in the stage of developing out of what is essentially an amateur interest in the field and are only slowly making progress toward professionalization. Young's pleas, not only for greater sophistication as historians, but also for more emphasis on studies in depth which are still very much lacking, are well taken. Indicative of this lack is the absence of any specialized publication source for studies which are monographic in nature. Just as it was in the period of pre-specialization, most current writing has been in the form of either books or articles. This is very much one of our most urgent needs.

Personally, I find myself too close to the period in question to evaluate the quality and significance of the individual publications that have appeared during the 1960s. It will have to suffice to say something about the quantity. In its first three years of publication (1965-1967) the *Journal of the History of the Behavioral Sciences* published forty-one articles devoted to the history of psychology, which may be compared to the thirty-eight over the twenty-year span (1938-1957) in the three journals. In the same three-year span, fifteen books primarily on the history of psychology were received for review from among the total of sixty-one books.

The results of a 1965-1966 questionnaire study by J. Brozek[35] reported on current research activities of fifty-seven members of the Division. Current works completed or nearly completed numbered thirty-one, while sixty-one works were in progress. Of the twelve books completed, nearly completed, or under way, only two appeared to be monographic in depth and scope.

Such then are the events of the long period of pre-specialization and the few years of self-conscious organization. Increased sophistication concerning the history of the field and that of related areas, recognition of the need for studies in depth, increased avenues of communication, and, above all, the appearance of a generation of specially trained historians of psychology will probably solidify some of these trends while changing others in ways beyond recognition.

---

35. Josef Brožek, "Current and Anticipated Research in the History of Psychology," *Journal of the History of the Behavioral Sciences*, 1968, 4: 180-185.

7. The History of Psychology as a Specialty: A Personal View of Its First Fifteen Years

I shall take this occasion to pay tribute to those individuals, living and dead, who helped to develop the specialization of the history of psychology within a broader context of the history of the behavioral sciences. I shall sketch the various themes that demonstrate the emergence of a new role for psychologists and other behavioral scientists arising from a new-found identification with the specialty, a maintained scholarly activity, and the presence of appropriate institutions to facilitate the activities of the new historical community that has made its appearance in the last 15 years. Each theme discussed will be followed through time to the present, but they will be presented in a rough chronological sequence of first appearance.

My role in these activities, such as it has been, I have presented in my recently published autobiography, and I need say no more about it. Nevertheless, I shall draw primarily upon personal experience with the individuals and events that figure in this account— much of it not available in the published literature. One obvious source of distortion is created by my greater immersion in activities connected with the history of psychology rather than with the broader contextual field of the history of behavioral sciences.

> This paper was originally presented at the annual meeting of Cheiron: The International Society for the History of the Behavioral Sciences, held in Durham, New Hampshire, May 31 - June 2, 1974. (Author's editorial comment: This article may serve as a means of placing the first ten years of the *Journal of the History of the Behavioral Sciences* in the perspective of the other activities of these years. Indirectly, it can be considered as a final summing up of the editorial activities now that the editorship passes into the capable hands of Dr. Barbara C. Ross.)

A compelling reason exists for consideration of the broader area of the history of the behavioral sciences. Nonpsychologists have contributed materially to the history of psychology as a professional entity. I have in mind Eric T. Carlson, psychiatrist, who was instrumental in the collaboration of advancing mutual interests, especially in connection with his interdisciplinary research group and the founding and maintenance of the *Journal of the History of the Behavioral Sciences*. There is also George Mora, psychiatrist, Book Review Editor of the *Journal* then and now, who has in some ways a more difficult function to serve than any other editor because he has responsibility for selecting books for review, securing the books, soliciting reviews and seeing that they meet professional standards. This last, his relationship with the review and the reviewer, requires firm statesmanship. Consider the delicacy involved in telling a reviewer, whom you have asked to write the review, that it requires modification. For no other recompense than the satisfaction of a job well done, he carried on his function in superlative fashion. There is John Burnham, historian, who, in the late fifties, attended meetings of the American Psychological Association in order to acquaint himself with the work being done in the history of psychology. Finding very little, he encouraged the launching of the forerunner of the Division of History of Psychology—the History of Psychology Group—and ever since has steadily maintained his sharp incisiveness in the service of high standards of scholarship. Remarks in a similar spirit could be made about Roscoe and Ghisella Hinkle of sociology, Otto Marx and Jacques Quen of psychiatry, Henry Guerlac, Uta Merzbach and Audrey Davis of the history of science and medicine, and members of the Editorial Board of JHBS to be mentioned a bit later. We cannot talk of the historians of psychology without speaking of historians of specialties other than that of psychology.

The situation prevailing prior to the 1960's is an appropriate point of contrast. In 1958, 60 psychologists, or about 1 out of 170, indicated through the Directory of the APA that among their interests was the history of psychology. By no means, however, did even these few psychologists imply that the history of psychology was a major interest or that they had published in this area. To illustrate the paucity of work in the field (excluding biographies and necrologies), there were more psychological articles published on the history of psychology in 1965–1967, the first three years of the existence of JHBS, than there had been in the twenty-five year span from 1938 to 1957 in those three American journals that accepted articles in this field.

Prior to the sixties, publication in the history of psychology was a nonsustained interest on the part of a particular psychologist. Practically all of the relevant books prior to 1960 were solo excursions into history by their authors. Stratton, Warren, Dennis, Peterson, Fearing, Gardiner and his associates, Heidbreder, Woodworth and Murphy each wrote a single, important volume and then turned to something else. There was also the occasional flurry of publications after the death of a Hall or a Hull, a Titchener or a Tolman, a Watson or a Woodworth. Most of these were prepared by individuals whose claim to historical expertise was some degree of association with the eminent individual. Before and after, they did not write in the historical mode. In addition to those once contemporary research studies which became historically significant with the passage of time, there was another sort of publication that came to be viewed as historical. These were once contemporary theoretical accounts which later became historical documents; for example, Harry Helson's important series of papers on Gestalt theory or the Murchison-edited volumes on the schools of psychology.

During these earlier years there was, of course, one exception to all that I have just said—Edwin G. Boring. He did not publish historically-oriented books and articles prolifically; he did maintain his interest in history; and he did identify with the field.

Garry was a complex person. It is perhaps the account by Julian Jaynes, in the April 1969 issue of JHBS, that best captures his complexity. I must content myself with saying that probably both his friends and his enemies were right in their appraisals of him. To some he was astonishingly broad, to others he was incredibly narrow; he was the soul of compassion, he was vindictive; he was certain, he was torn by doubts; he looked to the past, he was forever reaching for the future. And yet, within his own frame of reference, he was of a piece uniting the Fechnerian day-and-night sides into a personal monism. Activities in history were exposed only to the warmth of day—his enthusiasm, his generosity, his detailed helpfulness. Garry gave of his time to the first efforts toward making the study of the history of psychology a viable specialization: he sent a message to the first and came to the second meeting of the History of Psychology Group; helped the attempt to form a Division; published in the first issue of JHBS; and had hoped to come to the Durham Institute, but his last illness prevented this. There are several individuals who attended the 1974 Cheiron meeting who have been influenced by Garry's personality and work. He would have approved of the inevitable parting that must take place—that one must leave behind his teacher. It would not have mattered to him that we may no longer share his convictions, although he would hope we would remember that our positions, even in disagreement, are at least partially created from knowing him.

Before 1960, it is correct to say historical study was not a specialty for psychologists. Characteristic were short excursions into history, the need to pay homage to a prominent deceased psychologist and the accumulation of material, once contemporary in orientation, that became historically significant with the passage of time.

This, then, was the state of affairs in 1960. Early that year, David Bakan and John C. Burnham attended a meeting in Evanston, Illinois, in order to make arrangements to issue invitations to those interested in history to meet at the coming September APA convention. Through a provision of the APA program committee, "special interest groups" may announce meetings on the program, and the purpose in this instance was stated to be the encouragement of work in the history of psychology. That September, 36 people showed up! Much of the time of the meeting (later to be called the History of Psychology Group) was taken up with short descriptions of current work in history, identification of available sources, exploration of steps to open up new sources of publication, and suggestions on what means might be pursued to make history a more meaningful and viable scholarly activity. Strong complaints were voiced against university psychology departments not accepting dissertations on historical subjects because they did not involve data collecting in the usual sense. Concern about lack of pertinent archival sources also was expressed. It can be noted that this meeting was prophetic in giving expression to many of the problems met and surmounted in later years. At the meeting it was decided to continue to hold meetings in future years and to organize a newsletter. After the first years, in 1963 and continuing through 1965, a committee of Cedric Larson and Ron Mayer maintained and enlarged the Newsletter. It closed publication only with the appearance of JHBS.

In the meantime, a very important activity had been launched in psychiatry. It should be prefaced by some remarks on its earlier history. The program in the history of psychiatry and the behavioral sciences at the Payne Whitney Clinic and Cornell University Medical College considerably antedates the time span with which we are now dealing, since it can be considered to be based on the historical library which Dr. Oskar Diethelm began years before it became a separate library in 1958. To this very day Dr. Diethelm, the pioneer historian of psychiatry, maintains an active interest in this enterprise. In 1958 Eric T. Carlson developed a small research team in the history of psychiatry and related disciplines. Normal Dain was an early associate and, to select a representative year, 1966, besides Carlson and Diethelm, Jacques Quen was a clinical assistant professor, and Dorothy Ross and Meribeth Simpson research fellows in a staff perhaps twice as large as those that have just been mentioned. The library staff itself was the source of the *Journal*'s editors for bibliography: first Mary Andresen and now Liselotte Bendix Stern. Even before 1960, it was this same Eric T. Carlson who suggested the founding of a newsletter to the Committee on the History of Psychiatry of the other APA. In July 1960, this newsletter, signalizing by its very name its broadness of scope that was envisioned—the *History of the Behavioral Sciences Newsletter*—first appeared. The two newsletters came into relationship with one another through the appointment, to the board of the latter, of a consulting editor for psychology.

The *Journal of the History of the Behavioral Sciences* was a natural outgrowth of the two newsletters. A prospectus was planned in 1962; it was presented to the financial sponsoring agency in 1963; and solicitation of manuscripts began in 1964. The first issue appeared in January 1965. Press of other duties prevented Eric T. Carlson from participating as co-editor, but he did join the Editorial Board. Other members of that Charter Board were drawn primarily from individuals associated with the two newsletters. Included then and now were Paul Bohannan, Dell Hymes, and George W. Stocking, Jr., from anthropology; Mary Brazier and Edwin B. Clarke from neurology; Norman Dain from history; Oskar Diethelm from psychiatry; Alvin Gouldner and Robert Merton from sociology; and George Mora, psychiatry and book reviews. Only our deceased pioneers, Edwin G. Boring and Robert MacLeod, representing psychology, are no longer with the Board. Other psychologists who replaced them were Robert Weyant, Wilhelm Van Hoorn, and Frank Wesley. During recent years Meribeth Simpson has served as Editorial Assistant and, in turn, has been aided by Stephanie Ackerman Swift. This year, 1974, completes the tenth year and, despite a series of vicissitudes, JHBS seems accepted as an appropriate publication source.

One crucial problem was the short-lived installation of page charges, a step taken at the Annual Meeting of Stockholders of the Corporation at the Montreal Meeting of the APA in September 1973. This was done, despite the objections of the present Editor and his announced intention to resign over this issue (to take effect at the end of 1974). Robert Weyant, heretofore Associate Editor, stepped in as Editor to try to see if this step could be accomplished without destroying the *Journal*. It could not. A page-charge policy was followed for several months of 1973 and 1974; but it became increasingly clear that these charges were unpopular, and that the quality of the *Journal* could have been affected had they been allowed to remain indefinitely. Accordingly, the page-charge policy was rescinded by the Corporation in May 1974.

As the *Journal* enters on its second decade in 1975, it will be edited by Barbara Ross with the support of members of the present Board, including this author.

Now, going back again to 1961, it was in this year that disposition of the archives of the American Psychological Association received consideration. A committee was set up which included Leonard Carmichael and W. Clark Trow. After meetings with professional archivists, a plan for deposit with the Library of Congress was arranged; but financial stringencies prevented deposit at that time. Another activity was the sponsorship of a paper on the proper disposition of private papers for archival purposes with the senior author, Nathan Reingold. A new committee, organized a few years later under the chairmanship of the late Max Meenes, made arrangements for periodic deposit of APA papers with the Library of Congress.

Extending over the years of the early sixties was the implementation of the plans of John Popplestone for The Archives of the History of American Psychology. In these matters he had the services of consultants and the endorsement of the newly-formed Division of the History of Psychology. In November 1965, the Archives was officially established by the Board of the University of Akron. Since then, under his forceful and enthusiastic direction and aided by a

Board of Advisors including David Bakan, Josef Brozek, Bob Davis, the late Robert MacLeod, Wallace A. Russell, Solomon Diamond, Virginia Sexton and Michael Wertheimer, it has been accepted as *the* archive for papers of individual psychologists and organizations other than the APA itself. In all of John Popplestone's activities in connection with the Archives, he has had the inestimable help of his wife, Marion White McPherson.

Another type of archival activity was launched in 1973 at the University of New Hampshire. This is the research archive collection set up by Rand Evans. It is not the usual depository because material is sought only to the extent that there is considerable expectancy that, within a reasonable time, such material will lead to research efforts. The collection is exemplified by present holdings on Titchener, and the topics, not actually yet realized, on Max Wertheimer and Kurt Lewin.

It is necessary now to go back in time to another development attributable to the efforts of the History of Psychology Group. As attendance increased, it became obvious that the one way to assure program hours at annual conventions would be to attempt to develop a more formal organization. The American Psychology Association is organized on a divisional structure, making it possible for a group interested in a common theme to petition to become a division. Among division privileges is a specified amount of program time at annual meetings. It was decided in 1964 to proceed with a divisional organization. There was some reluctance about taking this step because many found the informal, almost casual, unstructured meetings a unique source of intellectual stimulation. The crucial argument for divisional structure was voiced by a young member, whose name is unfortunately lost, that, if we had a Division of the History of Psychology, he would feel his interest in work in this area was more "authentic" and established as an accepted part of psychology. This and other arguments led to a decision of the Group to carry on the necessary steps, primarily the securing of an appropriate number of signatures in a petition for a division. The following year was spent in carrying on the necessary preliminaries and, in September 1965, the Council of Representatives of the APA approved the formation of the Division of the History of Psychology. Since 1966 formal programs have been presented at the time of the annual meetings. The charter membership numbered 211, two years later the membership had increased to 300, and at the present time there are nearly 500 members.

The charter program of the Division took place at the New York APA meeting in September 1966, for which Josef Brozek had served as program chairman. Twenty papers were given, including those by David Krantz, Ted Mischel, Frank Wesley, John Popplestone, Eric T. Carlson, Robert Harper and Michael Wertheimer. Gardner Murphy was installed as President-elect for the following year, John Popplestone as Secretary-Treasurer, and Michael Wertheimer and Benjamin Wolman as Representatives to Council. Robert Davis served as Chairman of the Membership Committee. The years since have seen a maintained interest in the sessions. The informal give-and-take of the annual meetings of the History of Psychology Group was to become a fixture of these programs by a session now labeled "Happenings." Subsequent presidents have included Robert MacLeod, Karl Dallenbach, David Bakan, Mary Henle, Solomon Diamond and, currently, Josef Brozek.

During the years of the sixties, funds for research grants in the history of the behavioral sciences were obtained from Federal sources and some private foundations. The History of the Life Sciences Study Section of the United States Public Health began functioning sometime in the late fifties. Edwin G. Boring was one of its earlier members and later George Mora and Saul Rosenzweig served as members. Jeanne Brand, as a staff person, was of considerable help to all anxious applicants for funding. The National Institute of Health Career Fellowship Program, one of the country's most prestigious and sought-after sources of funding for a career in research and writing, was held by one of our psychiatric members, Otto Marx, for a considerable number of years. Funds in recent years, as we all know, have disappeared to all intents and purposes. At a more propitious time than the present, we must take steps to work for their return.

Although I already have excluded discussion of individual scholarly pursuits in this paper, two books and a considerable number of articles must be exceptions. There is the volume edited by George Mora and Jeanne Brand and appearing in 1970, *Psychiatry and its History: Methodological Problems in Research*, based upon a workshop devoted to methodology. There is also the volume of 1973 edited by Mary Henle, Julian Jaynes and John J. Sullivan, *Historical Conceptions of Psychology*, drawing in part upon papers delivered at earlier Cheiron meetings and with royalties to accrue to the Society. There has also been a class of historiographic papers exemplified by Josef Brozek's paper, "Current and Anticipated Research in the History of Psychology," and Robert M. Young's critique of scholarship in the history of the behavioral sciences. Josef Brozek serves still another important professional function: his papers and books make him the major source of information about what historical work is going on in the Soviet Bloc and, in this regard, we are all in his debt. In all of this, collaborative attention to methodology and historiography and cooperative publication within the field are indications of a professional centering in keeping with the theme of this talk.

The presence of reprint series devoted to the history of psychology and the behavioral sciences attests to the presence of a group of scholars able to supply and maintain an interest in republication of historically important books. The earliest of these series, attributable to efforts from within this group, is that published by Scholars Facsimiles & Reprints in which Jim Blight, James Cardno, Solomon Diamond, Ernest Harms, Paul McReynolds, Jacques Quen, Michael Sokal, Barbara Ross, John Sullivan, Thom Verhave, Anthony Walsh and Robert Weyant all have written introductions to various historically significant volumes. The newcomer in the field is the Heritage Press where Anthony Walsh, Michael Sokal and Ronald H. Mueller will have volumes.

Much of what I have had to say so far has had its geographical basis in the United States and Canada, but the invisible college in our midst has a network of informal relationships with individuals from other countries.

Robert M. Young, writing as he does from Kings College in Cambridge, offered his critique of our practices from that locus, perhaps in part because his own work otherwise had hardly begun, and there was very little in Britain on which to comment. But there is some. L. S. Hearnshaw of Liverpool spends a not inconsiderable proportion of his time in historical activities and has had, and will have, a variety of relationships with us. In some respects William O'Neil of Sydney, occasional visitor to the States (including Durham), is his opposite number for Australia. His interests and his work in history reach over into philosophy of science, but he again serves to help prevent us from becoming too provincial. James A. Cardno, in faraway Hobart, Tasmania, with still very strong intellectual ties to Edinburgh and Cambridge, has steadily maintained his interests in Victorian psychology and shares his wisdom with us. And there is Wilhelm Van Hoorn of Leyden, of the days of the first and second Institute, a member in good standing of Cheiron, exchange professor at San Diego with William Hillix of the second Institute. Mutual communication by letter, by visits, by attendance at national and international meetings, and by news and notes items, characterize this network of communication.

The graduate training program, including that in the history of psychology at the University of New Hampshire, was planned at the departmental level under the leadership of Eugene Mills, the historian of Ladd, supplemented by visits from outside specialists and then graduate school and higher administrative approval. In 1967 the graduate program was launched in earnest.

The would-be historian is given a thorough grounding in general psychology, statistics and research methodology. The first year includes courses in historical and systematic psychology, once required of all students but now electives with nine out of ten of the first-year students participating. In the second and subsequent years, the history major takes courses and seminars, tutorials and relevant work outside of the seminar. A considerable proportion of the third year is taken up with required practicum and experience in teaching. The dissertation (often, but not always, based on library research) is planned in the third and completed in the fourth year. Two years ago Rand Evans joined the departmental staff, and already his influence is bearing a fruitful impress upon the program. As of August 1974 there will be eight doctoral graduates: Barbara Ross with a dissertation on "Psychological Thought within the Context of the Scientific Revolution (1665-1700)" in 1970; Elizabeth Goodman on the "History of Marriage Counseling Research," and Kenneth R. Gibson who wrote on "The Conceptual Bases of American Psychology: A Content Analysis of the Presidential Addresses of the American Psychological Association, 1892-1970," both graduating sometime in 1972. On June 2 of this year, there were three graduates: Richard A. Bagg with a dissertation, "The Eminence of American Psychologists," Ronald H. Mueller, "The American Era of James Mark Baldwin," and Anthony Walsh on "Johann Christoph Spurzheim and the Rise and Fall of Scientific Phrenology in Boston, 1832-1842." In August, James G. Blight graduated. His dissertation dealt with the psychological aspects of the thought of Jonathan Edwards.

It also gives me pleasure to state that a second graduate program in the history of psychology has completed its first year. This is, of course, that at Carleton University in Ottawa, Ontario, which includes in its departmental staff Marilyn Marshall and A. B. Laver. Both will, I am sure, be glad to supply further information, in individual conversation or at our Cheiron business meetings which frequently serve as vehicles not only for the expected transactions but also for sharing of experiences. (In passing I might say to those who are not members of Cheiron, that they might judge the business meeting to be one item in the program to be cut at all costs. They would be wrong! Historiography, if not history, is made there!)

It was under the directorship of Josef Brozek that the First National Science Foundation Institute on the Teaching of the History of Psychology was held in Durham in the summer of 1968. The six-week institute was, I think, intellectually and emotionally satisfying. Staff members included Julian Jaynes, who planned to come for a week but stayed for two; Henry Guerlac, the historian of science; George Mora, David Krantz, Robert MacLeod, and guest speakers Joseph Agassi, Eugene Mills, Gardner Murphy, Thom Verhave, Richard Solomon, Robert Sears and Mary Henle. But it is the predoctoral participants that I wish to call particularly to your attention and to note briefly what they have accomplished during the six subsequent years. They were Barbara Ross, who served as recording secretary of the Institute and was the first graduate of the UNH program; Elizabeth Goodman, present Secretary of Cheiron, graduated soon thereafter; and Anthony Walsh, now of Dickinson, known for his work on Gall and Spurzheim. There were also Levy Rahmani, author of that fine book on Soviet psychology; Michael Sokal, later a graduate of the Case Western Reserve where he had worked with Robert Davis and now *the* authority on James McKeen Cattell; and Bill Woodward, now doctoral candidate at Yale, who still earlier worked with Julian Jaynes at Princeton and has several historical publications to his credit. These individuals are the first of those who have been directly and avowedly trained as historians of psychology or closely related fields. The rest of us were amateurs who eventually moved into a different status; they have been professionals from the start of their careers.

Of the thirty participants, seven lecturers and special lecturers at the Institute, according to my count 15 have attended the sixth annual meeting of Cheiron, a society proposed in spirit, if not by name, in the late hours of the 25th of July, 1968, by Julian Jaynes. Earlier that evening he had given a talk including the theme, "Why I am going to wear a tie for the photograph tomorrow morning." He indicated that the group picture to be taken was, in his estimation, sufficiently significant, despite the heat, to be dignified by this gesture, and he proposed consideration to be given to perpetuating the group which otherwise would disband. Most of this group met at Brozek's apartment that evening and what was later to be named Cheiron, The International Society for the History of the Behavioral and Social Sciences, was born. Barbara Ross became our first Secretary; other officerships up to now have been blithely ignored in favor of an annual town meeting chaired by the host from the institution sponsoring that particular meeting. Fittingly, the first meeting in 1969 was held at Princeton with Julian Jaynes as host, and attended by about forty, equally divided between charter members and newcomers.

John Popplestone invited us to the University of Akron for the second annual meeting. An obvious attraction was the presence of the Archives. But this was the year of Kent State, and all campuses of the Ohio State system were closed, so we did not get to see the Archives after all—except for some choice items smuggled off campus!

In 1971 the third annual meeting took place in New York City under triple auspices. Mary Henle of the New School, John Sullivan of NYU and Virginia Sexton of Fordham hosted the meetings, which were divided among the three campuses. It was decided to hold the fourth annual meeting at the University of Calgary with Robert Weyant as host, and where both the papers and the hospitality were positively brilliant. In 1973, Cheiron met at the University of the State of New York at Plattsburgh with Noel Smith as host. At that occasion, Rand Evans suggested Durham as an appropriate meeting place and subsequently served as host for the sixth meeting. Along with Mary Henle, Marilyn Marshall and Jacques Quen, the committee planned what might well prove to be one of our most interesting meetings.

The second NSF supported Summer Institute, again directed by Josef Brozek, took place in 1971 at Lehigh University, Bethlehem, Pennsylvania. I consider it significant that two participants in the first Institute, Robert G. Weyant and Wilhelm Van Hoorn, served as instructors; and Barbara Ross, John J. Sullivan and Michael Sokal, other first Institute participants, made appearances as guest speakers. Mary Henle, guest speaker at the first Institute, was an instructor at the second, while Julian Jaynes reversed these roles for the two Institutes. Thus, continuity and growth both were evident.

Perhaps the most recent event in our history is the recent appearance of Volume 1, Number 1, of the Cheiron Newsletter on the initiative of Cheiron's present secretary, Elizabeth S. Goodman. I am sure that it will prove to be a valuable source of communication, and I join Elizabeth in asking that you forward items to her for inclusion in future issues.

It is apparent then that the history of psychology as a specialization has made considerable progress in the last 15 years. Characteristics associated with a recognized and established community of specialists within the major psychological society, not present before, are now very much evident. There is self-identification with the field; there is continuity of publication on the part of a person working in history; there is recognition by one's colleagues as filling a role as a specialist; there are graduate training programs with graduates making significant contributions; there are job openings for historians of psychology; there is a specialist *Journal;* there are professional associations identified with the field; there is some governmental support, sparse though it may be; and there is a healthy and viable relationship with colleagues in the other behavioral sciences. Historians of psychology have merged with others to form a community of specialists, epitomized in the activities at the sixth annual meeting of Cheiron.

8. The Organization and Preservation of Personal Papers

Unpublished documents are the major source materials for historians. Before modern times they had to rely upon what amounted almost to happenstance for their supplies of source material. For some centuries documents concerned with political, military, and diplomatic history have been deliberately selected and preserved by archivists and others. More recently similar selection and preservation techniques have been applied to materials relevant to the history of the sciences. Interest in manuscript selection and preservation became sufficiently focused so that in 1960 a Conference on Science Manuscripts was held in Washington under the chairmanship of the senior author. The deliberations of this conference were published in *Isis* (Anonymous, 1962). There have been several important steps taken as the result of this conference although it is not a formal continuing body. In the United States and in Europe both national scientific societies and other organizations have concerned themselves with documentary preservation. For example, the American Historical Association, the American Institute of Physics, and the British Psychological Society have taken steps to help select and preserve documents of potential historical value in their respective fields.

Recently the American Psychological Association has concerned itself with both its own records and those of individual psychologists. An ad hoc Committee on Psychological Archives was appointed to

A report of the ad hoc Committee on Psychological Archives, Robert I. Watson, Chairman, to the Board of Directors. Expert advice was sought from Nathan Reingold, then of the Library of Congress, who collaborated in the preparation of this report.

consider the problem of the preservation of the Association's archives and other related matters. Preparation of this report was one of its tasks.

Suggestions relevant to the personal papers of psychologists will be offered concerning (a) how to find suitable sources for their deposit, and (b) the extent to which principles of orderly arrangement should be applied. It is important to note that personal papers by no means are to be saved only by persons of top rank. Preservation of a wide range of individuals is necessary to provide an experimental check, as it were, on conclusions about a period drawn solely from the "great." Papers of the rank and file are particularly valuable in studying routine activities and commonplace presuppositions of a profession, important because they are pervasive but not articulated.

Almost nothing directly concerned with the organization and preservation of private papers has appeared in archival literature. Failure on our part to cite literature is an unfortunate necessity. The annual bibliography of the *American Archivist* was searched from its first issue in 1943 through 1963. In the literature cited in the bibliographies there is considerable advice to organizations on maintenance of records and on how depositors are to arrange records after receipt from persons or organizations, but not a single reference specific to the present problems.

It is not unusual to contrast archives and private papers. However, these are relative terms lacking clearly defined boundaries. One may substitute "institutional" and "personal" papers respectively. Archives then become the records of institutions, private papers the records of individuals. In any given situation the distinction between institutional and personal will vary according to law, customary usage, and even unique circumstances. One can say that, in general, archives are much larger and have a more elaborate internal structure than private papers. These tend to be smaller in number and to have simpler structures.

Another way of looking at accumulations of records of the activities of men is in terms of how they came into existence. In this sense manuscripts can be divided into natural or artificial accumulations. The former comes into existence in the course of a sequence of activities which they in turn document. The documents served a role in these activities. Artificial accumulations or collections are deliberately brought together, after the fact, and represent attempts to provide documentation, often according to some specific subject scheme or some program of gathering evidence. A collection of autographs of psychologists is an example of the latter; the office files of a psychologist are an example of the former. In this frame of reference, personal and institutional records can be either natural or artificial collections depending on their nature.

Natural collections tend to be larger than artificial collections; to have arrangements reflecting the ways they were used, not any arbitrary subject scheme; and, in general, to provide better historical evidence in the sense of greater completeness, less subjectivity in selection, and closeness (historiographically) to the events involved. Artificial collections are human artifacts and can have virtues of considerable importance. Specific topics can be documented in great detail from many diverse origins. By bringing together documents normally not viewed in association, an artificial collection can place events in new frames of reference.

These comments were addressed to individual bodies of documents; they are also applicable to aggregations of collections, i.e., to depositories. There are very few depositories consisting of only the papers of one man or one institution and just as few consisting only of one artificial collection. The usual situation is a mixture of archival and private, of natural and artificial.

It follows from this discussion that disposition of personal papers is facilitated by making a distinction between a natural and an artificial collection. For the natural collection a natural depository is indicated, e.g., a psychology department's records to a university archive—for the artificial collection, a collecting institution gathering materials in the field in question. If there is no natural depository for a natural collection, the individuals involved have the option of trying to form one or of treating their collection as if it were artificial, i.e., seeking a collecting agency with signs of the proper subject orientation.

Universities have, or should have, a university archive which would contain papers of departments, committees, and the like. Often they also contain the papers of individual faculty members. (That is, they become not only the repositories of the records of an institution but also collectors of the sources for the history of the institution and ancillary topics.) Many, perhaps most, university archives are in the library whose director is usually the person one should consult. Many professional societies have archives or history committees which may advise on the disposition of papers. The history departments on campus often have knowledgeable individuals in their ranks.

Psychologists not associated with universities and colleges do not have as obvious a place to which to turn. In general they have to think of public libraries, historical societies, and possibly institutions specifically collecting in their field.

As the name implies, the Society of American Archivists is the national professional organization concerned with matters under discussion. The Society does not formally advise individuals. They will refer the inquiry to a suitable individual or organization. Officers of the Society are listed annually in the *American Archivist*, as are the committees. The administrative notes section in each issue contains relevant information.

The network of collecting institutions, as distinguished from natural depositories, is quite complex. University libraries have widely diverse collecting interests; state and local historical societies are interested in acquiring manuscripts pertaining, even remotely, to the regions they serve. The great public libraries, like the New York Public Library, have extensive manuscript holdings. The Library of Congress serves as a national manuscript depository. The Library of the American Philosophical Society in Philadelphia is a fine example of a subject-oriented organization—in this case the history of science. All will take in private papers if they are deemed both important enough and within whatever scope the institution sets for its holdings.

If a university professor feels that there is no particular interest at his university in his papers (which pertain to more than his years on the campus), he can turn to any one of the above. Even if they are not interested, these institutions will, if possible, probably refer him to a suitable depository.

In the event of uncertainty concerning available facilities an excellent source is the manual by Philip M. Hamer (1961), *A Guide to the Archives and Manuscripts in the United States*. Still another source is the *National Union Catalog of Manuscript Collections*, of which three volumes have appeared. It will eventually list all the manuscript collections in depositories in the United States.

Those psychologists who take steps to preserve their personal papers would expedite this step by specific attention to these matters in their wills. A specific clause concerning disposition of personal papers is indicated.

To give some general background to the problem of arrangement of personal papers the criteria for accessioning used by archivists will be sketched. It must be emphasized that these criteria are used in archival collections and are almost never strictly applied in the collecting of personal papers. Value, the most important criterion, is so general as to become impossible of application except against particular settings and circumstances. Some of the other criteria are age, absence of dilution with valueless material, noncurrency, absence of close restriction on their use, orderly arrangement already worked out, intelligibility to an outside examiner, and extent of relationship with work of other scientists of senior stature. These criteria are elaborated in the various writings of T. R. Schellenberg and in articles in the *American Archivist*.

In personal papers three factors seem to be involved: (*a*) an evaluation of the significance of the individual; (*b*) an evaluation of the richness of the collection; (*c*) the determination of collecting scope. The first two are purely subjective. The third criterion refers to the fact that the depository tends to define its holdings by drawing a boundary and excluding all outside and accepting most collections within the boundary offered to it. Only if there is a very high rating of a man and his collection from outside the boundary will the institution go out of scope. This does not apply to those rare organizations that are pure or nearly pure collectors of artificial collections. In such instances "anything goes."

In the light of the above comments, it will be noted that it is felt psychologists (or any others) should not "arrange" their papers (i.e., a natural collection) in any manner explicitly structured for the presumed convenience of future historians. Historical research is best served if the papers are reasonably complete and in the order in which they were used (so to speak, *in vivo*). The primary concern should be the convenience of the person creating the records. The types of orderly arrangement in use and which are recommendable are many if one worries about specific schemes. One great archivist, the late Sir Hilary Jenkinson, said that all records fall into three classes—records received from without, copies of records sent out, and records created and maintained internally (e.g., incoming letters, outgoing letters, and lab notebooks), referred to here as in, out, and internal. Traditionally these were kept separately. Today they are combined in many instances—with the exception of certain classes of internal records, like lab records. The schemes for combination are various (chronological, by correspondent, by subject categories, by particular events or functions as in project files). All that one cares to say is that after one realizes the value of records, a specific scheme should be adopted and followed consistently. For whatever it is worth, the trend among archivists concerned with institutional records is for the arrangement according to broad categories of function or administrative procedures. Within these categories, the documents are usually grouped in very simple patterns. Elaborate subject classifications are decidedly in disfavor.

The concepts and procedures that have been described are designed to present posterity with fragments of evidence as little changed in time as is humanly possible. There is a real parallelism between the preservation of historical documentation and an investigator's obligation to give an adequate description of method in a paper. Both are designed to provide a means for evaluation by independent observers. Preservation of historical source materials is consequently an act of intellectual integrity and of professional responsibility.

REFERENCES

Anonymous. The conference on science manuscripts. *Isis*, 1962, *53*, 3–157.
Hamer, P. M. *A Guide to the archives and manuscripts of the United States.* New Haven: Yale University Press, 1961.

II. Multidimensional Framework of the History of Psychology

9. The Historical Background for National Trends in Psychology: The United States

In the early nineteenth century before the impress of the new psychology, Scottish faculty psychology of the philosophy of common sense prevailed in the universities, while outside their walls phrenology exerted considerable influence, especially in medical circles (Watson, 1963). It is perhaps significant of a somewhat shamefaced attitude toward this pre-experimental period of our history that it is one about which we are uninformed. Parenthetically, I am not at all sure this attitude is justified, and an investigation is under way (Cardno and Watson).

Before the last twenty years of the nineteenth century, graduate education was in a sorry state. So superior was its European counterpart that in 1880 there were about as many Americans studying abroad as in all of our graduate schools (Albrecht). It was between 1880 and 1895 that many features of the German university system were introduced.

In the reform of university education, psychology spearheaded the attack upon what by then was regarded as the "old-fashioned" doctrine of faculties. Consequently, it was in a strategically favorable position; psychology was not only "new," it was "progressive." When introduced into the curriculum with the other new subjects, such as economics and political science, new departments were created for psychology in contrast to the European practice of a continued tie with philosophy.

A paper from a symposium given at the XVIIth International Congress of Psychology, Washington, D.C., August 20-26, 1963, under the Chairmanship of Ernest R. Hilgard, Stanford University, and organized by Robert I. Watson, Northwestern University.

In the general expansion and modernization of education, psychology profited mightily (Watson, 1963). In 1880 only two rather casually treated rooms at Harvard, first used five years before, could be called a laboratory; by 1895 there were 26 psychology laboratories. In 1880 no one could be called a full-time psychologist; by 1895 a flourishing American Psychological Association had been in existence for three years. As late as 1886 there was no psychological journal; by 1895 there were five. In fifteen short years psychology had emerged as a discipline.

Two individual architects of these changes were William James and G. Stanley Hall. James is the American psychologist most deserving of the name of genius in that he united within his person many diverse strands from the intellectual currents of his time to give forth something new, important, and exciting, which made psychology a subject to be respected. His *Principles of Psychology* serves as a refreshing stimulant for all succeeding generations. But he was neither an organizer nor an administrator, and not even an experimentalist.

G. Stanley Hall shared with James the ability to stimulate enthusiasm in others, but otherwise was of quite a different stamp. He was an organizer and administrator, and an enthusiastic spokesman for experimental research, but not a theorist. He founded the first journal, *The American Journal of Psychology*, and then still other journals; he organized the American Psychological Association; he founded laboratories at Johns Hopkins and Clark Universities; and he trained a considerable number of the second generation of American psychologists.

Other leaders emerged shortly after. One was James McKeen Cattell, who, while taking his degree with Wundt, had brought to Leipzig his own alien problems of individual differences in reaction time. It is also significant of his attitude that he said of Francis Galton that he was the greatest man he had ever known. In later years Cattell did much to emphasize the study of individual differences; through serving as our psychological statesman, brought psychology to the attention of other sciences; and helped to make applied psychology a characteristic enterprise.

Another leader was that Britisher with an unshakable allegiance to Wilhelm Wundt, Edward Bradford Titchener. His attempt to introduce and to refine the content of Wundtian psychology in this foreign clime was a magnificent failure. It could not be grafted upon an already flourishing tree indigenous to our particular climate. At any rate, quite apart from content, his lessons of exactitude and respect for the dignity of science did somehow hearten other psychologists and we have been the better for his presence.

The years of the schools of psychology—Functionalistic, Behavioristic, Gestalt and Psychoanalytic—extend from about 1910 through the early 1930's. Suffice it to say at this point that, today, American psychology has moved away from schools, each as a demarcated system with a body of theories unique unto itself, a claim of universal applicability of a particular set of tenets and ego involvement in that point of view. A distinguished exception is psychoanalysis, and to some extent Gestalt psychology.

It is not enough, however, to leave the period through the thirties as that of the schools alone. Far removed from their clamor was the careful quantitative work of L. M. Terman on intelligence tests, L. L. Thurstone on factor analysis, E. L. Thorndike on human and animal learning, K. S. Lashley on brain physiology and the first appearance of the definitive *History of Experimental Psychology* by E. G. Boring.

Today the American Psychological Association has 20,000 members. With the second edition of the *International Directory* expecting to record 10,000 entries for psychologists outside the United States, it appears that two out of three psychologists live and work in the United States.

Historical developments in psychology when they met certain social forces have given us the contemporary scene in psychology. Industrialization, secularization and urbanization have left their mark upon modern psychology and serve as the background for the professionalization and increased social orientation of American psychology.

World War II helped considerably to bring about an increase in professional orientation and in sheer numbers. It created a situation in which many of the then younger psychologists transferred their skills to work quite foreign to their earlier training. Since the public proved enormously receptive to these efforts, many psychologists continued peacetime pursuits related to these experiences; others returned to the universities and developed training programs in line with these experiences.

The number of psychologists now engaged in professional practice is revealing. In 1962 a representative sampling of American psychologists (Lockman) showed that 39 percent were employed in colleges or universities and that of the rest, 36 percent were in federal and local governmental agencies, 10 percent in private nonprofit agencies, 10 percent in industry and business, and 5 percent were self-employed. Assuming that in each group an equivalent proportion belied the nature of their work by their locus, it is possible to conclude that 6 out of 10 psychologists are primarily concerned with the applications of psychology.

There are various current indications of professional practice—the American Board of Examiners in Professional Psychology which issues diplomas certifying competence in several specialties, and state legislative action in the form of licensing or certification. The American Psychological Association, although spending a major portion of its income for publications, also has increased its budget to meet professional demands. Since my European colleagues expect it of me, I should mention that in 1962 the Association had assets of over two million dollars and an annual budget of over one million dollars.

Closely related to professionalization is the increased social orientation of American psychology, taking place both at the university and on the larger social scene. In our universities, psychology has a dual image. In the so-called divisional faculty structure into which departments are grouped based on presumed commonality of interest, some psychology departments are placed in the natural sciences while others are in the social sciences. At a national level, the American Psychological Association has representation both on the National Research Council (for the natural sciences) and on the Social Science Research Council. This dual representation signalizes that academic psychology is considered to be both a social and a biological science. The socially oriented phases will receive attention later.

The universities are the stronghold of the biologically oriented psychologists. Confining myself to members of the National Academy of Sciences, the universities have been the locus of the work of F. Beach on neural and hormonal behavior, C. H. Graham on sensory psychology, H. F. Harlow on primatology, D. Lindsley and C. Pfaffmann on psychophysiology, S. S. Stevens on the psychophysics of vision, and E. G. Wever on audition. Incidentally, hereafter I shall take the perhaps cowardly way out of referring by name to living psychologists only if they are members of this august body, roughly the equivalent of the Royal Society, or past presidents of the American Psychological Association—with three exceptions which I shall leave for you to detect.

If one uses as the criterion the social or biological *orientation* taken by an individual psychologist, and disregards self-consciousness about its locus, American psychology outside university walls is overwhelmingly social in orientation despite there being only a relatively small number who refer to themselves as "social" psychologists. The consent of the governed as a prerequisite to that governing requires that we secure considerable bodies of information from our citizens by psychological techniques. Moreover, almost all of the professional activities of psychologists are social in orientation. From prognostic and therapeutic work with patients, through management consultation to the selection of bomber crews, psychologists are involved with problems of social interaction.

Central to the organization of an important recent analysis by Kuhn (1962) of the history of the physical sciences is his use of paradigms, that is, those contentual models accepted at a given period of scientific development. A paradigm, Kuhn argues, defines to some extent the science in which it operates. One readily recognizes that a particular paradigm concerns chemistry, astronomy or physics.

Not too many years ago "convergent trends in psychology" was a theme in which we took comfort and pride. From today's perspective, I am not so sure that this is more than wishful thinking. The seven volumes, *Psychology: a study of a science*, edited by Koch, are an obvious source to which to turn because the intellectual climate of American psychology set the limits to the scope of the study. The general introduction to the project begins by stressing the diversity of tongues with which psychologists speak. Similarly, the preface begins with a comment that psychology proceeds along "several quite unsure directions" (Koch, 1959, p. V).

Psychology is still in the pre-paradigmatic stage. Contentually defined and internationally accepted paradigms do not yet exist in psychology.

Some term is necessary which allows for recognition of national differences, for opposition and counter-currents within the science, and, paradoxically, for a reference wider than that of one science. To convey these characteristics the term "prescription" will serve. As I shall use it, prescriptions are those prevailing inclinations or tendencies to behave in a definable way in a particular science in a particular country at a particular time. These ways of behaving are often of such general nature as to be shared with other sciences and to some extent with scientists in other countries. Some prescriptions can be identified as dominant, others as counter-dominant. Some of the latter exist as direct alternatives to dominant prescriptions; others do not stand in specific opposition, they are more generally counter to prevailing dominant prescriptions.

Unlike a paradigm, a prescription does not have to define contentually the field in question. Certain prescriptions, such as determinism, monism, and naturalism, are shared with the other sciences; environmentalism applies with equal force in biology; operationalism was borrowed from physics and the philosophy of science as well as having roots in our own past.

Prescriptions are also alternatives in that selection may be made from among them. Often, this does not occur deliberately; a prescription is apt to be first accepted by the young psychologist as immutable truth, alternatives being discovered only later when the prescription has set so firmly as to be changed with difficulty.

A prescription, when deeply ingrained, tends to be unverbalized and utilized as a matter of course, unless circumstances force one to see its inapplicability. As he begins a piece of research how often does an American psychologist say to himself that it must be quantified? He behaves in a way that shows he makes this an implicit assumption.

No more than other scientists do psychologists use these words often and fluently. Their significances are implicit in their activities as research workers but not part of their universe of discourse.

Some dominant prescriptions—determinism, naturalism, physicalism and monism—although characteristic of American psychology are mentioned only in passing. Freedom of the will, supernaturalism, spiritualism, and dualism are hardly serious counter-prescriptions. This is not the same as saying that these particular counter-prescriptions are not viable in disguised forms, as a fuller exposition would give me an opportunity to bring out.

A functional spirit had been very evident in James in his Monday, Wednesday, Friday self. When this spirit became a school it was represented most vocally by Dewey, Angell and Carr at the University of Chicago, but the more eclectic Columbia University functionalists, led by Cattell and then by Woodworth, were also influential. As a school, it expired gracefully; as a prescription, it is very much a part of our present scene. It is expressed in the stress on "activities" as utilities, in the acceptance and advancement of the applications of psychology, and in the utilization of the contingent meaning of function in research planning and interpretation. Following in the footsteps of Monsieur Jourdain, most of us speak functional prose whether or not we are aware of doing so.

After its disappearance as a school, the behavioristic spirit, with its crudities and brash crusading evangelicism refined away, continued to exert influence through stress on objectivity. A case could be made for referring to American psychology as objective, rather than subjective, in its emphasis, but in the interest of precision, it is perhaps preferable to refer to more specific manifestations in operationalism, quantativism and hypothetico-deductivism.

In the thirties, quite apart from the influence of Behaviorism, American psychology was in a receptive state for operationalism since a pragmatic attitude prevailed. The then currently popular definition of intelligence as whatever intelligence tests measure suffices as an illustration.

Operationalism is intimately related to Comte's positivistic efforts (1853), to Mach's experiential positivism (1914), and to the logical positivism of the Vienna Circle. American psychologists, however, were introduced to operationalism through a work first published in 1927 by the physicist P. W. Bridgman (1927).

In brief, concepts that are used must be tied to the conditions of observation. Instead of Machian experience, the ultimate primary data for most American psychologists turned out to be behavior, a belief to which most of them were already committed. Others, such as Boring, Gibson, Köhler and Rogers, in the spirit of Mach's experiential positivism would see variables having direct experiential reference as legitimate sources for systematic analysis. The operationalistic prescription serves as a credo, and as a means of evaluation, not as the slogan of a school. It is shared by psychologists of otherwise quite different theoretical orientations.

S. S. Stevens (1935a,b) and E. G. Boring (1933) were among the first to recognize operationalism's psychological implications and to bring it to the attention of psychologists. E. C. Tolman (1936) contributed the intervening variable as characteristic of what he called operational Behaviorism. C. L. Hull utilized "symbolic constructs, intervening variables, or hypothetical entities" (1943, p. 22) in his discussion of the principles of learning. After Tolman the intervening variable was soon elaborated by others. The meaning of operational validity was considerably clarified by the 1948 paper of K. MacCorquodale and P. E. Meehl (1948) concerned with the distinction between hypothetical constructs and intervening variables.

Desire to follow a quantitative prescription in research is very evident. The urge toward quantification—that is, "the assignment of numerals to objects or events according to rules" (Stevens, 1946, p. 677)—is drilled into all American psychologists. Speculation, no matter how brilliant, is apt to be considered worthwhile only if it be a prelude to a form in which it can be restated so as to be measured. Speculation leads to quantitative hypothesis formulation and is not an end in itself. S. S. Stevens' clarifying and classificatory papers on quantification have been influential (e.g., 1946, 1951).

There is little question that boldness and originality has characterized many of these quantifications. Consider the work of G. Murphy in psychometrics, of R. R. Sears in child development, of J. McV. Hunt, L. F. Shaffer, O. H. Mowrer, and E. L. Kelly in personality; of T. M. Newcomb in attitude study and L. J. Cronbach in test development. D. O. Hebb, a Canadian, also ranks among these men with his work on brain function and learning. The wide variety of fields in which they showed ingenuity in finding ways of quantifying without sacrificing complexity is noteworthy.

The present fervent attachment to the hypothetico-deductive prescription helps to account for American psychology following through from one research study to the next to the relative exclusion of the development of new theories. Deductive elaboration of already existing hypotheses is its metier. Hull's hypothetico-deductive theory of rote learning is a classic instance. With its powerful support, psychologists are more comfortable in dealing with systematic elaboration than in striking out in new directions. The "bandwagon effect" is characteristic of many psychological research areas. However, the hypothetico-deductive prescription is not without its challengers, among others, Skinner, Guthrie, and Tolman (Koch, 1959).

An environmentalistic prescription prevails. Although not derivable directly from Behavioristic tenets, Watson was the major voice in crusading for an uncompromising environmentalism. Potential adaptive variability at the expense of fixed innate propensities also owes something to functionalism. In a larger sense, the democratic, latitudinarian ideal in the United States contributed. In present-day research, if heredity is considered at all, it is apt to be as a variable to hold constant as in matching groups in intelligence. Even when intelligence is studied directly, it is characteristic to try to show the effect of some form of environmental influence.

The environmentalistic research problem *par excellence* is that of learning. Hence, it is not surprising that it is the research area attracting the most attention in the United States. The work of C. L. Hull, E. R. Guthrie, and E. C. Tolman in the recent past and that of K. W. Spence, B. F. Skinner, W. K. Estes, E. R. Hilgard, N. E. Miller, and D. G. Marquis in the present, along with all of the work that they stimulated, stands witness to this fact. The wide scope given to learning is shown by a tendency to equate learning with behavior in the titles selected for books and theories in which learning is used more or less synonymously for behavior. Even the increased interest in perception that some see as a prominent recent development does not weaken the point. This increased interest (e.g., Koch, 1959) turns out to be in perceptual *learning*.

The search for general laws, even if expressed within the modest limits of miniature theories, clearly marks American psychology as primarily nomothetic in character. There are, of course, staunch defenders of the idiographic, for example, in Gordon W. Allport and many clinical psychologists.

Certain counter-prescriptions deserve specific attention. While not having the greater specificity of the counter-prescriptions, so too do psychoanalysis and Gestalt psychology. They are similar in that they run counter to dominant prescriptions.

In many respects, psychoanalysis still stands apart, unintegrated into the psychological body as a whole. To be sure, there are individual neo-Freudian psychologists who have come to terms with psychoanalysis, but they are islands unique unto themselves. H. A. Murray has been most outstanding in uniting psychoanalysis with diverse strands from psychology and other related fields in a point of view that is shared by others. Nevertheless, his integration has not received national acceptance.

If psychoanalysis is to achieve scientific status, the majority of psychologists would insist that it must be tested by either the appropriate adaptations of available research methods or by the derivation of more appropriate ones. The operative word here is "appropriate," with strong differences of opinion over its meaning.

When Gestalt psychology arrived on these shores in the persons of M. Wertheimer, W. Köhler, and K. Koffka, we were ready to receive them—as psychologists of perception. There is no question today that configurations, patterns, and equipotentialities are accepted as commonplace. To this acceptance was later added their major contribution to what was to become contemporary field theory. Psychologists, generally, would say that the worthwhile facets of Gestalt psychology have now been assimilated. Gestalt psychologists themselves are not so sure about the integration and point to additive connectionism as a flagrant instance of the lack of integration. Just as there are articulated objects within a larger field, so, too, Gestalt psychology is distinguishable from the field of American psychology in general. In standing apart, it helps to maintain phenomenalism and to stave off contemporary molecular pressures.

Moving on to counter-prescriptions, there seems to be a somewhat amorphous objection to the dominant demand for rigor in theorizing. That which for its adherents is rigor, modesty or cautiousness becomes timidity, lack of imagination, lack of adequate complexity, or antitheoretical bias to its antagonists. Sometimes this position is taken, not because they object to the dominant prescriptions reflecting rigor as ideal, but because they consider psychology not far enough advanced to be ready for them (Royce, 1957). There are also those who appeal for more theory on humanist or other grounds.

There is also a counter-prescription calling for increased attention to philosophical matters (e.g., Misiak, 1961). Historically, the independent organization of our departments of psychology and, with the exception of William James, the lack of first-rate philosophers among our pioneers makes an antiphilosophical attitude understandable. It is doubtful if more than a handful of American schools insist upon or even encourage work in philosophy on the part of its graduate students. An exception to this lack of interest in matters philosophical must, however, be made of the philosophy of science, where Meehl, Bergmann and others have made important contributions, and in phenomenology and in existential psychology.

It seems worth mentioning that philosophical interests and theoretical boldness both seem to be on the increase in the last few years, attributable in part to the influence of phenomenology, existentialism and personality theory.

Another counter-prescription is psychological phenomenology, which calls for reconstructing the world of the other person so as to be able to understand it. This stands in contrast to a psychology interested only in the prediction and control of behavior (MacLeod, 1947). Words not welcome in a foreign country have a way of not being translated. Neither *Geisteswissenschaften* nor *Verstehen* have exact English equivalents. Existential psychology, also a counter-prescription, has recently stirred a relatively sharp increase in interest but again only among a small proportion of American psychologists (May, 1961).

Although strongly sharing in the social locus and environmentalistic prescription, the area of so-called personality theory otherwise is rife with counter-prescriptions, such as in self theory and those theories dependent upon unconscious motivation. Trends here defy brief summarization.

It has been seen that national trends in modern American psychology follow certain dominant prescriptions. Determinism, naturalism, physicalism and monism, although very much operative, are judged to incite relatively little opposition. Functionalism, operationalism, quantification, hypothetico-deductivism, environmentalism, and nomotheticism are likewise dominant, but there are counter-prescriptions which tend to oppose them. As for the schools of psychology, psychoanalysis, very obviously, and Gestalt psychology, less firmly, still stand apart. Serving as counter-prescriptions to those dominant in psychology are those calling for increased complexity in theorizing, for an increased attention to philosophical matters, for general acceptance of phenomenology, for increased attention to existential psychology and in a somewhat amorphous way almost all of the areas of personality theory call for counter-prescriptions of one sort or another.

REFERENCES

Albrecht, F. M. The new psychology in America: 1880–1895. Unpublished Ph.D. dissertation, Johns Hopkins, 1960.

Boring, E. G. *The physical dimensions of consciousness.* New York: Century, 1933.

Bridgman, P. W. *The logic of modern physics.* New York: Macmillan, 1927.

Cardno, J. A., and Watson, R. I. Affective and volitional concepts: 1797–1874. In progress.

Comte, A. *Positive philosophy.* (Trans. and condensed by Harriett Martineau) London: Chapman, 1853.

Hull, C. L. *Principles of behavior.* New York: Appleton-Century, 1943.

Koch, S. (ed.). *Psychology: a study of a science. I. Conceptual and* systematic. Vol. 1: Sensory, perceptual and psychological formulations. New York: McGraw-Hill, 1959.

Kuhn, T. S. *The structure of scientific revolutions.* Chicago: University of Chicago Press, 1962.

Lockman, R. F. Characteristics of APA members in the 1962 National Scientific Register. *American Psychologist*, 1962, *17*, 789–792.

MacCorquodale, K., and Meehl, P. E. On a distinction between hypothetical constructs and intervening variables. *Psychological Review, 19,* 1948, *55*, 95–107.

Mach, E. *The analysis of sensations.* (5th ed.) LaSalle, Ill.: Open Court, 1914.

MacLeod, R. B. The phenomenological approach to social psychology. *Psychological Review*, 1947, *54*, 193–210.

May, R. (ed.). *Existential psychology.* New York: Random, 1961.

Misiak, H. *The philosophical roots of scientific psychology.* New York: Fordham University Press, 1961.

Royce, J. R. Toward the advancement of theoretical psychology. *Psychol. Rep.*, 1957, *3,* 410–410.

Stevens, S. S. The operational basis of psychology. *American Journal of Psychology*, 1935a, *47*, 323–330.

—— The operational definition of psychological concepts. *Psychological Review*, 1935b, *42*, 517–527.

—— On the theory of scales of measurement. *Science*, 1946, *103*, 677–680.

—— Mathematics, measurement, and psychophysics. In S. S. Stevens (ed.), *Handbook of experimental psychology.* New York: Wiley, 1951, pp. 7–49.

Tolman, E. C. Operational behaviorism and current trends in psychology. *Proc. 25th Anniv. Celebr. Inaug. Grad. Stud.*, Los Angeles: University of Southern California Press, 1936.

Watson, R. I. *The great psychologists: from Aristotle to Freud.* Philadelphia, Pa.: Lippincott, 1963.

10. Psychology: A Prescriptive Science

In a recent analysis of the dynamics of the history of the older, more mature sciences, Kuhn (1962, 1963) holds that each of them has reached the level of guidance by a paradigm. In one of its meanings a paradigm is a contentual model, universally accepted by practitioners of a science at a particular temporal period in its development. With this agreement among its practitioners, the paradigm defines the science in which it operates. In a science where a paradigm prevails, one recognizes that a particular paradigm concerns chemistry, astronomy, physics, or the biological sciences. Illustrative in astronomy is the Ptolemaic paradigm which gave way to the Copernican paradigm, and in physics is the Aristotelian paradigm which gave way to the Newtonian dynamic paradigm, which, in the relatively recent past, was superseded by the paradigm provided by Einstein and Bohr. The great events of science which occur when a new paradigm emerges Kuhn calls a revolution.

The historical sequence Kuhn holds to be as follows: As scientists go about the tasks of normal science, eventually an anomaly, i.e., a research finding which does not fit the prevailing paradigm, is obtained. A normal science problem that ought to be solvable by the prevailing procedures refuses to fit into the paradigm or a piece of equipment designed for normal research fails to perform in the anticipated manner. Failures in science to find the results predicted in most instances are the result of lack of skill of the scientist. They do not call into question the rules of the game, i.e., the paradigm, that the scientist is following. Reiterated efforts generally bear out this commitment to the accepted paradigm that Kuhn calls a

Address of the President of the Division of the History of Psychology at its charter meeting at the American Psychological Association convention in New York City, September 1966. During 1966 earlier versions of the paper were given at colloquia at Cornell University and Knox College.

dogmatism. Only repeated failure by increasing numbers of scientists results in questioning the paradigm which, in turn, results in a "crisis" (Kuhn, 1963). The state of Ptolemaic astronomy was a recognized scandal before Copernicus proposed a basic change, Galileo's contribution arose from recognized difficulties with medieval views, Lavoisier's new chemistry was the product of anomalies created both by the proliferation of new gases found and by the first quantitative studies of weight relations. When the revealed anomaly no longer can be ignored, there begin the extraordinary investigations that lead to a scientific revolution. After sufficient acceptance of this anomaly is achieved from the other workers in the field, a new paradigm makes the place of the one overthrown and a period of normal science begins. Since a paradigm is sufficiently open-ended it provides a host of problems still unsolved. In this period of normal science, the task of the scientist is to fill out the details of the paradigm to determine what facts, perhaps already known, that may be related to the theory, to determine what facts are significant for it, to extend to other situations, and in general to articulate the paradigm. In short, it would appear that the activities of normal science are a form of "working through" in a manner somewhat akin to that task which occupies so much time in psychoanalytic psychotherapy.

When a new anomaly appears and is given support, the cycle then repeats.

The bulk of Kuhn's monograph is taken up with a historical account of the events leading up to scientific revolutions, the nature of these revolutions, and the paradigmatic developments thereafter, with many familiar facts of the history of astronomy, physics, and chemistry cast in this particular perspective. It is here that the persuasiveness of his point of view is to be found. The test of the correctness of Kuhn's views rests upon the fit of his data with the available historical materials. Kuhn uses the key concept of paradigm in several degrees of breadth other than contentually defining and it is difficult to know precisely what differentiates each of the usages. Fortunately, I can leave to the specialist in the history of the physical sciences, the evaluation of the correctness of his reading the details of their history and the various meanings of paradigm, for I am more concerned with what can be drawn from what he has to say about other sciences that he contends lack a contentually defining paradigm.

In all of its meanings, a paradigm has a guidance function. It functions as an intellectual framework, it tells the scientists with what sort of entities their scientific universe is populated and how these entities behave, and informs its followers what questions may legitimately be asked about nature.

What are the consequences in those sciences that lack a defining paradigm? Foremost is a noticeable lack of unity within a science, indications of which Kuhn acknowledges as one of the sources for his paradigmatic concept, which arose in part from his being puzzled about "the number and extent of the overt disagreement between social scientists about the nature of legitimate scientific methods and problems" (1962, p. 4) as compared to the relative lack of such disagreement among natural scientists.

That psychology lacks this universal agreement about the nature of our contentual model that is a paradigm, in my opinion, is all too readily documented.[2] In psychology there is still debate over fundamentals. In research, findings stir little argument, but the overall framework is still very much contested. There is still disagreement about what is included in the science of psychology. In part, at least, it is because we lack a paradigm that one psychologist can attack others who do not agree with him as being "nonscientific" or "not a psychologist," or both. Schools of psychology still have their adherents, despite wishful thinking. And an even more telling illustration, because it is less controversial, is the presence of national differences in psychology to such an extent that in the United States there is an all too common dismissal of work in psychology in other countries as quaint, odd, or irrelevant. National differences, negligible in the paradigmatic sciences such as physics and chemistry, assume great importance in psychology. A provincialism in psychology in the United States is the consequence, provincialism on a giant

---

2. Others have expressed themselves about the lack of unity in psychology. If one were asked what is the most comprehensive treatment of psychology since Titchener's *Manual*, the answer must be the multivolumed *Psychology: A Study of a Science,* edited by Sigmund Koch (1959). Its general introduction makes considerable capital of the diversity of tongues with which psychologists speak and the preface comments that psychology proceeds along "several quite unsure directions" (p. v). To turn to but one other source, Chaplin and Krawiec (1960) close their recent book on systems and theories with the prophecy that the task of the future is "to integrate all points of view into one . . ."; to provide "a comprehensive theoretical structure with the integrating force of atomic theory . . ." (pp. 454-455).

scale, to be sure, but still a provincialism which would and could not be present if a paradigm prevailed.

Before its first paradigm has served to unify it and while still in "the preparadigmatic stage" each physical science was guided by "something resembling a paradigm," says Kuhn. Since it was outside his scope, Kuhn said hardly more than this about the matter.

Psychology has not experienced anything comparable to what atomic theory has done for chemistry, what the principle of organic evolution has done for biology, what laws of motion have done for physics. Either psychology's first paradigm has not been discovered or it has not yet been recognized for what it is. Although the presence of an unrecognized paradigm is not ruled out completely, it would seem plausible to proceed on the assumption that psychology has not yet had its initial paradigmatic revolution. The present task is to answer the question—if psychology lacks a paradigm, what serves to take its place?

It would seem that it follows from Kuhn's position that whatever provides the guidance could not have the all-embracing unifying effect of defining the field in question since if it did so, a paradigm would exist. What seems to be required is some form of trends or themes, numerous enough to deal with the complexity of psychology and yet not so numerous as to render each of them only narrowly meaningful. Those which I have isolated follow:

The Prescriptions of Psychology Arranged in Contrasting Pairs

Conscious mentalism—Unconscious mentalism (emphasis on awareness of mental structure or activity—unawareness)

Contentual Objectivism—Contentual subjectivism (psychological data viewed as behavior of individual—as mental structure or activity of individual)

Determinism—Indeterminism (human events completely explicable in terms of antecedents—not completely so explicable)

Empiricism—Rationalism (major, if not exclusive, source of knowledge is experience—is reason)

Functionalism—Structuralism (psychological categories are activities—are contents)

Inductivism—Deductivism (investigations begun with facts or observations—with assumed established truths)

Mechanism–Vitalism (activities of living beings completely explicable by physiochemical constituents—not so explicable)

Methodological objectivism–Methodological subjectivism (use of methods open to verification by another competent observer—not so open)

Molecularism–Molarism (psychological data most aptly described in terms of relatively small units—relatively large units)

Monism–Dualism (fundamental principle or entity in universe is of one kind—is of two kinds, mind and matter)

Naturalism–Supernaturalism (nature requires for its operation and explanation only principles found within it—requires transcendent guidance as well)

Nomotheticism–Idiographicism (emphasis upon discovering general laws—upon explaining particular events or individuals)

Peripheralism–Centralism (stress upon psychological events taking place at periphery of body—within the body)

Purism–Utilitarianism (seeking of knowledge for its own sake—for its usefulness in other activities)

Quantitativism–Qualitativism (stress upon knowledge which is countable or measurable—upon that which is different in kind or essence)

Rationalism–Irrationalism (emphasis upon data supposed to follow dictates of good sense and intellect—intrusion or domination of emotive and conative factors upon intellectual processes)

Staticism–Developmentalism (emphasis upon cross-sectional view—upon changes with time)

Staticism–Dynamicism (emphasis upon enduring aspects—upon change and factors making for change)

The overall function of these themes is orientative or attitudinal; they tell us how the psychologist-scientist must or should behave. In short, they have a directive function. They help to direct the psychologist-scientist in the way he selects a problem, formulates it, and carries it out.

The other essential characteristic is that of being capable of being traced historically over some appreciable period of time. On both counts, the term "prescription" seems to have these connotations.[3] It is defined in the dictionaries as the act of prescribing, directing, or dictating with an additional overtone of implying long usage, of being hallowed by custom, extending over time.[4]

3. A fortunate historical precedent for using prescriptions in this way is to be found in a quotation from Leibniz in his *New Essays Concerning Human Understanding* (1949). It may help to make clear what is meant. "The discussions between Nicole and others on the *argument from the great number* in a matter of faith may be consulted, in which sometimes one defers to it too much and another does not consider it enough. There are other similar *prejudgments* by which men would very easily exempt themselves from discussion. These are what Tertullian, in a special treatise, calls *Prescriptiones* . . . availing himself of a term which the ancient jurisconsults (whose language was not unknown to him) intended for many kinds of exceptions or foreign and predisposing allegations, but which now means merely the temporal prescription when it is intended to repel the demand of another because not made within the time fixed by law. Thus there was reason for making known the *legitimate prejudgments* both on the side of the Roman Church and on that of the Protestants" (Book IV, Ch. 15, pp. 530-531).

4. Something akin to the prescriptive approach has been suggested in the past. In the early part of the last century Victor Cousin (1829) followed by J. D. Morell (1862) developed a synthetical system of the history of philosophy based upon a division into the four aspects of sensationalism, idealism, scepticism, and mysticism.

In the '30s, Kurt Lewin (1935) was groping toward something similar in his discussion of the conflict between the Aristotelian and Galilean modes of thought. Lewin's shift of modes of thought from the Aristotelian to Galilean, although admitting of partial overlap, impress me as too saltatory, too abrupt in movement from qualitative appearance to quantitative reality, from search for phenotypes to search for genotypes, from surface to depth, from disjointed descriptions to nomothetic search for laws. They are, in my opinion, not so much a matter of qualitative leaps as they are gradual changes with the older views still very much operative. Lewin's conceptualizing in relation to the historic facts seems similar in spirit to Piaget's brilliant strokes on the process of development. I suspect that if we were to take Lewin as seriously as did the American investigators who followed the leads of Piaget into painstaking detailed research, we would find that there was much blurring and overlap of these Lewinian shifts, as there seems to be at the Piagetian levels.

In applying the shift in modes of classification from the Aristotelian to Galilean syndrome, Brunswik (1956) placed psychology as showing the shift between Titchener in 1901 and Lewin in 1935. It is unfortunate that an arbitrary impression of finality emerges. Prescriptions, at any rate, are not conceived as emerging with such definitiveness; they appear gradually and tentatively to disappear and then to reappear.

Brunswik (1955, 1956) also casually used the term "Thema" in somewhat the same broad sense that I use prescription, but without working out its meaning or scope. He also used the same term to apply to the seeking of analogical

It is for the reason of persisting over relatively long periods of time that prescriptions can be of historical moment. In fact, in choosing the particular prescriptions with which I deal the presence of historical continuity over at least most of the modern period was a major decisive factor. If an instance of some conception serving a directive function was of relatively short temporal dimension, it was

---

similarity to the content of another science (1955) and even to psychological content, as such (1956).

In his *Historical Introduction to Modern Psychology* through the 1932 revision but not his 1949 revision, Murphy (1932) in his summing up of the decades of 1910 and 1920 utilized quantification as the integrating theme to unify psychology but gave serious consideration to such trends as from structural to functional, from part to whole, from qualitative to quantitative, and from experimental to genetic-statistical. It is important to reiterate that these were used as guiding themes only for a summary of 2 decades, and not for the earlier history of psychology. When Murphy faced the task of summarizing from the vantage point of the late '40s, he abandoned this form of summarization.

Bruner and Allport (1940) analyzed the contents of psychological periodicals for the 50-year period 1888–1938, in terms of individual "author's problem, his presupposition procedure, explanatory concepts and outlook in psychological science" (p. 757). The material provided the basis for Allport's 1939 Presidential Address to the American Psychological Association. In his summarization, Allport (1940) indicated that his survey showed an agreement with an earlier one by Bills and not only stated that psychology is "increasingly empirical, mechanistic, quantitative, nomothetic, analytic and operational," but also pleaded, should not psychology be permitted to be "rational, teleological, qualitative, idiographic, synoptic, and even non-operational?" (p. 26). Thus, Allport and I show substantial agreement since five out of six "presuppositions," as he calls them, are among those in my schema of prescriptions. The reason that one exception, operational-nonoperational presuppositions, is not included in my schema is that I consider it, as explained before, historically rooted in other older prescriptions.

Allport and Bruner's work cries out for follow-up and I hope to have someone working on it in the near future. Allport did, however, use something akin to his schema in a comparison of American and European theories of personality published in 1957.

A more recent related publication is that of Henry Murray, who in the course of an overview of historical trends in personality research, made a plea for "a comprehensive and fitting classification of elementary trends" (1961, pp. 15–16), which he then classified as regional, populational, theoretical, technique, data ordering, intentional (pure or applied), and basic philosophical assumptional trends. This last, the basic philosophical assumption, was not in any way spelled out so there is no way of knowing what he had in mind.

102 : SELECTED PAPERS

not considered a prescription. It is for this reason that some prominent trends in psychology today do not appear as prescriptions. Physicalism and operationalism are very much part of the current *Zeitgeist* in psychology but because they are relatively new upon the psychological scene, they are not considered prescriptions. Instead, they serve as challenges to utilize the prescriptions for their explanation. It is characteristic of prescriptions that modern, more specifically formulated versions of the more general historically rooted ones may appear. Empiricism-rationalism have modern descendents in environmentalism-nativism.

To arrive at a reasonably complete and appropriate categorization of the prescriptions, I carried out two separable, although actually intertwined steps. I considered the present scene, for example, in a paper on national trends in psychology in the United States (1965), in order to ascertain what seemed to characterize psychology today, and then turned to the very beginning of the modern period in the history of psychology in the seventeenth century to see if these themes were then discernible in recognizable form. In the 300-page manuscript that I have so far prepared, I can say that I find encouraging indications of the historical roots of these prescriptions somewhere in the contributions of Bacon, Descartes, Hobbes, Spinoza, Leibniz, Locke, and Newton, and in those of the lesser figures of the seventeenth century.

Turning to its directive-orientative function, it will be remembered that this theory of prescriptions is more than a classificatory system, more than a convenient means for a particular historian to order his account. These prescriptions were and are part of the intellectual equipment of psychologists. Psychologists are always facing problems, novel and otherwise. They do so with habits of thought, methodological and contentual, which they have taken from the past. This applies today with just as much force as it ever did in the past. In short, they are dynamic because psychologists accept, reject and combine prescriptions, thus thinking in certain ways and not in others.

In the above list, prescriptions have been presented in one of the ways they function—as contrasting or opposing trends.[5] At some

5. There is a precedent for considering the trends studies in terms of antithetical pairs. In his critical study, *Biological Principles*, J. H. Woodger (1929) considered the problems of biological knowledge to center on six antitheses: vitalism and mechanism, structure and function, organism and environment,

point in their history most of these prescription pairings have been considered as opposed, even irreconcilable, for example, naturalism as opposed to supernaturalism, and empiricism as opposed to rationalism.

A summarization, such as the list gives, inevitably distorts its subject matter. Especially pertinent here is the false impression of tidiness this arrangement of antithetical isolated pairs gives. Consider the dichotomy mechanism-vitalism. Does this oppositional way of presenting them exhaust the matter? By no means, mechanism bears relation to molecularism, and molecularism may come in conflict with supernaturalism, which in turn relates to certain forms of dualism.

Prescriptions are by no means simple, dominant, isolated themes moving monolithically through history. In a recent analysis of the history of mathematical concepts in psychology, George Miller (1964) warns expressly against this kind of oversimplification. His treatment of what he calls the "varieties of mathematical psychology" (p. 1), that I consider to bear considerable relation to the quantitavistic prescription, is further subdivided into several categories and subcategories. As he indicates, a more extensive treatment would require still others.

Their oppositional character does lead to explication of another characteristic of prescriptions. At a time, past or present, when both of the opposed prescriptions had or have supporters, it is possible to

---

preformation and epigenesis, teleology and causation, and mind and body. His emphasis was upon examining the current views circa 1929. Although he showed a lively appreciation of their historical roots, his task was not essentially historical.

W. T. Jones (1961) also has developed a means of evaluation of so-called "areas of bias" of order-disorder, static-dynamic, continuity-discreteness, inner-outer, sharp focus-soft focus, this world-other world, and spontaneity-process. Content high on the order axis shows a strong preference for system, clarity and conceptual analysis while that for disorder shows a strong preference for fluidity, muddle, and chaos. Illustrative applications to samples of poetry, painting and documents in the social and physical sciences were made. Syndromes for the medieval, the Renaissance, the enlightenment, and the romantic periods were developed. The last, receiving the most attention, was characterized as showing soft-focus, inner-disorder, dynamic, continuity, and other-world biases. The results so far reported show it to be a promising technique.

Brunswik (1956) also speaks of the survival of dichotomizing doctrines, such as the four temperaments as illustrative of a prescientific syndrome in psychology.

make some sort of an estimate of their relative strength; in other words, we may speak of dominant and counterdominant prescriptions. Rationalism dominated in seventeenth-century England; Locke was nearly alone in advocating empiricism. Nomotheticism dominates today in the United States; an idiographic prescription is sufficiently viable to make itself heard in protest against the prevailing state of affairs. Hence, idiography is counterdominant.

The presence of dominant and counterdominant prescriptions helps us to see how competitions and conflict may result. Whether purism or utilitarianism dominates in American psychology today, I would be hard put to say, but we can be sure of one thing— both prescriptions have sufficient protagonists to make for a prominent conflict. Dominance may shift with time; at one time supernaturalism dominated decisively; there followed centuries of conflict; and today naturalism dominates almost completely.

Although important, their oppositional nature is not always present. Empiricism-rationalism has been presented as a contrasting pair, yet at least to the satisfaction of some psychologists and philosophers of science, they have been reconciled today at a higher level of synthesis. Induction and deduction were also considered antithetical once. In actual practice today, the scientist often sees them as aspects of an integrated method which permits him to weave them together. Sometimes prescriptions, rather than being contradictory, are contrary; there may be gradations, or relationships of degree, as seems to be the case with methodological subjectivity-objectivity.

Reinforcing its directive character is the fact that prescriptions sometimes are "prejudgments," presuppositions or preconceptions that are acted upon without examination, that are taken for granted.[6] Some prescriptions are characterized by their being tacit presuppositions taken as a matter of course and even operating without explicit verbalization. What psychologist today says to himself that the

---

6. Of course, implicitness of historical trends is not a novel idea. Whitehead (1925) remarked that when one is attempting to examine the philosophy of a period, and by implication to examine a science as well, one should not chiefly direct attention to those particular positions adherents find it necessary to defend explicitly but to the assumptions which remain *unstated*. These unverbalized presuppositions appear so obvious to their adherents that it may even be that no way to state them has occurred to them. In similar vein, Lovejoy (1936) has observed that implicit or incompletely explicit assumptions operate in the thinking of individuals and ages.

problem he is considering is one that I must decide whether I should or should not quantify? Instead he immediately starts to cast the problem in quantitative terms without further ado. Similarly, most psychologists are monists. That many psychologists would react to being called monists with a sense of incredulity and even resentment nicely illustrates my point. We think monistically without using the term. Similarly we are apt to follow empiricistic and naturalistic prescriptions without much thought to the fact that we do so. But there was a time when the issues of quantitativeness-qualitativeness, of monism-dualism, of empiricism-rationalism, and of naturalism-supernaturalism were very much explicit issues, occupying the center of the psychological stage. Often their implicit character seems to have come about when one became so dominant that the other no longer stirred argument. Sometimes no clean-cut agreed-on solution was verbalized, instead they were allowed to slide into implicitness. A shift of interest, rather than resolution with a clearcut superiority of one over the other seems characteristic. Old prescriptions never die, they just fade away. Naturally, at some times and to some extent a prescription became less relevant to psychology, but these are matters of degree.

Much of psychology's early history is, of course, a part of philosophy. Many of these prescriptions had their roots in philosophical issues, and are even still stated in what is current philosophical terminology as in monism-dualism and empiricism-rationalism, to mention the two most obvious. I do not hesitate to use philosophical terminology because psychology cannot be completely divorced from philosophy either in its history or in its present functioning. This state of affairs is cause for neither congratulation nor commiseration. Psychology is not the more scientific by trying to brush this sometimes embarrassing fact under the rug, as do some of our colleagues, by teaching and preaching psychology as if it had no philosophically based commitments. They are psychology's Monsieur Jourdaines who deny they talk philosophical prose. Denying there is need to consider philosophical questions does not solve the problem. The very denial is one form of philosophical solution.

Since they were originally philosophical issues, it will be convenient to refer to some prescriptions as "contentual" problems. To bring home this point, the areas of philosophy in which certain of the prescriptions fall might be identified. Rationalism and empiricism have their origins in epistemology, monism and dualism in ontology (nature of reality), molarism and molecularism in cosmology (structure of reality).

A major task in the history of psychology is to trace how the field individuated from the philosophical matrix. In this process, the prescriptions that served as major guidelines in the emergence of psychology as a separate discipline originally had a philosophical character, which took on a general scientific character with the emergence of the physical sciences in general, and psychological science in particular. It is in this sense that they can be referred to as philosophically contentual in character. Moreover, consideration by psychologists and others in the sciences transformed them sometimes in ways that only by tracing their history can one see the relation to their parentage.

Often the traditional terminology used herewith, for example, its dualistic and mentalistic locus, has had to give way to objectivistic and monistic terminology. Confused and confusing though these terms might be, they still referred to something relevant to psychology. As they are formulated, psychologists may be repelled by the "old-fashioned" air of the statement of many of the prescriptions. Justification is found in the fact that these are the terms in psychology's long history until a short 50 years ago.

Lacking a paradigm has meant that psychology looked to other scientific fields for guidance. It is characteristic of prescriptions that borrowing from other fields has taken place. Psychology's heritage from philosophy could be viewed in this manner. But there are other forms of borrowing which have entered into prescription formation. There has been noteworthy borrowing from biology, physiology in particular, signalized by Wundt's calling his work "physiological psychology" in deference to the methodological inspiration it was to him. But physics, highest in the hierarchy of the sciences, has just as often served as the model science. Psychology has had its dream of being a challenging prince. The rejected child of drab philosophy and low-born physiology, it has sometimes persuaded itself that actually it was the child of high-born physics. It identified with the aspiration of the physical sciences and, consequently, acquired an idealized version of the parental image as a super-ego, especially concerning scientific morality, i.e., the "right" way for a scientist to behave.

Psychologists looked to these other sciences for methodological guidance.[7] This methodological cast is particularly evident in the prescriptions concerned with nomothetic law, inductivism-deductivism, quantitativism-qualitativism, methodological objectivism and subjectivism, and determinism-indeterminism. It follows that these prescriptions apply in varying degrees to other sciences. So, too, does the puristic-utilitarian prescription, and working through the naturalistic-supernaturalistic problem.

Some of the contentual prescriptions have counterparts in other sciences. Salient to all biological sciences are developmentalism-statisticism, functionalism-structuralism, mechanism in its various guises, and molecularism-molarism. It is also at least possible that many of these prescriptions would be found to have counterparts in other nonscientific areas of knowledge, such as literature, religion, and politics. After all, man's reflective life, as the "Great Ideas" of Adler and Hutchins and their cohorts show, has much more interpenetration into the various compartmentalizations of knowledge than is customarily recognized. But to explore this further would be to extend discussion beyond the scope of the paper.

In the preparadigmatic stage of a science, a scientist may also become an adherent to a school, that is to say, he may accept a set of interlocking prescriptions espoused by a group of scientists generally with an acknowledged leader. Functionalism, behaviorism, Gestalt psychology, and psychoanalysis are representative.

The orientative character of prescriptions is also present in a school. As Marx and Hillex (1963) recognize, each school seems to follow a directive—you should be primarily concerned with the study of the functions of behavior in adapting to the environment and the formulation of mathematical functions relating behavior to antecedent variables: *functionalism*—you ought to study the stimulus-response connections through strict methodological objectivism: *behaviorism*—you can arrive at useful formulations of psychological principles through consideration of molar units of both stimulus and response, i.e., configurations or fields: *Gestalt*—you should be concerned with the interplay and conflict of the environment and native constituents of the disturbed personality with special attention to its unconscious aspect: *psychoanalysis*.

Salience or nonsalience of particular prescriptions characterize schools. Behaviorism is both contentually objectivistic and environmentalistic (empirical). However, the former is salient; the latter is nonsalient. Contentual objectivism is central and indispensable, environmentalism is not crucial to its central thesis. Behaviorism would still be behaviorism even if all behaviorists were nativistic in orientation.

In broad strokes based on salient prescriptions, functionalism is functionalistic, empiricistic, quantitativistic and molecularistic. Behaviorism has, as salient orientative prescriptions, contentual objectivism and molecularism. Gestalt psychology may be said to make salient molarism, subjectivism, and nativism. The salient directive prescriptions of psychoanalysis seem to be dynamicism, irrationalism, unconscious mentalism, and developmentalism.

The differing patterns of salient prescriptions of the schools serves also to make more intellgible their differing research emphases upon particular contentual problems—the functionalists, with their empiricistic salience, upon learning; the behaviorists, with their peripheralism upon motor activity (including learning); Gestalt psychology with its molarism and nativism, upon perception; and psychoanalysis, with its dynamicism and irrationalism, upon motivation.

There is an even broader level of prescriptions, that of national trends, exemplified by the Symposium on National Trends at the XVIIth International Congress, to which reference already has been made (Watson, 1965). Here greater diversity than that of the schools is expected. Instead of patterns, it is most meaningful to couch their discussion in terms of dominance and counterdominance.

Immersion in the current scene as a participant-observer adds immeasurably to the already complicated task of the historian, who is apt therefore to approach the present with a great deal of trepidation. What will be hazarded is inclusive, broad, therefore crude, overall characterization of the current scene of psychology in the United States. It will serve as another exercise in the application of the prescriptive approach. Although couched in terms of a somewhat different array of prescriptions than now is being used, for reasons explained earlier, I will quote from the concluding summary of my paper on this Symposium:

> It has been seen that national trends in modern American psychology follow certain dominant prescriptions. Determinism, naturalism, physicalism and monism, although very much operative, are judged to incite relatively little opposition. Functionalism, operationalism, quantification, hypothetico-deductivism, environmentalism, and nomotheticism are likewise dominant, but there are counter-prescriptions which tend to oppose them. As for the schools of psychology, psychoanalysis, very obviously,

and Gestalt psychology, less firmly, still stand apart. Serving as counterprescriptions to those dominant in psychology are those calling for increased complexity in theorizing, for an increased attention to philosophical matters, for general acceptance of phenomenology, for increased attention to existential psychology and in a somewhat amorphous way almost all of the areas of personality theory calls for counterprescriptions of one sort or another. (p. 137)

It is important to note that most national prescriptive trends have been stated in terms of dominance and counterdominance, which reflects diverseness, not integration. Indeed, the highest level of integration in psychology is still that of the schools, not that of the nation. Different patterns of dominance and counterdominance are present in different countries. For the sake of brevity, but at the risk of oversimplification, we may say that methodological and contentual objectivity, particularly in the form of operationalism, prevails in the United States, while methodological and contentual subjectivity, especially in the form of phenomenalism, does so in large segments of Continental Europe.

It follows that patterns of dominant prescriptions characterize a given temporal period and geographical area. When we wish to emphasize the then current intertwined pattern of dominant prescriptions as having a massive cumulative effect, we refer to the *Zeitgeist*. The *Zeitgeist* in itself is empty of content until we describe that which we assign to a particular *Zeitgeist*. The strands that enter into the *Zeitgeist* include the dominant prescriptions of that time. So the *Zeitgeist* and the prescriptive concepts are considered complementary. One of the puzzling facets of the *Zeitgeist* theory is just how to account for differential reaction to the same climate of opinion. The prescriptive approach may be helpful in this connection. Plato and Aristotle, Hobbes and Spinoza, Hume and Rousseau, each experienced the same *Zeitgeist* but also had idiosyncratic, nondominant prescriptive allegiances.

What I have said about prescriptions by no means exhausts this complexity. Prescriptive trends fall and rise again, combine, separate, and recombine, carry a broader or narrower scope of meaning, and enter into different alliances with other prescriptions, change from implicitness to explicitness and back again, and concern themselves with different psychological content and its related theories. Beyond this, I hesitate to go, except to say I am confident there are probably other as yet unrecognized ramifications. Prescriptions endure while the psychological facts, theories, and areas which influenced their acceptance are ephemeral and ever-changing.

If I have stressed the directing and guiding phase of the effect of prescriptions on a scientist's thinking, it is not because of blindness to the other side of the coin, the originality of the scientist. A scientist not only is guided by but also exploits both paradigms and prescriptions. He does so in terms of his originality, and other factors that make for individuality.

My enthusiasm for prescriptions may have left you wondering whether this is all that I can see in the history of psychology. Let me reassure you at this point. The usual contentual topics of psychology most broadly summarized as sensation, learning, motivation, and personality and the hypotheses, laws, and theories to which their investigations give rise are still considered very much a part of its history. As differentiated from philosophically oriented contentual prescriptions, it is these and related contentual topics which show that a concern for psychology is the subject matter of historical investigation. These contentual topics are the vehicles with which all historians of psychology must work. Even here there is another point about prescriptions that I might mention. There seems to be some historical evidence of an affinity between certain prescriptions and certain contentual topics, e.g., dynamicism with motivation, developmentalism with child and comparative psychology, personalism, idiographicism, and irrationalism with personality, and empiricism with learning. Individual psychologists who have been strongly influenced by particular prescriptions are apt to reflect them in their work. Although the evidence has not yet been sought, it is quite plausible to believe that, reciprocally, choice of problem area may influence allegiance to certain prescriptions. In similar vein, I suspect that prescriptions tend to cluster in nonrandom fashion. Offhand, acceptance of supernaturalism seems to have an affinity for teleology, indeterminism, and qualitativism; naturalism with mechanism, determinism, and quantitativism; nomothesis with determinism; rationalism with deduction; empiricism with induction.

To return to extraprescriptive aspects of psychology, the methods of psychologists—observation and experiment—cannot be neglected in a historical account. Psychologists' use of these methods are an integral part of that history. However, certain prescriptions, particularly those identified earlier as methodological in nature, allow casting considerable historical material in the way that has been sketched.

Any adequate history of psychology must consider the personality characteristics of individual psychologists and the extrapsychological influences, such as social circumstance, which have been brought to bear upon each psychologist. Can one imagine that Hobbes' psychological views were independent of his detestation of organized religion, adoration of a strong central government, and fear of the consequence of political disorders?

I would like to summarize briefly some of the functions that I consider prescriptions to serve. They provide classification and summarization through a conceptual framework which can be applied historically. Prescriptions provide principles of systematization which are related to, and yet to some extent are independent of, the particular contentual or methodological problem of the individual psychologist. They are also mnemonic devices which make it possible to summarize and convey a maximum of meaning with a minimum of words. Going beyond anything even hinted at in the paper, prescriptive theory might also help to make history a tool for investigation of the psychology of discovery, and also serve as a framework for studies using content analysis applied to historical documents.

Prescriptions are characterized by an oppositional character manifested in dominance and counterdominance, an implicit as well as explicit nature, a philosophically based contentual character, a methodological character borrowed from the other sciences, a presence in other fields, an interlocking in schools of psychology with some salient and others nonsalient, a clash of prescriptions at the national level, and a participation of prescriptions at the national level, and a participation of prescriptions in the *Zeitgeist*. Since psychology seems to lack a unifying paradigm, it would seem that as a science it functions at the level of guidance by prescriptions.

REFERENCES

Allport, G. W. The psychologist's frame of reference. *Psychological Bulletin*, 1940, 37, 1-28.

Allport, G. W. European and American theories of personality. In H. P. David and H. von Bracken (ed.), *Perspectives in personality theory*. New York: Basic Books, 1957, pp. 3-24.

Bruner, J. S., and Allport, G. W. Fifty years of change in American psychology. *Psychological Bulletin*, 1940, 37, 757-776.

Brunswik, E. The conceptual framework of psychology. In O. Neurath, et al. (eds.), *International encyclopedia of unified science*. Chicago: University of Chicago Press, 1955, pp. 655-760.

Chaplin, J. P., and Krawiec, T. S. *Systems and theories of psychology*. New York: Holt, Rinehart and Winston, 1960.

Cousin, V. *Cours de l'histoire de la philosophie*. 2 vols. Paris: Pichon and Didier, 1829.

Jones, W. T. *The romantic syndrome: Toward a new method in cultural anthropology and history of ideas*. The Hague: Nijhoff, 1961.

Koch, S. (ed.), *Psychology: A Study of a science*. Study 1. *Conceptual and systematic*. New York: McGraw Hill, 1959.

Kuhn, T. S. *The Structure of scientific revolutions*. Chicago: University of Chicago Press, 1962.

Kuhn, T. S. The function of dogma in scientific research. In A. C. Crombie (ed.), *Scientific change*. New York: Basic Books, 1963, pp. 347-369.

Leibniz, G. W. *New essays concerning human understanding*. (Trans. by A. G. Langley.) La Salle, Ill.: Open Court, 1949. (1704)

Lewin, K. The conflict between Aristotelian and Galilean modes of thought in contemporary psychology. In *A dynamic theory of personality*. New York: McGraw Hill, 1935, pp. 1-42.

Lovejoy, A. O. *The great chain of being*. Cambridge: Harvard University Press, 1936.

Marx, M. H., and Hillix, W. A. *Systems and theories in psychology*. New York: McGraw Hill, 1963.

Miller, G. A. (ed.), *Mathematics and psychology*. New York: Wiley, 1964.

Morell, J. D. *An historical and critical view of the speculative philosophy in Europe in the nineteenth century*. New York: Carter, 1862.

Murphy, G. *An historical introduction to modern psychology*. 3rd rev. ed. New York: Harcourt Brace, 1932.

Murray, H. A. Historical trends in personality research. In H. P. David and J. C. Brengelmann (eds.), *Perspective in personality research*. New York: Springer, 1961, pp. 3-39.

Watson, R. I. The historical background for national trends in psychology: United States. *Journal of the History of the Behavioral Sciences*, 1961, 1, 130-138.

Whitehead, A. N. *Science and the modern world*. New York: Mentor, 1925.

Woodger, J. H. *Biological principles: A critical study*. New York: Harcourt, Brace, 1929.

11. Prescriptions as Operative in The History of Psychology

Over the last decade or so, the history of psychology as a scholarly discipline has been making considerable strides. Early in this period the refrain was heard that we were all amateurs attempting to pull ourselves up by our own bootstraps and eager to learn our trade from our more experienced confreres in other historical disciplines. It would, of course, be a serious mistake if we were ever to lose this eagerness to learn from workers in related fields. More recently, coincident with an increasing confidence in our own abilities, there has come to the psychologist a realization that, by the very nature of his training and background, he brings to the study of history certain positive skills in which he may well be better equipped than is the typical historian. Instances of these skills are expertise in quantitative procedures, knowledge of social psychology, and familiarity with personality research and theory— all of which bring a direct enrichment to historical research. Just as knowledge of history adds a depth to one's knowledge of psychology, so, too, psychology can help to add another dimension to history.

This is an account of the search for a psychologically authentic approach to historical study which draws upon the already established thought patterns of a psychologist. It is motivated by a desire to extend psychological thinking to historical approaches. Although a means of teaching of the field to students is one of my

---

Earlier versions of this paper were given at the Annual Meeting of the American Psychological Association, September, 1970 in Miami, Florida, and as the Presidential Address at the Annual Meeting of the New England Psychological Association, November, 1970 in Boston, Massachusetts.

considerations, I am more desirous of providing a framework in which to carry on research and to write in the field. Illustrations, in fact, will ignore teaching in favor of research stimulation and writing.

I have found this framework for historical research in what I have called prescriptive theory (Watson, 1967). A prescription is an attitude taken by a psychologist toward one or another aspect of his psychological concerns. By conceiving prescriptions in attitudinal terms, in effect, I am opening up the possibility of placing them in the setting of social psychology. The major function of prescriptions is conceived to be orientative or attitudinal in that it tells the psychologist how he should behave. A quantitative prescription is manifested by a psychologist when, faced by a psychological problem, he forthwith starts to ask how he might quantify it without necessarily first inquiring whether the problem is suitable for quantification. Moreover, in order to be of historical value, the prescriptions isolated for study must have existed over some appreciable period of time. The rational and empirical prescriptions have served a guidance function for centuries while more specific manifestations such as logical empiricism have been of historical moment for much shorter temporal periods. Empiricism and rationalism then are the prescriptions; logical empiricism a manifestation of them.

Before expanding upon this summarization of the prescriptive approach something should be said about other approaches to history that are current.[1] A new approach had become imperative because in using at least some of the earlier ones I became aware of certain weaknesses they exhibited. In almost all instances I found them useful but in a limited way, so that I now make them supplementary to the prescriptive approach. I shall deal with them one by one saying only enough to identify the approach, and then indicate what appears to me to be its major weakness. Later in this paper I shall attempt to show how prescriptive theory helps to overcome the weaknesses they show.

Curiously enough, one major approach to history can be said to be severely psychological in nature. This is the Great Man approach,

---

1. The paradigmatic approach to history associated with the name of Kuhn I have considered in the earlier paper. Despite the stimulation I have received from Kuhn, I agree with him that psychology is a preparadigmatic science and for the reasons I have stated. I will say no more about it.

in which the burden of history is conceived as being borne by the eminent men who made history. My textbook *The Great Psychologists* (1968) leans heavily upon this approach. Quite apart from the simplistic invitation it extends to make psychology's cast of characters either good guys, "true scientists," or bad buys, "superstitious charlatans," or, save the mark, "philosophers," this way of conceptualizing history is too limited in scope. While not going so far as to conceive psychology's eminent men as serving only as placebos, as did E. G. Boring, I do agree that the individual, while he does have an effect, cannot carry the burden of history alone. The difficulty is this. The Great Man theory is psychological but not *social* psychological in nature. In its extreme form it denies any influence whatsoever to environmental factors. In short, when used in isolation, it does not allow us to see the individual in a social-intellectual context.

To move to its polar opposite, the social-intellectual context approach to history is often referred to as the *Zeitgeist* theory. To use one of Boring's definitions, it is "the total body of knowledge and opinion available at any time to a person living within a given culture" (1955, p. 106). When some great scientific discovery is made it is attributed to the *Zeitgeist;* the time was propitious and, as someone said, if it hadn't been Einstein who made the advance, Zweistein or Dreistein would have come along shortly. To speak of the *Zeitgeist* and to mention a prominent characteristic has a certain summarizing value. Most often appeals made to the *Zeitgeist* evoke a mood in the hearer but they often suffer from being extraordinarily empty of content. Attributing something to the *Zeitgeist* is often nothing more than a slogan for our ignorance, or a way of saying what will be, will be. When given more specific meaning, it characteristically attempts to do so in terms of very broad trends—urbanization, frontier mentality, democracy, and the like.

When the *Zeitgeist* is studied at a more detailed level, say that of the academic community, it does take on more meaningfulness. In fact this speaker found this to be so when he investigated how the social, educational, economic and political conditions under which pioneer investigators of individual aptitude differences—Binet, Galton, Cattell, Stern, and others—functioned (Watson, 1968). By comparing them with the typical breed of academic psychologists of their time it was possible to establish that their academic *Geists* differed in certain characteristic respects. For example, these pioneers tended to be free from the more stifling aspects of the academic atmosphere by what might appear to be the somewhat dubious advantage of not having regular academic appointments.

I would argue, then, that there is some value to a *Zeitgeist* approach but all too often it is so generally stated as to be meaningless. By explaining everything it explains nothing. When used without supplementation by other approaches, it also may be said to be profoundly ahistorical. That is to say, often the *Zeitgeist* account of a particular period is stated in such fashion that historical continuity is impossible. One *Zeitgeist* is seen as succeeding another with the characteristics attributed to the former bearing little or no relation to those of the latter.

But what about that well-worn approach to conceptualizing history in terms of the content of relevant research and speculation at a given temporal period? For example, Helmholtz's major work might be examined in terms of the speed of neural impulse, theory of color vision, an account of space perception and exploration of pitch discrimination. This approach seems, at first glance, to have much to recommend it since it solves the problem of needing a framework by dismissing it as unnecessary. It seems as if all one had to do was just report the facts and nothing but the facts. But here, as always, there is some principle of selection operating through the historian since he never does report *all* of the facts. There is an inevitable selection.

What seems to be the most common principle of selection by historians is to emphasize presentation of historical material most relevant to the content of current science. It was this characteristic of fact collection that caused Agassi (1963) to call misdirected efforts along this line the inductive approach to history. This approach he traced back to Francis Bacon and his impossible demand that collection of facts be made without appeal to preformed opinions. We know now that we are always guided by some implicit or explicit hypothesis. Quite apart from the weakness that the contentual inductivist who says he is only collecting facts is actually being guided by some implicit hypotheses which by that very fact weakens his grasp of the material, there are certain traps to the unwary historian to which this approach makes him susceptible. Agassi based his central attack upon what is often referred to as presentism (e.g., by Stocking, 1965), that is, the view that the past facts lead to the present facts, the past is to be judged as it leads to the highest point of development and normative point of departure, the present. Agassi took somewhat savage delight in arguing that much practice in the writing of history is guided by comparing the past to the truth as reported in the latest textbook in the particular field. Inductive historians were seen as behaving as if they were grading compositions—those in the past who were seen as being precursors of present truths were given good marks while those who held different or contrary views were given bad marks and often charged pejoratively with being "nonscientific," philosophical, and perhaps most damning of all, "metaphysical."

There are practicing historians who stand sturdily opposed to presentism but still follow an inductive-contentual approach. In denying presentism, they say, in effect, we must report the facts as the individual at the particular historical period in question saw them. We must not anticipate, we must play fair, immerse ourselves in the past and see it as they did. In my view, this is much truer to the historian's craft than is presentist variation of inductivism and yet can we ever free ourselves from the present? I doubt we can. Moreover, the more the antiquarian goal, the past for its own sake, is achieved by historical workers, the more difficult it is for contemporary readers to find it either comprehensible or relevant. We all have had the experience of reading history, including the history of psychology, and finding the material almost meaningless, and certainly dull. We might have even congratulated ourselves for not being psychologists at the time of Wundt, when we would have to have been trained as introspectors and report our sensory experiences. Did the psychologists of that time find the material dull and meaningless? Not at all. Just as we do, they paid rapt attention to their work and engaged in vehement controversies about events, research problems, pieces of apparatus, and theories that today are forgotten, considered insignificant or even found incomprehensible. To mention only two or three examples, the Beast-Machine controversy, imageless thought and the influence on the speed of reaction time of the attitude taken toward it, were as vital and gripping to psychologists then as behavior therapy, computer programming and student involvement are today. Something must be wrong, then, if history to be true to the past must be dull and meaningless to those of us of the present. At the moment, we seem to be trapped between the enticing evils of contentual presentism and the dullness of contentual antiquarianism.

What I have said to this point applied to the history of science in general as well as the history of psychology in particular. In order to be able to turn to a variant of the noncontentual presentist approach based on a decision as to what is its current subject matter, I will now turn specifically to psychology as a field which in some way or another we must distinguish from and relate to other disciplines, such as physiology, philosophy or physics. At first glance the question might be framed as to what is psychology's subject matter—an account of the kind of things with which it deals. With Popper, I hope that there is no subject matter—be it physics or psychology—distinguished by the subject matter that its practitioners investigate. Disciplines are distinguished partly for administrative convenience such as organization of academic departments and partly because problems we investigate tend to grow into a system of interrelated problems and theories. These are not salient means of demarcating a field. *We are not students of some subject matter but students of problems.* And problems may cut right across the borders of any subject matter of discipline. This is the reason that physiology and philosophy are inescapable parts of our heritage insofar as they have dealt with the same problems as we do.

I am now in a position to turn to a presentist but noncontentual approach to history. In an attempt to answer the question of what is relevant to its history, some historians of psychology (e.g., Kantor, 1963) concluded that the appropriate solution is to first decide about the nature of psychology of today on other grounds than content. What they do is this. They judge psychology today as possessing certain characteristic trends. If today's scientific psychology is judged to be objective, monistic and interpersonal, then *any material from the past that is objective, monistic, and interpersonal was scientific psychology then.* In short, these historians search the past theories, problems, methods and trends that support selected current conceptions and ignore or decry the rest on the ground that it was not part of scientific psychology then because, as they see it, it is not part of psychology now. This way of limiting scope is of course a fertile ground for exercise of special pleading and straining, and results, for example, in attempting to prove that Plato, insofar as he was a psychologist, was a behaviorist. It arrives at its delimitation of the field by excluding many facets that at least some psychologists to this very day think is part of the field. Limiting myself to only the polar opposites of the three trends mentioned, i.e. subjectivism, dualism, and for lack of a better term on my part, nonpersonalism, each surely have some contemporary supporters among psychologists. To marshal evidence to show that psychology has become increasingly objective, quantitative, or whatever is entirely defensible. (Indeed, with similar and even identical prescriptions I do precisely this.) To the extent that the selected trends leave out some aspects of psychology and yet claims to be the whole field, the view is short-sighted and limited, not only in denying that other trends may have been at work in shaping psychology of the present, but also in denying that they did so in the past, and, implicitly at least, in denying that these other trends might also function in the future.

Table I presents the prescriptions arranged in terms of contrasting pairs—only one among several ways that they relate to one another. Some manifestations of prescriptive function can be no more than mentioned on this account. Instead of polarity, gradations may be exhibited as often happens in the setting of rationality-irrationality. Some prescriptions are held implicitly at a particular temporal period as is the case with monism at the present time despite being a very explicit prescription in the past.

THE PRESCRIPTIONS OF PSYCHOLOGY ARRANGED IN CONTRASTING PAIRS

Conscious mentalism—Unconscious mentalism (emphasis on awareness of mental structure or activity—unawareness)
Contentual objectivism—Contentual subjectivism (psychological data viewed as behavior of individual—as mental structure or activity of individual)
Determinism—Indeterminism (human events completely explicable in terms of antecedents—not completely so explicable)
Empiricism—Rationalism (major, if not exclusive, source of knowledge is experience—is reason)
Functionalism—Structuralism (psychological categories are activities —are contents)
Inductivism—Deductivism (investigations begun with facts or observations—with assumed established truths)
Mechanism—Vitalism (activities of living beings completely explicable by physio-chemical constituents—not so explicable)
Methodological objectivism—Methodological subjectivism (use of methods open to verification by another competent observer— not so open)

Molecularism–Molarism (psychological data most aptly described in terms of relatively small units–relatively large units)

Monism–Dualism (fundamental principle or entity in universe is of one kind–is of two kinds, mind and matter)

Naturalism–Supernaturalism (nature requires for its operation and explanation only principles found within it–requires transcendent guidance as well)

Nomotheticism–Idiographicism (emphasis upon discovering general laws–upon explaining particular events or individuals)

Peripheralism–Centralism (stress upon psychological events taking place at periphery of body–within the body)

Purism–Utilitarianism (seeking of knowledge for its own sake–for its usefulness in other activities)

Quantitativism–Qualitativism (stress upon knowledge which is countable or measurable–upon that which is different in kind or essence)

Rationalism–Irrationalism (emphasis upon data supposed to follow dictates of good sense and intellect–intrusion or domination of emotive and conative factors upon intellectual processes)

Staticism–Developmentalism (emphasis upon cross-sectional view–upon changes with time)

Staticism–Dynamicism (emphasis upon enduring aspects–upon change and factors making for change)

When their oppositional character is exhibited in the same temporal period, one can make an estimate of relative strengths. Thus dominance and counterdominance come into play. At the time of Locke, rationalism dominated in England despite our justified emphasis on his major contribution to empiricism. At the time, empirical leaning was perhaps just strong enough to be called counterdominant. Both he and his contemporary rationalists agreed on emphasizing methodological and contentual subjectivism in psychology. Today Locke's stress on empiricism is shared by us but we have shifted to a dominant adherence to methodological and contentual objectivism. Nevertheless, still viable on the current scene and therefore counterdominant are rationalism and contentual and methodological subjectivism.

This polarity can and does occur among them but often at a given temporal period some other more complicated relationships hold. For example, a synthesis may occur. A moment ago mention was made of a current *stress* on empiricism in psychology. Neither for Locke long ago nor today was or is this an unrelieved empiricism. For centuries, empiricism and rationalism presented what was interpreted to be irreconcilable rival claims as sources of knowledge. It is not long since that their synthesis, logical empiricism, i.e., "rational" empiricism, captivated psychologists. Indeed, there is every reason to believe that there are instances where, instead of being antithetical, prescriptions are complementary with both being simultaneously present. For example, in the thinking of a given person there may be both structural and functional aspects as will be the case with Descartes mentioned in a moment.

There is some merit in distinguishing between contentual and methodological prescriptions as is done in identifying some of the prescriptions in that the attitudes they express are oriented toward one or another of these two facets of the psychologist's task. I will illustrate through the methodologically oriented prescriptions. The modern period, in fact, was ushered in with an emphasis on method. Bacon, Descartes, Hobbes, Leibniz and Locke each differed widely in their answers but agreed that their quest was for the correct method to gain knowledge. As the source of knowledge, empiricism with its emphasis on experience, and rationalism with its stress on reason, are particularly salient. So too are deductivism and inductivism. Also important in influencing the methods used are methodological objectivism and methodological subjectivism. This emphasis on methodology continues to this very day with logical empiricism and phenomenology each claiming to be the most valid and relevant method for securing psychological knowledge, while drawing upon their respective prescriptions. Instead of trying to decide which of these predominates today (and is supposed therefore to be characteristic of psychology), say, empiricism and methodological objectivism, and then ruling out rationalism and methodological subjectivism as nonpsychological, I treat them both as contributing to the history of psychology, thus handling the matter differently than would a noncontentual presentist.

Of course, the same prescription changes with time. The inductivism of Bacon and the inductivism of Skinner differ, to be sure, but I would argue that a line of descent could be traced. So too does the rationalist attitude of Descartes differ from that of Husserl, but a historical continuity seems to be present.

By use of prescriptive theory, I try to preserve the values each expressed as the individuals concerned saw them in their own time but to relate these views to those of the present through demonstrating a basically related prescriptive attitude.

The contents and the methods associated with prescriptive attitudes—the nonsense syllable of Ebbinghaus in the service of objectivism and quantification, the search for certainty through systematic doubt of Descartes as a means of establishing rationalistic truth, the free association of Freud to bring out the dynamic unconscious irrationalisms of his patients—give flesh and blood to the story we tell which is history. They are not then just contents or hardware, or investigatory methods or statistical techniques, but set so far as possible in the context of the thought processes of the individuals concerned. This would be my way of "telling it like it was" and yet showing the relation of the past to contemporary interest.

This helps to solve the presentist-antiquarian issue. Presentistic interest is preserved by showing the relation to the present. The value of antiquarianism is preserved by presenting the content of the time in its context as seen by the contributors concerned.

At the charter meeting of the International Society for the History of the Behavioral Sciences in May, 1969, at Princeton University, I presented a paper (1971), "A Prescriptive Analysis of the Psychological Views of René Descartes," lifted more or less bodily from the prescriptively oriented history of psychology on which I am working. As you might expect, I paid considerable attention to Descartes' adherence to a deductive rationalism which led to a sharpening of the prevailing dualistic prescription, but at this juncture I chose to focus on aspects not perhaps quite so obvious. Descartes was inspired, in some measure at least, by Harvey's work on circulation, which successfully fostered a mechanistic prescription, i.e., Harvey had shown how a bodily function is intelligible in terms of its own mechanisms. On this problem Descartes worked at two prescriptive levels—the molar level through his argument that an animal is an automaton and the body of man a machine, and at the molecular level through his espousal of a corpuscular theory, so-called because it is not, strictly speaking, an atomic theory since he accepted no limit to spatial divisibility and denied the void. His treatment of mind as substance led to a discussion of his use of the structural prescription while his view of mind as exhibiting faculties showed his simultaneous adherence to a functional prescription.

Hardly more than under way is another book in which I apply prescriptive theory to the problem of the history of personality theory. I mention it at all because it gives me the opportunity to show how prescriptive theory may provide a framework before actually turning to writing on a historical subject. The concept of salience was first applied to the various prescriptive possibilities. An emphasis on the idiographic attitude rather than the nomothetic seems essential to any examination of personality theory. Moreover, since the self-concept is an aspect of many personality theories, contentual subjectivism must also be explored. Similarly, the attempts to rule out the subjective component expressed contentually by objectivistic views of personality also must receive attention. Combining the two, we have individuality objectively and subjectively viewed. Many personality theories lay almost comparable stress upon unconscious mentalism, dynamicism, irrationalism and developmentalism. With this as the preliminary heuristic framework I am ready to go more deeply into the matter, referring, of course, to men, social conditions, contentual problems and methodologies.

I have already referred in passing to how I met the objection to noncontentual presentism and how I attempt to preserve the values of both presentism of a noninductive sort and antiquarianism. I would like to say something about the other approaches. The principal objection I have advanced to the Great Man theory, its simplistic isolation making impossible sole reliance upon it, has been met by working with prescriptive constructs yet dealing with them as expressed by individuals. Supplementation by the limited *Zeitgeist* approach that I outlined earlier also serves as a needed corrective. Only one approach remains to be considered: inductivism as such. This I avoided by being primarily deductive at the onset. My deductive hypotheses of prescriptive theory are spread out for all to see. Prescriptive theory is analytic in the sense that it tries to specify the dynamic components that are to be found in the history of psychology.

Since the psychological study of history is a relatively new area of inquiry for psychologists, I might call your attention to some of the values of a theory in this context. As is customary, theories serve as mnemonic aids in that "facts" become more manageable when subsumed under a theory. Theory, here as elsewhere, guides observations and search.

One of the difficulties of the study of history in the customary artistic fashion is the ease with which one can slip into circular reasoning. Historians approach their task with preconceptions, of course, but they are not always verbalized. A fertile field for special pleading and overlooking of contrary evidence is thus created. To be sure, one's fellow historians will be quick to step in to point out the obvious errors, but at best this is a wasteful procedure, since in the meantime the falsified evidence has been introduced into the stream of scholarship perhaps undetected by all except the specialist. I am reminded in this connection of how often the layman will find his ideal historian in a person that he discovers the professional regards as suspect.

If a research design approach is adopted to study history, the data collected stands between the plan of attack and the conclusions drawn. An adequate theory has the tremendous advantage of making possible its disproof by its promulgator. Without an explicit theory, which historians often lack, this safeguard is not possible within the context of his own work. Related if not identical with this, explicating a theory in some detail in advance of study has the advantage of making it possible to see more clearly than otherwise would be the case when deliberate or accidental deviations are made.

I have reached the last aspect of this paper—research studies in the narrower sense of data collection and analysis that have been generated by prescriptive theory. Over-determined in my own behavior by an allegiance to quantitativism and methodological objectivism in the setting of a more general empirical bent, several studies have served to submit prescriptive theory to test other than that of validation by the method of plausibility. Prescriptive categories are judged sufficiently testable to permit investigation including the possibility of finding results that call for their own demise or modification, a not inconsiderable virtue not always present even in theories in research areas much more explored than is that of history.

The first dissertation in our doctoral program in the history of psychology used prescriptive theory as a major aspect of its framework. Completed by Barbara Ross, now of the University of Massachusetts, Boston, it is entitled "Psychological Thought within the Context of the Scientific Revolution, 1665-1700." Contrary to general opinion, which places the beginning of the scientific study of man in the nineteenth century, she hypothesized that events of the seventeenth century served to place psychology in the same conceptual framework as that of the other sciences. This, of course, does *not* conflict with the incontrovertible fact that the major interests of the seventeenth-century scientists were in the problems of the natural sciences.

The scientific literature of the period scrutinized was the papers in the *Philosophical Transactions* of the Royal Society during the years mentioned. Although not replacing the hard intellectual labor of the historian, content analyses provided the major tool. It allows organization of the complex framework of prescriptions in a systematic way through the definition of the categories, treatment of the data and interpretation of the findings.

Two judges, other than Dr. Ross, were given definitions and trained in their application with some material similar to but not identical with the papers in the *Transactions*. The judgment made about each paper was whether or not a category under consideration was relevant or not relevant. Intra-coder and inter-coder reliabilities were in the range of .80 to .96. The information the coding provided was used in a computer analysis through a joint frequency matrix and an association matrix for the 125 variables as well as for each of seven five-year periods.

Of the over 1900 papers published in the *Transactions*, 367 or 19 percent were judged to be relevant to psychological thought and the study of man. These papers formed the basis of further study. Something should be said about general findings before considering what was found about prescriptions. Many of the principles accepted as basic assumptions of nineteenth-century psychology were found to be embedded in these papers. These include the beginnings of the physical science model for psychology and physiology, the natural mechanical explanation applied to the study of the body of man and also applied to that of abnormal behavior, mechanical treatment of animal motion leading to the concept of reflex and explanation of body motions residing in the nervous system, independent and separate functions of parts of the brain, including systematic examination of removing parts. Increased attention to voluntary and involuntary motion took place, comparative studies of men and animals led to discussion of evolutionary concepts, and mechanical philosophy provided most of the fundamental knowledge in the areas of sensation and perception, and cultural differences were studied by examination of the history of language and religion.

Findings on subject matter categories in which the papers from the *Transactions* fitted must be mentioned. Physiological problems were discussed in 46 percent of the papers, while sensation and social phenomena accounted for 36 and 33 percent respectively. Perception, abnormal, and comparative problems also received major attention, while thinking, personality, learning and development received somewhat less attention. In a few minutes, to do justice to the evidence presented in a manuscript of nearly 500 pages is an almost impossible task. Remarks hereafter need therefore be restricted to those pertinent to prescriptive theory.

"Prescriptively, the new science [i.e., of the seventeenth century] reflected quantitativism, nomotheticism, methodological objectivism and probabilistic determinism. The same prescriptive emphases underlie modern science." Thus Dr. Ross completes the first paragraph of her concluding summary. It was these particular prescriptions (and no other) that were hypothesized as reflecting the prevailing scientific attitude in the latter half of the seventeenth century. Accordingly this quotation forms the basis of what I shall have to say about the findings concerning prescriptions.

A major source of evidence for this contention was the relatively high percentage of papers judged as showing their presence, namely methodological objectivism 70 percent, quantitativism 40 percent, nomotheticism 51 percent, and probabilistic determinism 59 percent.

In most instances Dr. Ross had supplemented the definitions given on the hand-out in her instructions for coding and consequently the meanings she attributed to the prescriptions. But there are some deliberate deviations. The pertinent prescription here is so-called probabilistic determinism. In preliminary analysis and planning of the study Dr. Ross found it necessary to broaden indeterminism—an event not always completely determined by its antecedents, as I defined it, to include probabilism—that it is possible with some degree of probability to predict sequences of events. In this instance, there is a deviation from the original formulation of prescriptions but one which she is at pains to justify. It may eventuate in modification in my theoretical position. It is too early to tell.

We at this point might focus on one of the advantages of a multivariable approach. There were other prescriptions with equally high percentages of appearance than she had predicted! If she had reached only for evidence applicable to her hypothesis, i.e., investigated only the variables called for by her hypothesis, then she would not have known of what was at first glance disconcerting contrary evidence. Suffice it to say here, she explained their presence satisfactorily without weakening her argument very much.

The conception of prescriptions as opposing pairs was supported by the association coefficients (of Kendall and Stuart), which reflects relative frequency of two variables occurring together in that they demonstrated a high negative relationship. That between methodological objectivism and methodological subjectivism was -0.8323, indeterminism and strict determinism -1.000, strict determinism and strict indeterminism -1.000, nomotheticism and idiographicism -0.8627, and quantitativism and qualitativism -0.8868. Indeed the 21 contrasting pairs yielded negative coefficients in all but one instance (functionalism and structuralism) in which a low positive correlation obtained, a not surprising state of affairs when the earlier illustration of expected simultaneous presence is recalled.

A proposal for a dissertation, "A prescriptive analysis of the Presidential addresses of the American Psychological Association, 1892-1970," reached the level of preliminary orals a few months ago. Kenneth Gibson of UNH proposes to study the frequency of acceptance, rejection and irrelevance of the prescriptions using the 76 presidential addresses as the material for content analysis. Dominance and counterdominance, explicitness and implicitness, the presence and absence of patterns and of cycles of prescriptions will be studied. Patterns across all presidential addresses will be obtained through a correlation matrix of 648 entries. Development of a manual, coding and rating, calculation of reliabilities and so on, although extremely detailed tasks, need no description here since they will be carried on more or less conventionally.

Without realizing it, some of you served as respondents to a rating study conducted by Joseph Mirabito for his master's thesis at UNH, since he wrote to all members of the Divisions of History of Psychology and of Philosophical Psychology, a total of 711 when overlap was eliminated. He wanted to investigate by content analysis the dimensions of certain psychological theoretical positions held by contemporary psychologists, drawing upon variables suggested by Coan and by Watson. Each person rated his opinion of each variable along a five-point scale ranging from marked positive emphasis on a given variable to marked rejection. Usable returns were obtained from 389 or 55 percent. He had used most of the prescriptive variables. After completion of the study I made arrangements for still another factor analysis involving only data from prescriptive variables.

As before, the Bio-Med General Analysis Program was used which yielded a principal components solution with rotations to provide orthogonal factors. This analysis extracted 9 factors which accounted for 58 percent of the total variance.

The first factor could be called *methodological objectivism* since its heaviest positive loading was precisely on this variable, with a negative loading on methodological subjectivism. Quantitativism, nomotheticism and inductivism received positive loadings on this factor. The second factor is associated with positive loadings on irrationalism, unconscious mentalism, developmentalism and centralism, and perhaps is best described as irrationalism. The fourth factor also includes developmentalism but not irrationalism while it is also positively weighted with molarism, dynamicism, functionalism and idiographicism. This seems to be a *molaristic-dynamic-idiographic* factor. The fifth factor involves only a positive weighting on purism and a negative weighting on utilitarianism. A preference for pure, rather than applied, science seems to be the only suitable way of describing it, and therefore it is called the *puristic* factor.

The third factor was reserved for final discussion because while "hanging together" so far as the variables involved were concerned, it was a quite unexpected finding. It can only be described as a *supernaturalistic* factor since it has positive loadings on indeterminism, vitalism and supernaturalism and negative loadings on their polar opposites—naturalism, mechanism and determinism. That part of the sample supplying the data were members of the Division of Philosophical Psychology and a not inconsiderable proportion of the Division of History of Psychology also have membership in this Division may help to account for this finding. That a humanistic emphasis could account for these findings seems plausible. Needless to say, it suggests further investigation, as do all the results.

In closing, the evidence in support of prescriptive theory seems to me to be encouraging. However, each of the approaches, including prescriptive theory, provides understanding and explanation of only part of that which influences the history of psychology. For me, prescriptive theory seems to provide a satisfactorily integrative framework as an approach to the history of psychology.

REFERENCES

Agassi, J. Towards an historiography of science. *History and Theory*, 1963, *2*, Beiheft 2.

Boring, E. G. Dual role of the *Zeitgeist* in scientific creativity. *Sci. Mon.*, 1955, *80*, 101-106. (Reprinted in *Psychologist at large*. New York: Basic Books, 1961, pp. 325-337.)

Kantor, J. R. *The scientific evolution of psychology*. Vol. 1. Chicago, Ill.: Principia Press, 1963.

Ross, Barbara. Psychological thought within the context of the scientific revolution, 1665-1700. Unpublished doctoral dissertation, University of New Hampshire, 1970.

Stocking, G. W., Jr. On the limits of "presentism" and "historicism" in the historiography of the behavioral sciences. *J. hist. Behav. Sci.*, 1965, *1*, 211-217.

Watson, R. I. Psychology: a prescriptive science. *Amer. Psychologist*, 1967, *22*, 435-443.

Watson, R. I. *The great psychologists: from Aristotle to Freud*. (2nd ed.) Philadelphia: Lippincott, 1968.

Watson, R. I. The individual, social, educational, economic, and political conditions for the original practices of detection and utilization of individual aptitude differences. *Rev. de Synthèse*, 1968, 49-52, 355-368.

Watson, R. I. A prescriptive analysis of Descartes' psychological views. *J. hist. Behav. Sci.*, 1961, *7*, 223-248.

12. Prescriptive Theory
And the Social Sciences

According to the prospectus for this Conference, one facet of our concern is a theory of scientific development in terms of its conceptual and methodological presuppositions. I propose to emphasize prescriptions—one form of presuppositional attitudes which I consider to be an extremely significant factor in the dynamics of the history of psychology. Some thoughts also about the extension of this view to the other social sciences will be offered.

I participate as a working historian in psychology, not as a philosopher of science. I follow May Brodbeck (1953) in considering the philosophy of science as talking about science and not as a part of science. Since I am "talking about" history rather than "doing" history and since I am relatively unversed in the philosophy of science, it is inevitable that I draw upon personal experiences—my reactions to what I know about the philosophy of science and the philosophy of history. I will not go as far as B. F. Skinner (1959), who, when asked to give his theoretical position following a detailed outline conformed to by all other participants in a cooperative, many-volume critique of the current state of the science of psychology, responded by writing his autobiography! Nevertheless, there are certain consequences of my professional career that influence my view of my historical task. One direct consequence of being a

Paper originally presented at an international working conference on "Determinants and Controls of Scientific Development" held in Graz, Austria, June 1974, under the auspices of the Institute for Advanced Studies, Vienna. Published in *Determinants and controls of scientific development* (Dordrecht, Holland: D. Reidel, 1975), pp. 11-35.

psychologist is adherence in historical endeavors to methodological individualism.

Indeed, the prescriptive approach, the major focus of this paper, is part of a more general emphasis on methodological individualism—a position that calls for the concepts used to be interpretable in terms of characteristics of individual human beings, a position peculiarly fitting to a psychologist who is concerned with experience and behavior of *individuals* whether they be in isolation or in groups. Now, all historians must come to terms with the inescapable fact that they are concerned with individuals; but here, historians divide into those who see this as a trivial statement and those who consider it a basic one. I take it seriously but not so one-sidedly that I would argue, as did Watkins (1953), that *all* concepts in social science are to be based on this doctrine.

In part, prescriptive theory was a reaction to evidence presented by Kuhn (1962) that some sciences possess a paradigm, i.e., a universally accepted contentual model that guides the activities of the practitioners of that science for an appreciable time. Although he has said relatively little about it, he did indicate the existence of preparadigmatic sciences, either as historically earlier stages of what are now paradigmatic sciences or as contemporary sciences which have yet to achieve paradigms. What little he said about contemporary preparadigmatic sciences showed that he had psychology and other social sciences in mind. Although what is to follow most often refers specifically to psychology, you would be correct in presuming that I am inclined to believe that other preparadigmatic social sciences face the same issues. As I proceed, you may wish to ask yourself whether or not this is the case.

In the original paper on prescriptive theory published in 1967, it was contended that psychology lacks a paradigm as demonstrated by our vociferous failure to agree about fundamentals, the continued presence of schools of psychology despite their weakened appeal, and the presence of national differences which make it possible to speak of German psychology, Russian psychology, and the like.

It would seem that American sociologists, too, share a conviction that their field does not have a unitary, over-arching theoretical posture; or, as I would put it, it lacks a paradigm. Thirty eminent sociologists, including Kingsley Davis, Everett Hughes, Daniel Katz, P. F. Larzarsfeld, Seymour Lipset, Talcott Parsons, David Riesman and Neil Smelzer were queried on this point by Popovich (1966).

Twenty-four took the position that sociology had no general, inclusive theory. Six believed that sociology had a prevailing view as expressed in the functional-structural approach. Moreover, on the issue of whether there was a close relationship between general theory and empirical research, only two thought the relationship to be very close, while twenty-two thought it to be very loose.

Turning to the European scene, I imagine, from the point of view of a European scholar, that this lack of a universal contentual model can be most expeditiously recognized in the provincialism, massive though it may be, that he attributes to American psychology. Moreover, European psychologists, when speaking of their countrymen's work, share my view about the lack of a contentual model. The French historian of psychology, Reuchlin, in an article published in 1972 and entitled "Psychology or psychologies?", characterized psychological activities as exhibiting increasing divergencies and contradictory viewpoints, while Graumann (1972), speaking as Past President of the German Society of Psychology, contended that psychology lacks the coherence of the exact sciences and went on to support a pluralistic view of the field.

Psychology and sociology, and perhaps the other social sciences, tend to avoid grand or large-scale theories, and, instead, seek small-range or middle-range theories. But the brute fact is that many of the old controversies which were integral aspects of the larger theories of the past have not been resolved; we pass over them in silence or are even ignorant that they are merely latent, not nonexistent. But, in renouncing all-inclusive theory almost to substitute an untidy eclecticism, are we not also saying that we make no claim to have adherence to a broad enough position to be acceptable as an all-embracing paradigm?

One expansive tendency does seem to contradict this interpretation. Since my original paper (1967), there have been several articles, also stimulated by Kuhn's work, which argue that psychology *does* indeed possess a paradigm. However, what seems to have happened is that these individuals are arguing that present adherence to a limited paradigm is the forerunner of psychology's paradigm-to-come.

Limited paradigms do have their place in nonparadigmatic sciences. Kuhn himself distinguishes between paradigms as universally accepted contentual models and "part" paradigms, accepted for a time by specific groups within a particular science. Acceptance of contentual models of less than universal character does occur in psychology and other social sciences. The Skinnerian model, adopted by an appreciable number of American psychologists, is illustrative of a perhaps even more inclusive Behavioristic model which embraces it. A functional paradigm might be seen as acceptable by a considerable number of American sociologists; but the study by Popovich referred to earlier would show it is by no means universally accepted; hence, it is a "part" paradigm.

Because a paradigm as a contentual rallying-point is lacking, the preparadigmatic stages of a science are those in which different subject matters of the field are either to be explained from widely different points of view or one remains content to work with what is acknowledged to be but a segment of that field. To embrace the scope of the field calls for a considerable degree of complexity and a plurality of themes or trends. These themes I have called prescriptions.

As aspects of the dynamics of the history of a science, prescriptions are orientative or attitudinal: "telling how a psychologist-scientist must or should behave. . . . They help to direct the psychologist in the way he selects a problem, formulates it, and the way he carries it out" (Watson, 1967:437). And, to avoid becoming entangled with ephemeral themes, it is also essential to have evidence that interest in these particular themes had been maintained for appreciable lengths of time, preferably from the beginnings of the modern period. Therefore, the second distinguishing feature of a prescription is the maintenance of a trend over a considerable temporal period, despite changes in how and why it is manifested.

Far removed from the formal programmatic research design that is occasionally espoused in the textbooks, my search for these themes more resembled oil-prospecting than anything else. My first sounding, before any formalization of the theory, was taken on the occasion of a paper delivered at the Seventeenth International Congress of Psychology in 1963 at a symposium which had been organized to discuss national trends in psychology in several European countries and in the United States. To quote from my final paragraph concerning the contemporary scene:

> It has been seen that national trends in modern American psychology follow certain dominant prescriptions. Determinism, naturalism, physical-

ism and monism, although very much operative, are judged to incite relatively little opposition. Functionalism, operationalism, quantification, hypothetico-deductivism, environmentalism, and nomotheticism are likewise dominant, but there are couter-prescriptions which tend to oppose them. . . . Serving as counter-prescriptions to those dominant in psychology are those calling for increased complexity in theorizing, for an increased attention to philosophical matters, for general acceptance of phenomenology, for increased attention to existential psychology and in a somewhat amorphous way almost all of the areas of personality theory calls for counter-prescriptions of one sort or another. (Watson, 1965:137)

It might be added parenthetically that I later saw that some of these just quoted trends, operationalism and physicalism for example, were short-time attitudinal expression of changes in thinking and better incorporated in more general prescriptions of longer duration.

I then began another book on the history of psychology beginning with the seventeenth century and based on prescriptive theory. As I wrote, I found I could organize my thinking in prescriptive terms when dealing with the content of the thinking by Descartes, Locke, Leibniz, Hume and others. This book is still incomplete, and the only related publication is a published paper devoted to Descartes (Watson, 1971). In effect, prescriptive theory at this point consisted of finding the approach meaningful for two temporal periods: the seventeenth century and contemporary psychology. I found the same prescriptions appearing in relevant and significant fashion in the thinking of individuals separated by centuries. I was therefore emboldened to consider that prescriptions, in addition to a guidance function, could be characterized as persisting over long periods of time—despite many changes in detail and context—and that they thus fulfilled the dictionary connotations of the term: both something of a directive character and something hallowed by long usage.

In this search for a framework of themes for the history of psychology, I arrived at the list, given in Table 1, which summarized prescriptions, that are at present isolated, in terms of contrasting pairs. Although there is a heuristic value to presentation in terms of bipolar opposites since each extreme helps to explain the other— what one pole is, the other is not—it is necessary to immediately dispel any belief that this is the only or even the major way they are related to one another. All I hold on this point is that at some temporal period they were seen as opposed. Prescriptions also show

TABLE 1

The Prescriptions of Psychology Arranged in Contrasting Pairs

Conscious mentalism – Unconscious mentalism (emphasis on awareness of mental structure or activity – unawareness)
Contentual objectivism – Contentual subjectivism (psychological data viewed as behavior of individual – as mental structure or activity of individual)
Determinism – Indeterminism (human events completely explicable in terms of antecedents – not completely so explicable)
Empiricism – Rationalism (major, if not exclusive, source of knowledge is experience – is reason)
Functionalism – Structuralism (psychological categories are activities – are contents)
Inductivism – Deductivism (investigations begun with facts or observations – with assumed established truths)
Mechanism – Vitalism (activities of living beings completely explicable by physiochemical constituents – not so explicable)
Methodological objectivism – Methodological subjectivism (use of methods open to verification by another competent observer – not so open)
Molecularism – Molarism (psychological data most aptly described in terms of relatively small units – relatively large units)
Monism – Dualism (fundamental principle or entity in universe is of one kind – is of two kinds, mind and matter)
Naturalism – Supernaturalism (nature requires for its operation and explanation only principles found within it – requires transcendent guidance as well)
Nomotheticism – Idiographicism (emphasis upon discovering general laws – upon explaining particular events or individuals)
Peripheralism – Centralism (stress upon psychological events taking place at periphery of body – within the body)
Purism – Utilitarianism (seeking of knowledge for its own sake – for its usefulness in other activities)
Quantitativism – Qualitativism (stress upon knowledge which is countable or measurable – upon that which is different in kind or essence)
Rationalism – Irrationalism (emphasis upon data supposed to follow dictates of good sense and intellect – intrusion or domination of emotive and conative factors upon intellectual processes)
Staticism – Developmentalism (emphasis upon cross-sectional view – upon changes with time)
Staticism – Dynamicism (emphasis upon enduring aspects – upon change and factors making for change)

many other relationships. As they change at some point in time, both of the "opposing" pairs may be accepted according to circumstances, as would be inductivism and deductivism in contemporary research according to whether one was proceeding from observations-empirical generalizations to theories or from theories to hypotheses derived therefrom; synthesized, as is rationalism-empiricism in logical empiricism; ignored, as are supernaturalism or vitalism in large measure today; conceptualized, as degrees of difference, as in quantitativism-qualitativism; or practiced in different settings, as are purism and utilitarianism. Other relationships also hold. Some are implicit—for example, as was the molecular constancy hypothesis, which was unidentified until the Gestalt psychologists, the critics of the older structural view, brought it into being. Sometimes it will be possible to speak of one or another prescription as being dominant, or of others as being counterdominant but viable, as I did in the quotation from the earlier paper. Other usages, especially of patterns of prescriptions, will become clearer as I proceed.

I find myself in agreement with Skinner about the primacy of attitude. To quote, "Science is first of all a set of attitudes. It is a disposition to deal with the facts" (Skinner, 1953:12). However, I lack his assurance as to what precisely are the "facts" because I do not adhere to the admirably consistent and explicit part paradigm that guides him in his choice of truth values. While accepting attitudes as primary, to me they are prescriptive in nature. In terms of one of the themes of the Conference and central to this paper, prescriptive attitudes are to be presented both as a unit of change and as a cause of change in the history of psychological science.

Prescriptive attitudes are a cause of change because prescriptions are motivational in character. Conception of prescriptions as attitudes make it possible to characterize them as, in keeping with contemporary usage, favorable or unfavorable. Prescriptive allegiance or rejection is not often a bloodless, neutral affair. Emotion, feeling and wishful thinking enter. A behavioral scientist, for example, who has a favorable attitude toward quantification of data and the use of objective means, views unfavorably investigations that do not have these characteristics. His attitudes may extend to the persons and the materials which he judges in these terms: Professor Smith (a humanist), whom he views unfavorably; a computer (a tool of quantification) that he likes to use whenever possible; and Rorschach cards (dubiously quantifiable), which he views with mixed feelings.

Attitudes, however, are not confined to affective responses; they have a considerable cognitive component as well. A psychologist may not only prefer to use quantitative approaches or to consider that his task as a psychologist be an empirical one, but he also has a considerable cognitive component from which he may defend the essential rightness of his attitudes. As for latent attitudes, there at first may be no cognitive component. But when a cherished, heretofore unverbalized attitude is brought to his attention, this gap is soon filled with either "wishful" or "real" reasons for the belief.

Generally when one refers to theory, one has reference to a principle supported by data from the content of the discipline under discussion. Disregarding the data content for a moment, I submit that some important and remaining aspects of the theories that are espoused are colored by prescriptive attitudes toward them. For example, having somewhat less a tendency in this direction, it seems to me that some colleagues, when responding to a problem, a behavior, or an experience that strikes them as worthy of scrutiny, immediately turn to the question of how it can be quantified. They do not, mind you, stop to ask if it is suitable for quantification or whether it might be premature or even impossible to do so. Adherence to a quantitative prescription is probably the basis for the tremendous appeal that operationalism has had for American psychologists: What you measure *is* its meaning, which you must admit is rather neat—if you can do it. When one holds this view, one *perceives* the measures used differently.

Negative attitudes find prescriptive expression through what individuals are against. The phenomenologist Buytendijk (1957) nearly twenty years ago wrote a short paper, with a still-contemporary ring, in which he challenged the overwhelming concern in experimental psychology with objectivity and causality. He advocated as being more appropriate what he referred to as the manipulation of personality theory from models and schemata to reach the objective of understanding not in the laboratory but in meaningful situations. What I have called methodological and contentual objectivity, determinism and molecularism, are being criticized. Even from his short critique, one may hazard that Buytendijk supports at least a contentual subjectivity, some form of indeterminism, and a molaristic approach to psychological problems. What he affirmed may be said to involve some aspects of a phenomenological approach.

The relation of a pattern of prescriptive attitudes to a particular theory helps us to understand incongruous or nonsalient elements in a theory and thus helps to distinguish between prescriptions and theories other than on the basis of content. Despite the possibility of their being confused, a pattern of prescriptions is not a theory. Within the history of psychology there has been more than one instance where particular patterns of prescriptive allegiances are formed by an individual and, once brought together around contentual problems, have become inseparable—despite any necessity for them to be related—and are seen in historical perspective as a "theory." A personal pattern of prescriptions does not a theory make.

Early behaviorism in the hands of John B. Watson and others can be characterized as being militantly objective in its rejection of the mind as subject matter for psychology, empirical in espousing learning as the core problem, and violently nonhereditarian. This pattern, or some approximation of it, is often referred to as behavioristic *theory*. There is confusion here: they are not a logically coherent set of propositions; their juxtaposition is derived from Watson's pattern of prescriptive allegiances. They were simultaneously present in the thinking and writing of Watson; but if the objectivity he espoused is to be considered salient to behaviorism, it does not follow that behaviorism must also be antihereditarian. A behaviorism with an allegiance to a hereditarian prescription would still be behavioristic.

Since attitudes are means of expressing prescriptions and vice versa, it follows that one can appeal to role theory for their elucidation. In society, maintenance of groups depends to some degree upon the functioning of the majority of the participants toward shared goals, with only some individuals performing certain tasks (such as those performed by social scientists). There are implicit and explicit expectations held about other members of a particular group. In the setting of the present discussion, one or another of the social sciences is that group. Not only members of society in general but also fellow social scientists and the individual social scientist expect members of his and other social sciences to behave and think in certain ways. These expectancies are attitudes. It would seem that prescriptive-role theory could be used in demarcating science from nonscience. Psychologists, sociologists and other social scientists are members of social groups; there are certain expectations held by each kind of social scientist, as well as by others, by virtue of their respective roles. For example, social scientists would reject as being foreign to their role expectancies that among their tasks was the writing of fiction about society—social-science fiction as it were. A behavior to be expected when one is involved in the role of a novelist is rejected when one is performing in the role of a social scientist.

Analysis in terms of roles is commonplace in social psychology and sociology with, for example, Parsons and Shils (1951) referring to the social system, at least in one sense, as a variety of roles. Nor has it escaped attention that among the roles in the social system are those that are identified with the social sciences themselves. Indeed, much of the work in social psychology and sociology of science is cast in terms of roles shared by members of a community. Ben-David and Collins (1971) in their study of social factors in the origin of psychology in Germany, France and England argue that a new role is necessary for a new scientific community to come into existence. Prescriptive theory would ask what were the prescriptive attitudes the members associated with their emerging roles. Tacitly, what I have just been saying answers one question raised by the organizing committee: sociology of science *is* relevant to the historian. I leave to others to define more precisely the nature of this relationship between sociology of science and history; but I would add that the bridge between the two, the mutual use of role concepts, suggests that it would be worthwhile to also look for cross relationships through those concepts from each which might be shared with the other.

Although it would be interesting to examine the literature dealing with psychologists' conceptions of their roles, I will content myself with asking you to picture what psychologists would say when asked to recount their attitudes toward themselves as psychologists. Is it not plausible that their accounts would touch upon at least some matters that might be subsumed under prescriptive rubrics? "I work with people for their own sake, not to find generalized laws of human nature." Is it not plausible to think that idiographic and utilitarian attitudes are being expressed?

The content of research must often be distinguished from the attitudes which it, relevantly or irrelevantly, reflects. A typical content of research may be the rate of verbal learning by timed practice trials, with the number of trials to learn to a specified level of proficiency used as the score. Prescriptive attitudes adhered to by the psychologist carrying out the study may include quantitativism, empiricism, contentual objectivism and methodological objectivism but with no direct reference being made to any of the terms or to any of the concepts. By the very nature of the study, there is dependence upon knowledge that is quantifiable; qualitative findings, if noted at all, are relegated to the debriefing session or to an occasional note. The perhaps implicit assumption is made that it is experience, i.e., practice, that is important, while nativistic possibilities of influence are tacitly ignored. (Nativism is considered to be a historical outgrowth of rationalism after an intermediate step of adherence to innate ideas espoused by rationalists.) Contentual objectivism, the behavior of the individual, is that which is being observed with no attempt being made to infer what is experienced. Methodological objectivism is expressed through using a method open to repetition by other competent research men.

Prescriptions may have been contentual issues in philosophy or in earlier psychology: say, a defense of empiricism against rationalism by Locke or the explicit advocacy of contentual objectivism by John B. Watson. There are also theoretical discussions by contemporary psychologists directly on these topics or on their modern counterparts; but this is but a small fraction of the total productivity of psychologists. This larger productivity does not deal with prescriptions as content but, instead, reflects them attitudinally.

Aside from the semantic shock that occurs when a contemporary psychologist is faced with the contention that his thinking is still influenced by such antiquarian entities as dualism or rationalism, it is not considered a disadvantage that many of the trends concern what is or was contentually aspects of philosophical study. On the contrary, a field that grew out of some of the contentual problems of philosophy should be expected to show its influence.

Kuhn (1962) has held that scientific revolutions depend upon a shift in the fundamental image scientists have upon their *subject-matter* paradigm.[1] A psychologist lacks this unified subject-matter contentual image; and therefore, he has to fall back in part upon his image of himself as a particular kind of scientific agent. Prescriptions, then, concern roles.

1. Although not of direct relevance to this paper, it is probable that prescriptions are operative in so-called paradigmatic sciences but that their influence is probably less crucial. The presence of a paradigm makes it less necessary and, with some individuals, even reprehensible to be concerned with attitudinal components since to do so is both subjective and, heaven save the mark, philosophical. Practitioners of a paradigmatic science, secure in its data base, can eschew philosophy more easily than preparadigmatic scientists. A case in point is the sheer inability of some practitioners of a natural science even to see that philosophical problems are involved.

Since prescriptive theory involves roles, it makes possible the utilization of the subconstructs usually discussed in connection with roles, such as role expectation and role perception. It would not be too difficult to devise methods to study how a particular kind of social scientist holds certain prescriptive expectations about the nature of his role, to investigate what he pays attention to, to what behaviors he emits qua social scientist.

Role perception of another person is also germane to the task of the historian-sociologist of science. Here he asks the question, what role or roles does a particular individual or a particular identifiable group take? This has been investigated for characteristic groupings of psychologists—the schools of psychology.

A study by Fuchs and Kawash (1974) inquired into patterns of prescriptions adhered to by the various schools of psychology. They took as their point of departure a definition I had suggested for schools of psychology as "a set of interlocking prescriptions espoused by a group of scientists, generally with an acknowledged leader" (1967:441).

Seven-point scales to indicate ratings, ranging from "no" (1) to "great" (7) significance, were prepared for each extreme of the bipolar arrangement, resulting in a doubling of the prescriptive terms to 36. All members of the Division of the History of Psychology of the American Psychological Association who replied to their questionnaire by a certain date, numbering 68, rated the degree of significance they perceived the adherents of the five schools would attach to each prescription. Aided by a glossary of the meanings of the prescriptive terms, structuralism, functionalism, behaviorism, Gestalt and psychoanalysis were so rated. Despite the many obvious deficiencies of this exploratory study, the results have some interest.

In order to reduce the amount of data given in Table 2, results are reported only on those twenty-five prescriptions which would allow each school to have at least three significant prescriptions available for presentation. To do this, it was found that the lowest mean rating selected for further discussion to be 5.50. Since even in this lowest case the standard deviation is about 1.10, practically all individuals rated adherents of the schools as considering the prescription as significant, i.e., above the midpoint of four on the seven-point scale. For higher mean ratings, say of 6.5, practically everyone had rated their estimation of adherence as 6 or 7 and

TABLE 2
Average Rater Judgments on Five Schools of Psychology as Found by Fuchs and Kawash (1974)

Scale	Behaviorism	Functionalism	Gestalt Psychology	Psycho-analysis	Structuralism
Centralism	3.07	4.35	*5.75*	*5.82*	5.25
Conscious Mentalism	1.73	4.60	5.07	3.68	*6.41*
Contentual Objectivism	*6.43*	4.82	3.43	2.78	2.65
Contentual Subjectivism	1.40	4.13	5.10	*5.93*	*5.90*
Determinism	*6.66*	4.93	4.72	*6.15*	5.37
Developmentalism	4.75	5.19	3.91	*5.87*	2.01
Dynamicism	3.85	4.94	4.85	*6.01*	2.18
Empiricism	*6.28*	5.63	4.57	4.12	*5.81*
Functionalism	4.84	*6.84*	4.13	4.41	2.07
Idiographicism	2.37	3.40	3.56	*5.97*	2.19
Inductivism	*5.91*	5.41	4.68	4.18	5.43
Irrationalism	2.58	3.03	3.09	*6.48*	2.13
Mechanism	*6.33*	4.06	3.56	3.68	4.06
Methodological Objectivism	*6.85*	5.01	4.50	2.50	3.87
Molarism	2.82	4.54	*6.44*	5.19	2.43
Molecularism	*5.73*	3.41	1.79	2.60	5.96
Monism	6.22	3.50	3.88	3.56	2.87
Naturalism	*6.51*	5.63	5.35	5.19	*5.48*
Nomotheticism	*6.46*	5.40	*5.50*	4.57	*5.98*
Peripheralism	*5.58*	3.93	2.68	1.98	3.24
Purism	4.46	3.18	4.94	2.91	*5.81*
Quantitativism	*6.28*	4.62	3.34	1.68	4.91

	Behaviorism	Functionalism	Gestalt Psychology	Psycho-analysis	Structuralism
Structuralism	1.86	2.44	3.34	3.88	*6.90*
Unconscious Mentalism	1.63	2.82	2.85	*6.81*	2.13
Utilitarianism	5.06	*5.74*	3.22	5.28	2.37

(Standard deviations of those singled out for discussion average 1.10.)

hence of "great" significance to the particular school in question. Significant prescriptions for behaviorism, the school offering the largest array of prescriptive allegiances, were found to be adherence to a contentual and a methodological objectivism, determinism, empiricism, inductivism, mechanism, molecularism, monism, naturalism, nomotheticism, peripheralism, and quantitativism. Psychoanalysis showed high and unique positive emphasis on developmentalism, dynamicism, idiographicism, irrationalism and unconscious mentalism, and shared with one or the other schools emphasis on centralism, contentual subjectivism and determinism. Its idiosyncratic pattern of prescriptive adherences confirms the view that it is more isolated within the psychological field than are the other schools under discussion. Functionalism, as might be expected, showed high ratings on functionalism, along with the relatively common empiricism and naturalism, but also displayed a positive utilitarian attitude. Gestalt shares with psychoanalysis an emphasis on centralism, but most emphatically was seen as emphasizing molarism. It was the Gestalt psychology rating of 5.50 for nomotheticism that supplied the lowest rating singled out for attention in the decision to draw the line so that at least three prescriptions for this school were mentioned. It follows that it was the school that seemed to supply the least in the way of pronounced peaks of adherence. It was followed by functionalism, which was considered to emphasize four prescriptions. Structuralism, in common with other schools, they saw as showing emphasis on empiricism, naturalism and nomotheticism, but also shown was high acceptance for conscious mentalism, purism, contentual subjectivism, and, highest of all, structuralism at 6.90. All of the latter, except contentual subjectivism, are unique to this particular school. Aside from psychoanalysis, it appeared to be the most unique school in terms of prescriptive allegiances.

The results of this study also provide something akin to divergent validity. If one considers the eleven prescriptions which have not yet appeared in discussion and were omitted from the Table because they did not qualify to appear, the evaluators are saying that less or nonrelevant to the schools of psychology, at least in the immediate past in the United States, are prescriptive adherences to deductivism, dualism, indeterminism, methodological subjectivism, qualitativism, rationalism, staticism, supernaturalism and vitalism. The lesser relevance accorded them seems appropriate, although the relative irrelevance accorded deductivism may be somewhat harder to account for.

Is this a study of stereotypes or of role perception? There may be few surprises and our prejudices may seem to have been confirmed by the results, but I prefer to think of this as a study of role perception. It is *not* a monolithic characterization of the schools and hence does not have this characteristic of a stereotype. Instead, considerable complexity of characterization emerges from the patterns. Moreover, this study is independent in the sense that it was not carried on by one of my students and it does confirm that prescriptive dimensions may be illuminating concerning views held about the various schools of psychology.

In hearing of such guiding concepts as rationalism, dualism, mechanism, and naturalism, many of you will be reminded that these and the other themes are the very fabric of the approach known loosely as the "history of ideas." Again, as a methodological individualist, I find the history of ideas, as usually expressed, to be an unnecessarily disembodied reflection of our intellectual heritage from Plato, Descartes and Kant. Ideas are too often treated as having a ghostlike life of their own with ideas propagating, contradicting, or supporting other ideas as if we had explained them when we had sorted out their chronology. Attitudes, however, have both a firmer personal reference and a more compelling character than do ideas. To be sure, there are ideas of reference as well as compulsive ideas; but it is precisely the point that to convey this, modifying terms must be employed. From the perspective of prescriptive theory, the history of ideas is a rich reservoir from which to draw materials for studying change in history.

Direct from the mythology of science is the notion that the scientist is a disinterested observer who, without emotion, allows the results of his findings or those of other scientific workers to decide the truth. Enough has already been said to show that I do not subscribe to this view. Rather, in their search for truths, scientists *try* to be as impersonal and knowledgeable about their motives as human nature permits. In a Hobbesean vein, one could even say that our instruments, our statistical and experimental controls, are necessary because we are venal or stupid or both. We are so unable to grasp the meaning of raw data, so open to wishful thinking, that we introduce external controls and conventions of statistical significance to protect us—we hope—from errors of interpretation. Investigation of prescriptive attitudes enters as part of this pattern of controls. Dualism as an idea may be neutral; one's attitudes toward it are not!

It is appropriate at this juncture to remind ourselves that the historian as a social scientist is human too! He, too, needs the sobering effect of methodological controls. He, too, must allow his cherished beliefs, his fond anticipations, to be exposed to the possibility of contrary evidence. Thus, with this in mind, I am going to address myself to methodology pertinent to the study of prescriptions *and* particularly to the historian as social scientist.

My somewhat crude but workable distinction between functions of a psychologist per se and those of a psychologist-historian is that in the latter role I am confined primarily to interacting with documents, not persons.

In all historical writing there is the inevitable selection that the historian makes among the available documents. History is a humanistic discipline, with the narrative depicting not only the contents of the documents but the selection that the skills of the historian emphasize and otherwise make from them. Their organization by the historian, his ability to penetrate into them, are crucial to the art of writing history. I value the artistic aspects of historical writing. I would not wittingly denigrate or destroy them. As I see it, my task is to walk that narrow line between falling victim to my enthusiastic interpretation of the historical material and committing the equally excessive error of distorting the material by overobjectification to the point that idiosyncratic light and shadow, depth, perspective and feeling have been squeezed from the historical material: "The goal . . . is rigor, but not rigor that distorts."

One of the tendencies that marks the historian as human is that he has to resist projecting into these documents what he would like to find in them. Some historians are recognized by their peers as more successful in resisting projection than others. We refer to them as "fair," "judicious," and "well-balanced." At a collective level, criticism of a particular brand of historical writing as unfair takes such forms as referring to the "Whig theory of history." Aspiring to fairness, I would supplement, not supplant, this art with objective techniques.

Potentially at least, a document may have both an overt and a latent content—what is actually said, and what is implied. To search for implicit meanings, a task on which all historians embark whether they have made this explicit to themselves or not, is not to be undertaken lightly. What I have just stated about documents should be placed in a larger context no matter how one "does" history.

It would be naive for historians to rest content with what men of the past have had to say explicitly about a particular problem. One does not have to accept the existence of an unconscious of the dynamic psychologies to appreciate the possible correlative functioning of unverbalized, implicit assumptions in historical events. Whitehead (1925) has remarked that, when one is examining the philosophy of a period and, by a not unreasonable extension of this view, the history or problem areas in a science, one should not direct attention primarily to those statements that have been made, but rather to search for the assumptions which have remained unstated. Unverbalized presuppositions may have seemed so obvious to those of the period as not to have required statement. Prescriptive theory, in which the attitudes being expressed are not necessarily overt and consciously held, may be helpful in this regard.

Prescriptions conceived as attitudes render relatively easy and straightforward the transition from theoretical discussion to application of content analysis. Commonly accepted definitions of this technique often refer to it as being a means of assessing the relative extent to which specified *attitudes* permeate a given set of documents.

One level of application is informal or qualitative. Quantification is not attempted. Instead, the historian examines the pertinent documents while continuously asking himself whether the material can be interpreted in prescriptive terms. An informal application of prescriptive theory was used by Ronald Mueller in his doctoral dissertation (1974) devoted to James Mark Baldwin and his era at the turn of the century in the United States. One phase of this study concerned Baldwin's three major books: *Mental Development,*

Social and Ethical Interpretations, and *Development and Evolution*. Familiar with prescriptive theory, Mueller examined the contents of these books and found developmentalism and functionalism to dominate. Developmentalism is manifested in Baldwin's genetic method, his dialectic of personal growth and his adherence to recapitulation theory. Functionalism was Mueller's means of integrating Baldwin's theory of imitation, his views on suggestion, habit and accommodation, organic selection and social heredity. As Mueller used prescriptive theory, quantitative findings were not sought; rather, the theory helped him to integrate the material meaningfully.

To serve as an introduction to quantitative research with more formal application of this approach, I turn to an equally straightforward application of prescriptions. Prescriptions, as categories for content analysis to the seventy-five Presidential addresses of the American Psychological Association between 1892 and 1970, were chosen by Kenneth R. Gibson (1972) as indicators of change in the conceptual bases of American psychology. These addresses were believed to be important documents because of the eminence of those who had delivered them, their presumed sensitivity to the then current issues, and their continuity from 1892 to the current time. Three raters, using prescriptions as content categories, made a blind analysis of their contents. Although ratings were made for neutral stands and for rejections, 78 percent of the codings were for acceptance. These acceptances form the basis for what further discussion time considerations permit.

One of the characteristic struggles through which psychology passed during the years encompassed was the shift from psychology as the science of the mind to psychology as the science of behavior. This had most direct expression in contentual objectivism–contentual subjectivism. In the decades 1891 to 1900, 1901 to 1910, acceptance of contentual subjectivism dominated, appearing in 85 or 90 percent of the papers; contentual objectivism was accepted in less than 20 percent. In the decade 1911 to 1920, that of John B. Watson's famous manifesto of 1913, acceptance of *both* was characteristic, with 70 to 80 percent of the papers paying explicit, positive attention to them. The decade 1921 to 1930 actually showed a puzzling drop in contentual objectivism to 40 percent, while contentual subjectivism almost held its own. Nevertheless, there was a steady drop in contentual subjectivism, although it never fell below 40 percent right up to the last decade. This degree of acceptance seems to contradict the oft-repeated generalization that American psychologists had little use for subjective phenomena. Nevertheless, contentual objectivism did dominate from 1931 on.

The findings are even more dramatic when *methodological* objectivism and subjectivism are considered. In the first two decades, acceptance of both was about equal, ranging between 35 and 45 percent. In 1911 to 1920, methodological objectivism surged forward to 80-percent acceptance, while subjectivism dropped to 30 percent. This drop in adherence to methodological subjectivism continued until it hit a low point of 5 percent in 1931. For the immediate past three decades, there has been a slight resurgence of acceptance of methodological subjectivism, but never more than acceptance by 10 percent. From 1911 on, methodological objectivism has clearly dominated.

As an indication of contemporary American psychology, using the last two decades from 1951 to 1970, Gibson found empiricism to be the most generally accepted prescription. While methodological objectivism, quantitativism and nomotheticism are very widely accepted, methodological subjectivism, qualitativism and idiographicism are sufficiently viable to be counterdominant. More or less equally and widely accepted are both deductivism and inductivism, purism and utilitarianism, and molarism and molecularism. Almost disappearing from expression on the current scene were supernaturalism, irrationalism, indeterminism, and monism and dualism. It would seem that prescriptive attitudes can be used as a unit of scientific change.

It is one of the myths of our history that psychology emerged from the matrix of philosophy as late as the nineteenth century with previous consideration of psychological matters being essentially philosophical or prescientific in character. Barbara Ross (1970) in her doctoral dissertation questioned this and turned for evidence to the pages of the pioneer scientific journal, *The Philosophical Transactions*, from its founding in 1665 to 1700, despite omission in its policy statement of any concern with psychological or social phenomena.

Distortion is inevitable when one tries to summarize in two or three pages a dissertation that totals 520 pages. What will be most conspicuous by its absence in what follows will be the narrative itself which fleshes out the bare outlines of the findings to be mentioned here. Her method otherwise was content analysis, using the services of two raters other than herself, with the content categories being the prescriptive variables. The raters were given practice in understanding the directions through a manual and pilot study on materials from the *Philosophical Collections*, which had been published for the years 1679 to 1682 when the *Transactions* had lapsed publication. Adequate reliability being established (summarized as over .80), she classified all the articles in the *Transactions* (from 1665 to 1700) and found that 367 of 1,924 papers, or 19 percent, were relevant to the study of man.

To arrive at these papers, she used twelve major content categories of indices of interest in man, each with more specific subcategories, which combined to give the 367 papers relevant to man. The six largest of these categories were, successively, human physiology, sensation, social phenomena, physiology, perception, abnormal and comparative phenomena. About 30 percent of these papers made reference to social phenomena, more specifically identified by its subcategories: social habits, language, value systems, somatic characteristics of various peoples, their intellectual systems, aspects of their material culture, interpersonal behavior, sub- and intercultural behavior. The overall results supported her first hypothesis: that men in the latter half of the seventeenth century sought reliable scientific knowledge about man, his experiences, and his behavior.

These 367 relevant papers were those to which the prescriptive categories were then applied. In prescriptive terms, the second hypothesis was that the prevailing scientific attitude of the late seventeenth century reflected methodological objectivism, probabilist determinism, nomotheticism and quantitativism. The third hypothesis, more specific to psychology, was that a behavioral view of man predominated in the scientific literature. This involved these same prescriptions and, in addition, mechanism, *new* empiricism and *new* rationalism.

Instead of talking about the overwhelming support for these hypotheses that the date engendered, let me discuss two points which, at first glance, might seem to be either discrepancies between her hypotheses and her findings or a weakening of prescriptive theory itself. Prescriptions other than those hypothesized were found to be present to a statistically significant degree since the entire array of prescriptions were studied. Nonpredicted emphases in over 70 percent of the papers were found in acceptance of contentual objectivism, an inductive approach, and a naturalistic emphasis.

Dr. Ross might well have demonstrated the presence of the predicted emphases by the usual narrative, qualitative approach; but then she would not have been forced, as she was, to use the entire repertoire of prescriptions to consider nonhypothesized prescriptions that emerged in a significant way. This safeguard in historical document analysis reduces the subjectivity of interpretation that is a characteristic of historical study. The unpredicted findings became a challenge to broaden and modify her view, which, without being able to go into further detail, as I see it, she did successfully.

What appeared to be novel prescriptions, i.e., "probablistic" determinism and the "new" rationalism and "new" empiricism, as she called them, emerged in her preliminary analysis of the factual data. In her opinion the data called for introducing them as prescriptive categories while still investigating "old" rationalism and empiricism as defined in the table. To describe only one of these, new empiricism, while agreeing that the source of knowledge is experience, also was concerned with, as she put it, "what was really there, not only what seemed to be on the basis of everyday experience with careful observation and accurate recording" (1970:328).

Locke, for example, would in this sense be a rationalist despite his vaunted empiricism. Her results bore out her contentions. The raters coded only 19.3 and 11.7 of the papers in terms of acceptance of the old, but 65.1 and 66.8 in terms of the new empiricism and rationalism, respectively. It is still possible, however, that if the new categories had been omitted, the raters would have coded them in the original categories.

These results illustrate not only the kind of modification or expansion that prescriptive theory permits, but also that more subtle meanings can be sought with adequate, advanced planning. It is intriguing, for example, that there has been found within empiricism and rationalism in the seventeenth century what Dr. Ross referred to as "rational considerations of the empirical data" (1970: 320). This can only be seen as a beginning of synthesis of rationalism and empiricism to which modern logical empiricism was to be a culmination.

Prescriptive theory, it is being said, is capable of modification and refinement when a particular combination of historical circumstances demand it, thus partaking of the advantage often attributed to models of discarding or modifying, if the findings seem to so indicate without thereby falsifying the theory.

The relation of prescriptive theory to the other social sciences demands consideration. Prescriptive theory itself is a cross-discipline venture since the constructs, attitude and role are at a point of interaction of the disciplines of psychology and sociology. The relation, however, of prescriptive theory to the social sciences has not been explored heretofore, and what I have to say is no more than illustrative and very tentative.

To me, the most convincing line of evidence in support of the supposition that prescriptive theory is relevant to the other social sciences is to be found in our common heritage. Before the emergence of the specializations that are the social sciences, each of them was a more or less discernible strand in the history of philosophy. Surely psychology and the other social sciences share something today from our forebears, and prescriptions are rooted in this heritage. It is conceivable that the particular patterns of prescriptions suggested have limited application in the other social sciences, but I hope I am forgiven for believing that there is at least somewhat more relevance than that. Even if *all* specified prescriptive attitudes that have been demonstrated to some extent to be relevant in psychology are rejected in the other social sciences, there would still be the formal phase of prescriptive theory—pluralistic attitudes held by practitioners within a given social science that shape to some extent the nature of the field.

I will now try to sketch some possible investigations from the social sciences. This is perhaps a foolhardy thing to do since I am stepping out of whatever area of expertise I can claim as my own. I ask only for the forbearance that might come from your remembering that details of my illustrations may be naively, poorly or even falsely expressed without thereby vitiating prescriptive theory itself.

Time permits but three vignettes of possible studies and one somewhat more detailed proposal. The culture-concept approach in anthropology is one in which molaristic contentions might be expected to predominate with the apparent decline in this approach being traceable to the intrusion of more and more molecular considerations. Jeremy Bentham's indeterministic, rationalistic (as opposed to irrationalistic), utilitarian, dynamic, nomothetic approach to human nature would seem particularly appropriate for prescriptive study since it was an effort to supply a view of man appropriate for economics. The nature of the functionalistic approach in sociology might be investigated prescriptively, not for its functional character alone, but to ascertain what patterns of other prescriptions cluster within this view as distinguished from patterns of prescriptions held by individuals opposed to this view.

A detailed illustration may be chosen from the work and influence of Durkheim. That he refused to acknowledge the relevance of individual psychology to sociology lends a certain piquancy to this choice. The immediate setting for my illustration is the recent, stimulating discussion by Terry N. Clark (1973) on the rise of the French university.

Clark argued that the basic unit of academic organization in the French universities was the cluster or informal grouping of a dozen or so persons "who shared *a minimal core of beliefs about their work* [italics mine] and who were prepared to collaborate to advance research and instruction in a given area." Their professional tasks included working for the advancement of one another, placing men in strategic places, universities, committees, journals and the like. The cluster around Durkheim Clark considers typical, and he proceeded to document this contention in considerable detail. I would now focus on that "minimal core of beliefs" that was present only as incidental background for Clark's study.

Durkheim's quasi-positivism,[2] engendered in part by admiration for Wundt, would suggest that he would be found to stress empiricism. His strong belief in progress and his use of a comparative method and a general evolutionary hypothesis would lead to a prediction that his position would show stress on developmentalism. Durkheim's finding of a molar social level beyond individual minds at the molecular level challenges us to answer his stricture that "Every time a social phenomenon is directly explained by a psychic phenomenon, one may be sure that the explanation is false." That he is a functionalist in one sense or another, I believe I can, for the sake of brevity, take for granted.

One of the challenges that this study would face rests in

---

2. I speak of quasi-positivism because of his epistemological sophistication influenced by Kant and his categories and Durkheim's belief in the reality of the categories of understanding which, according to the rationalist, are inborn or come from divine reason and a position he could not accept fully either. Social origins in collective representations was his answer. Moreover, as Parsons has pointed out, Durkheim's stress on goals, values and sentiments as social phenomena of great importance are not susceptible to sense observation as demanded by the positivist.

Durkheim's stress on social solidarity. Does this call for a social preference-individual preference prescriptive attitude not yet predicted? The path of caution would be to postulate it and see whether it turns out to be essential or whether the findings can be more parsimoniously explained without it.

My intent to formulate the relationship of prescriptive theory to the study of the history of the social sciences in no sense implies rejection of the other aspects that make up a reasonably complete pluralistic approach to history. To place sole reliance upon a prescriptive approach would give only a segmented and therefore distorted picture of the study of the historical process.

In my original paper on prescriptive theory (Watson, 1967), in point of fact, it was indicated that historians must concern themselves with the contentual topics of psychology, such as motivation and learning; the hypotheses, laws and theories that have been stated, defended and criticized; the methods used, observations and experiments, to state them in broadest terms; other personal characteristics of individuals with whom one is involved; and the social circumstances in which these events take place. Content, in the conventional sense, theory, methods, personal characteristics and social circumstances require attention. In a later paper (1971) a description was given of how prescriptive theory could be related to and utilized with the Great Man and *Zeitgeist* approaches. And, as I indicated earlier in this paper, I have since grown to appreciate the significance of contentual part paradigms.

Implicit in what I have been saying has been a stress on internal determinants of history considered central for the Conference Topic B, scientific development.

Sciences are what scientists do and think. Scientists are influenced by their scientific heritage *and* by external social influences beyond the boundaries of the individual or scientific community. It is an empirical problem to determine the extent to which they are influenced from beyond their own personally-held traditions. To go beyond my topic for a moment, to an aspect of Topic B, it may even be that prescriptive pattern studies could be extended to questions of organized scientific research. To take a clue from research on marriage, I would find intriguing to investigate whether successful research organization shows complementarity or congruence in acceptance or rejection of prescriptive attitudes.

One of the advantages of preparation for participation in a

cross-discipline conference is the reminder it gives that perspectives other than one's own have a legitimate and vital role, and one's own personally satisfying position is perhaps no more than an area of the ground with a different figural emphasis.

Speaking more generally, psychologists wearing methodologically individualistic spectacles, as it were, make the individual the figure, while sociologists and most other social scientists would see the social circumstances as the figure and the individual aspects as the background. Sectarian dangers arise when figures are perceived as a unity segregated from the ground. The contour, the boundary where figure and ground meet, becomes crucial if it is to become possible to shift figure and ground.

I accept as a methodological imperative to attempt to reconcile the social and the individual approaches by trying occasionally to become flexible, to see as figure what comes naturally as ground! Perhaps other participants may be stirred in a reciprocal fashion to consider using the prescriptive approach in our common search for the dynamics of history and social science.

REFERENCES

Ben-David, J. *The Scientist's Role in Society: A Comparative Study.* Englewood Cliffs, N.J.: Prentice-Hall, 1971.

Brodbeck, May. "The nature and philosophy of science," in H. Feigl and May Brodbeck (eds.), *Readings in the Philosophy of Science* (New York: Appleton-Century-Crofts, 1953), pp. 3-7.

Buytendijk, F. J. J. "Femininity and existential psychology," in H. P. David and H. v. Bracken (eds.), *Perspectives in Personality Theory* (New York: Basic Books, 1957), pp. 197-211.

Clark, T. N. *Prophets and Patrons: The French University and the Emergence of the Social Sciences.* Cambridge: Harvard University Press, 1973.

Fuchs, A. H., and G. Kawash. "Prescriptive dimensions for five schools of psychology." *Journal of the History of the Behavioral Sciences, 10* (1974), 352-366.

Gibson, K. R. "The conceptual bases of American psychology: A content analysis of the Presidential addresses of the American Psychological Association, 1892-1970." Unpublished doctoral dissertation, University of New Hampshire, 1972.

Graumann, C.-F. "The state of psychology." I. *International Journal of Psychology, 7* (1972), 123-134.

Kuhn, T. S. *The Structure of Scientific Revolutions.* Chicago: University of Chicago Press, 1962.

Mueller, R. "The American era of James Mark Baldwin (1893-1903)."

Unpublished doctoral dissertation, University of New Hampshire, 1974.

Parsons, T., and E. A. Shils. *Toward a Theory of Action*. Cambridge: Harvard University Press, 1951.

Popovich, M. "What the American sociologists think about their science and its problems." *American Sociologist, 1* (1966), 133-135.

Reuchlin, M. "Psychologie ou psychologies?" *Psychologie 31* (1972), 181-196.

Ross, Barbara C. "Psychological thought within the context of the scientific revolution, 1665-1700." Unpublished doctoral dissertation, University of New Hampshire, 1970.

Skinner, B. F. *Science and Human Behavior*. New York: Macmillan, 1953.

Skinner, B. F. "A case history in scientific method," in S. Koch (ed.), *Psychology: A Study of a Science*. Vol. 2. General Systematic Formulations, Learning and Special Processes (New York: McGraw-Hill, 1959), pp. 359-379.

Watkins, J. W. N. "Ideal types and historical explanation," in H. Feigl and May Brodbeck (eds.), *Readings in the Philosophy of Science* (New York: Appleton-Century-Crofts, 1953), pp. 723-743.

Watson, R. I. "The historical background for national trends in psychology: United States," *Journal of the History of the Behavioral Sciences, 1* (1965), 130-138.

Watson, R. I. "Psychology: A prescriptive science," *American Psychologist, 32* (1967), 435-443.

Watson, R. I. "A prescriptive analysis of Descartes' psychological views," *Journal of the History of the Behavioral Sciences, 7* (1971), 223-248.

Watson, R. I. "Prescriptions as operative in the history of Psychology," *Journal of the History of the Behavioral Sciences, 7* (1971), 311-322.

Whitehead, A. N. *Science and the Modern World*. New York: Mentor, 1925.

13. A Prescriptive Analysis of Descartes' Psychological Views

Of all the men in the early seventeenth century—Francis Bacon, Thomas Hobbes, Galileo Galilei and William Harvey among others—René Descartes stands out as the most significant contributor to the psychology that was to be. This takes on added significance because it was at this time that the earliest lines of development were initiated which have a continuous traceable history to today's psychology. And it was Descartes, more than any other, who provided the background and framed the problems that were to become salient for psychology.

Much of what the men of his age had to say about the contentual problems of psychology—sense, mind, passion, and the like—from today's perspective seems alien or irrelevant. To examine Descartes' significance in psychology's history, it is necessary to place his thinking in a framework which is intelligible and recognizable today while doing as little possible violence to his own intentions. Accordingly, broader issues, expressed in attitudinal perspectives, such as subscribing to a dualistic rather than a monistic tradition or expressing a rationalistic as contrasted with an empiristic attitude are more meaningful and influential. Basic orientative assumptions and modes of conceptualization, referred to hereafter as prescriptions, provide directive functions which help to decide how, at a given temporal period, a person—such as Descartes—will think about matters related to psychology.[1]

A modified version of an invited address given at the meeting of the International Society for the History of the Behavioral Sciences at Princeton University in May 1969.

1. Watson, R. I. Psychology: a prescriptive science. *American Psychologist*, 1967, *22*, 435–443.

Recognizable continuity over considerable periods of time is another salient attribute that characterizes a prescription. Each prescription, however, shows shifts in time in its various characteristics and manifestations—shifts in dominance, shifts in contentual form, shifts in relation to other prescriptions and a variety of other relationships. This characteristic of a prescription is, of course, less evident in a paper devoted to the contributions of one man than would be the case when larger temporal periods were involved. Work with other men and other times gives me some assurance that these prescriptions have relevance to psychology throughout the entire modern period up to the present.

Although salient to a thoroughgoing prescriptive analysis of Descartes and, indeed, being carried out in another context,[2] it is necessary to forego discussion of prescriptive influences arising from the social and religious aspects of his intellectual matrix—his somewhat limited support for the utilitarian prescriptive aims fostered so enthusiastically by Bacon and his unorthodox defense of supernaturalism while advancing the naturalistic prescription as well as his reaction to influences arising from physical problems as he struggled with manifestations of and offered solutions to problems arising from the teleological, deterministic, nomothetic and qualitative prescriptions.

Consideration will first be given to the influences arising from physiological problems expressed through his handling of mechanistic, vitalistic and molar-molecular prescriptions. Attention will then be given to the methodological prescriptions expressed in a deductive rationalism. His sharpening of the prevailing dualistic prescription will next receive consideration. Last to be considered is his primary treatment of mind, in terms of a structural prescription wherein mind is treated as a substance, and his secondary view of mind as exhibiting faculties and his consequent adherence to a functional prescription.

PRESCRIPTIVE INFLUENCES FROM PHYSIOLOGICAL PROBLEMS

The seventeenth century saw the foundation of microscopic anatomy and considerable work in optics, plant physiology, and genetics. However, investigations in human physiology are most

2. Watson, R. I. Modern psychology in the seventeenth and eighteenth centuries: a prescriptive approach (in process).

directly relevant. In this area the quantitative measurement and demonstration of the circulation of the blood by William Harvey was most important.[3] So long as the blood in the arteries and veins was considered as carrying vital spirits and to be in the setting of a theory with animistic overtones, then these mysteries effectively blocked the way to inquiry into the function of the various organs. With Harvey's research, the "spirits" were found to be mere quantities of blood and no longer a hindrance to research. Harvey had treated the problem of blood circulation as one in mechanics and solved it in mechanical terms without appeal to the soul, which so long had been defined as that which serves as the principle of movement. Harvey had showed how a body function was intelligible in terms of its own mechanisms.

Harvey's example was not lost on Descartes. Aside from Galileo, Descartes in his Discourse on Method[4] alluded only to the work of Harvey. He saw him as bridging the barrier which had separated into two disparate realms the animal organism and the inanimate mechanical system. The principles of mechanics apply, he now could say, to the behavior of all material things. It could no longer be held that, in principle, it is impossible to describe organic processes in mechanical terms. He saw Harvey's research as serving as a model which contributed a great deal to strengthening the mechanistic prescription.

In the seventeenth century a major contribution to the physical sciences was the vigorous support given to the view that its task was the study of mechanical movements of objects in space, the mechanistic prescription, as it shall be called. Central to these emerging physical sciences was a concept of a material something, existing independently of the observer and, while showing varying guises, remaining essentially unchanged. The spirits, the qualities of the Middle Ages were being pushed aside. During earlier centuries the "substantial forms" and "real qualities" were much more than properties of bodies; they were the true causes of sense properties, rooted as they were in Aristotle's thinking of hot, cold, wet and dry

3. Harvey, W. *An anatomical disquisition on the motion of the heart and blood in animals.* (1628) (Trans. by R. Willis.) In R. M. Hutchins (ed.), *Great Books of the Western World*, vol. 28. Chicago, Ill.: Encyclopaedia Britannica, 1952, pp. 265-304.

4. Descartes, R. *Discourse on the method of rightly conducting the reason.* (1637) Unless otherwise noted, citations to Descartes are the works in Elizabeth S. Haldane and G. R. T. Ross (Trans.), *The philosophical works of Descartes.* (2 vols.) Cambridge: University Press, 1911.

as intertwined with the elements of fire, earth, water and air. No longer were these occult qualities considered the entities of scientific endeavor. Galileo insisted that the physical world consisted of material entities in motion with the laws of their relations being discoverable, and once discovered, possessing absolute certainty. Instead of an appeal to Divine intervention or to vague Aristotelian substantial forms, this way of regarding matters called for the tracing of the antecedents of some event back to simpler circumstances where presumably the event's action would be better understood.

There was not yet an unalloyed mechanistic approach. Complete mechanism was contradicted by the Christian complex of beliefs which involved not only man's soul and his free will, but also his mind. These crucial exceptions imply that while physics might proceed without too much opposition to develop along mechanistic lines, psychology still faced a major problem in assimilating the mechanistic prescription.

The mechanistic prescription is considered here as it applies to biological phenomena, since to do so is in keeping with the present interest in psychology. It takes on particular relevance because Descartes utilized concepts derived from a mechanistic view in differentiating living and nonliving things.

There are two levels of mechanistic theory—that of atoms or corpuscles as basic units of matter, and that of machines as larger levels of organization—the molecular and molar levels respectively. Although the two levels cannot be completely separated, the theory of atoms will first be considered with later shift of emphasis to the more molar level of machines.

Greek atomists, particularly Democritus, had explained substances without any assumption of a nonmaterial nature, and had held that the only realities are the atoms, small bits of matter, moved in the void by blind chance. Later the atomic philosophy had been fostered by the Epicureans, not for scientific purposes, but as a weapon to attack established religion as delusory.

It is not unnatural, then, that in the seventeenth century atomism was seen by many as an affront to religious beliefs. However, atomism was too attractive a concept to be ignored, so it was revived in a setting of attempts to reconcile it with religious orthodoxy in its application to man. On the continent, it was Pierre Gassendi (1592–1655), a priest, mathematician and scientist, who did much to popularize and make acceptable for the religiously

160 : SELECTED PAPERS

orthodox a comprehensive but nonmathematical theory of the atomic composition of man.[5] Never as baldly as will now be put, he tried to reduce all phenomena to atoms—excepting the immortal soul.[6] In agreement with the orthodox belief, Gassendi held that the soul was not material. Consequently, the soul, or, rather, the highest aspect of it, was exempt from the principles of mechanics.[7] This aspect is the spiritual soul from which comes rational insight. It is vastly superior to the corporeal soul and, consequently, beyond the province of his atomistic inquiries. After admitting the soul's existence but disposing of it as nonrelevant to his scientific interests, Gassendi then proceeded as if the corporeal soul alone existed.

In general, seventeenth-century workers made a decisive advance over the Greek atomists in conceiving atoms as aspects of regular dynamic systems capable of formulation in law-like statements. Instead of the abhorred fortuitous blind chance, their movements were conceived to be ordered and having a direct influence upon the properties of matter.

MOLAR MECHANISMS AND DESCARTES

The pioneer modern formulation of mechanistic theory at the molar rather than the molecular level was the work of Descartes. It was with the mathematical concepts of number, motion, and extension that Descartes proposed to reconstruct both the physical and biological sciences. The essential property of matter was extension in space, by which Descartes meant length, breadth and depth.[8] Descartes' physics called for bodies and extension to involve each other, and therefore empty space—or what in his terms would be extension without body—would be a contradiction in terms which must be rejected. Matter, he held, is extension, it fills all space, there is no vacuum. What is commonly referred to as space, Descartes conceived to be nothing more than a form of extended

---

5. Boas, Marie. The establishment of the mechanical philosophy. *Osiris*, 1952, *10*, 412-541.

6. Gassendi, P. Syntagma philosophicum. (1658) In F. N. Magill (ed.), *Masterpieces of world philosophy in summary form*. New York: Salem Press, 1961.

7. Ibid.

8. Descartes, R. *Rules for the direction of the mind*. (1701) XIV.

substance comparable to an infinitesimally fine dust. For him there was no limit to the spatial divisibility of bodies whose essence was extension. Thus the doctrines both of the void and of the indivisibility of atoms were denied. In a strict sense, Descartes was not an atomist, since both doctrines are integral aspects of classical atomic theory. To distinguish his view from that of the atomists it has been referred to as "corpuscularian." Nevertheless, his corpuscular theory was essentially closer in nature to atomist than it was to the Aristotelian theory of forms and qualities, which held that there were real, existing entities residing in the object, a contention which Descartes denied vigorously.

We need not follow Descartes into his specific physical theory of vortices that was destined to be an attractive and stimulating influence, but a blind alley nevertheless, doomed to be overthrown quickly by its Newtonian rival. Our interest, rather, is how his mechanical model of the universe is related to living things. Are living things one with the rest of nature, or are they an exception? Descartes took a clear, unequivocal position. Everything in nature, including animals and the bodies of men, he said, is mechanical, everything, that is, except the rational thought of the mind.[9] Governed by no other laws than those of matter in motion, the animals and the bodies of men are particles of matter in various combinations and movements. The human body is a machine:[10] ". . . the body is nothing else than a statue or machine of clay . . ."[11] The body-machine is governed then by laws of mechanics and biology is a branch of mechanics.

The deliberate use of the physical sciences as a model for physiology and psychology began with Descartes. His mechanical model for the human body was destined to be the prototype for the hypothetical model, one of the most powerful present-day tools of psychological research.

Several considerations led him to advance this model. He proceeded from physics to physiology because his physical theory had given him certain principles which, since they were considered basic, should apply to the human body as well. He conceived his task as that of reasoning what the body *must* be like according to

9. Descartes, R. *Treatise on man.* (1662) In R. M. Eaton (ed.), Selections. New York: Scribner's, 1927, pp. 350-354; *Discourse, op. cit.*, V.
10. *Ibid.*
11. *Ibid.*

his already established physical principles. He had before him the powerful inspiration of demonstration of the mechanical circulation of the blood by Harvey. Another source for the mechanical model came from the deep impression made on him by the intricate clockwork statues on display in the ornamental gardens of his time in which the figures moved themselves, made sounds and even played music.[12] As he conceived it, the flow of water that moved the statues made the pipes through which it flowed similar to nerves and its engines similar to the muscles. Sensing in humans, he claimed, is akin to a visitor to the gardens stepping upon certain tiles in the walk which would cause the statue of Diana at her bath to withdraw into the reeds and, if the visitor continued to pursue, similar mechanical apparatuses would cause the statue of Neptune brandishing his trident to appear and block his path.

To Descartes, the human body functioned in this mechanical way. Not only functions, such as digestion, the beating of the heart, respiration, sleeping and waking, but also sensing of light, taste, heat, the impression of these upon the common sense and imagination, the appetites and the passions, and external movement follow from the arrangement of the parts of the machine, just as naturally as the movement of a clock comes from the arrangements of its parts. This renders unnecessary the concept of man as possessing a sensitive and vegetative soul.[13]

During the period now under consideration, the proponents of the mechanical philosophy proceeded as if oblivious to a potential rival explanation of the same phenomena—a vital principle. The acceptance of a teleological perspective contributed to this lack of sharp distinction because it made the acceptance of analogies between the causes of motion in living and nonliving bodies relatively easy. Stones fell or water flowed as if seeking their natural position at the center of the earth; conversely, flames and smoke rose to seek their position in the heavens, just as in the same way birds sought to reach their nests. This point of view did much to blur distinction between animate and inanimate objects. A sharp distinction between mechanism and vitalism was not to emerge until the end of the century, with the defense of the latter prescription by Stahl.

Nevertheless, Descartes anticipated crucial aspects of the controversy by giving an unequivocally mechanistic answer. Being of

12. *Ibid.*
13. *Ibid.*

the body, life phenomena are mechanical. Life is due to "fires without light."[14] This fire, he said, is in no way different from that generated when hay heats up, when shut up before it is dry. Descartes' meaning is clear—he considered living bodies to show no essential difference from nonliving things. His conception of death reinforced this view. The departure of the soul is not the cause of death.[15] It is not that the soul passes out of the body, and then the body dies; rather, when the natural heat, which is of the body, ceases, the soul departs. Death comes from some fault of the body, not of the soul. A life source or vital principle does not maintain life; the interrelation of the parts of the body does so, and death is due to a failure of these parts.

Man, he argued, already had considerable ability to make automata or moving machines.[16] Descartes predicted that the bodies of animals one day could be simulated so perfectly that we could not tell them from machines. Indeed, he went on, animals are machines and lack any crucial differentiation from lifeless machines. The human machine, however, can be distinguished from automata even if its outward resemblance is that of man.[17] While a machine may do some things well, some even better than man, it does not have as versatile a range of activities. Machines have to be adjusted for each particular action; man has reason, an instrument universal for all contingencies. In contrast to the soulless brutes, which are automata, man has the capacity to initiate action.

In conceiving animals as automata, Descartes made for a pronounced break with tradition. To Descartes, animals are directed not by thought but by forces of nature.[18] The return of the swallows in the spring is comparable, he said, to the movements of clockwork. Although animals are automata, feeling and sensations are ascribed to them, but not thinking.[19] Animals were denied thoughts and anything similar to consciousness or mind. They could not, for example, feel genuine pangs of pain; their eyes saw only that which

14. *Discourse on method, op. cit.*, V.
15. Descartes, R. *Passions of the soul.* (1649) Arts. 2-6.
16. *Discourse on method, op. cit.*, V.
17. *Ibid.*
18. Descartes, R. *Letter to Marquis of Newcastle.* (1646) In Eaton, *op. cit.*, pp. 355-357.
19. Descartes, R. *Letter to Henry More.* (1649) In *ibid.*, pp. 358-360. Descartes, R. *Meditations on first philosophy and objections against the meditations and replies.* (1641) Reply to fourth set objections.

a human in reverie sees when he gazes on things with a glassy stare, apprehending nothing. They yelp for pain, they visually avoid and seek objects, but do not think.

PHYSIOLOGICAL PROBLEMS AND DESCARTES

To demonstrate how the body might function if his mechanical conceptions were correct, Descartes utilized available anatomical and physiological knowledge and further supported it with a variety of assertions and assumptions, selected or invented to support his beliefs. To his credit, he knew that he was describing a hypothetical, not a real, body and thus to show appreciation of the ultimate value of a model—that it may be discarded when it is no longer serviceable.

For Descartes, the motive power for the body-machine lay in the heat innate to the heart, which, when rarified, became animal spirits.[20] Animal spirit was consistently treated by him as if it were a fluid, a subtle rarified fluid, to be sure, but still a fluid. It was no more distinguishable from blood, say, than the spirits of wine are distinguishable from wine itself. In consistently treating animal spirits as material in nature he differed from most of his predecessors. To him, spirit was governed by physical laws and hence became a part of the bodily machine. Muscle action is determined by the sheer amount of animal spirits carried to the muscle because the muscle that moved is the one of the opposed pair that received the greater amount of animal spirits.[21] In short, muscles contract because animal spirits inflate them.

In order to illustrate his theory of neuromuscular action he reproduced in his *Treatise on Man* a picture of a man kneeling near a fire. The fast-moving particles of fire coming near the foot ". . . have the power to set in motion the spot of skin at the foot which they touch, and by this means pulling upon the delicate thread which is attached to the spot of skin, they open up at the same instant the pore against which the delicate thread ends, just as by pulling at one end of a rope one causes to strike at the same instant a bell which hangs on the other end. When this pore is opened, the animal spirits of the cavity enter into the tube and are carried by it partly to the muscles which pull back the foot from the fire, partly to those which turn the eyes and the head in order to regard it, and partly

---

20. *Treatise on man, op. cit.*
21. *Passions, op. cit.*, Art. 11.

to those which serve to advance the hands and to bend the whole body in order to shield itself."[22]

Descartes accounts for some sensory-motor activity in mechanical terms without appeal to consciousness or mind. This correctly suggests he might have some conception of reflex activity.

That he had a clear conception of the involuntary nature of some human actions is shown in his discussion of dilation of the pupil with far fixation.[23] If we only think of dilation, we cannot enlarge it; only by looking at objects far away can we do so. This is because nature has not provided the movements required for this action to take place.

Descartes specifically identified a variety of involuntary automatic activities—such as a man thrusting out his hands to break a fall—as those in which the soul or mind was not involved.[24] As another example, he points out that we cannot stop our eyes from closing when someone playfully strikes toward them, which, he goes on, is an act carried out without the intervention of the mind as demonstrated by the fact that it is performed against our will.

How close did Descartes come to identifying reflex responses in the modern sense, and to what extent does he deserve credit for a pioneer formulation? First it must be noted that his was a more inclusive view than today's conception of reflex. In addition to the illustrations given earlier, he also mentioned walking, talking, and singing, providing we do so ". . . without the mind attending to them."[25] These are activities which violate modern criteria for a reflex since they are not unlearned, involuntary, nonconscious, and predictable. Most telling of all, while Descartes gave a description of how the reflexes might function, he did not demonstrate that they did so. As Richet was to say many years later, he conceived of the reflex but did no experiments.[26] But he did conceive of it. We must date from Descartes the beginning of the modern concept of the reflex.

    22. Quoted in F. Fearing, *Reflex action: a study in the history of physiological psychology*. Baltimore, Md.: Williams and Wilkins, 1930, p. 24.

    23. *Passions, op. cit.*, Art. 44.

    24. *Passions, op. cit.*, Art. 13; *Meditations, op. cit.*, Reply to fourth set objections.

    25. *Ibid.*

    26. Cited in E. G. T. Liddell, *The discovery of reflexes*. Oxford: Clarendon Press, 1960, p. 105.

The senses are always stimulated by some sort of contact.[27] The senses perceive passively; this is to say, they do not reach out to the objects perceived.[28] It is as if each sense was a wax into which a seal is impressed. We do not see the torch or hear the bell, rather we sense movements that come from these objects.[29]

Although forms of touch,[30] each sense has distinctive characteristics. In vision, for example, light particles come into contact with the nerves leading to the brain. The channel for sensations are the nerves and the nerves alone; the skin is no more an organ of touch than are gloves worn in handling some object.[31]

In connection with vision, Descartes, following earlier work by Kepler, performed a noteworthy experiment.[32] First he scraped away the coats at the back of the eye of a bull to the point it became transparent. Then, while standing in darkness with the light emitted through the eye as the only source, he saw on paper behind the eyeball the inverted image of the world outside. Thus he both demonstrated how retinal images are formed and likewise corroborated Kepler's demonstration of the function of the lens.[33]

Descartes rejected the so-called copy or representative image theory of perception—the theory that a picture of the object was deposited on the brain so that a perception resembles the object. He argued that tickling and pain are in no way similar to the stimulating objects and that the word-names are totally different from the objects they signify. Both of these contentions, he argued, would be called for if perceptions were copies of objects.[34]

Descartes also gave one of the first systematic accounts of the psychological cues to the visual perception of size, shape and distance.[35] He compared the feeling out of distance by convergence of the eyes to a blind man feeling out distance with a stick in each

27. *Meditations, op. cit.*, Reply to fourth set objections.
28. *Rules, op. cit.*, XII.
29. *Passions, op. cit.*, Art. 23.
30. *Ibid.*, Art. 191.
31. Descartes, R. *Dioptric*. (1637) In N. K. Smith (Trans.) *Descartes' philosophical writings*. London: Macmillan, 1952, pp. 167–179.
32. *Ibid.*
33. Kepler's research is given in his *Dioptric*. (Augsburg: Frank, 1611.) It is described in E. G. Boring's *Sensation and perception in the history of experimental psychology*. (New York: Appleton-Century-Crofts, 1942.)
34. *Passions, op. cit.*, Art. 197; *Dioptric, op. cit.*
35. *Ibid.*

hand. When the man felt the two sticks touch an object, he could tell its distance by how much the two sticks were bent inward, since a relatively more distant object would require turning of the sticks to a more parallel position. Man, Descartes said, had an ability to carry on a natural geometry of this kind and, incidental to this, he suggested that he had a kinesthetic sense. Accommodation and the secondary cues of aerial perspective and of relative size were also related by him to visual perception.[36] A physiological mechanism was postulated so as to relate memory to sense. For the mind to have memory, it is necessary for traces of sensed objects to be impressed upon the brain.[37]

He also gave a physiological explanation for memory. An act of volition causes the pineal gland to drive animal spirits to the various parts of the brain until they reach the part where that which we wish to remember has left its "traces."[38]

At the physiological level, Descartes reinforced the distinction that he made between innate and acquired ideas by commenting that the arrangement of the little threads of the brain may be either native or acquired.[39] He also made a distinction between nature and habit.[40] Movements of the pineal gland are related to movements either by nature, as in the contraction of the pupils in order to look at a near object, or by habit, as in the learned activity of speaking. In this formulation there can be seen to be a beginning of a distinction between innate and acquired characteristics, later to become important in psychology.

Descartes used the concept of instincts only incidentally and sparingly, referring to them as natural dispositions.[41] Natural appetites are treated in the same fashion. He indicated that certain drives are determined by the "union" of the body and mind, such as hunger and thirst,[42] and that they may be called natural dispositions.[43]

36. *Ibid.*
37. *Meditations, op. cit.*, Reply to fifth set objections.
38. *Passions, op. cit.*, Art. 42.
39. *Treatise on man, op. cit.*
40. *Passions, op. cit.*, Art. 44.
41. *Ibid.*, Art. 50.
42. *Meditations, op. cit.*, VI.
43. *Ibid.*, Reply to second set objections.

While Descartes' primary interest was philosophical, he did render the emerging field of physiology a considerable service. By conceiving the brain and body as an automaton, Descartes made it possible to examine nervous and bodily functions as a mechanical system without going outside that system. A separate science of physiology discriminable from other fields was being proposed and made more plausible. Although his specific model had little impress, his thesis of a mechanical model of the body did gain support that, because of him, resulted in sounder evidence being found.

METHODOLOGICAL PRESCRIPTIONS AT THE BEGINNING OF MODERN SCIENCE

In the seventeenth century there was no universally accepted scientific method with experiments and observations methodologically similar being conducted by those interested in science. It almost seemed as if there were as many methods as there were people who thought and wrote about scientific matters. Lacking guidance from a scientific paradigm, each man worked out his particular way of coming to terms with the older speculative traditions.

It was not unnatural that Descartes and his contemporaries Bacon and Hobbes each would believe that his particular intellectual formulation was the result of the methods he used. A dogmatic methodism, a belief that technique had an inherent quality of ensuring success, was especially prominent in Descartes.

From our vantage point, we can see that along with the others of this time, Descartes had two sets of choices to make—one concerning what was considered to be the major source of knowledge, to follow the rational or the empirical prescription, and the other concerning the priority to be given either to general principles or individual facts, to follow the deductive or the inductive prescription.

Rationalism, his choice in one of these pairs, is a concept with many shades and variations of meaning. In its broadest sense, rationalism is the belief that in thinking logically a man's mind works the same way as does the universe, making it possible that ultimately man can understand everything, just as he understood in Descartes' time simple mathematical or physical problems. In the present context, the more specific meaning intended is that of an adherent to the rationalistic prescription who finds the primary, if not the exclusive, source of knowledge to lie in reason.

If, on the other hand, one follows the empirical prescription, knowledge is found in experience. Experience, however, does not come from the senses alone, a narrower doctrine that came to be known as sensationalism. In addition to analysis of sensory experience, often some form of introspective analysis was accepted by the empiricist. To use the formulation of John Locke, the first great modern adherent to empiricism, "reflection" by which we are informed concerning the workings of our minds is operative in addition to the effect of experience. Empiricism, although only counterdominant, was never completely dormant, and was to receive a strong impetus from the success of the emerging experimental method.

During the period now under consideration, the rationalistic prescription was dominant. Apart from this being a heritage from the past, in earlier periods as well as at the beginning of the modern age, rationalism lent itself more readily than did empiricism to support of religious doctrines, since rationalism in lay and religious matters reinforced one another in their common insistence upon independence from sense perception.[44] This helps to account for the adoption and adaptation of Greek rationalistic systems by Christian theologians. Rationalistic dominance received further support from the increased scope and precision that new mathematical discoveries were beginning to provide at this time. Such was the inspiration of mathematics to the men of this age that, after Descartes, if a particular philosophical or scientific issue could not be solved mathematically, it would at least be treated in the "spirit of mathematics." What is this spirit? It was to arrive at what were considered to be unchallengeable premises and then proceed to elaborate them by deductive reasoning.

DEDUCTIVE RATIONALISM AND DESCARTES

Descartes[45] was deeply interested in the problem of finding precisely the right method to obtain knowledge and thereby to bring about an essential reform. Descartes' solution was intertwined with his conviction of the certainty of the operations of mathematics.

---

44. Reichenbach, H. *The rise of scientific philosophy.* Berkeley, Calif.: University of California Press, 1951.
45. *Rules, op. cit.; Discourse on method, op. cit.*

The solution of uniting method and mathematics came in a revelation in a very literal sense. It occurred as part of a dream on St. Martin's Eve, 10 November 1619. One of the insights it gave him was that of applying algebra to geometry—the basic conception of analytic geometry. In effect, this unites algebra to spatial relationships. But it was more than a mathematical advance, tremendous though it was, that occurred that night. There was also another insight—that the method of mathematics could be extended to other fields of knowledge. His aim, however, was not to produce a mathematical interpretation of the universe, but rather to develop a point of view in likeness of mathematics in the way described a moment ago. His first task became the rationalistic one of finding self-evident truths, and once these were established, his second task would be to deduce the other truths that they implied. As did the men of the Middle Ages, he wanted to begin with accepted truths. There was to be this difference: they had begun with accepted truths based on religious pronouncements; he wished to begin with accepted truths based on reasoning.

It is unnecessary with this audience to trace Descartes' skeptical journey to the bed rock of "I think, therefore I am" and his triumphant return with his beloved basic principles, now not matters of mere belief but rationally established truths. One consequence, however, must be indicated. Descartes thereafter was to have a profound faith in the ability of reason to discover the true principles of any problem which he chose to investigate. Never thereafter did he waver in this conviction, never did he even consider that reason might be inadequate for any task to which it legitimately be put (on which ground he excluded little besides revealed dogma).

Descartes supported his rationalism by insisting that the clear, compelling, not to be doubted, and inevitable principles are innate. Before we experience the ideas of God, self, the axioms of mathematics, the figure of the triangle, we have the corresponding ideas. God simultaneously established laws of nature and endowed our minds with them so that, provided we used the right method, we would arrive at them. The innateness of ideas is stated time and again. It is variously spoken of as "certain primary germs of truth implanted by nature",[46] "naturally existent",[47] and "imprinted . . . in our minds."[48]

46. *Rules, op. cit.*, IV.
47. *Discourse on method, op. cit.*, VI.
48. *Ibid.*, V.

Ideas are not created by the process of thought; rather, they are *discovered* as the content of thought. A clear indication is given when Descartes was challenged by a critic to explain how a man would have an idea of God if he were to be born without the use of his senses and therefore without sensory experience. Descartes answered that he would not only have an idea of God and self, but, since he lacked sense experiences, he would hold them in an even more purified and clear fashion because these ideas existed for him without the adulteration of sense experience.[49] Sources of error found in everyday sensory experience serve to stifle knowledge of innate ideas, a handicap from which a person born without sense would not suffer.

Descartes' earlier statements about innate ideas had given his critics the impression that he was saying that we are born with them in ready-made, complete form. Under their criticism, he modified his view to say that what he meant by innate ideas is the potentiality of thought that is actualized by experience. Innate ideas are not always present; rather, we have the capacity of summoning up such ideas.[50] When we are exposed to extraneous things, it is the faculty of thinking, not those extraneous things themselves, that transmits ideas to our minds. They transmit something which gives "the mind occasion to form these ideas, by means of an innate faculty."[51] An innate idea is a "propensity." To drive home the point, he argued that, just as generosity or disease may run in families, so too there may be a familial disposition for certain ideas.[52] Neither ideas nor any other innate characteristic appear fullblown, they await experience to bring them out. Formulation in terms of propensity was something which was later to lend itself readily to adaptation for use in discussing nature versus nurture.

Inept as they are, Descartes held that sense experiences are of some use since they provide the occasions for the arousal of our ideas of mathematical entities and other simple notions. The role of perception is that of bringing innate ideas to consciousness. The mind then discovers ideas which it already implicitly possessed.

Descartes' position on innateness of basic principles is in agreement with his dualistic separating of mind and body. In thinking the

49. *Meditations, op. cit.*, Reply to fifth set objections.
50. *Ibid.*, Reply to third set objection, reply to objection X.
51. Descartes, R. *Notes directed against a certain programme* (1648), p. 443.
52. *Ibid.*, p. 442.

mind may function entirely independently of body.[53] When the mind functions in this independent fashion, it has pure ideas, i.e., pure activities as contents of thought without any dependence for their truth upon the world of objects. As would Kant after him, Descartes held that the mind provided the ground for certain structuring principles which were therefore *a priori.*

Knowledge of truth and falsity come from thinking alone.[54] The senses contribute to the materials of thought, but neither sensation alone nor imagination alone could ever assure us of their truth value. Thinking must intervene.[55] Sensory experiences, as he warns again and again, are fallible,[56] and, because sensory experiences are omnipresent, it is no easy task for the judgments made by the human mind to be free from their erroneous impressions. This, he admits, makes it hard to follow the rules of correct thinking which occupied so much of his attention in the *Rules for the Direction of the Mind* and *Discourse on the Method of Rightly Conducting the Reason.* But with faithful adherence to these rules, one can do so, Descartes had no doubt.[57] It follows that his was to be a deductive procedure, the beginning of investigation with already formulated principles.

Descartes gives a clear summary statement of how he would use this deductive method in order to find further principles in his short statement, *Rules for the Direction of the Mind.*[58] Besides intuition, he says, the other fundamental operation of the mind is deduction. Intuition had supplied the first principles of truth safeguarded as to their validity by the already familiar test of clarity so that knowledge comes first from intuition. Deduction that follows is the process of making inferences from this certain knowledge. It is the process whereby the mind allows inferences to be drawn from basic principles in successive steps. These remote deductively derived conclusions have the characteristic of being derived step by step, which intuitive truths do not have.

Descartes relied primarily on deduction but in the broader

---

53. *Meditations, op. cit.,* II.
54. *Rules, op. cit.,* VIII.
55. *Discourse on method, op. cit.,* IV.
56. *Rules, op. cit.,* VIII, XII, XIII; *Meditations, op. cit.,* I, VI. Reply to second set objections, reply to fifth set objections.
57. *Rules, op. cit.,* II.
58. *Ibid.,* III.

sense made evident in earlier discussion. No more than to Bacon was deduction as he conceived it dependent upon the Aristotelian syllogism, which is useful only in restating that which is already discovered. This dependence upon deduction is not exclusive. He specifically denied the charge that he always deduced particular truths from universal proposition. Instead, he said, he always started with particular propositions as he indicated in replying to a critic. He argued that in order to discover the truth, we should always start with particular notions, in order to arrive at general conceptions subsequently, though we may also proceed in the reverse way, after having discovered the universals, deduce other particulars from them. Thus in teaching a child the elements of geometry, we shall certainly not make him understand the general truth that *"when equals are taken from equals the remainders are equal,"* or that *"the whole is greater than its parts,"* unless we show him examples in particular cases.[59] The mind's knowledge, then, is such that general propositions are formed from particulars, and Descartes cannot be said to exclude induction. Nevertheless, beyond a certain irreducible minimum, he preferred to depend upon deduction.

Descartes did not, as legend would have it, believe that all physics could be deduced from first principles. "We cannot determine by reason how big these pieces of matter are, how quickly they move, or what circles they describe . . . [this] is a thing we learn from observation. Therefore, we are free to make any assumptions we like about them so long as all the consequences agree with experience."[60] Hypotheses must be framed and experiments must be used in order to select from among competing equally deductively and rationally plausible interpretations.

The intellect's unaided powers were not enough; "experiments [are] necessary to me in order to justify and support my reasoning."[61] Descartes would experiment—but only to fill out the details, to show from among the alternatives the way God has chosen to produce.[62] Experiment, therefore, had a subordinate but acknowledged place in his scheme. As he conceived it, the more

59. *Meditations, op. cit.*, Letter to M. Clerselier, *op. cit.*
60. Descartes, R. *Principles of philosophy.* (1644) In V. Cousin (ed.), *Oeuvres*, Vol. 3, Paris: Levrault, 1824.
61. *Ibid.*, Author's letter.
62. *Discourse on method, op. cit.*, VI.

advanced the knowledge became, the more necessary experiments became.[63] It not unexpectedly follows that experiment is stressed by Descartes in connection with biological and physiological problems.[64]

To some slight extent, Descartes practiced what he preached. There is evidence that he did make some observations, collected some specimens, and made vivisections.[65] Moreover, he himself exhibited his method by exercises in optics and geometry appended for that purpose to the *Discourse*. Neither in these studies nor anywhere else did Descartes, or any other person, for that matter, employ his method in all of its details. Instead, he behaved as did other scientists: he discovered experimentally the equality of the sines of the angles of incidence and of refraction in 1626 and only later did he fit it into the deductive proofs of the *Dioptric* first published in 1637.

Looking back over Descartes' rationalistic and deductivistic system from our vantage point shows it to be open to serious qualification and criticism. An unvarying system in which each step is laid out in advance may be suitable for exposition of scientific procedures in general terms for the interested reader. It is not a method of scientific discovery because there is no one method of scientific investigation; there are many.

Descartes' method is that of the philosophical system builder rather than that of the scientist. He rejected experimental proof if it could not be assimilated into his system. This explains how he could be so blind as not to be content with Harvey's demonstration that the heart was a contractible muscle and insisted, instead, that the heart was a heated container, as it was called for to be by his primary principles. Similarly, after praising Galileo for freeing himself of the errors of the schools and for using mathematics, Descartes went on to say, ". . . he has merely sought reasons for certain particular effects without having considered the first causes of nature; and thus he has built without a foundation."[66] He was criticizing Galileo for not having "theoretical," i.e., "metaphysical"

63. *Ibid.*
64. *Ibid.*, XI.
65. Haldane, Elizabeth S. *Descartes, his life and times.* New York: Dutton, 1905.
66. Descartes, R. *Letter to Mersenne*, March 1638. In *Oeuvres et lettres.* (Intro. by A. Bridoux.) Paris: Gallimard, 1953, p. 995.

presuppositions as a "foundation" for his work—a standpoint that we see to be its precise strength.

The clarity and distinctness of the postulates followed, Descartes held, are important in any deductive system. But then and now, one can argue that they do not tell the whole story. Dependence on self-evident truths is not characteristic of scientific advance. In fact, regarding postulates as tentative, not certain, to be discarded when they disagree with observations or experiments is a lesson scientists had to learn many times over the centuries. In this methodological sense, Galileo was right and Descartes wrong. In Descartes' hands, the hypothetic-deductive method of Galileo lost its hypothetical to retain only its deductive character.

Despite the defects, Descartes' rational and deductive analysis of the order of nature following mathematical methods was one of the most influential ideas of the seventeenth century. It overshadowed by far Bacon and his adherence to induction and empiricism. With such different views neither could have appreciated the significance of the work of the other. They could not see, as we do from our vantage point, that induction and deduction, and rationalism and empiricism, could and would be integrated in the course of scientific endeavor.

DUALISM AND DESCARTES

Against the general scientific background of the early seventeenth century and Descartes' methodological and attitudinal conceptions and presuppositions, it now becomes appropriate to examine his way of regarding the relationship between mind and body and the nature of mind itself.

Before Descartes, body and mind had not been seen clearly as opposing entities. Influenced by Aristotle, medieval theologians had conceived living bodies as so imbued with soul that no chasm between soul and body could be seen. It was Descartes who established, for all of those who came after to see, the distinction between a spiritual mind and a mechanistic body. Indeed, a sharply defined dualism was a problem that he did much to create.

Descartes conceived of two substances—mind, whose essential character is thinking, and body (matter), whose essential quality is extensiveness (length, width and depth).[67] With the distinction asserted, it becomes necessary to show how he arrived at this conception.

Cartesian dualism followed directly from his deductive search for certainty. Acceptance of his dictum "I think, therefore I am" made thinking separate from matter, since in the course of his search for certainty, it will be remembered, matter had been recovered at a separate later step.

A host of other arguments supported his absolute distinction between mind and body: matter can easily be divided into parts, while mind cannot;[68] the mind, the independent substance, can "act independently of the brain: for certainly the brain can be of no use in pure thought. . . .";[69] mind moves the body, since "the most certain and most evident" experience makes us "immediately aware of its doing so";[70] and the mind and body can exist apart from one another, and therefore are distinct and separate.

But one argument, above all, was to be important for the future of psychology. This was a distinction between an objective and subjective prescription first given scientific sponsorship by Galileo and to be known from the day of Boyle and Locke[71] as the distinction between primary and secondary qualities.[72]

Without too much attention to the matter, the scholastic philosophers of the past had assumed that in sense perception the mind was directly in touch with real things.[73] To them, things were entities having "qualities" that were inherent in objects. So long as science was content to remain Aristotelian with things being just what they appeared to be, with water being wet, the fire hot, there

67. E.g., *Meditations, op. cit.*, IV.
68. *Ibid.*, VI.
69. *Ibid.*, Reply to fifth set objections.
70. Descartes, R. *Letter to Arnauld*. (1648) In N. K. Smith (Trans.), *Descartes' philosophical writings*. London: Macmillan, 1952, pp. 280-281.
71. Galileo, G. *Il Saggiatore*. (1623) Quoted in Joan W. Reeves, *Body and mind in Western thought*. London: Penguin Books, 1958, Question 48.
72. It would seem that the actual terms "primary" and "secondary" in this context were introduced by Robert Boyle in 1666 in his "Origin of Forms and Qualities According to the Corpuscular Philosophy." T. Birch (ed.), *Works* (Vol. 3), London: Johnson *et al.* 1773. (1666) Details are given in Sir William Hamilton's edition of the *Works of Thomas Reid, D.D.* (Edinburgh: Machlachlan and Stewart, 1863), Vol. II, p. 825, Note D.
73. Wiley, B. *Seventeenth Century background*. London: Chatto and Windus, 1934.

was no problem. But now Galileo had begun to uncover a new universe, a particular pitch was a certain number of vibrations and water was material particles in motion. The sound of the string, the coolness and wetness of the water, seemed no longer to be properties of the string or of water itself. But whence came these properties? The answer was that it must be the mind that heard the sound or felt the water.

This issue was brought into sharp focus by both general scientific developments and by a specific relevant distinction made by Galileo. During these early modern days, measurements had been made of weight, size and motion almost to the exclusion of heat, color and sound. The fascination that their mathematical manipulation had for the scientist of the day made the former seem somehow more real than the latter. In the interest of clarifying the nature of the scientific task by setting the limits of physical science and in furthering his mathematical apriorism, Galileo made a sharp distinction between the objective and mathematical and the subjective and sensitive world. Discussions occurred in the setting of a consideration of Aristotle's contention that motion is the cause of heat. This Galileo denied, saying that an object or substance has shape, quantity, and motion, and only these. These are the "primary qualities"; they cannot be separated from things. But warmth (and, by logical extension, a color, a taste, a sound, and a smell) do not inevitably accompany objects. These are, Galileo said, "mere names, having their location only in the responsive body . . ."[74] If the sensing persons were taken away, these qualities would no longer exist. These "secondary qualities" do not have the status of physical reality. Take away the sensing person and these qualities disappear. In short, they are qualities of sensation, not of things; they are subject rather than object. They have no reality apart from experience. To Galileo, their subjectivity meant that they are to be banished from natural science.

Galileo had made a highly novel contribution which served to place physical science on a more methodologically objective footing. In the interest of *methodological* objectivity in the physical sciences Galileo was arguing that a *contentual* subjectivity existed concerning the psychology that was to be. Objectivity was being denied to sensory experiences, since they were not external to the individual.

74. *Il Saggiatore, op. cit.*, p. 107.

Instead, sensory experiences were subjective, occurring only within an individual. There is no question that this distinction, useful though it may have been at the time, prolonged the period before psychology was to emerge as a science, since the "subjectivity" of sense qualities has been a problem to be overcome ever since.

What was merely a methodological distinction for Galileo became for Descartes an argument for a dualism of two worlds. In support of the immateriality of the mind, he happily enlisted the distinction between primary and secondary qualities and phrased it that odors, smells, and tastes became mere sensation, "existing in . . . [one's] thought."[75] Bodies exist only in the shape and motion. He goes so far as to say that sensations represent nothing outside of our minds.[76] They are not in the objects, but in our minds. Instead of sensible qualities residing in bodies, actually it is quite possible that sensible qualities and the objects are not at all similar.[77] In approaching fire and first feeling heat, then moving still closer and feeling pain, far from compelling one to believe that "heat" and "pain" are somehow in the fire itself, on the contrary, suggests that they are not. The upshot, then, was that secondary qualities were relegated to the mind of the perceiver, while primary qualities were the properties of nature and the features of the world requiring mechanical explanation and to be, by definition, the only essential properties of the scientific concern.

A rigid separation of body and mind, contrasted and separated entities, was insisted on by Descartes. All reality of the human being, Descartes was saying, is either spatial (body) or conscious (mind). The relationship is disjunctive; what is spatial is not conscious, what is conscious is not spatial. It follows that mind or body each can be studied without reference to the other. The physical world, including body and its mathematically measurable relationships, is in one realm, the mind with its thoughts, sensations and free will is in another. The body's behavior is determined by mechanistic laws, but in the mind there is purpose and freedom of will, making a person's actions subject to praise and blame. As distinguished from body, man's mind then cannot be reduced to an aspect of a mechanical system because man's mind transcends the material world and the efficient causality which governs therein.

75. *Meditations, op. cit.*, Reply to sixth set objections.
76. Descartes, R. *Principles of philosophy.* (1644)
77. *Meditations, op. cit.*, VI.

Descartes' dualism had important implications for the sciences in general and for psychology in particular. Matter, including body, was to be treated mathematically and explained mechanically. The two-substance view, mind and matter, simplified physical science by means of what it excluded, while at the same time it introduced a major problem for psychology. From the present perspective the effect of dualism was more pernicious than helpful. The dualistic view of psychology, so firmly established by Descartes, was to dominate even into the twentieth century. Ever since Descartes, psychologists have had the problem of dealing with the relation between mind and body. Descartes himself offered one solution.

While laboring mightily to separate mind and body, Descartes was acutely aware there was an interaction and union between them. Evidence so prevalent in nature that he could not ignore it attested that the mind influences the body and the body influences the mind. His answer was to postulate a point of interaction—the pineal gland.[78] His choice of what is now known to be a vestigial organ of no functional significance whatsoever was based entirely on speculative reasoning. The gland's location, deep in the center of the brain, was seen as befitting its central role, while its uniqueness among brain structures is not being divided into hemispheres served to emphasize its unitary nature.

With a point of interaction selected on these grounds, Descartes proceeded to speculate on how it acted to bring about interaction of body and mind. He postulated that the slightest movement of the pineal gland can alter the flow of the animal spirits, and, reciprocally, the animal spirits can alter movements of the gland.[79] According to its direction of inclination, animal spirits are directed to bring about responses in that region. The sources of stimulation for these inclinations of the pineal gland are not only external sense impressions, but also those arising from the two internal senses, the natural appetites (hunger, thirst, and the like) and passions (love, hate, fear, etc.).

Selecting a point of interaction, any point of interaction, however, created the necessity of explaining how mind, a nonmaterial substance, can influence a material body, and vice versa. The mind, answered Descartes, directs the *course* of motion flowing through the body without in any way altering the *volume* of motion. In his

78. *Passions of the soul, op. cit.*, Arts. 31-32.
79. *Ibid.*, Art. 31.

opinion, this way of understanding the relationship did no violence to the separation of the mental and physical, since, as he saw it, the mind did not exert a physical force. The weakness of this argument is all too obvious today, since we realize this explanation violates that which came to be called the principle of the conservation of momentum. Altering direction is just as much a result of physical energy as is alteration of quantity. Descartes has raised a problem of how the mind and body influenced one another, but had by no means solved it.

He also considered the general nature of the union of mind and body. That there is, in his opinion, a union he leaves no doubt.[80] This union is not accidental, Descartes insisted.[81] "Accidental" to Descartes meant something which, if absent, would still not destroy the object, such as man's clothing, which is "accidental" to the man. The relationship is much closer than, say, that of a sailor to a ship.[82] Pain is felt by the mind when the body is hurt, which is a more intimate relation than the concern the sailor feels when his ship is damaged. The union of mind and body, it would seem, is an integral one for Descartes.

Although related to body, mind possesses a unity denied to body.[83] If one takes away a part of the body, the body is decreased, but this does not thereby take away part of the mind. Moreover, corporeal objects can be subdivided into parts, which is not the case with mind. Instead, mind is united with all parts of the body so as to form a whole.[84] This is to say, the mind is united with an integrated assemblage of organs, which, precisely because the organs are interrelated, makes for a kind of unity.

It now becomes appropriate to focus upon the mind as affected by the body, rather than the reverse, which will be discussed in considering prescriptive influences from physiological problems. Perception, imagination and passion are prominent themes which he uses in this connection.

Sensing has three aspects: (1) the effect on the motions of the

---

80. *Meditations, op. cit.*, Reply to fourth set objections, Reply to sixth set objections; *Passions, op. cit.*, Art. 30.

81. Descartes, R. Letter to Regius. (1641) In N. K. Smith (Trans.), *Descartes' philosophical writings*. London: Macmillan, 1952, pp. 269–270.

82. *Meditations, op. cit.*, VI.

83. *Ibid.*

84. *Ibid.; Passions, op. cit.*, Art. 30.

bodily organs by external objects; (2) the mental result, as in the perception of pain, color or sound, and the like, due to an intermixture of mind and body; and (3) "judgment" made on the basis of the past experiences with things sensed.[85] Since the first has already been discussed in the setting of his physiology, it is the second and third aspects that receive attention. Descartes contends that the first and second aspects, just mentioned, cannot be false. It is the third aspect of judgment which, if not used reflectively, brings about errors which only understanding—and mature understanding at that—can correct.

By introducing the aspect of judgment into discussion of "sense," it is apparent that Descartes is using "sensing" in a manner similar to others who would refer to "perception" of things, that is, the "sensing" of external objects, of hunger, thirst, and other natural appetites. In order to avoid terminological confusion, the term "perception" will be used hereafter. It is also evident that some perceptions go beyond the body, since judgment, which is of the mind, has been introduced in explaining the third level of sensing. As he put it elsewhere, perception is not by sense alone, but involves reason (thinking) exercised upon the sensed object.[86]

Imagination is also related to body. In imagining, the mind contemplates a material form, as distinguished from understanding when the mind employs itself alone. Imagination is not essential, since with understanding—but without imagination—one can still find truth.[87] Imagination is sometimes useful, he admits, as a supplemental aid when one is considering material things. The difference between understanding and imagination is shown by the fact that images are produced without contribution on the part of the person and, indeed, sometimes against his will, neither of which characterize understanding.

Much of philosophy before Descartes had emphasized an interest in the contemplative and intellectual, rather than in the active and emotional. In considering "passions" in some detail, Descartes struck a heretofore long neglected note. His was one of the earliest attempts to isolate and to understand the primary constituents of emotional life.

As Descartes conceived the "passions," they concerned more

85. *Meditations, op. cit.*, Reply to sixth set objections.
86. *Principles, op. cit.*, Part I, 73.
87. *Meditations, op. cit.*, VI.

182 : SELECTED PAPERS

than what we call emotions. "Passion" is derived from the so-called passivity of the mind, a term introduced to stand in contrast with the mind's own initiation of activity through understanding. Passions of the mind, then, arise from bodily movements. The brain was their physiological seat. Descartes admitted that the heart, then accepted by many as their center, is thought to be affected by the passions, but this is a mistake arising from the close connection between animal spirits and blood.

In the broadest sense, every conscious state that arises in the mind occasioned by bodily movements is a passion.[88] Passions, he indicated, were of three kinds: perceptions referable to the external world, such as the light of a torch and the sound of a bell; appetitive perceptions referable to the body, such as hunger, thirst, and other appetites; and perceptions referable to the mind, such as anger and joy. These last, the emotions as such, are those on which Descartes concentrated—that is, those ". . . perceptions, sensations or emotions of the soul (mind) which we specifically relate to it, and which are caused, maintained and fortified by some movement of the animal spirits!"[89] These "passions of the mind," the emotions, are those which are referred to the mind alone in the sense that their effects are felt there. For the passions, there is usually no known proximate cause to which they can be attributed as is the case with the perceptions and the appetites. Sadness, a passion, is experienced in the mind itself, and even though, as in all perceptions, there is a physical cause, it cannot be attributed directly to some definite object.

Surprisingly enough, Descartes had a considerable amount to say about the external indices of the passions.[90] He took the position that we can learn about the passions from study of external behavior. He comments on such matters as the effect of the passions on changes of color, in blushing and pallor of the face, and on trembling, languor, fainting, laughter, crying and sighing.

Although objects moving the body are innumerable, he conceived that the passions they excite affect us only in a limited number of basic ways. His analysis caused him to arrive at six primary passions—admiration (wonder), love, hatred, desire, joy, and

---

88. *Passions, op. cit.*, Arts. 17, 18, 19, 41.
89. *Ibid.*, Art. 27, pp. 121-122.
90. *Ibid.*, Arts. 112-124, 128, 130, 135.

sadness.[91] Wonder is the intellectual passion; all of the rest are forms of "desire." He was now using this latter term in a broader sense than for the passion of desire itself. Passions, whenever they incite to action, become desires in this broader sense.[92]

Primary passions give rise to related secondary passions. To admiration are related the secondary passions of esteem, contempt, generosity, pride, humility, veneration, and disdain. Passions of desire (in the narrower sense) include hope, fear, jealousy, confidence, courage, and cowardice, while from joy and sadness arise derision, envy, anger, shame, regret, and joyfulness.

The passions of joy and sadness are the vehicles for his advancing a theory of pleasure and pain. Joy is agreeableness, while sadness is disagreeableness.[93] Pleasure and pain are the predecessors of these passions and serve to produce them.[94] Feelings of pleasure occur when experiencing that which is beneficial, and pain when experiencing that which is harmful.[95]

Joy and sadness come from a consciousness of self-perfection or imperfection.[96] The passions function to incite the mind to consent to "actions which may serve to preserve the body, or make it more perfect in some way."[97] This call for personal fulfillment and maturity contains more than a hint of what we would today call a self-actualizing approach to personality.

THE MIND AND DESCARTES

At long last, the problem of mind, the salient issue of the emerging psychology, is at hand. The conceptions of the mind's structure, its faculties, its relations to will, the problem of objectivity and primary and secondary qualities will be of major concern. But before considering them, something must be said about the use of meditation as the method for the study of mind.

Meditation as a Method for the Study of Mind. It is instructive to compare meditation, as Descartes used it, to the method of

---

91. *Ibid.*, Arts. 51-97.
92. *Ibid.*, Art. 144.
93. *Ibid.*, Arts. 91, 92.
94. *Ibid.*, Arts. 94, 137.
95. *Meditations, op. cit.*, VI.
96. *Passions, op. cit.*, Art. 137.
97. *Ibid.*

introspection which was to be so characteristic of later psychology. From our temporal perspective the classic introspective method has proven to be a cooperative enterprise drawing upon the work of many men in an effort to find the structure of mind. It has been found to proceed by analysis of the contents of this structure into parts according to one schema or another.

In spite of his faith in reason, Descartes clearly took an impatient view about learning from the introspections of others. Meditation was not a collective enterprise. He denied categorically that we need to borrow observations from others concerning the passions because, as he put it, we feel them ourselves.[98] Moreover, Cartesian meditation did not lend itself to molecular analysis of mental states into component parts or aspects. Innate ideas, for example, once achieved, were given to consciousness in all their self-contained unity from which Descartes then proceeded without any attempt to analyze them. So on both counts, Cartesian meditation was dissimilar to the later method of introspection that was to be the dominant method in psychology for a considerable period of time.

The Structure of Mind. Descartes clearly regarded the mind as a substance, as previous discussion attests. It was he, along with Hobbes, who made the conception of mind as substance, structure or content prominent on the modern scene. Although the same substance in each case, Descartes considered the mind to show different structural emphases—mind as thought, mind as ideas, mind as consciousness and mind as self-consciousness.

Mind as Thought. Time and again, Descartes stressed that mind is identical with thinking.[99] As he put it, "the human mind . . . is a thinking thing, and not extended in length, width, and depth, nor participating in anything pertaining to body."[100] Mind is not a process but a substance, immaterial though it may be. He meant it quite literally when he called it a "thing." The ideational content of the mind, discussed later as still another view, will bring this out even more clearly.

When Descartes wished to be especially precise about mind as a spiritual substance, or "single agency," he would refer to "understanding" rather than thinking.[100] When the mind is engaged in

98. *Passions, op. cit.,* Art. 1.
99. *Meditations, op. cit.,* Preface to reader.
100. *Ibid.,* IV.
101. *Rules, op. cit.*

understanding, the body is an intruder. In these instances, sense, imagination, and memory serve but to obscure and falsify the intuition of ideas, of basic principles or their deductive elaboration, giving further support to his contention that a man born without sense would have the greatest appreciation of these ideas. In this restricted meaning, the mind is almost no more than a passive spectator in the world of objects, encapsulated, self-contained, and static.

In addition to this narrow meaning just considered, in which the mind is in contact with basic principles, Descartes used thinking more broadly to refer to all of which we are consciously aware, including not only "understanding" but also will, imagination and sense, and memory.[102] This broader view comes about when mind in interaction with body is considered. In this perspective, the mind is related to objects—and relation to objects is expressed through the body. The brain, not involved in understanding, now comes into use.

All perceptions, images, emotions, and volitions, then, are related to thinking and aspects of thinking. The mind senses, imagines, remembers, feels emotions, and carries out acts of will. The traditional Aristotelian distinction between a sensitive and a rational soul, between sensing and imagining in contrast to thinking, is no longer operative. In effect, the sensitive soul is merged with the thinking mind.

While mind as thinking is fundamental for Descartes, several subsidiary views are discernible in which mind is conceived as ideas, as consciousness, and as self-consciousness.

Mind as Ideas. Ideas make up the content of this mind substance for Descartes. There are three kinds of ideas. Above all are the ideas which arise directly from the mind—the innate ideas, those basic, most certain principles, which are the supreme achievement of the mind.

There are also ideas that form a link between the mind and natural objects, the ideas the mind has through sense, memory, and imagination. An idea may represent in the mind an object in the world which is its cause. It is not the eye that sees but the mind, although through the intervention of the brain. Ideas of the mind relating to objects may also be false. Ideas may or may not conform to external reality.[103] Indeed, a major source of human error is to forget that ideas do not always conform to external objects.

102. *Principles, op. cit.*, Part 1, 9; *Rules, op. cit.*, VIII, XII.
103. *Meditations, op. cit.*, III.

Another category of ideas are those manufactured by the mind, such as ideas of imaginary objects which make sleepers and madmen have ideas of objects which do not exist. We all, he asserts, experience ideas of the mind as being within the mind itself.[104] Such are the passions, the feeling of joy, anger, and the like, and perceptions of volition, that is, awareness of oneself as willing.

Ideas are not to be confused with images which arise from motion imparted to the senses. Ideas arise from the mind uninfluenced by the body, except as it serves as the instigator to trigger their appearance. But what is sensed cannot give rise to the idea itself and there is no direct correspondence between sensing and ideation.

Mind as Consciousness. The mind underlies consciousness; it is not identical with consciousness. Consciousness is a substance, a thing, an aspect of the structure *of* the mind. Regarding it as a function was yet to appear. The concept of consciousness as substance is neatly illustrated by Descartes' two types of memory—memory of material things, leaving traces of preceding excitations on the brain, and memory of mental things, which leave permanent traces in consciousness itself.

Thought in the extended sense (as differentiated from understanding) covers everything in us of which we are immediately conscious.[105] Ideas in this context are the forms of thoughts.[106] Ideas are immediate awareness of what the mind perceives.[107] Ideas include willing and fearing, for example, since in so doing one perceives, one wills, or one fears.

Awareness is an awareness of consciousness. Despite his acceptance of the potentiality of innate ideas, nothing exists in the mind of which it is not conscious.[108] This follows because the mind contains only thought. Indeed we must be conscious of thought for it to exist. Even infants, he argues, are conscious of their thoughts, although afterwards they might not remember them. An inconscious mind would have been a contradiction in terms for Descartes. In fostering the prescription of conscious mentalism, he did so without

---
104. Haldane, Elizabeth S. *Descartes, his life and times.* New York: Dutton, 1905.
105. *Meditations, op. cit.*, III.
106. *Ibid.*, Reply to third set objections.
107. *Ibid.*, Reply to fourth set objections.
108. *Ibid.*, Reply to sixth set objections.

even the slightest consideration of a mental life of which one is unaware, i.e., an unconscious mentalism.

Mind as Self-consciousness. In advancing his *cogito ergo sum*, Decartes had made self-consciousness his primary datum. He could conceive of the world being nonexistent and of not having a body, but he could not conceive of not having a mind which is unaware of itself. Indeed the criterion of truth for things other than the mind is that it be as clear and distinct as that of the mind's own existence.

The mind thinks and it is conscious of itself. Knowledge of self is immediate and occurs whenever a person first asks himself that particular question, claimed Descartes.[109] The very moment that there is awareness in consciousness, he added, that instant there is awareness of one's own existence.[110]

Descartes also used self-consciousness as an explanatory concept. For example, the continuity of personal identity is used to characterize the waking state and distinguish it from that of sleeping.[111] Self-consciousness also relates to self-evaluation. Self-blame and esteem arise in his opinion through exercise of free will and the control or lack of it we have over our volition.[112] It is for these reasons that a man can be praised or blamed.

Although only a beginning, a concept of unity or self can be found to be emerging in Descartes. The unity of the mind is at the same time the unity of the self. The arguments for unity of mind then became arguments for unity of self as well, although this is a point he did not make explicit.

An important caution must be offered concerning his accounts of mind. Although they were to lead psychologists with different aims and presuppositions than his own toward the particular perspectives just given, Descartes' aim, in contrast, was essentially philosophical, or, to be more specific, epistemological. He wished to demonstrate unequivocally that we are thinking beings.

The Faculties of Mind. A conception of mental phenomena as processes or activities—the functional prescription, as it shall be called—was also discernible in his thinking, although mind as content (the contentual prescription) dominated. The functional conception was a tradition traceable at least as far back as Augustine, for whom

109. *Ibid.*, Reply to fifth set objections.
110. *Meditations, op. cit.*, IV.
111. *Meditations, op. cit.*, III.
112. *Passions, op. cit.*, Art. 152.

memory, will, and imagination were to be attributed to the respective faculties, powers, or agencies of the mind. Faculties were supposed to produce the various mental activities to which human beings were prone. Faculty psychology was a forerunner of functional psychology insofar as it conceived of the mind as having specifiable function or functions.

Descartes specifically claimed authorship of the view that the mind consists of only one thing, the "faculty" of thinking.[113] The mind has unity so that faculties are not parts of that mind, since it is one and the same mind which employs itself in these faculties. They are, as he put it, ". . . modes of thinking peculiar to themselves. . . ."[114]

The substantial nature of mind, "a thing that thinks,"[115] made it relatively easy for Descartes to espouse a faculty point of view. Hence, his easy reference after the above quoted words to go on ". . . or a thing that has in itself the faculty of thinking."[116]

The faculties useful in cognition are stated by Descartes somewhat casually and inconsistently. One account he gave called for thinking in the form of understanding and imagination, sense and memory.[117] Of these, only understanding can give the truth; the others are auxiliary. Thinking, already familiar as a "power . . . (that is) purely spiritual,"[118] uses the bodily-based faculties by applying itself to them or it may cooperate and thus use them. Elsewhere, feeling and willing are also treated as faculties by Descartes. Discussion of willing will be indicative of will as a power.

WILL AND ITS FREEDOM

Speaking generally, two extreme positions may be discerned concerning the freedom of the will. There is the view that, since man possesses a nonmaterial mind or spiritual soul endowed with the power of free choice, he transcends the material world and therefore the system of causality. There is the opposed view that would extend the scientific conception of the material universe

---

113. *Notes against a programme, op. cit.*
114. *Meditations, op. cit.*, VI.
115. *Ibid.*, Preface to the reader.
116. *Ibid.*
117. *Rules, op. cit.*, XII.
118. *Ibid.*

to include man, in which free will would be seen as an epiphenomenon and freedom of will denied. Between these extremes there are a number of views which would offer qualification and elaborations.

Descartes accepted clearly and unequivocally the reality of the freedom of the will. After stating that all men possess the faculty of willing, he went on to say that it is the power of choosing or not choosing to do a thing.[119] In another place, he referred to judging or refraining from judging as an act of will, which, he adds, is under our control.[120] There is freedom of the will, then, shown in choosing or judging.

This freedom is evident, innate, and found by self-examination,[121] claimed Descartes. The very capacity to apply methodic doubt, the starting point of his method, he holds, is evidence of this freedom. In doubting all things, he perceived liberty to do so to exist. Man's freedom of will is received from God.[122] Man's will is free in the same sense and from the same source in God as are miracles, since in both instances there is a suspension of causality.

But what is the relation of the will to the mind? Despite his repeated references to understanding as the only function of mind, a position that has been accepted as his up to this point, when dealing with the relation of mind to will, he introduces the latter as a faculty. Besides understanding, he now says, there is also the will, in contradiction to his position that mind is pure thought.[123] Statements to the contrary were, he now argues, a matter of emphasis; will is also of the mind. He was perhaps influenced in acceptance of this position by the Church, for to follow its dictates, he had to accept both the will as influencing the mind and its freedom.

His position concerning will as a faculty of the mind is made especially clear when we examine the question of the cooperation and conflict of the will and the understanding. In a setting of considerations of man's ability to distinguish between the true and the false,[124] he argues that error arises from misapplication of the will which consists of extending it beyond understanding. Understanding does not cause errors; incorrect exercise of one's will does. Will

---

119. *Meditations, op. cit.*, IV.
120. *Ibid.; Letter to Clerselier, op. cit.*
121. *Principles, op. cit.*, Part I, 39.
122. *Meditations, op. cit.*, IV.
123. *Principles, op. cit.*, Part I.
124. *Meditations, op. cit.*, IV.

exceeds understanding in that we can will many things that we do not understand and therefore err.[125] If we understand (which is God given), we cannot err in willing, but if we do not understand and will nevertheless, we can commit error.

The relation of the will to the passions is important to Descartes because to show how to control the passions is Descartes' didactic and moral aim for considering them.[126] The first step toward this control is to understand them, which he believed his book on the passions to give.[127] When passions are aroused, we can divert ourselves until the agitation calms and then, and only then, should we make a judgment as to what is to be done. Then the freely acting mind can influence the workings of the bodily machine by the process of willing, which can cause the pineal gland to incline in the manner necessary for the appropriate bodily action.[128]

As distinguished from the passion or desire, will is that which gives or withholds consent to desire.[129] In this context, the principal effect of the passions is to incite the mind to will.[130] The agitation of the animal spirits, especially if it be violent, is of the body, and, just as a clap of thunder must be heard whether we want to or not, so too the mind cannot completely control the passions. The will, however, can quickly gain control of the passions by not permitting their effect to proceed further than the first beginnings.[131] Through the will, the hand that rose to strike in anger can be restrained before the blow is struck; running away in fear can be stopped after the first involuntary movements. Most actions originate with the will, reflex responses being a major class of exceptions. The activity of the will, or rather its failure yet to act, is shown in involuntary action described earlier in connection with the functioning of the nervous system.

In sum, the mind is free since it initiates action through the will and thus transcends causality. Since to be free is to be without laws, Descartes was denying that there can be a science of psychology. The material world was rigidly determined. Physical

125. *Ibid.*, Reply to Fifth set objections.
126. *Passions, op. cit.*, Art. 212.
127. *Ibid.*, Art. 211.
128. *Ibid.*, Art. 41.
129. *Ibid.*, Art. 80.
130. *Ibid.*, Art. 40.
131. *Ibid.*, Art. 46.

processes and everything about animals and the bodies of men fall within this material world. The one exception was the human mind, which has volition.

METHODOLOGICAL AND CONTENTUAL OBJECTIVITY-SUBJECTIVITY

To his successors, Descartes was to be a rich source for various combinations of methodological and contentual objectivity and subjectivity. His conception of matter as extension furthered an objective quantitative science and opened the way to a view of man as a machine. Through his concept of an animal as an automaton and, more specifically, though his concept of reflex action, Descartes contributed to the beginnings of both physiological and animal psychology. It was this sort of thinking that led a modern commentator, Randall, to say that Descartes ". . . held to a thoroughly mechanistic biology and psychology."[132] This is true for the latter only if one is thinking of psychology today. It is not true for the centuries between, during which psychology was conceived to be the study of mind. In historical perspective, the psychological side to the story is to prove to be quite a different matter. A nonmechanistic phase in the history of psychology was about to be entered upon because of Descartes. His contentually subjective position concerning the mind was to dominate in psychology well into the first years of the twentieth century. Although Descartes insisted on a contentual subjectivity for the mind, in so doing, he was searching for a methodological objectivity and, hence, his view should not be confused with "subjectivism" in this sense. He wanted desperately to attain a truth comparable to the impersonal truth of mathematics. He wished to distinguish the reality of consciousness from the world "outside" of which consciousness is not a part. In consciousness, we each are alone with ourselves. Reality, including other persons, is reached only by an inference, a step in itself that emphasized the distance between subject and object.

Descartes' *Meditations*, as Husserl[133] asserts, is the prototype

---

132. J. H. Randall, Jr., *The career of philosophy: from the Middle Ages to the Enlightenment*. New York: Columbia University Press, 1962, p. 381.

133. Husserl, E. *Cartesian meditations: an introduction to phenomenology*. The Hague: Nijhoff, 1964. (1936)

of philosophical reflection in that he turned within himself for immediate experience. In so doing, he fostered the phenomenological approach which calls for mind to be studied in precisely this fashion.

Descartes must be given credit for a consistent, maintained attempt to examine "the sheer facts of experience," as MacLeod[134] put it recently. Just prior to the quotation MacLeod had explained that two German words, *Erlebnis* and *Erfahrung,* give a convenient distinction that the English word "experience" does not convey. *Erlebnis* refers to present experience, that which is immediately given without reference to origin; *Erfahrung* refers to an accumulation of experiences. This makes it possible to speak of Descartes as stressing experience in the sense of *Erlebnis* without implying he was empirical, i.e., depending upon accumulated experience as the source of knowledge, which, as is very obvious, he was not. As a consequence of this emphasis, he contributed to a phenomenological point of view.

Those who came after Descartes could find in him support for that which they wished to stress, whether it be contentual objectivity or subjectivity or methodological objectivity or subjectivity.

---

134. MacLeod, R. B. Phenomenology: a challenge to experimental psychology. In T. Wann (ed.), *Behaviorism and phenomenology: contrasting bases for modern psychology*. Chicago: University of Chicago Press, 1964, pp. 47–78.

III. Fields and
Selected Aspects of Psychology

14. A Brief History of Clinical Psychology

Clinical psychologists have been very surprisingly ahistorical. Very little thought has been given to, and less written about, the origin and development of clinical psychology. In the literature there are articles and books which interpret historically various special aspects or evaluate related fields, some of which have been of considerable help in preparing this paper. Nevertheless, whatever the reasons, there is not available a general account of the history of clinical psychology from the perspective of today.

In part, this neglect is due to the upsurge of interest in clinical psychological activity during and following the second World War. Since then, clinical psychologists have had little time to spend inquiring into their origins. Then too, their day-to-day activities impress them as so new and vital that they are hardly to blame for tacitly accepting the belief that they are pioneers and that somewhere in the chaos of war and its aftermath was born a new profession having little or no relation to what went before. The state of affairs today is curiously reminiscent of the situation found by Kimball Young in 1923 in tracing the history of mental testing. He remarked, "Making history on every hand as we are, we have a notion that we somehow have escaped history" (121, p. 1).

To capture in full measure the sweep and continuity of the history of clinical psychology is beyond the competence of the reviewer, to say nothing of space limitations. In order to do justice to all aspects of the subject one would have to deal with the complex history of the psychology of motivation and dynamic psychology.

This article was written while the author was at the Washington University School of Medicine.

Similarly, all the ramifications of the relation of clinical psychology to the rest of the field of psychology, of which it is an integral part, as well as an account of the history of test development would have to be considered.

The present account, perforce, presents an examination of men and ideas influential in shaping clinical psychology. But, since psychology is now a profession, attention must also be devoted to those internal and external controls which characterize a profession and to the settings in which the professional practice is conducted.

In presenting a historical account the question arises concerning the most appropriate date at which to begin. With some justification it was decided that since clinical psychology, as we know it, arose at about the turn of the present century, it would be appropriate to begin with the immediate forerunners of this first generation of clinical psychologists. The origins of clinical psychology, the first major section of this account, are to be found in the psychometric and dynamic traditions in psychology; the psychologist in the settings of the psychological clinic, child guidance, mental hospitals, institutions for the mentally defective; and the beginnings of psychology as a profession. Somewhat arbitrarily this early pioneer work is considered to come to a close with the end of the second decade of this century. This is followed by a section concerned with clinical psychology in the twenties and thirties. The same topics just mentioned, e.g., the dynamic tradition and psychology as a profession, are again considered. The work of psychologists in the armed services during the second World War and its effect upon psychology in the postwar period are next evaluated. A brief overview of clinical psychology today closes the account.

THE ORIGINS OF CLINICAL PSYCHOLOGY

The Psychometric Tradition in Psychology. This tradition, one of the headwaters from which clinical psychology sprang, was, in turn, a part of the scientific tradition of the nineteenth century. With all the limitations with which it is charged today, it is to this movement that the clinical psychologist owes much of his scientific standing and tradition. Whenever a clinical psychologist insists upon objectivity and the need for further research, he is, wittingly or otherwise, showing the influence of this tradition. Moving from Galton through Binet and Terman, this tradition met the demand that psychology, if it was to become a science, must share with other sciences the respect for measurement.

Psychometrics as a tool for clinical psychology owes its beginnings to Francis Galton (53) in England. Grappling as he was with the problem of individual differences, he and his followers did much to lay the groundwork for the investigation of ability by using observations of an individual's performance for information on individual differences. He thus founded mental tests.

In 1890 Cattell (29) introduced the term "mental tests" in an article describing tests which he had used at the University of Pennsylvania. Even at that date he was pleading for standardization of procedure and the establishment of norms. From the time of his days as a student of Wundt's, Cattell was interested in the problem of individual differences and did much to stimulate further investigation. Along with Thorndike and Woodworth, he also stressed dealing with individual differences by means of statistical analysis—a really new approach at this time. Some of these investigations, both from Cattell's laboratory and from others in various parts of the country, made positive contributions to various facets of the problem of psychometric measurement. For example, Norsworthy (82) in 1906 compared normal and defective children by means of tests and found the latter not a "species apart," pointing out that the more intelligent of the feebleminded were practically indistinguishable from the least intelligent of the normal.

Most of the investigations of the time were concerned with simple sensorimotor and associative functions and were based on the assumption that intelligence could be reduced to sensations and motor speed, an attempt which, as is now known, was doomed to failure. Furthermore, although more suitable verbal material was used, the studies of college students at Cornell, such as Sharp's (95), and the Wissler study (113) at Columbia, were found to be essentially nonpredictive. What the workers failed to take into account was the fact that college students are a highly selected group having a considerably restricted range. The negative finding of these studies effectively blocked further investigation at the college level for years. When one stops to consider that the dominant systematic position of the day was the structuralism of Titchener, who had banished tests as nonscientific, it is no wonder that "tests" were viewed with at least a touch of condescension.

In the meantime Binet had been working in France developing

his tests based on a wider sampling of behavior than had yet been used. His success in dealing with the intellectual classification of Paris school children is well known and needs no amplification at this point. The translation of his tests and their use in this country followed shortly after the turn of the century. It was Goddard (simultaneously with Healy), a student of G. Stanley Hall, who introduced the Binet tests to this country. Through a visit abroad and contact with Decroly, he became acquainted with Binet's work (121). In 1910 he began publishing findings with the test and in 1911 published his revision of the 1908 Binet Scale. This revision, along with Kuhlmann's, also published in 1911, gained some popularity among clinicians, but the subsequent development by Terman far overshadowed their work.

Probably the test that had the most influence upon trends in clinical psychology was the Terman Revision of the Binet Scale (83). In fact, for years the major task of the clinical psychologist was to administer the Stanford-Binet. In view of the importance of this test it is desirable to present in some detail the background of its development.

Lewis M. Terman (101) received his graduate training at Clark just after the turn of the century under Hall, Sanford, and Burnham. As Terman put it, "For me, Clark University meant briefly three things: freedom to work as I pleased, unlimited library facilities and Hall's Monday evening seminar. Anyone of these outweighed all the lectures I attended" (101, p. 315). This influence of Hall's was more from the enthusiasm he inspired and the wide scope of his interests than from his scientific caution and objectivity. Sanford was his doctoral adviser, but Terman chose his own problem in the area of differentiation of "bright" and "dull" groups by means of tests and worked it through more or less independently.

By a severely limited survey such as this it would be easy to give the impression that little or nothing else was being done along the lines under discussion except that reported. Terman was not alone in his interest in the development and standardization of tests by any manner of means. In his autobiography Terman (101) mentions as known to him in 1904 the work of Binet, Galton, Bourdon, Oehrn, Ebbinghaus, Kraepelin, Aschaffenburg, Stern, Cattell, Wissler, Thorndike, Gilbert, Jastrow, Bolton, Thompson, Spearman, Sharp, and Kuhlmann.

At the suggestion of Huey, who had been working in Adolf

Meyer's clinic at Johns Hopkins, Terman, undeterred by the prevailing hostile attitude of most psychologists, began work with the 1908 Binet Scale and in 1916 published the Stanford Revision of the Binet-Simon tests. Terman's interest in both the test and results from it continued unabated, resulting in still another revision in 1937.

Performance tests, so necessary for work with the linguistically handicapped, actually antedated the Stanford-Binet. The Seguin, Witmer, and Healy form boards and other performance tests were already in clinical use. Norms, although not lacking, were undeveloped, and the directions placed a high premium on language. What seemed to be needed was a battery of performance tests sampling a variety of functions and not as dependent upon language. Among the earliest to appear and to come into fairly common use was the Pintner-Paterson Scale of Performance Tests (85), published in 1917. Included in this scale were several form boards, a manikin and a feature-profile construction test, a picture completion test, a substitution test, and a cube-tapping test.

Another major step was the development of group tests under the impetus of the need for large-scale testing of recruits in World War I. This testing program is described with a wealth of detail by Yerkes (120). Although group tests were not unknown before the war, as witness those described in Whipple's *Manual of Mental and Physical Tests* (110), the need for quick appraisal of the basic intelligence of a large number of men provided the impetus for extensive development. The *Alpha* scale for literate English-speaking recruits and the *Beta* scale for illiterates and non-English-speaking recruits were developed rapidly under this demand. The Woodworth Personal Data Sheet (118), the first of a long line of psychoneurotic inventories, also was a product of military needs. So successful were these tests in overcoming the prejudices against testing both within the field of psychology and in the general public that after the war a veritable flood of group tests appeared. Many extensive surveys in the public schools were made for classificatory purposes. Further developments in this tradition during the twenties and thirties will be appraised after examination of other aspects of the origin of clinical psychology.

The Dynamic Tradition in Psychology. A major source of influence contributing to the growth of clinical psychology was the thinking and writing of the "Boston group" who promulgated "the new psychology"—William James, G. Stanley Hall, and their associates.

Although in no way could they be labeled clinical psychologists, their thinking was much closer to the heart of the clinical psychology movement and to progressive psychiatry than was the structural point of view of Titchener. Heresy though it may be, it cannot be denied that at that time academic psychology had relatively little to contribute to clinical psychology. Psychology, to be sure, had been placed by Fechner, Helmholtz, Wundt, Kraepelin, and others upon a scientific, quantitative foundation instead of being permitted to remain an indistinguishable cohort of philosophy. This was an essential step without which there could have been no clinical psychology; nevertheless, a sensationalistic approach to conscious intellectual experience offered relatively little for the clinical method and the profession with which it was to be associated.

The psychiatry of the day was in the main concerned with pathology and the search for an explanation of mental disturbances in disease processes. Kraepelin (68) had introduced clarity through his classification of mental disease, but at the expense of deeper understanding. Based upon symptoms and primarily descriptive in character, his classification served to diminish—even to discourage—in its users any urge toward understanding of psychological dynamics.

French psychiatric thinking and research profoundly influenced James (80). The work of Janet and Charcot was particularly important in this connection. With Morton Prince, he did much to stimulate interest in the phenomena of dissociation, feeling as he did that it was a fruitful method of investigation of personality functioning. Early in his career he recognized the value of a clinical approach which led him "whenever possible to approach the mind by way of its pathology" (77, p. 20).

The influence of James was expressed primarily through his *Principles of Psychology* (65), published in 1890, and to a lesser degree by his *Varieties of Religious Experience* (66), published in 1902. Both of these works were sufficiently removed from the otherwise prevailing psychological thinking of his day to be considered major pre-Freudian, dynamic influences. The choice of the term "dynamic" in this context is neither idle nor wishful thinking. James himself used the term to distinguish his point of view from the structural approach of Titchener (86).

Concerning the influence of the *Principles*, Morris had this to say:

> Great books are either reservoirs or watersheds. They sum up and transmit the antecedent past, or they initiate the flow of the future. Sixty years after its publication, the *Principles* appears to be one of the major watersheds of twentieth-century thought. Directly or indirectly, its influence had penetrated politics, jurisprudence, sociology, education and the arts. In the domain of psychology, it had foreshadowed nearly all subsequent developments of primary importance. Viewed retrospectively, the permanent significance of the *Principles* was incentive. It explored possibilities and indicated directions. These led, eventually, into social, applied and experimental psychology; into the study of exceptional mental states, subliminal consciousness and psychopathology. Because of its extreme fertility in the materials for hypothesis, most of the competitive schools of psychological theory that arose during the first half of the century could claim common ancestry in the *Principles* for at some point it implied their basic assumptions (77, p. 15).

This aptly catches James's influence on clinical psychology, not through work directly in the field or with the method, but through the fertile (and contradictory) character of his thinking.

In addition to the stimulation of his writings, James did take specific action of direct relevance to clinical psychology in his support of Clifford W. Beers, whose book, *A Mind that Found Itself* (19), did so much to further the mental hygiene movement. This he did through an endorsing letter which appeared in the first edition and, according to Henry James, his son, by departing from his fixed policy of "keeping out of Committees and Societies" (64, p. 273). In addition, he was interested in psychical research and in the efforts of Freud and Jung, although dubious about both of these trends (64).

Obviously it is impossible to capture the full flavor of William James in a paragraph or two, but this "defender of unregimented ideas" is at least the eccentric brilliant uncle of the men in clinical psychology who followed after.

Another of the pioneers of this time and place was G. Stanley Hall. He was more influenced by the evolutionary concept stemming from Darwin than by French psychopathological thinking. Shakow, in considering Hall's influence on psychiatry, so well summarizes his contributions that they may be seen as contributions to clinical psychology as well. He writes that it was

> Hall, the propagandist, who gave Freud his first academic hearing, who gave courses in Freudian psychology beginning in 1908 and whose pressure for its consideration remained life-long; Hall, who influenced Cowles in establishing the psychological laboratory at McLean Hospital which had

as directors following Hoch, Franz, Wells and Lundholm; Hall, who stimulated Adolf Meyer, by his early interest in child study, to write his first paper on a psychiatric topic—*Mental Abnormalities in Children during Primary Education* . . .—and who did so much to make the country child-conscious; Hall, whose students Goddard and Huey (also Meyer's students at the Worcester State Hospital) did the early pioneer work on feeblemindedness . . . Hall, whose bravery in handling the problem of sex did so much to break down the first barriers, thus greatly facilitating the later child guidance handling of this and related problems; Hall, whose student Terman achieved so much in the development of the Binet method in the United States and whose student Gesell did so much for other aspects of developmental psychology; Hall, whose journals regularly published material of psychopathological interest; Hall, the ramifications of whose psychological influence are most pervasive in fields related to psychopathology . . . (92, p. 430).

Certain other factors might also be mentioned. Before his period as president of Clark University, Hall, while at Johns Hopkins, held weekly clinics at Bay View Hospital and, until its medical staff was organized under his direction, served as lay superintendent. For a period of years he taught and demonstrated for psychiatrists at Worcester State Hospital, handing over the actual instruction in 1895 to Adolf Meyer, but continuing his interest in the field (74). Other students of this period who made substantial contributions to clinical psychology included Blanchard, Conklin, Kuhlmann, and Mateer.

Something of the spirit and activity of the associates of these men may be captured by an examination of the journal that was begun early in the century. *The Journal of Abnormal Psychology*, later called *The Journal of Abnormal and Social Psychology*, was a major source of publication of the more enlightened efforts of its time. Until 1913, when the *Psychoanalytic Review* was founded, it was the only journal in which psychoanalytic papers were published (32). Founded in 1906 for the express purpose of serving both medicine and psychology, it had as its editor Morton Prince, later professor of psychology at Harvard University, and numbered among its associate editors Hugo Münsterberg, James Putnam, August Hoch, Boris Sidis, Charles L. Dana, and Adolf Meyer. The papers in the first issue aptly catch the various influences at work in the psychology and psychiatry of the day. The first is a paper by Janet and thus represents the French psychopathological school; the second concerns hypnosis; the third, a critique of Freud by Putnam (the first article in English calling attention to Freud's work); and the fourth, a paper by Morton Prince concerning his most famous case of multiple personality, Miss Beauchamps. The first book review in this new journal was that of Freud's *Psychopathology of Everyday Life*, which had been published in Germany in 1904. So far as this writer is aware, the first critical article concerning psychoanalysis by an American psychologist appeared in the February 1909 issue of this journal. It was entitled "An Interpretation of the Psychoanalytic Method in Psychotherapy with a Report of a Case so Treated" (90). This is apparently the second instance of a report of personal psychotherapeutic experience by a psychologist.[2] Its author, known for endeavors in fields far removed from this, was Walter Dill Scott, the psychologist, later president of Northwestern University.

The situation in the official psychiatric journal may be used for contrast. The first psychoanalytic paper to appear in the *American Journal of Insanity* was in the October 1909 issue. This paper was by Ernest Jones of Toronto and deplored the fact that Freud's methods had been neglected. None of Freud's books was reviewed in this journal for some years and, indeed, the first review to appear was that of Brill's *Psychoanalysis* in July 1914.

Isador Coriat (32), in presenting some reminiscences of psychoanalysis in Boston, attributes the interest in psychotherapy there to the stimulation of William James. Although A. A. Brill began psychoanalytic practice in New York in 1908, he was the only psychiatrist in the United States at that time engaging in such practice. He, Putnam, and Ernest Jones, then of Toronto, were the first in America to do active work with psychoanalytic methods. The first English translation of a work by Freud, *Selected Papers on Hysteria*, appeared in 1909 according to Coriat (32). It was in this same year that G. Stanley Hall, as president of Clark University, invited both Freud and Jung to come to the United States to lecture on the occasion of the twentieth anniversary of Clark University. Both by attendance and by subsequent publication of these lectures in the *American Journal of Psychology* (51) psychologists became more familiar with their work. In the meantime, Brill (23) was

---

2. Before taking a medical degree, Boris Sidis, then a psychologist, published in 1907 in the *Boston Medical and Surgical Journal* (96) a series of cases of what he called hypnoidal states treated by his particular method of suggestion.

translating Freud's works, and other psychoanalysts began practice. By 1911 there was enough interest that the first psychoanalytic association, the New York Psychoanalytic Society, was founded.

In view of these factors in the history of clinical psychology, it is possible to offer the interpretation that actually it was partly the psychologists and not psychiatrists alone, as is commonly supposed, who offered the first support to psychoanalysis in the United States. To be sure, in the twenties the psychiatrists in increasing numbers became interested and during the following twenty years became so firmly identified with the field that it is only today that psychologists, as psychologists, are again beginning to assume any prominence in psychoanalytic thinking and practice.

THE PSYCHOLOGIST AND THE PSYCHOLOGICAL CLINIC

It has been accepted by psychologists quite generally that the case leading to the founding of the first psychological clinic was treated by Lightner Witmer (114) at the University of Pennsylvania in March 1896. Witmer was the first to speak of the "psychological clinic," of "clinical psychology," and the "clinical method in psychology" (26). The history of his clinic has been discussed elsewhere (26, 27, 93, 107, 114) and is quite well known. It is, therefore, unnecessary to dwell upon it. Instead, after very briefly examining its functioning, attention will be given to the extent of its influence upon the history of clinical psychology.

Even a cursory examination of the early issues of the *Psychological Clinic*, a journal founded and edited by Witmer, will show that the work attempted in this clinic included referral to medical sources, the presence of social workers, and many other "modern" innovations discussed by the writer elsewhere (107). On the other hand, although the juvenile court and social agencies referred cases to Witmer's clinic, the great majority came from the school system. Much attention was paid to the relation of physical defects and neurological conditions to behavior problems. Cooperation with special teachers of the blind and deaf and the mentally defective was stressed. In general, intellectual aspects of children's problems were emphasized, using a biographical approach. Relatively few psychologists published in the *Psychological Clinic* in the early years. Educators, either teachers, principals, or professors, wrote the majority of the articles during this period. In later years the publications of psychologists predominated. The articles are chiefly of antiquarian interest today.

The clinic founded by Seashore (91) at the University of Iowa about 1910 was modeled after Witmer's clinic, and others, such as that founded by J. E. W. Wallin of the University of Pittsburgh in 1912, undoubtedly owe part of their impetus to it, but many other psychological clinics and activities seemed to grow up independently and with little knowledge of the development of this first clinic (97). For example, Seashore (91) speaks of his as the "second" psychological clinic. And yet in 1914 Wallin (105) found about 20 psychological clinics to be in existence, of which some at least must have developed under a different tradition except in the rather unlikely event that the great majority were founded after 1910 but before 1914. Although the Witmer clinic has been functioning continuously since its inception, it is quite difficult to find evidence of its effects upon clinical psychology today. This has not been due to lack of local support; rather it is because its influence did not spread beyond Philadelphia to any considerable degree. The reasons for this relative lack of influence will be discussed after considering a related development: the child guidance movement.

THE PSYCHOLOGIST IN CHILD GUIDANCE

Still another stream which merged into the torrent that is clinical psychology today came from the so-called child guidance movement. In this effort William Healy (59), a psychiatrist, was the most important early figure. The beginnings of this movement arose from the conviction that antisocial behavior was treatable by psychiatric means. A subsequently discarded tenet which went hand in hand with this conviction was an emphasis upon pathology. Hence the first "child guidance" clinic, at the time of its founding in Chicago in 1909, was called "The Juvenile Psychopathic Institute." It is perhaps prophetic that the selection of Healy for the position of director was "as a pupil of James and a free lance in competition with a more rigid Wundtian and experimentally and statistically minded psychologist" (76, p. 242). Its first staff was very small, consisting of Dr. Healy, as psychiatrist, Dr. Grace M. Fernald, as psychologist, and one secretary. It is important to note that no social worker was a paid member of the staff, but Healy indicates that social workers from cooperating agencies worked with them from the very beginning. Only later did the specialty of psychiatric social workers, as such, emerge. Mental testing by Fernald, and later by Augusta F. Bronner, emphasized performance testing and other instruments of local origin. In 1910, however, Healy introduced the Binet-Simon tests into the United States (as did Goddard at Vineland simultaneously and independently). A direct outgrowth of the use of this and other instruments was the publication in 1927 of a *Manual of Individual Tests and Testing* (25) by Bronner, Healy, and their co-workers. Both Healy and Bronner had migrated eastward, organizing in 1917 a clinic in Boston under the name of the Judge Baker Foundation, later changed to the Judge Baker Guidance Center. This venture was enormously successful and resulted in still further important work in the field of delinquency. Many publications, including several books upon problems of the delinquent, had considerable influence upon patterns in this field.

In contrasting the relative success of Healy's venture and its continuity with the present with the relative lack of influence of Witmer's clinic, Shakow (92) presents a thoughtfully detailed statement, one or two points of which can be mentioned. The psychologist Witmer was concerned with intellectual aspects of the functioning individual, worked primarily with mental defectives or school retardation problems, when concerned with medical aspects focused more on the physical or neurological, and, most important of all, identified himself with the Wundt-Kraepelin point of view. On the other hand, the psychiatrist Healy was concerned with affective aspects of the personality, worked primarily with behavior problems and delinquency, when concerned with medical problems stressed the psychiatric, and, again most important of all, was profoundly influenced by James and Freud. Although a pioneer, Witmer turned his back on almost all that was to predominate in the later days of clinical psychology and became of historical significance only. Healy is still a contemporary.

THE PSYCHOLOGIST IN MENTAL HOSPITALS

The importance of McLean Hospital in Waverly, Massachusetts, has never been fully appreciated in the history of psychiatry and psychology. Founded in 1818, its superintendent at the turn of the century was Dr. Edward Cowles, a former surgeon in the Union Army.[3] Years later he took some incidental training in psychology at Johns Hopkins (57). In many ways he was a man ahead of his time. He encouraged research and brought to this hospital biochemists, pathologists, physiologists, and psychologists. One could date the beginnings of conjoint medicine as taking place at McLean Hospital since these approaches were used in its laboratory some time before 1894. In that year Hall described the laborabory as follows: "The work of this laboratory was begun in 1889, for the clinical purposes of the hospital. It is sought to combine neurological studies in the departments of psychiatry and physiological psychology, and their relations with anatomical and chemical pathology, etc." (57, p. 358). Only a quotation from Cowles will bring out the contemporary ring of his words:

> The purpose of establishing and developing the laboratory has been carried on under much difficulty, naturally due to the newness of the attempt to combine with psychiatry the other departments of scientific medical research. The pathology of the terminal stages of insanity must be studied as heretofore, and it is necessary to add that of the initial conditions which lead to mental disorder. Such studies must therefore be combined with physiological psychology in the attempt to determine the exact nature and causes of departures from normal mental function. Also, in the dependence of these changes upon general physiological processes, and in order to take into account all the elements of vital activity involved, it is supremely necessary to study both physiological and pathological chemistry in their direct and indirect relations to mental changes (57, p. 363).

Research efforts along these lines apparently first emerged from this laboratory. In presenting the history of psychiatric research, Whitehorn (111) recognized this contribution and first described McLean Hospital and its work before dealing with any other developments.

Cowles, in a review of the progress in psychiatry at the time of the fiftieth anniversary of the American Psychiatric Association in 1894, emphasized the importance of what he referred to as the systems of "new psychology" as one of the "most hopeful signs of progress" to bring about advancement in the understanding of mental diseases (34). Either as frequent visitors from nearby Boston or as members of the staff of McLean Hospital at this time were

---

3. Shaffer, P. A. Personal communication, 1952.

Morton Prince, August Hoch, Boris Sidis, and Adolf Meyer. Interest in psychology is shown by the fact that Cowles and William Noyes, of the same hospital, were among the approximately 13 to 18 individuals who were present at the founding of the American Psychological Association at Clark University in 1892 (36).

In 1893 August Hoch (75) was selected by Cowles to be psychologist and pathologist at McLean. The use of the term *psychologist* was neither idle nor esoteric. Having previously received a medical education, he now was sent abroad for further training, and it would appear that much of his training was in psychology with Wundt, Külpe, Marbe, and Kiesow. He also worked with Kraepelin. On assuming his post at McLean he turned to work with the ergograph in clinical problems and in the first volume of the *Psychological Bulletin* (62) summed up experimentation in this field. Subsequently, as professor of psychiatry at Cornell and director of the Psychiatric Institute, he turned to more narrowly psychiatric problems, but there would appear to be little doubt that during this period at McLean he functioned, in part at least, as a psychologist.

It was in this atmosphere that a psychological laboratory was founded. This laboratory was begun in 1904 at McLean Hospital by Shepard Ivory Franz (50). It was influential in the *rapprochement* of psychology and psychopathology, although often interested in matters more physiological than psychological. The laboratory became established under the direction of Franz, and on his leaving for what is now St. Elizabeths Hospital of Washington, F. Lyman Wells was appointed his successor and remained there until 1921.

Franz continued his interest while in Washington, not only writing such articles with a modern ring, although published in 1912, as "The Present Status of Psychology in Medical Education and Practice" (25), but also introducing in 1907 a routine clinical psychological examination of all new patients in a mental hospital setting. This was probably the first instance of routine psychological testing of psychiatric hospital patients. Among Franz's associates during the early period were Grace H. Kent and Edwin G. Boring, both of whom published on learning in dementia praecox. Although Boring, as is well known, returned to other fields, he nevertheless felt that the summer he spent in the hospital was a very valuable, broadening experience (22). From 1906 to 1921 Grace H. Kent was psychologist at Philadelphia Hospital, Kings' Park State

Hospital, and St. Elizabeths, respectively. In 1922 she went to Worcester State Hospital, remaining there until 1926 (79). Thereafter, for many years she was at Danvers State Hospital.

THE PSYCHOLOGIST AND INSTITUTIONS FOR THE MENTALLY DEFECTIVE

It was Goddard's laboratory at the Vineland Training School that was the second center to be devoted to the psychological study of the feebleminded.[4] Henry H. Goddard became director of psychological research at this institution in 1906 and was influential in the establishment of the psychologist as a person working with the mentally defective. As mentioned earlier, he first translated and used the Binet in this country. For practical purposes, the use of the Binet was at this time almost exclusively restricted to the feebleminded. It was from this center that the Binet spread to other institutions (84). Goddard's directorship continued until almost the twenties.

PSYCHOLOGY AS A PROFESSION

It was as early as 1904 that Cattell (30) made the prediction that there would eventually be a profession as well as a science of psychology. Actually professional action preceded this pronouncement.

For purposes of this presentation the relevant characteristics of a profession include establishment of commonly agreed upon practices concerning relationship with colleagues and with the public served. The questions of competency and the means of controlling competency immediately arise. Traditionally, a profession controls competency among its own members. Thus, self-determined control of its members is the hallmark of a profession.

The first stirrings of attempts at control arose in the American Psychological Association and took the form of considering control of clinical procedure through evaluation of test data. In 1895, only three years after the founding of the Association, J. Mark Baldwin, in the words of Fernberger, "proposed the formation of a committee

---

4. In 1898 Wylie, a physician, began psychological testing at the state institution for the feebleminded at Faribault, Minnesota (98).

to consider the feasibility of cooperation among the psychological laboratories for the collection of mental and physical statistics" (43, p. 42). The committee that was appointed, chaired by Cattell, called itself "The Committee on Physical and Mental Tests," but the battery of tests they proposed for try-out to develop norms gained little acceptance so that after 1899 no further word was heard from this committee. Another committee for the purpose of establishing methods of testing was appointed in 1907 and continued until 1919. It made some progress, for example, sponsoring research on the Woodworth-Wells Association Tests, but it fell far short of the ostensible goal.

In 1915, on the motion of Guy M. Whipple, the Association went on record as "discouraging" the use of mental tests by unqualified individuals. In 1917 a committee to consider qualifications for psychological examiners was appointed, and two years later one to consider certifying "consulting" psychologists. In 1919 the Section of Clinical Psychology within the American Psychological Association was formed (43). In large measure, it was a "special interest group" concerned wit arranging programs at the annual meetings and the like. Its members were, however, drawn into the discussion, pro and con, of the merits of certification. After much maneuvering, favorable action on certification of clinical psychologists finally resulted, and the first certificates were granted after the 1921 meeting. However, only twenty-five psychologists applied, and the project was abandoned. The death blow was dealt by an APA policy committee which considered that certification was not practicable and, on vote of the APA membership in 1927, discontinued certification. In some measure, at least, the decision was influenced by the realization that with certification went the problem of enforcement of the standards instituted, especially on psychological workers outside the membership. Thereafter, according to Fernberger (43), there was a period of some years without important action within the American Psychological Association on these problems.

Internship training, as distinguished from academic course work, is a manifestation of professional training. Morrow (78) indicates that Lightner Witmer was apparently the first to suggest practical work for the psychologist through training school and laboratory. However, the first actual internships were those offered by the Training School in Vineland, New Jersey, under the supervision of H. H. Goddard. This program began in 1908 and has continued down to the present time. In 1909 William Healy began accepting graduate students at the Juvenile Psychopathic Institute in Chicago, while the first internship in a psychiatric institution for adults was established in 1913 at the Boston Psychopathic Hospital under the direction of Robert M. Yerkes. Other earlier internships include those at Worcester State Hospital, McLean Hospital, the Western State Penitentiary in Pennsylvania, and the New York Institute for Child Guidance.

CLINICAL PSYCHOLOGY IN THE TWENTIES AND THIRTIES

In the twenties and thirties clinical psychology left the period of its lusty, disorganized infancy and entered its rather undernourished but rapid and stormy adolescence. As late as 1918 only 15 members or 4 percent of the APA listed the field of clinical psychology as a research interest (44). This rose to 99 members or 19 percent in 1937. In that year the newly instituted membership category of Associate showed 428 or 28 percent interested in clinical psychology, the largest field of interest for this class of membership. In increasing numbers clinical psychologists were employed in hospitals, clinics, schools, penal institutions, social agencies, homes for the feeble-minded, industrial plants, and the entire gamut of agencies concerned with human welfare. For example, Finch and Odoroff (46), in a survey concerning employment trends, indicate that of 1,267 members of the American Psychological Association in 1931, 286 or 26.9 percent were not in teaching positions. In 1940 the number of nonteachers had swelled to 888 or 39.3 percent of the membership. Clinical nonteachers increased from 95 to 272 during this ten-year period.

It was during this period that many psychologists did yeoman service for clinical psychology without being primarily identified with the field. Carl E. Seashore (91) may be used as an illustration. It has already been noted that he founded a psychological clinic at the University of Iowa about 1910. During the period now under consideration he was interested in the relationship between psychology and psychiatry and took the lead in organizing a national conference on this topic. He also aided in founding the Iowa Psychopathic Hospital and worked with Samuel Orton, Edward Lee Travis, and Wendell Johnson in speech pathology. Many other men such as

Gardner Murphy, Goodwin Watson, Horace B. English, Albert T. Poffenberger, Kurt Lewin, Carney Landis, Robert M. Yerkes, Walter R. Miles, Gordon W. Allport, and Kurt Goldstein, although primarily associated with some other aspect of psychology, also performed services for the clinical field.

In spite of such developments as those just described, Loutitt (70) could indicate during the same period that "American Psychology, generally speaking, has not been greatly interested in practical problems of human behavior" (70, p. 361). This contention applied to clinical psychology with as much force as, or more than, it did to other applications of psychology. Most of the difficulties that clinical psychology went through during this period as it groped toward professional stature were internal to the field itself. Both rapid growth and some hostility from the dominant entrenched forces in psychology are imbedded in the history of the period and influence many of the specific developments now to be discussed.

The Psychometric Tradition. The period of the twenties was, in the words of Merrill, a "plateau . . . [following] the initial impetus given to testing when these first tools of the clinician were being subjected to evaluation, and the exaggerated expectations of over-enthusiastic users were being reduced in the crucibles of research" (73, p. 283). Studies of validity, investigations of the constancy of IQ, applications of the tests to new populations, studies of individual differences, the nature-nurture controversy, racial differences, the development of group testing, achievement tests, interest measures, and personality testing of the questionnaire variety occupied this and the following decade and helped to consolidate the gains of the previous period. Theories of intelligence and factor analysis are also intimately related to this trend. It was a period, as the term plateau implies, of masked gain which prepared the way for the present period.

More and more objections began to be raised to the limitations entailed by this approach. The development of group tests during and after World War I placed a premium on easy reproduction, rigid standardization down to the slightest detail, and emphasis on the score obtained to the exclusion of all else. Measures of personality with these same characteristics were developed during the twenties and thirties. To some psychologists the results obtained were considered disappointing and sterile.

In 1927 F. L. Wells published *Mental Tests in Clinical Practice*

(108), in which he stated vividly the major objection to a rigid psychometric approach:

> An intelligent South Sea Islander, observing a psychometric examination, would be likely to regard it as a magic rite designed to propitiate friendly spirits in the patient's behalf. Should he observe a conscientious examiner in the apprentice stage, tightly clinging to forms prescribed, his idea would be confirmed, for none knows better than himself how slight a departure from the required formulae will not only destroy their beneficence but may well deliver the hapless sufferer into the hands of the malignant ghosts. Over against such esoteric views of psychometric methods is the customary and pragmatic one. The function of psychometrics is not the accomplishment of a ritual, but the understanding of the patient. The ceremony of mental tests is valuable so far as it serves to reach this end. When it fails, or stands in the way of doing this, proper technique demands that it be modified. Ability to do this intelligentely is what distinguishes the psychologist, properly so called, from the "mental tester" (108, p. 27).

Further objections to exclusive reliance upon a psychometric approach arose with the emergence of projective techniques as an aspect of the dynamic tradition next to be considered.

The Dynamic Tradition. Many of the present developments in clinical psychology—the emphasis on understanding of personality functioning, the attempt to relate present behavior to experiences of which the patient is unaware, the evaluative use of incidental verbalizations and physical behavior of the patient, and the artistic element in psychodiagnostic appraisal—stem in large measure from the dynamic tradition.

In terms of the sources of these influences, Sigmund Freud, of course, looms largest. He and his fellow analysts profoundly affected the thinking of many clinical psychologists, who were for the most part passive recipients of this influence. No longer did they share leadership with their medical colleagues as during the first twenty years of the century. The influence of psychoanalysis was felt directly on three of the specific manifestations of the dynamic tradition directly involving the psychologist—projective techniques, the Harvard Psychological Clinic, and the American Orthopsychiatric Association. The first, an approach to personality, the second, a clinic, and the third, a professional organization, share responsibility as the most important manifestations of the dynamic tradition in psychology of the day. Each will be considered in turn.

Hermann Rorschach, a Swiss psychiatrist, published with

Oberholzer on the specific but intricate relationships which exist between his inkblot technique and psychoanalysis. The technique itself occupied much of his time between 1911 and his untimely death in 1922. In the United States pioneering work with the Rorschach was done by David M. Levy, a child psychiatrist, with whom Samuel J. Beck became associated beginning in 1927. In 1930 Beck presented the first Rorschach study in this country as his doctoral dissertation, and during the thirties the Rorschach technique came more and more into prominence in clinical circles. Along with Beck, pioneer American psychologists who made major contributions to Rorschach literature during this period were Bruno Klopfer, Marguerite Hertz, and Zygmunt Piotrowski.

Two reasons are given by Beck (18) for the increasing preoccupation of psychologists with the Rorschach technique as compared to psychiatrists. There is, first, the division of labor with the Rorschach as one of the diagnostic testing instruments and, second, the fact that its use spread outside the narrowly psychiatric area into the schools, work with delinquents, industry, and the like. Other projective techniques, notably the Thematic Apperception Test, also appeared during the thirties.

In the meantime the psychodynamic emphasis began to be a part of the intellectual armamentarium of the psychologist. The article by L. K. Frank, "Projective Methods for the Study of Personality" (48), published in 1939, offered a rationale for the projective approach and stimulated both research and theoretical efforts in the decades to follow. Merrill summarizes other reasons for the rapid spread of projective testing as having

> . . . had to do with significant changes that have been occurring in the clinician's self-concept and his changing perception of his role as his social responsibilities grow and expand. Projective tests have become important tools for the psychotherapists. These tests command the attention and respect of our colleagues in the medical fraternity, the psychiatrists. They constitute moreover, the basic technological structure upon which is being built a new systematic point of view, projective psychology with its own theory of personality. This new projective psychology has been aptly characterized as a psychology of protest. As both behaviorism and Gestalt psychology came about as protests against the established psychologies called structural, so this emerging projective psychology runs sharply counter to the traditions that have characterized individual psychology in America. Having something to push against, it can move (73, p. 286).

In 1927 the Harvard Psychological Clinic was founded by

Morton Prince. Its express purpose was to bring together academic and clinical psychology. Henry A. Murray took over headship of the clinic early in the thirties and with a large group of collaborators, including Donald W. MacKinnon, Saul Rosenzweig, R. Nevitt Sanford, and Robert W. White, carried on a brilliant research project in personality functioning. This culminated in 1938 in the well-known *Explorations in Personality* (81).

The American Orthopsychiatric Association is an organization with ties to child guidance in particular and to the dynamic tradition in general. It was founded in 1924 with many of the leaders of the child guidance movement present (71). William Healy was elected president during this year and served through 1926. Later presidents included Karl Menninger, David Levy, and, in 1931, the first psychologist to be president, Augusta F. Bronner. Other psychologist presidents were Edgar A. Doll, Samuel Beck, and Morris Krugman. After thinking through the problem of membership, originally restricted to psychiatrists, the pattern emerged in 1926 of having as full members "psychiatrists, psychologists, and other professional persons whose work and interest lie in the study and treatment of conduct disorders" (71, p. 199). Both the letter and the spirit of this method of organization for work interchange, support, and advance have continued to the present day. However, there has never been any question, as might have been foretold from the original organization, but that psychiatrists were dominant in it. For example, twenty-one of the first twenty-six presidents held the M.D. degree, only four being psychologists and only one a social worker. This organization continues to wield much influence both through its journal, *The American Journal of Orthopsychiatry*, and through its annual meetings, which are characteristically attended by far more nonmembers than members.

Psychological Clinics. This was a period during which psychological clinics reflected the plateau of the psychometric tradition. Some new clinics appeared; others closed their doors (70). In 1934 a survey report of a questionnaire of psychoeducational clinics by Witty and Theman (115) appeared. On the basis of their returns they estimated that there were about 50 such clinics. This figure may be contrasted with the approximately 20 found by Wallin in 1914 (105). In 1932 the median length of time the clinics had been in existence was four years. Located in colleges, universities, teachers colleges, and normal schools, their stated purposes involved (a) providing schools, social agencies, and individuals with diagnostic test services and remedial methods in order to bring about educational, vocational, and social adjustment; (b) training students in giving and interpreting tests; and (c) research with emphasis on the study of deviates, causes and treatment of learning difficulties, and work with remedial materials. It would appear that this survey epitomizes the work of psychological clinics of the day, featuring emphasis on testing and remedial education.

Child Guidance. The period 1922–1927 was one in which the National Committee for Mental Hygiene on behalf of the Commonwealth Fund established demonstration clinics in a variety of cities and rural areas for the purpose of showing both their need and the work they could do (99). For the first time they were called "child guidance clinics." Eight clinics were permanently established directly as a result, and many others were at least partially stimulated by this effort. It was the announced intention from the very beginning that eventually expenses for their maintenance would be absorbed by the community in which they were located. Deliberate experimentation as to method of organization in relation to other agencies was carried out—some were attached to the courts, others to local charities, to university and to teaching hospitals. The child guidance clinic plan of organization called for the professional personnel to include at least a psychiatrist, a psychologist, and a social worker. These activities in their formative stages continued roughly over the decade 1920–1930. To be sure, their influence and organization continued thereafter, but this period marked the heyday of their unique contribution.

An important shift of focus of attention had been occurring during this period. No longer was the delinquent of primary interest. Nor was there much concern with mental defectives, epileptics, or neurological cases. Instead, emphasis was placed upon maladjustment in school and home, especially that centering around parent-child relationships. The clinics began to concentrate upon problems of the individual who may be spoken of as falling within the normal range of intelligence, the roots of which may in some measure be traced to emotional difficulties.

The Psychologist in Mental Hospitals. In 1921 Wells left McLean Hospital for Boston Psychopathic Hospital, where he served as head psychologist until 1938. This hospital also became a center of clinical activity and training. A pioneer in present-day clinical psychology, David Shakow, now of the Illinois Neuropsychiatric Institute, is still very active. For a period of nearly twenty years, Shakow served as director of psychological research at Worcester State Hospital. His activities, along with his research efforts, included direction of an internship training program. It apparently was the closest in spirit to the modern internship program, and his experience derived in this setting was of great value in formulating present-day practices concerning internship.

A gradual increase in the number of clinical psychologists in mental hospitals was taking place. However, the geographical isolation of most such hospital psychologists apparently accentuated an isolation on other grounds so that the effect of this aspect of the development of clinical psychology was not as important as it was to be in the decades to come. Nevertheless, some psychologists were beginning to suspect that their approach was unduly limited. As a result, there were serious attempts at broadening the scope of testing efforts, to escape the atomistic tradition by means of search and theorizing concerning the personality of their patients.

Mental Deficiency. In 1919 Goddard was succeeded by Stanley D. Porteus as director of the Vineland Laboratory. Under both his direction and the subsequent direction from 1925 until 1949 of Edgar A. Doll the clinical problems of feeblemindedness received intensive and extensive study.

It was precisely in the field of intelligence testing that clinical psychology was most advanced during this period. Psychometric testing of suspected mental deficiency was widely accepted, and the psychologist was the authority in this field (28). Nevertheless, as Buck (28) indicates, appreciation of the complexity, rather than the simplicity, of the diagnosis of mental deficiency emerged during these two decades.

The fact that a person was doing clinical psychological work with mental defectives unfortunately indicated almost nothing about the nature of the training and experience of the practitioner in question. In 1940 Hackbusch (56) reported an inquiry concerning psychological work in state and private institutions for the mentally defective. Of the approximately 100 institutions which replied, apparently all were doing some form of psychological testing. However, less than half had a psychologist on their staff. The remainder had their testing done by outside sources, or by teachers, social workers, and physicians on their own staffs. It is also noteworthy that the "psychologists" apparently varied widely in the nature of their background. Some had less than an A.B. degree, while others had an A.B. or an M.A. in addition, but very few held the Ph.D. degree. Therefore, despite the acceptance of their work, the status of psychologists and psychological work in the twenties and thirties was somewhat confused.

Psychology as a Profession. The origins of professional activity, as has been indicated, were centered within the American Psychological Association. This period extended from 1895 to the mid-twenties. Founded to advance psychology as a *science,* the Association had not been singularly successful in reflecting the interests of its members either in applications of psychology or in their professional aspirations. The twenties and thirties were characterized by the advent of other organizations more directly concerned with professional problems.

In 1917 a group of psychologists interested in the advancement of the practice of psychology met in Pittsburgh, Pennsylvania. Leta S. Hollingworth took the initiative in bringing the group together, and prominent charter members included Bronner, Fernald, Healy, Kuhlmann, Pintner, Terman, Whipple, Wells, and Yerkes. To quote Symonds, "After a brief history of two years, during which a bitter struggle went on in the American Psychological Association over the question of authority for certification of psychologists for clinical work, the American Association of Clinical Psychologists became defunct through the adoption by the APA of a report recommending the establishment of the AACP as a Section of Clinical Psychology" (100, p. 337). According to the same writer, the next step was the slow development of various local groups concerned with applied and professional matters in several states.

In 1930 the Association of Consulting Psychologists was reorganized from a still earlier association founded in 1921 (40, 52). Gradually it extended its membership beyond New York and environs and became one of the more important elements later to merge into the American Association for Applied Psychology (AAAP). The organization meeting of this association took place in 1937. Many of the difficulties in organizing centered upon the standards for membership. Then, as now, there was the dilemma of maintaining standards and yet not setting them so high as to exclude the majority of those doing work in the applied fields. Eventually this was settled, and a national organization concerned with all aspects of the application of psychology came into being and became the dominant national professional organization. A divisional structure was followed with clinical, educational, industrial, and consulting sections.

The Journal of Consulting Psychology was at first a publication of the Association of Consulting Psychologists and then of the AAAP. Papers in clinical, educational, industrial, and consulting psychology appeared, but a considerable portion of space was devoted to organizational and professional matters (100).

Thus, there existed at the close of the thirties two major psychological societies—one dedicated to the advancement of psychology as a science and the other to its application. Generally speaking, members of the latter also had membership in the former but sincerely felt the essential nature of their applied organization. The Psychometric Society and the Society for the Psychological Study of Social Issues were also founded during this period. In part, at least, these organizations arose because of similar dissatisfaction with the adequacy of representation of some of their interests in the American Psychological Association. So the thirties closed with at least the possibility of dangerous rifts in the ranks of psychologists. However, as is well known, this danger passed in the forties with all of these organizations integrated into the reorganized American Psychological Association (116). In 1945 this reorganization went into effect. Both in spirit and in practice the American Psychological Association represents psychology as a science and as a profession.

The Psychologist and Therapy. During the twenties and thirties there appeared to be a gradual increase in the number of clinical psychologists engaging in therapy. From the time of Sidis and Scott at the turn of the century some psychologists had been so employed. In many instances psychotherapeutic practice grew out of the psychologist's educational function. Considered as expert both in matters of learning as a subject of investigation and in education as a field of endeavor, the psychologist worked with patients, particularly with children, with whom remedial education was necessary. A similar process took place to a lesser extent in psychiatric clinics. It was in the hospitals that this development lagged, partly because the sheer press of numbers of patients confined the psychologists to psychodiagnostic tasks and partly because psychotherapy, except at a few institutions, was not practiced at all.

There was relatively little difficulty in interprofessional

relations with psychiatry during this period. In large measure this was because there were few psychologists practicing therapy, and these few were doing so under institutional auspices and exceptional circumstances. Then, too, the psychiatrist himself was more isolated both from his medical colleagues and from the public than he is today. More concerned with the psychotic and the adult than with the neurotic and the child, his path did not as often cross that of the psychologist as it did in the forties and fifties.

No continuity in the development of psychotherapists among psychologists is discernible from generation to generation. Neither Sidis nor Scott stimulated psychologists to work with psychotherapeutic problems. In later years individual psychologists prominent in psychotherapy gained in stature, not unaided to be sure, but also not from the combined efforts of any group or from the work of one senior individual. Phyllis Blanchard, for example, an acknowledged leading therapist, as attested to by her presence in leading symposia and by books on the topic, neither received her training in therapy from psychologists nor participated in the training of psychologists in therapy. Other therapist-psychologists, also, developed along individual lines. The work of Carl Rogers, although begun in the thirties, did not reach national prominence until the forties.

PSYCHOLOGISTS IN THE ARMED SERVICES AND THEIR EFFECT UPON PSYCHOLOGY IN THE POSTWAR PERIOD[5]

About 1,500 psychologists served in the armed services during World War II. About one out of four psychologists thus was called upon to function in an applied field—that is, psychology applied to the very practical problem of war. Moreover, this group was predominantly young, averaging about 32 years of age (24), thus including many individuals just reaching professional maturity. It is not unduly optimistic to suppose that some of their experiences during these tours of duty carried over in attitude and practice to the postwar years.

To appreciate properly certain changes of attitude, it must be remembered that a considerable number of psychologists in uniform

---

5. This section of the article is a modification of a section of a chapter in a book edited by the writer (106). The permission of Harper and Brothers, publishers, to include this section is acknowledged gratefully.

were products of an academic tradition whose isolationist tendencies in regard to professional application prior to the war they were quite willingly and even complacently furthering. In fact, Andrews and Dreese (16) found that almost 90 percent of the psychologists in military service were in academic or governmental work prior to the war.

From the process of learning to apply their psychological training to the military situation, later consideration revealed at least two major trends that have had, and will continue to have, profound effect upon contemporary psychology. They discovered to their mild surprise, and to the considerable amazement of their colleagues from other disciplines, that their general training in psychological methods was capable of application to many problems which at first seemed utterly alien to their background. From aircraft instrument-panel design to selecting underwater demolition teams, psychologists found that they, in collaboration with specialists from other fields, had something valuable to contribute. Realization was forced upon them that an experimental background in psychology is capable of transfer to intelligent and capable handling of many sorts of problems.

Paradoxically, however, they gained added respect for the clinical approach. In this connection it must be realized that almost half of the psychologists used clinical and counseling procedures during some part of their period in uniform (24). Many psychologists, willy-nilly, were placed in a position where they functioned in selection and assignment, sat as members of discharge boards, worked as members of clinical teams, conducted therapeutic sessions, both group and individual, and in these and many other ways used diagnostic and treatment methods. Concrete expressions of this interest can be found in an article by Britt and Morgan (24) concerning the results obtained from a questionnaire mailed to every psychologist in uniform. They conclude that there was an overwhelming interest in having more practical postwar graduate training. Nearly 24 percent of the suggestions for new courses for graduate study were clearly within the general clinical field. At least some of the armed services psychologists who had previously not been particularly receptive came to understand and appreciate the contributions, past and potential, of the clinical method. This impression is verified by the finding in a survey by Andrews and Dreese (16) that three times as many military psychologists engaged in clinical work after the war as had done so in the prewar period.

CLINICAL PSYCHOLOGY TODAY

With the coming of the forties and World War II, one leaves the realm of history and enters the present. It would be both hazardous and presumptuous to attempt to trace in detail the events from this time on. Nevertheless, certain factors in the foregoing account may be related to present trends. Clinical psychology as a method, as an attitude, and as a field of endeavor is reflected in its past.

It would appear that clinical psychology and academic psychology have influenced each other markedly, with a reciprocal, symbiotic relationship having been formed. Other disciplines, notably the medical and particularly the psychiatric and psychoanalytic, influenced and vitalized clinical psychology.

Through the thirties certain predominant aspects may be referred to as "child," "psychological," and "clinical" as contrasted with "adult," "psychiatric," and "institutional" functions. Distinctively psychological clinics and work with children are not only important because of their service and scientific value, but also for the community orientation that they manifest and the preventive emphasis that they maintain. And yet since the thirties the emphasis has shifted.

The "adult," "psychiatric," and "institutional" aspects of clinical psychology appear to be dominant today, but this is by no means an unmixed blessing. Many of the more vocal leaders of the field, including to some extent the official committees of the American Psychological Association, have fostered emphasis upon the former. The extremely valuable support rendered by the Veterans Administration to our training and practice has emphasized the current trend. Work with adults in a psychiatrically oriented institution is a specialty, albeit an important one, in the broader field.

With the forties also came the domination in the history of clinical psychology of one of the trends previously sketched. This was the emergence and implementation of a concept of a profession of psychology. One illustration will suffice. Until after World War II, there was relatively little demonstrable agreement about the training, nature, duties, or status of the clinical psychologist. To quote

Eysenck, "A person who called himself a "clinical psychologist' might be someone of great eminence, highly qualified academically and with 20 or 30 years of practical experience in the fields of diagnostic testing, research, and therapy, or he might be a student just graduated from the University, without any kind of relevant experience, capable only of grinding out Binet I.Q.'s without even an adequate understanding of their relevance to the clinical problem presented" (41, p. 711). The facet of the professionalization of a psychologist, although not completely defined today, has reached a degree of precise formulation undreamed of a few years ago.

Current issues and accomplishments, stabilizing trends, and unresolved problems may be related to the emergence of psychology as a profession. Factors making for the present stabilization include the agreement of the great majority of interested parties concerning diagnostic appraisal as a task of the clinical psychologist (7, 9, 12, 55, 94), the present organization and function of the American Psychological Association (4, 116), current efforts directed toward the training of clinical psychologists (9, 10, 12, 14), present activities looking toward codification of ethical problems (5, 6, 17, 21, 61), and the influence of such institutions as the American Board of Examiners in Professional Psychology (2, 3), state societies (11), the United States Public Health Service (42, 104), the Veterans Administration (1, 58, 103), and the armed services (102). On the other hand, currently unresolved issues face the profession today. The problems on which there are differences of opinion both in psychology and in other professions include psychotherapy as a task of the psychologist and the nature of the relation of psychology to psychiatry and medicine (7, 13, 54, 55, 72, 87, 94), the nature of the relation of psychology to social work (33), the question of the advisability of certification and licensure (31, 47, 60, 109, 112, 117), the question of the desirability of private practice (38, 39), the position and function of non-Ph.D.'s in clinical psychology (15, 20, 35, 67, 69, 98), and the "imbalance" in psychology between scientific and professional demands (63, 87, 88, 89). Not only do these problems have roots in the past, but they are also an expression of the period of professionalization of large segments of psychology today.

World War II focused the needs and demonstrated what could be done in clinical psychology; the period after the war is still feeling the pressure of these social needs and is witnessing the reactions, adaptive and otherwise, of a beginning profession to these demands.

REFERENCES

1. Adler, M. H., Futterman, S., and Webb, R. Activities of the mental hygiene clinics of the Veterans Administration. *J. Clin. Psychopath.*, 1948, 9, 517-527.
2. American Board of Examiners in Professional Psychology, Inc. *Official Bulletin*, 1948, No. 1.
3. American Board of Examiners in Professional Psychology. The work of the American Board of Examiners in Professional Psychology: annual report of the Board to the members of the APA. *Amer. Psychologist*, 1951, 6, 620-625.
4. American Psychological Association. By-laws for the American Psychological Association (as amended through September, 1951). In *Directory, American Psychological Association*. Washington, D.C.: American Psychological Association, 1951.
5. American Psychological Association. *Ethical Standards for psychologists*. Vol. 1: *The code of ethics*. Washington, D.C.: American Psychological Association, 1952.
6. American Psychological Association. *Ethical standards of psychologists*. Vol. 2: *Source book of ethical problems, incidents, and principles*. Washington, D.C.: American Psychological Association, 1952.
7. American Psychological Association, *Ad Hoc* Committee on Relations between Psychology and the Medical Profession. Psychology and its relationships with other professions. *Amer. Psychologist*, 1952, 7, 145-152.
8. American Psychological Association, Committee of Clinical Section. I. The definition of clinical psychology and standards of training for clinical psychologists. II. Guide to psychological clinics in the United States. *Psychol. Clin.*, 1935, 23, 2-140.
9. American Psychological Association, Committee on Training in Clinical Psychology. Recommended graduate training program in clinical psychology. *Amer. Psychologist*, 1947, 2, 539-558.
10. American Psychological Association, Committee on Training in Clinical Psychology. Annual report of the Committee on Training in Clinical Psychology. *Amer. Psychologist*, 1951, 6, 612-617.
11. American Psychological Association, Conference of State Psychological Associations. *CSPA Newsletter*, April, 1952. (Mimeo.)
12. American Psychological Association, Conference on Graduate Education in Clinical Psychology, Boulder, Colorado. *Training in clinical psychology*. New York: Prentice Hall, 1950.
13. American Psychological Association, Divisiosn of Clinical and Abnormal Psychology, Committee

on Psychotherapy. Report. *Newsletter, Div. clin. abnorm. Psychol.*, 1950, *4*, No. 2, Suppl. (Mimeo.)
14. American Psychological Association, Education and Training Board. Doctoral training programs in clinical psychology. *Amer. Psychologist*, 1952, *7*, 158.
15. American Psychological Association, Policy and Planning Board. Annual report: 1951. *Amer. Psychologist*, 1951, *6*, 531–540.
16. Andrews, T. G., and Dreese, M. Military utilization of psychologists during World War II. *Amer. Psychologist*, 1948, *3*, 533–538.
17. Anon. Discussion on ethics: a little recent history. *Amer. Psychologist*, 1952, *7*, 426–428.
18. Beck. S. J. Rorschach's test in this anniversary year. In L. G. Lowrey (Ed.), *Orthopsychiatry, 1923–1948: retrospect and prospect*. New York: American Orthopsychiatric Association, 1948. Pp. 422–455.
19. Beers, C. W. *A mind that found itself*. New York: Longmans Green, 1908.
20. Black, J. D. A survey of employment in psychology and the place of personnel without the Ph.D. *Amer. Psychologist*, 1949, *4*, 38–42.
21. Bobbitt, J. M. Some arguments for a code of ethics. *Amer. Psychologist*, 1952, *7*, 428–429.
22. Boring, E. G. Edwin Garrigues Boring. In E. G. Boring, H. S. Langfeld, H. Werner, and R. M. Yerkes (Eds.), *A history of psychology in autobiography*. Vol. IV. Worcester: Clark Univer. Press, 1952. Pp. 27–52.
23. Brill, A. A. Introduction. In A. A. Brill (Ed.), *The basic writings of Sigmund Freud*. New York: Modern Library, 1938. Pp. 3–32.
24. Britt, S. H., and Morgan, Jane D. Military psychologists in World War II. *Amer. Psychologist*, 1946, *1*, 423–437.
25. Bronner, Augusta F., Healy, W., Lowe, Gladys M., and Shimberg, Myra E. *A manual of individual mental tests and testing*. Boston: Little Brown, 1927.
26. Brotemarkle, R. A. (Ed.) *Clinical psychology: studies in honor of Lightner Witmer*. Philadelphia: Univer. of Pennsylvania Press, 1931.
27. Brotemarkle, R. A. Clinical psychology 1896–1946. *J. consult. Psychol.*, 1947, *11*, 1–4.
28. Buck, J. N. The present and future status of the psychologist in the field of mental deficiency. *Amer. J. ment. Def.*, 1949–1950, *54*, 225–229.
29. Cattell, J. M. Mental tests and measurements. *Mind*, 1890, *15*, 373–381.
30. Cattell, J. M. Retrospect: psychology as a profession. *J. consult. Psychol.*, 1937. *1*, 1–3; 1946, *10*, 289–291.
31. Combs, A. W. A report of the 1951 licensing effort in New York State. *Amer. Psychologist*, 1951, *6*, 541–548.
32. Coriat, I. H. Some personal reminiscences of psychoanalysis in Boston: an autobiographical note. *Psychoanal. Rev.*, 1945, *32*, 1–8.
33. Cowan, E. A. Correspondence. *J. consult. Psychol.*, 1945, *9*, 64–65.
34. Cowles, E. Progress during the half century. *Amer. J. Insanity*, 1894, *51*, 10–22.
35. Darley, J. G., Elliott, R. M.,

Hathaway, S. R., and Paterson, D. Are psychologists without Ph.D. degrees to be barred from membership in the APA? *Amer. Psychologist*, 1948, *3*, 51-53.

36. Dennis, W., and Boring, E. G. The founding of the APA. *Amer. Psychologist*, 1952, *7*, 95-97.

37. Doll, E. A. (Ed.) *Twenty five years: a memorial volume in commemoration of the 25th anniversary of the Vineland Laboratory, 1906-1931.* (Publ. Ser. 1932.)

38. Ellis, A. The psychologist in private practice and the good profession. *Amer. Psychologist*, 1952, *7*, 129-131.

39. Ellis, A. (Chm.) Report of the Committee on Private Practice. *Newsletter, Div. clin. abnorm. Psychol.*, 1952, *5*, No. 4. (Mimeo.)

40. English, H. B. Organization of the American Association of Applied Psychologists. *J. consult. Psychol.*, 1938, *2*, 7-16.

41. Eysenck, H. J. Function and training of the clinical psychologist. *J. ment. Sci.*, 1950, *96*, 710-725.

42. Federal Security Agency. *National Mental Health Act. Five years of progress, 1946-1951.* Washington, D.C.: 1951. (Mimeo.)

43. Fernberger, S. W. The American Psychological association: a historical summary, 1892-1930. *Psychol. Bull.*, 1932, *29*, 1-89.

44. Fernberger, S. W. The scientific interests and scientific publications of the members of the American Psychological Association. *Psychol. Bull.*, 1938, *35*, 261-281.

45. Fernberger, S. W. The American Psychological Association, 1892-1942. *Psychol. Rev.*, 1943, *50*, 33-60.

46. Finch, F. H., and Odoroff, M. E. Employment trends in applied psychology. *J. consult. Psychol.*, 1941, *5*, 275-278.

47. Fowerbaugh, C. C. Legal status of psychologists in Ohio. *J. consult. Psychol.*, 1945, *9*, 196-200.

48. Frank, L. K. Projective methods for the study of personality. *J. Psychol.*, 1939, *8*, 389-413.

49. Franz, S. I. The present status of psychology in medical education and practice. *J. Amer. med. Ass.*, 1912, *58*, 909-911.

50. Franz, S. I. Shepard Ivory Franz. In C. Murchison (Ed.), *A history of psychology in autobiography.* Vol. II. Worcester: Clark Univer. Press, 1932. Pp. 89-113.

51. Freud, S. The origin and development of psychoanalysis. *Amer. J. Psychol.*, 1910, *21*, 181-218.

52. Fryer, D. (Chm.) The proposed American Association for Applied and Professional Psychologists. *J. consult. Psychol.*, 1937, *1*, 14-16.

53. Galton, F. *Inquiries into human faculty and its development.* London: J. M. Dent, 1883.

54. Gregg, A. The profession of psychology as seen by a doctor of medicine. *Amer. Psychologist*, 1948, *9*, 397-401.

55. Group for the Advancement of Psychiatry, Committee on Clinical Psychology. The relation of clinical psychology to psychiatry. *Amer. J. Orthopsychiat.*, 1950, *22*, 346-354.

56. Hackbusch, Florentine. Responsibility of the American Association on Mental Deficiency for developing uniform psychological practices in schools for mental defectives. *Amer. J. ment. Def.*, 1940-41, *45*, 233-237.

57. Hall, G. S. Laboratory of the McLean Hospital. *Amer. J. Insanity*, 1894, *51*, 358-364.
58. Hawley, P. R. The importance of clinical psychology in a complete medical program. *J. consult. Psychol.*, 1946, *10*, 292-300.
59. Healy, W., and Bronner, Augusta F. The child guidance clinic: birth and growth of an idea. In L. G. Lowrey (Ed.), *Orthopsychiatry, 1923-1948: retrospect and prospect.* New York: American Orthopsychiatric Association, 1948. Pp. 14-49.
60. Heiser, K. F. The need for legislation and the complexities of the problem. *Amer. Psychologist*, 1950, *5*, 104, 108.
61. Hobbs, N. The development of a code of ethical standards for psychology. *Amer. Psychologist*, 1948, *3*, 80-84.
62. Hoch, A. A review of psychological and physiological experiments done in connection with the study of mental diseases. *Psychol. Bull.*, 1904, *1*, 241-257.
63. Hunt, W. A. Clinical psychology—science or superstition. *Amer. Psychologist*, 1952, *6*, 683-688.
64. James, H. (Ed.) *The letters of William James.* Vol. II. Boston: Atlantic Monthly Press, 1920.
65. James, W. *The principles of psychology.* New York: Holt, 1890.
66. James, W. *The varieties of religious experience.* New York: Longmans Green, 1902.
67. Kelly, G. A. Single level versus legislation for different levels of psychological training and experience. *Amer. Psychologist*, 1950, *5*, 109, 111.
68. Kraepelin, E. *Lehrbuch der Psychiatrie.* Leipzig: Verlag von Johann Ambrosius Barth, 1899.
69. Longstaff, H. P., Speer, G. S., McTeer, W., and Hartson, L. D. A survey of psychologists in four midwestern states. *Amer. Psychologist*, 1950, *5*, 422-423.
70. Louttit, C. M. The nature of clinical psychology. *Psychol. Bull.*, 1939, *36*, 361-389.
71. Lowrey, L. G. The birth of orthopsychiatry. In L. G. Lowrey (Ed.), *Orthopsychiatry, 1923-1948: retrospect and prospect.* New York: American Orthopsychiatric Association, 1948. Pp. 190-216.
72. Menninger, W. C. The relationship of clinical psychology and psychiatry. *Amer. Psychologist*, 1950, *5*, 3-15.
73. Merrill, Maude A. Oscillation and progress in clinical psychology. *J. consult. Psychol.*, 1951, *15*, 281-289.
74. Meyer, A. G. Stanley Hall, Ph.D., LL.D. *Amer. J. Psychiat.*, 1924-25, *81*, 151-153.
75. Meyer, A. August Hoch, M.D. *Arch. Neurol. Psychiat.*, 1919, *2*, 573-576.
76. Meyer, A. Organization of community facilities for prevention, care, and treatment of nervous and mental diseases. *Proc. First Inter. Cong. Ment. Hyg.*, 1932, *1*, 237-257.
77. Morris, L. *William James: the message of a modern mind.* New York: Scribners, 1950.
78. Morrow, W. R. The development of psychological internship training. *J. consult. Psychol.*, 1946, *10*, 165-183.
79. Murchison, C. (Ed.) *The psychological register.* (2 vols.) Worcester: Clark Univer. Press, 1929, 1932.
80. Murphy, G. *Historical introduction to modern psychology.*

(Rev. Ed.) New York: Harcourt Brace, 1949.
81. Murray, H. A., *et al. Explorations in personality: a clinical and experimental study of fifty men of college age.* New York: Oxford Univer. Press, 1938.
82. Norsworthy, Naomi. The psychology of mentally deficient children. *Arch. Psychol., N.Y.,* 1906, No. 1.
83. Peterson, J. *Early conceptions and tests of intelligence.* Yonkers, N.Y.: World Book Co., 1925.
84. Pintner, R. *Intelligence testing: methods and results.* (New Ed.) New York: Holt, 1931.
85. Pintner, R., and Paterson, D. G. *A scale of performance tests.* New York: Appleton-Century, 1917.
86. Roback, A. A. *History of American psychology.* New York: Library Publishers, 1952.
87. Rogers, C. R. Where are we going in clinical psychology? *J. consult. Psychol.,* 1951, *15,* 171-177.
88. Rosenzweig, S. Imbalance in clinical psychology. *Amer. Psychologist,* 1950, *5,* 678-680.
89. Rosenzweig, S. Balance in clinical psychology: a symposium in correspondence. *Amer. Psychologist,* 1951, *6,* 208-212.
90. Scott, W. D. An interpretation of the psycho-analytic method in psychotherapy with a report of a case so treated. *J. abnorm. Psychol.,* 1909, *3,* 371-377.
91. Seashore, C. E. *Pioneering in psychology.* Iowa City, Iowa: Univer. of Iowa Press, 1942.
92. Shakow, D. One hundred years of American psychiatry: a special review. *Psychol. Bull.,* 1945, *42,* 423-432.
93. Shakow, D. Clinical psychology: an evaluation. In L. G. Lowrey (Ed.), *Orthopsychiatry, 1923-1948: retrospect and prospect.* New York: American Orthopsychiatric Association, 1948. Pp. 231-247.
94. Shakow, D. Psychology and psychiatry: a dialogue. *Amer. J. Orthopsychiat.,* 1949, *19,* 191-208, 381-396.
95. Sharp, Stella E. Individual psychology: a study in psychological method. *Amer. J. Psychol.,* 1899, *10,* 329-391.
96. Sidis, B. Studies in psychopathology. *Boston med. & surg. J.,* 1907, *156,* 321-326, 357-361, 394-398, 432-434, 472-478.
97. Smith, T. L. The development of psychological clinics in the United States. *Ped. Sem.,* 1914, *21,* 143-153.
98. Speer, G. S. A survey of psychologists in Illinois. *Amer. Psychologist.,* 1950, *5,* 424-426.
99. Stevenson, G. S., and Smith, G. *Child guidance clinics: a quarter century of development.* New York: Commonwealth Fund, 1934.
100. Symonds, J. P. Ten years of journalism in psychology, 1937-1946; first decade of the Journal of Consulting Psychology. *J. consult. Psychol.,* 1946, *10,* 335-374.
101. Terman, L. M. Trails to psychology. In C. Murchison (Ed.), *A history of psychology in autobiography.* Vol. II. Worcester: Clark Univer. Press, 1932. Pp. 297-332.

102. U.S. Dept. Army, Office of the Surgeon General. The U.S. Army's senior psychology student program. *Amer. Psychologist*, 1949, *4*, 424-425.
103. Veterans Administration. Cooperative training program for clinical psychologists in association with part-time work in VA stations where neuropsychiatric cases are treated. *V.A. Tech. Bull.*, 1948, TB 10A-146.
104. Vestermark, S. D. Training and its support under the National Mental Health Act. *Amer. J. Psychiat.*, 1949, *106*, 416-419.
105. Wallin, J. E. W. *The mental health of the school child.* New Haven: Yale Univer. Press, 1914.
106. Watson, R. I. The professional status of the clinical psychologist. In R. I. Watson (Ed.), *Readings in the clinical method in psychology.* New York: Harper, 1949. Pp. 29-48.
107. Watson, R. I. *The clinical method in psychology.* New York: Harper, 1951.
108. Wells, F. L. *Mental tests in clinical practice.* Yonkers, N.Y.: World Book Co., 1927.
109. Wendt, G. R. Legislation for the general practice of psychology versus legislation for specialties within psychology. *Amer. Psychologist*, 1950, *5*, 107-108.
110. Whipple, G. M. *Manual of physical and mental tests.* Baltimore: Warwick and York, 1910.
111. Whitehorn, J. C. A century of psychiatric research in America. In J. K. Hall (Ed.), *One hundred years of American psychiatry.* New York: Columbia Univer. Press, 1944. Pp. 167-193.
112. Wiener, D. N. The Minnesota law to certify psychologists. *Amer. Psychologist*, 1951, *6*, 549-553.
113. Wissler, C. The correlation of mental and physical tests. *Psychol. Monogr.*, 1901, *3*, No. 6 (Whole No. 16).
114. Witmer, L. Clinical psychology. *Psychol. Clin.*, 1907, *1*, 1-9.
115. Witty, P. S., and Theman, Viola. The psycho-educational clinic. *J. appl. Psychol.*, 1934, *18*, 369-392.
116. Wolfle, D. The reorganized American Psychological Association. *Amer. Psychologist*, 1946, *1*, 3-6.
117. Wolfle, D. Legal control of psychological practice. *Amer. Psychologist*, 1950, *5*, 651-655.
118. Woodworth, R. S. *Personal Data Sheet.* Chicago: C. H. Stoelting, 1917.
119. Wyatt, F. Clinical psychology and orthopsychiatry. In L. G. Lowrey (Ed.), *Orthopsychiatry, 1923-1948: retrospect and prospect.* New York: American Orthopsychiatric Association, 1948. Pp. 217-230.
120. Yerkes, R. M. (Ed.) *Psychological examining in the United States Army.* (Memoirs of the National Academy of Sciences, Vol. 15.) Washington, D.C.: U.S. Govt. Printing Office, 1921.
121. Young, K. The history of mental testing. *Ped. Sem.*, 1924, *31*, 1-48.

15. Progress in Orthopsychiatry: Psychology

My task today is to sketch progress in orthopsychiatry so far as psychology has contributed to it and profited from it. Several possible frameworks for presentation were open. One possibility would have been to focus upon the specific psychological contributions of individual members within our Association exemplified by their reports in the American Journal of Orthopsychiatry. The review of anthropology and orthopsychiatry by Jules Henry (6) in the 1948 anniversary volume comes to mind as an illustration of this approach. I do not follow his example partly because I decided I did not possess his skill in making vivid current problems through specific references to the literature published in our journal. Another approach would have been to follow the example of Frederick Wyatt (23) and David Shakow (15) in the same anniversary volume and focus upon clinical psychology in relation to orthopsychiatry. They did such an admirable job that anything I could have prepared using clinical psychology as a framework would have been but a six-year supplement to their statements. In reaching the conclusion to follow neither their example nor that of Henry, I was also influenced by what will emerge as one of my principal theses. Orthopsychiatry's influence and reciprocal relation is with psychology as a whole. Important though the approach to this problem either through clinical psychology or through orthopsychiatric literature may be, a broader perspective is allowed when the problem is conceived as a consideration of the relation of orthopsychiatry and psychology.

There are many indications, some of which will be briefly sketched, that psychology as a science and a profession is becoming more closely united today than it has been in the past. There is an increasing recognition on the part of psychologists and others on the essential unity of the field. "Schools of psychology" which used to plague us are almost nonexistent. I do not mean there are no differences of opinion, but often these differences rest upon this or that specific point, not upon some fundamental principle which would tear the fabric of the field into small bits. There is, to be sure, a "latitudinarian" left and a "rigorous" right, an issue to which I shall return in a moment, but such a distinction is a quantitative, not a qualitative, one.

What orienting approaches to the relation of psychology to orthopsychiatry are open to me? I have chose to use two approaches. I shall first trace the history of child psychology as a branch of and specialty in psychology and examine its *rapprochement* with orthopsychiatry. At first glance it may appear that the decision to center upon child psychology contradicts my earlier assertion that I intended to discuss the relation of orthopsychiatry and psychology as a whole. Child psychology is an integral aspect of psychology differentiated from the whole field only by its focus on a limited age range. Clinical psychology, on the other hand, not only has its own unique approaches, but also it was both earlier and more vigorously subject to influences outside the field (21). In orthopsychiatry's relation with psychology there must be a point of focus, and I have chosen to make it child psychology. Secondly, in the light of these considerations, I shall examine some of our current interprofessional issues in relation to orthopsychiatry.

In choosing to consider child psychology in relation to orthopsychiatry I am influenced by the fact that, by and large, members of the American Orthopsychiatric Association are specialists in work with children. To some extent we draw upon a common scientific-theoretical heritage. In a sense all orthopsychiatrists depend upon child psychology. Let me hasten to add I realize that what we in orthopsychiatry would mean by the term child psychology varies considerably. Some would mean by the term clinical research and observation in one or another psychoanalytic tradition. Others would lean almost exclusively upon the rigorous tradition of general psychology. As Hebb puts it: "There appears to be a left wing and a right wing in psychology . . . the Right favors parsimony of explanatory ideas, a simple or mechanical account of behavior, and definiteness even at the cost of being narrow. The Left is prepared to postulate more fully and can better tolerate vagueness and lack of system in its account of behavior" (5, pp. 47-48). Relevant to your evaluation of this review of child psychology, your present speaker places himself somewhat left, but not too far left, of center.

What do I and presumably many other psychologists encompass by child psychology? It is pertinent to examine the history of child psychology not only for other psychologists but also for members of related disciplines. This is especially pertinent in times when interprofessional strife is high. Such strife between individuals is always reflected in the ideologies they hold. If we can understand the background on which an individual forms his convictions, even if these be ones with which another individual disagrees, we are taking a step toward understanding these difficulties and thereby making a step toward solution. This becomes mandatory for me when I admit I have a strong conviction that there is a possibility that there are among us, as busy people, individuals who have outdated and distorted views of the present status of child psychology.

Before the advent of child psychology as a branch of science, certain attitudes were held toward the child. Individuals sharing these attitudes had in common an interest, not in the child as such, but in what he had been or was to become. Thus in historic times the child was variously viewed as a miniature adult, a future citizen, innately depraved, inherently good, or a stage of evolution.

The beginnings of child psychology occur, as is inevitably characteristic of any discipline, in the work of investigators from other fields. The beginnings of systematic observation in child psychology are to be found in the work of Preyer, an embryologist, and his method of the baby biography, the day-to-day observation of a single child starting at or near birth. Indicating as it did the necessity of careful observation and detailed study, it served as an inspiration for subsequent psychological workers. But the baby biography was also subject to methodological weakness in that bias was very tempting and it offered little opportunity for check on reliability or validity of the observations.

The next major development in the history of child psychology is to be found in the work of G. Stanley Hall, the same Hall who in 1909 invited Freud to the United States. One facet of interest of this many-sided individual was expressed in collecting information about children through questionnaires. Using teachers and parents as sources of data collection, he pursued this method for many years.

The interest and enthusiasm he engendered resulted in the so-called child study movement which swept the country shortly after the turn of the century. Its uncriticalness, superficiality, and application by entirely untrained workers led to the collapse of the movement from its own weight. Despite its intrinsic weaknesses, it made definite contributions to the psychological study of the child in that it increased recognition of the importance of childhood per se, led to realization of the importance of empirical study, and stimulated critical evaluation of the methods used.

It fell to Alfred Binet to make the next major contribution. In 1904, at the request of the French Minister of Education, he set upon the task of developing an instrument to be used in deciding whether Paris school children suspected of mental retardation should be eliminated from regular school classes. Having had experience with the artificially simplified laboratory tasks used in mental tests up to this point, he turned away from these short, simple, discrete tests heretofore used, such as estimation of distance, speed of reaction, and rate of tapping. He chose, instead, to use the more complex and realistic tasks of everyday life, such as items requiring verbal knowledge of objects, repetition of digits, memory for designs, and definitions of abstract terms. In the second, or 1908, Binet test, he made his second great contribution—the grouping of tests according to the age at which they are usually passed. Thus a logic for interpretation of the results of intelligence tests, the mental age, was established. The restandardization of the Binet Scale in the United States by Lewis M. Terman, called the Stanford Revision, followed in 1916. This soon became the standard testing instrument in the United States for the measurement of intelligence of children. It is no exaggeration to say that the major task of the early clinical psychologist was to administer Binet after Binet. As Goodenough (3) indicates, the rapidity with which Binet testing was seized upon in the United States can be traced to a number of conditions which made the times right for its usefulness. Compulsory school attendance was being vigorously enforced and the period of schooling increased in length. Backward students in the schools thus became an increasingly important problem. Juvenile delinquency as a social problem came into active prominence, and emphasis upon social welfare and prevention of emotional and mental defect was becoming part of the American scene. Such problems called for large-scale assessment by means of a standardized instrument, a need which was admirably fulfilled by the Binet scales.

Another of the foundation stones of child psychology is to be found in the work of John B. Watson on emotional responses of infants during the second decade of this century at the Phipps Psychiatric Clinic in Baltimore. His specific research findings were found wanting in many respects later but he made a definite impress upon the field. By championing behavioral aspects and dismissing introspection he made young children appropriate subjects for psychological investigation by the then current techniques.

It was through the work of such men as Preyer, Hall, Binet, Terman, and Watson that child psychology came into being. Although working with different problems in different countries, they all had something in common—a desire for quantitative findings through scientific research. And, although interpreting objectivity in research with varying standards of exactitude, each turned his back on philosophical and theological discussion and worked toward this common goal. Each is identified with a technique of child study emphasizing to a greater or lesser degree exactitude and repeatability of observations—the true beginnings of the scientific study of the behavior of the child.

We now leave these early pioneers and turn to the twenties and thirties. Certain characteristics stand out. No longer were there isolated giants, as in the past, but rather many capable workers collectively making a considerable contribution to our knowledge of the child. These decades were characterized by specialized studies of the different capacities of the child. For child psychology the years were a period of piecemeal measurement. The soil was so rich that it encouraged snatching examples of behavior here and there and then hurrying to the next bauble. The times were also characterized by turning to the parent field, general psychology, for inspiration on both methods and problems to be investigated. Sensory capacity, motor performance, emotion, language, and thinking were investigated extensively. But studies of learning and intelligence were most vigorously investigated while whatever may be meant by the term "personality study" was relatively neglected. Many of the studies were normative in that they charted measurements of some segment of behavior by age. The hundreds of titles concerning measurement of intelligence by tests grouped according to age are characteristic.

It was during this period that some voices of doubt could be heard. "Where in this mass of facts," they asked, "is the child?" The segmentalized, compartmentalized approach to the child which characterized the period was noted with some misgivings by parents, educators, and others who dealt with children in everyday situations. They asked for general principles that would make the behavior of the individual child intelligible, that would make the facts cohere. In short, they asked for general principles of personality organization. Their questions were, at this time, being asked prematurely. What such critics neglected to see is that normative data were a necessary first step before moving on to this more global problem.

Concomitant with these developments, other fields and other men were beginning to have an influence upon child psychology. It is to these other fields and men I now turn because they also influenced orthopsychiatry. Undoubtedly one of the greatest influences upon modern child psychology has come from the work of Sigmund Freud. His eminence in child psychology is to be judged not only in the direct utilization of psychoanalytic concepts and findings in the field, but also in the subtle, indirect, and sometimes unnoticed effect upon child theory and practice. His influence is so self-evident as to not need detailed examination with this group.

Influence on child psychology also came from another worker in a psychoanalytic tradition, Hermann Rorschach. The greatness of his contribution lies not in the inkblots themselves, which had been used before, but in the conceptual system of interpretive significance which in broad outline at least has stood the test of time. The examination was introduced in this country in the early twenties. It is Samuel Beck who has probably had the greatest influence in the United States through his work with the blots. He published in 1931 the first original article in English about the Rorschach. Significantly, it was concerned with children. Since that time over 1200 studies using the Rorschach with children and adults have appeared (2).

The child guidance movement has also contributed a great deal to child psychology. As is well known, the first child guidance clinic to combat juvenile delinquency was founded in Chicago in 1909 under the name "The Juvenile Psychopathic Institute." From the beginning a unique characteristic of this and subsequent clinics was the so-called team approach, or the coordinated services of the three specialties the members of our society represent. The prevailing conviction was that delinquency was treatable by psychiatric and psychological means. There was a gradual broadening of scope as it was recognized that substantially the same means of treatment could be applied to the emotionally disturbed nondelinquent child. With this audience, many of whom know more about the topic than I, it is obviously unnecessary to attempt to trace in detail the history of child guidance. I shall now turn for a moment to clinical psychology.

Some of the same influences brought to bear upon child psychology were operative in helping to shape the history of clinical psychology. The psychometric tradition exemplified by Binet and Terman, the projective tradition exemplified by Rorschach, the influence of psychiatry and psychoanalysis, and the child guidance movement had their effect upon its development. Some of the details of the history of clinical psychology have been discussed elsewhere by your speaker (21). My friend and colleague, William A. Hunt, in his recent Salmon Lectures (7) examined in broader sweep the trends that shaped the specialty of clinical psychology from general psychology. Only two or three especially pertinent points concerning its history will be made here.

The opening in 1896 of the Psychological Clinic at the University of Pennsylvania is said to mark the advent of clinical psychology. Lightner Witmer, the founder and director of the clinic, became interested in helping the educationally retarded and handicapped child. As a consequence the great majority of the cases came from the school systems. This clinic, the first of many founded at universities and teachers colleges, found its particular area of competence in the everyday problems of the child, particularly those relating to academic success such as reading. This is not to say that emotional, nonschool problems were ignored; rather, less stress was placed upon them (perhaps because at that time there was less understanding of them).

The major task of the clinical psychologist was originally in large measure conceived to be administration of psychological tests. In this early period before World War II the Stanford-Binet Intelligence Scale and a variety of less verbal "performance" tests made up his principal tools. A somewhat narrow concept of the function of the clinical psychologist prevailed. But the stirrings of the beginning of a broader, more dynamic concept could be noted among these early pioneers. Three of our members, Augusta Bronner,

Frederic Wells, and Simon Tulchin, are among this distinguished group. For example, Tulchin (17) in 1934 demonstrated through analysis of Binet-Simon results that emotional blocking and reading and language handicaps must be considered in interpreting intelligence test results. Commonplace though this thought may be in the present day, it was a courageous step for a man to take in the days when a rigid psychometric tradition prevailed. The advent of projective personality measures, such as the Rorschach, considerably broadened the clinical psychologist's repertory, and thus the scope of his activities.

A gradual extension of his diagnostic functions in other spheres also took place. From the very beginning of his clinical work the psychologist was expected to be an expert on educational matters. It is no wonder, then, that remedial matters such as school difficulties were his to work with not only in psychological clinics but in other settings as well. This separation of "intellectual" from "emotional" aspects of the patient's life came eventually to be regarded as artificial, and there gradually came about psychotherapeutic work of a more inclusive character. In this broadening of psychotherapy Phyllis Blanchard, Dorothy Baruch, and Carl Rogers among our members were important early figures.

This tradition of close cooperation with the schools still has a respected place in the activities of the clinical psychologist. Nevertheless, for good or for ill, clinical psychology as a specialty has outgrown its beginning in a quasi-educational setting. In addition to the child guidance clinic it has found its place in mental hospitals, industry, homes for the mentally defective, and many other settings (19). Thus many psychologists who are members of our organization, in addition to their work with children, have distinguished themselves in other fields. In this connection Edgar Doll, Hyman Meltzer, Albert Rabin, David Rapaport, Saul Rosenzweig, David Shakow, Percival Symonds, and David Wechsler come to mind.

Pediatrics, also, has had some effect on and has been affected by child psychology and orthopsychiatry. According to Senn in our anniversay volume (14), interest by pediatricians in psychological aspects was slow to develop, not reaching any proportions until the end of the first quarter of the present century. Thereafter psychological factors received more attention. Specifically he mentions the influence of Binet and Terman through their work in intelligence testing, Gesell and his co-workers through their research on the infant developmental sequence, and John B. Watson through his studies of infant learning and conditioning.

Concerning subsequent developments this authority refers to the rise of psychiatric-pediatric collaboration, and the appearance of child guidance clinics, in which there was a provision for pediatric service. Now many medical schools arrange for some pediatrics to be taught collaboratively with psychiatrists, with at least some attention to the personality of the child.

In many ways child psychology and childhood, as education and educational psychology view them, owe their development to the same forces. The early attitudes toward the child previously mentioned are as much the heritage of education and educational psychology as they are of child psychology. These fields also share in the beginnings of child psychology. Preyer, Hall, and Binet are part of their history. Naturally the emphasis of the educator and educational psychologist was upon the processes of learning and teaching.

In the modern period two individuals stand out as influencing studies of children's learning and of methods of teaching them—John Dewey and Edward L. Thorndike. John Dewey, philosopher, psychologist, and educator, probably had a more profound influence upon education than any other man of this century. His educational philosophy is widely known, though not always put into practice. Through his followers his work led to the progressive education movement, which, as Krugman (10) reminds us, really consists of the application of mental hygiene to education. The studies of Edward L. Thorndike on learning and related topics are part of this common heritage. Sharing, through his own research in learning, in the discovery of the individual child as an individual, he did much to document the newly appreciated fact of individual differences. The existence of individual differences was now established by research instead of being part of the intuitive grasp of the gifted few "born" teachers. Thorndike's first book on educational psychology was published in 1903, and in the next year his *Mental and Social Measurements* was the first book to make generally available the budding tool of statistics. His emphasis upon drill as a means of learning, although influential for many years, is now seen in a broader perspective and is of less influence than formerly.

The work of the educational psychologists and that of their colleagues in other disciplines has led to a concern with the growth and development of each child in spite of the educator's major responsibility for large groups of children. Differentiated curricula, the activity program, the advent of elective subjects, concern with each individual student's interest and motivation, and the appearance of learning readiness programs all attest to education's concern with the individual child and his emotional as well as intellectual needs, as Krugman's account in our anniversary volume (10) so ably indicates.

Sociology, too, but in lesser measure, has contributed to child psychology. This discipline, centering as it does upon the behavior of groups, touches upon present interests through the medium of the family. In connection with the family and its problems, sociology considers such matters as courtship, divorce, the nature of family life and education for it, marriage as an institution, and planned parenthood. In this field the work of no one man is sufficiently outstanding to require mention; instead, a considerable number of workers have made collectively a significant contribution to our understanding of the child in the family.

Findings in cultural anthropology also have influenced child psychology. Workers in this field attempt to understand man as a social being. In the main they study the different so-called primitive cultures throughout the world, although some anthropologists have begun to interest themselves in contemporary cultures such as our own. Impressed with the necessity of describing the primitive cultures still not altered or destroyed by European influences, the anthropologist in the early years of this century spent much of his time in the field collecting "facts." In a way, this collection of facts was something similar in both form and spirit to the collecting of the artifacts—the baskets and spears for the museums—that accompanied it. Each bit of behavior was carefully noted and to some extent catalogued, but an understanding of the over-all pattern was lacking because theory was lacking. Gradually a new point of view emerged. It is not the behavior in itself as an independent unit but its meaning, the assumptions underlying it, the way it is patterned, the motivation for it, and the satisfactions it brings that give the particular behavior unit its vitality and relevance. Working within such theoretical frameworks, whether psychoanalytically or non-psychoanalytically oriented, and recognizing the implication of the units of behavior for an understanding of broader social processes are characteristic of modern cultural anthropology.

Many of the recent contributions of such distinguished anthropologists as Margaret Mead and Jules Henry have been directed by a desire to test psychiatric-psychological hypotheses in other cultures (9). Often such studies focus attention on younger subjects as avowedly developmental in character and thus of influence upon child psychology. For example, Mead's *Coming of Age in Samoa* and *Growing Up in New Guinea* reveal in their very titles a concern with the developmental sequence.

Certain consequences of these trends characterize present-day child psychology. Their relevance to the present topic lies in their similarity to what I consider to be the spirit of orthopsychiatry. In talking about child psychology, in some measure I am talking about it as well. Let me document this remark concerning the considerable similarity by briefly examining orthopsychiatry. I hope that you find it a fair summarization. If not, it is all the more necessary that I give it, since it expresses my personal conviction concerning the field. To the extent that I fail to capture orthopsychiatry in this account, to that extent may my discussion of its relation to child psychology be false.

A few weeks ago, in the course of securing volunteers to work at this convention, I had the experience of attempting to explain to my class in child psychology what the American Orthopsychiatric Association is and what it stands for. After quoting excerpts from the Constitution and By-laws conveniently given in our 1954 Membership List, I felt the need of supplementation so that I attempted to formulate my own impressions. What I offered was substantially this:

> The American Orthopsychiatric Association is made up of about 1000 psychiatrists, psychologists, and social workers who are united both in theory and practice in furthering their joint coordinated efforts in understanding and working with emotionally disturbed individuals, particularly children, in what loosely may be called a dynamic tradition. Broadly speaking, orthopsychiatrists are interested in personality development in the total situation in which the child is found. For some members research, although of considerable interest, is a secondary consideration to clinical endeavors. Nevertheless, all accept as vital to their work an interplay of science and practice. Because of high membership requirements, generally speaking it is composed of older, more experienced members of the professions.

These themes, just mentioned, of personality development, total situation, and the interplay of science and practice will now be examined as they appear in child psychology.

We in child psychology and orthopsychiatry share with others the American tradition of emphasis on the worth and value of the developing individual. Development is the common interest of all of these varied fields sketched earlier and of child psychology. It is this theme of development which can be made central in discussions of child psychology both as a concept and as a means of presenting the facts and theories concerning the psychological study of the child. It can be discerned that that which can make the concept more specific and meaningful is an emphasis upon *personality* development. Although variously defined, personality is concerned with the molar behavior and experience of the person.

The present era is one in which *personality* investigation is paramount both in child psychology and in orthopsychiatry. We have on one hand certain views of personality long in theory but short on facts; on the other hand we have various scientific findings short on theory but long in facts. Sometimes an individual child psychologist or a member of another field interested in the child reacts by slavishly accepting a certain theoretical position, say psychoanalysis, and then planning investigations which, provided one accepts the major tenets, can be said to further the knowledge of personality functioning as psychoanalysis views it. Others refuse to see any problem and ignore theory while normatively mapping personality as a separate entity in the same way as in other areas such as learning or intelligence. But there is a middle ground representing, in my opinion, the most fruitful one. Without allowing any one rigid theoretical position to pervade all of one's thinking, one can use theoretical constructs as a guide to hypothesis-making. With continuing research a picture gradually will emerge based upon scientific verification. As these particular facets merge into larger structures a more unified picture combining theory and science can be seen. In the meantime, unverified but plausible hypotheses can be used to fill in the missing gaps *provided that they are recognized for what they are—as yet unverified assumptions*. In this task of balance of science and theory the child psychologist, I hope, plays an important part.

It is characteristic of the modern period in child psychology that the child is seen as having his psychological significance as an individual in a total situation. The child functions as he does not only because of individually determined forces but also because of the environmental circumstances pressing upon him. The beginnings of this point of view were apparent in the earlier periods. Indeed, it is present in the psychoanalytic point of view where Freud stressed the effect of adverse circumstances upon personality development, and even more clearly in the child guidance movement where William Healy's first major work, significantly entited *The Individual Delinquent*, showed that delinquency was a situational phenomenon, not characteristic of the child himself, and subject to change if circumstances are changed. Within child psychology itself this stress upon total social situation gave us the flourishing field of the social psychology of childhood. In these areas Harold Anderson, Robert Sears, L. Joseph Stone, and other members of our Association have taken a leading part.

This emphasis upon the whole child in a total situation and on interdisciplinary research has made inevitable another trend characteristic of the modern period—the development of multidiscipline child research institutes. Although often psychologists predominate, the personnel of such institutes include individuals of different areas of specialty and representatives of other fields such as psychiatrists, pediatricians, nutrition experts, and physiologists.

The Institute of Child Welfare at the University of California is typical. Two of our members, Harold Jones and Jean W. Macfarlane, are senior members of the staff. In operation for many years, its research is directed along several lines (8). It is dedicated to the investigation of the physical, pphysiological, and psychological development of children and adolescents. The Adolescent Growth Study conducted by this Institute is concerned with a representative sample of school children from Oakland, California. The major dimensions of this study concern physical growth, physical abilities, and physiological functions on the one hand, and psychological changes in interests, attitudes, and social relationships on the other. The Berkeley Growth Study, another major endeavor, is devoted to records on the medical and psychological development of Berkeley children monthly during nursery school days and at 6-month intervals during early childhood and adolescence. The Guidance Study, still another research interest, samples every third child born in Berkeley during an 18-month period. In this study they are concerned with studying developmentally these children from nursery school and on to maturity with special emphasis upon personality development. Other divisions of the Institute include a nursery school which carries on a study of social discrimination and prejudices in children and a series of studies in autonomic functions. The

Institute is dedicated to research, the development of theory, the training of students, the preparation of reports concerning the implications of their findings for schools, and practical problems in child training.

It is characteristic of the modern period in child psychology that there is an interplay of science and practice. The healthy integrating exchange thus coming about is borne out by many of the facets of history previously outlined. Clinical-child psychologists or, if you prefer, child-clinical psychologists are one manifestation. Still other child psychologists are to be found within education, home economics, pediatrics, parent education, marriage, correctional work, and the gamut of children's agencies. Research stations such as those outlined before are very sensitive to questions of practice. It is recognized today that you cannot wrench apart the fabric and artificially separate science and practice. Nevertheless there can be a division of labor.

The clinical psychologist working with children may on this basis be distinguished from the child psychologist. The former is interested in working with disturbed children. The child psychologist, although cognizant of what his brother is doing and sometimes assuming the uneasy role of his brother's keeper, is more concerned with scientific advance and sees the problems of the child in a broader perspective. He sometimes pays for this breadth by less appreciation of individual dynamics.

This résumé may be perhaps considered partisan. It is pertinent to report the opinion of others. One authoritative source is the *Annual Review of Psychology* in which current research is critically examined by experts in each of the specialties. In the 1955 volume, the Yarrows, who write the review of child psychology, have this to say:

> Rather slowly, but very perceptibly, a new point of view is emerging in child psychology. It is not a point of view which is an irresponsible, radical departure from the conservative empiricism which has epitomized this discipline, but it is a reformulation of the problems in terms of a more dynamic conception of behavior and development (24, p. 1).

After examining briefly earlier developments in child psychology in a fashion not too different in spirit from my presentation they go on to summarize the modern era as follows:

> Childhood re-emerged as a crucial field of study (the fourth phase) when testable hypotheses based on clinical (mainly psychoanalytic)

theories began to be formulated by systematically oriented researchers, when psychological theory and cultural anthropology converged, and when the genius of Kurt Lewin trained the experimental method upon meaningful social psychological questions within a framework of dynamic field theory (24, p. 2).

That we are not alone in taking this stand concerning the importance of the current dynamic-theoretical phase of child development is also borne out by the analysis of the United States Children's Bureau bulletin on current research in progress (18). In the problem areas of personality dynamics, personality deviations, and parent-child relationships fall 41 percent of all studies in progress reported in this presumably nearly exhaustive review. This is all the more significant when it is noted that clinical case studies are omitted. On the other hand, studies of physical growth, motor development, perception, hereditary and constitutional factors, and learning make up slightly more than 10 percent combined. Evidently the current research scene reflects at least some aspects of the present contentions.

It would be impossible to say precisely how much and in what manner orthopsychiatry has contributed to these developments in child psychology. Even if there be no relation of antecedent and consequent, we as orthopsychiatrists should take considerable satisfaction from the congruence of our views and that of this discipline.

Concerning the reciprocal relationship between child psychology and orthopsychiatry, I will hazard only one generalization. Orthopsychiatry, by and large, has supplied more of the theoretical climate to our efforts while child psychology per se has supplied leads on research design and a greater rigor of interpretation. It will be an indication of even greater unification when there is greater balance in these reciprocal contributions.

In the themes of unification, development, personality, the total situation, interdisciplinary research and activity, and the interplay of science and practice we find the *rapprochement* of psychology and orthopsychiatry.

The situation, then, in regard to relations between psychology and orthopsychiatry at this level shows considerable integration and unificiation. I will now turn to interprofessional problems. It must be remembered that psychology has relatively recently emerged as a profession with the hallmark of a profession, independence to decide its own course of development but with the coresponsibility to guide its progress by a sense of social responsibility, including that toward other professions. What are some of the accomplishments of professional psychology? Time-space requirements do not permit more than a cursory mention of them—but they have been more fully documented elsewhere (e.g., 22). There is a strong national organization in the American Psychological Association with about 13,000 members. General agreement about the nature of training in psychology has been reached. A code of ethics has been worked through empirically. The American Board of Examiners in Professional Psychology has been established and has received wide support. Responsibility to the public has been a major concern and within the profession there is a strong base of reciprocal understanding.

Such, then, are some examples of present accomplishments of professional psychology. But by no means are there no unresolved issues facing psychology. Within the profession we are still working out the balance of professional and scientific influences and facing the intricate problem of psychological practice at the subdoctoral level. However, these need not concern us here. Unresolved interprofessional issues are more relevant to a discussion of the relations of psychology and orthopsychiatry. It is impossible to consider psychology in relation to orthopsychiatry without considering these current tensions. These can be stated variously, legal control through certification and/or licensure, the moratorium on legislative action proposed by the committees of the two APA's, and so on. Within the area of the mechanics of settling these interprofessional differences much can be and is said. These problems, however, important though they may be, are symptomatic of the difficulties. As I see it, the essential problem for us is summarized as the *independent practice of psychotherapy with the ill by the psychologist*. Let me hasten to emphasize I am stating a problem, not proposing a stand on the issue! I am sure you will agree with me that the three words "independent," "psychotherapy," and "ill" are words that cause battle lines to be drawn. Let me consider each of these in turn, although to do so wrenches them apart artificially.

Independent practice is carried on by psychologists in many settings, as business consultants, reading experts, and so on in aspects of psychology far removed from medical concern. Guidance activities of the counseling psychologist, although one step closer to our present concern, are not crucial to our interest in the matter. These forms of independent practice are outside the present scope of discussion. We are talking about private practice by clinical psychologists without collaborative and/or supervisory medical relationships. Even within the scope of our interest it is not private practice per se that is cause for concern because diagnostic specialists such as experts with the Rorschach may be in private practice. If they confine themselves to the diagnostic phase they inevitably are in a collaborative relationship with whoever carries on therapeutically. Private practice is not necessarily independent practice. Nor is private group practice a source of concern. Independence of practice as an interprofessional issue concerning psychologists, then, occurs when there is not a collaborative relationship with medical men concerning treatment methods used by psychologists.

Orthopsychiatry is committed to joint coordinated efforts insofar as practicable. We represent group practice in clinics and elsewhere and consultative relationships. By and large independent practice, no matter the discipline, is not characteristic of our membership. Long before independent practice of psychologists became anything approaching a problem, we were committed to these forms of working together. It would be quite proper for us to take a stand that the most socially desirable and efficient method of working out our common problems is through such relationships as are expressed in our membership requirements. I would submit that our course would be to do everything we could to support collaborative practice—a positive aim of the American Orthopsychiatric Association.

If independent practice is not the most desirable pattern then we must work in the direction of collaborative practice. But I also submit that the way to achieve our goal is not through restriction but through education. As a profession, psychology has independence of action and will defend the right of its members to enter independent practice, though many, as I do, consider collaborative practice more desirable in the best interests of the profession and of the patient.

Sometimes in theory, but even more often in practice, psychiatrists encourage psychologists' engaging in psychotherapy when it is in a medical setting. Most psychologists in this situation recognize that medical responsibility is necessary. The only ethical course open to a psychologist who cannot accept this state of affairs is to withdraw. Generally speaking, the question of responsibility is worked out satisfactorily. Personally, at least, I hear little or nothing about intensive warfare in hospitals or .psychiatric clinics over psychotherapeutic cooperation, supervision, or whatever you choose to call it. So far as I know, psychologists working in orthopsychiatrically oriented clinics are not being adversely affected either personally or professionally by these pressures. In fact, only a very few scattered instances are known where there was a possibly direct connection between the repercussions of these issues and what happened to individual psychologists. Not that all is a bed of roses; struggles of a sort, subtle and obvious, continue. But these are difficulties in interpersonal relations, presumably related to the personality dynamics of the individuals concerned and the specific situation, not directly a result of the aspects of the climate of the times under discussion. This, of course, is as it should be. I think we can be a bit proud that there is little or no confusion of the roles of a particular psychologist, social worker, or psychiatrist with the larger issues of the professions. And yet, there is another kind of confusion created by a paradox.

The psychologist often faces a paradox of tolerance. Sometimes, if a psychiatrist knows and respects the work of a particular psychologist in a medical setting, he is apt to encourage him enthusiastically in his therapeutic activities in this setting. If perchance this psychologist turns to independent practice, this psychiatrist, although distressed, is not unduly disturbed. In fact, he may make referrals despite some doubts on the matter. But it is a different matter if "psychologists in independent practice" as a general proposition is broached. Then a different and relatively uncompromising stand is taken. I am not suggesting that this is right or wrong—our problems don't permit such easy solution—I only call your attention to this confusion.

I can see no justification for objecting to the psychologists' doing something called "psychotherapy." They do so in medical settings with varying degrees of approval on the part of physicians. There is also no question that they carry on psychotherapeutic activities outside of a medical setting. Often, although not always, it takes one or another specific form differently labeled according to the background and identification of the psychologist concerned. As an illustration may I offer a quotation from a current textbook in clinical psychology. What is under discussion for the moment is omitted.

. . . generally involves a shorter rather than a longer series of sessions, deals with reactive problems rather than intrapsychic conflicts, may stress intellectual factors rather than emotional ones, is likely to deal with non-incapacitating rather than severely disturbing and involved maladjustments, often places the symptom or symptoms in the center of focus, is likely to deal with relatively normal people rather than neurotics or psychotics, and is based upon a rapport rather than a transference relationship (20, p. 585).

I have used this quotation as a projective device, asking both counseling psychologists and clinical psychologists what is under discussion. Almost invariably counseling psychologists call the procedure described "counseling," while clinical psychologists call it "supportive psychotherapy." I can only conclude that both are right. I am led to the position that it is not what is done but with whom it is done that is the crucial factor.

I doubt if psychotherapy can be restrictively defined in a fashion that will make for clarity and understanding as it includes a host of interactive situations. I might add that I am, of course, dismissing that circular interpretation used by some physicians who define psychotherapy as psychological methods with the ill and then, on hearing psychotherapy is used by a psychologist, reason that he is practicing medicine. I mention it at all because it brings into crucial prominence the meaning of "ill."

Detailed consideration must be given to the meaning if illness. I consider this to be the crux of the matter. In thinking this I find that I am in substantial agreement with William Hunt's formulation in his recent Salmon lectures where his evaluation led him to the same conclusion. Emphatically the problem is not settled by baldly quoting from an American Psychiatric Association report that "mental illnesses are well defined disease entities and these definitions of terms are officially recognized by the medical profession" (11, p. 862)—as the statement quoted at our last business meeting would have it. If this refers to the psychiatric nomenclature, may I remind you that the Diagnostic and Statistical Manual (1) among other categories refers to so-called transient situational personality disorders including habit disturbances and conduct disturbances, as well as personality disorders such as inadequate personalities, emotionally unstable personalities, learning and speech disturbances. One classification is that of "Personality trait disturbance, other," in which one is advised that "instances in which a personality trait is exaggerated as a means to life adjustment (as in the above diagnoses), not classifiable elsewhere, may be listed here" (1, p. 37). Quite a bit of the territory of human behavior and experience appears to be included which may legitimately, on occasion at least, fall outside the medical province. It is also pertinent to point out that this same manual differentiates "disorders" and "illness." For example, quoting from the description of compulsive personality: "While their chronic tension may lead to a neurotic illness, this is not an invariable consequence" (1, p. 37). Illness and disorders are, it would appear, not the same. This distinction and its significance for the present issue also must be explored.

We are all aware of the complexities and subtle interplay entering into the individual's psychodynamics. Psychiatrists and psychologists should consider working together on the thorny, multifaceted problem of the operational definition of illness. It might well take the form of clearly demarcating the extremes of illness and nonillness (strange as the latter term may sound), with the necessary tolerance of ambiguity of the middle region.

One example and suggestion for exploration of this question of illness might take as its point of departure an issue which at first glance may appear far afield, namely, current thinking on comprehensive medicine. For example, there is the work of Halliday on etiology (4), Saslow and his collaborators on comprehensive medicine (13), and Karl Menninger (12) on changing concepts of disease. Thinking such as theirs on this problem might be directed along lines of easing and integrating interprofessional activity. These and other workers have been working for some time on what is, in effect, a definition of illness sufficiently broad, complex, and in accord with modern conceptions of psychiatry to be useful in the present' controversy. Of course, I do not mean to imply that any or all have said the last word, nor that I would agree forthwith to leave to the physician all territory sketched in these and similar discussions. Their statements could, however, serve as a base line for a psychiatric formulation. Certainly their level of approach does more justice to the complexity of the problem than would an approach on the dualistic level of mind-body. In this connection, false though this dichotomy may be, I cannot forbear mentioning that after two thousand years the issue suggested by our "dualism" must now actually be settled at a professional level! It may be that Aristotelian thinking is going to have an effect on a psychologists' certification bill in Iowa or New Hampshire!

Illness is the province of medicine. Psychologists really do not question this despite occasional remarks to the contrary. Psychologists who disagree almost certainly have in mind a very extended concept of "illness" held by some psychiatrists. So any apparent disagreement is in part semantic. I feel, however, that the position expressed here will ultimately be found to be the clear and just position to take. What we do question then is the nature of the definition and the dividing line to be drawn. Hence, a focal problem to work out is what is illness and what is not. Legislative definition of illness, insofar as it touches upon these matters, should be deferred until adequate understanding and at least an attempt at agreement are worked upon. This consultation with others is difficult, I know, but seems indicated by the importance of the matter.

Such then are some personal opinions on these complex issues. They cannot necessarily be expected to reflect the opinions of other psychologists, let alone the membership of AOA. I may be wrong on any or all of these statements.

On one matter, however, I cannot be wrong. We can expect leadership in the American Orthopsychiatric Association in defense of interdisciplinary collaboration. It was on this basis that concern was expressed by the Board of the Association about the proposed bill to amend the Medical Practices Act submitted in the New York State legislature last year, since it was possible that this bill would have "eliminated or jeopardized the use of our collaborative teamwork functioning" (11, p. 864). This particular action may have been misinterpreted by some of our members, but the spirit which prompted the Board to take this action cannot be a source of disagreement. On this the Board reflected our concern with positive interdisciplinary activity.

I have already mentioned one of the reasons I can assume such leadership to be forthcoming—our dedication to joint collaborative relationships among the disciplines. Another facet of this same pattern should be mentioned. To put it baldly, we have had more experience as an organization in wrestling with how to get along with our neighbors than either the American Psychiatric Association, the American Psychological Association, or the American Association of Psychiatric Social Workers. Extreme partisanship of any sort has not been too popular in AOA, for which I am thankful. Talk among our members of rump sessions of representatives of one discipline I hope will not be heard again.

Second, we can expect a defense of collaborative relationships because our councils are still led by men and women who have the wisdom of maturity and experience which serves to remove them from the ferventness of youthful identification. If I may appear to digress a moment, have you ever considered the really unique phenomenon at our professional meetings of the overwhelming preponderance of nonmember attendance? The usual answer to the question of why they are not members is that they lack the experience to meet membership requirements. Our standards are high, and this means that our ranks are not filled to overflowing by younger members, as are those organizations standing for but one discipline, like the two APA's. This is but a partial answer. They are those younger members of our professions who are most likely to be attracted to our common aims and aspirations and, as such, they should be encouraged. Their exclusion from the membership, however, does mean that more individuals in the last stages of tolerance —tolerance of closely competitive fields—are among our members. I would like to develop this theme for a moment.

Drawing upon some years' experience in medical schools and in graduate schools of psychology, I am impressed with how both medical and psychology students make complete and intense identification with their particular field of study, a point Stillman (16) has made concerning certain other fields. The novice's identity becomes merged with his discipline and criticism of it is interpreted personally and rejected derisively. There is no zealot like a young zealot! One facet of what Stillman refers to as academic imperialism is very obvious in both psychology and medicine. This is the student's discovery of the remarkable reaches of human experience which his discipline is in the position of best explaining. Starting with what in the larger scheme of things is but a pitifully minute issue or a segmented aspect of some theory, this new convert is ready to meet the world and its problems. Often in psychology it is expressed in the presenting of a Ph.D. topic too big and cumbersome, which, once cut to size by the hard-hearted adviser, still permits the young enthusiast to reach conclusions of earth-shaking consequences. I say this not in derision nor in impatience but affectionately and regretfully. Young students have an unsullied faith in the power of their field of endeavor. Gradually the horizon of tolerance of other fields may widen but, in a curious way, from the periphery inward, so to speak. The fields and problems most remote and peripheral are seen objectively and accepted for their contribution to the field. Quoting Stillman: "Only in the last stages of tolerance, bordering on desertion itself, does tolerance extend to disciplines most clearly competitive" (16, p. 77). Orthopsychiatry has been a training ground for speeding this growth of tolerance.

In this interdisciplinary activity in all of its complexity and very human troubles, we can see as we did in examining the problem in historical perspective that there is an essential unity. To be sure, each child specialist quite appropriately sees the child from a different perspective. Each has a partial view, embracing perhaps in limited proportions the other views, but each with a different emphasis. Since we in orthopsychiatry are charged with seeing the child steadily and seeing him whole, our present task demands application of all these views of the child because they affect behavior and experience. It is characteristic of the present era that insularity in all of these fields is on the wane. In orthopsychiatric and in psychological science and practice the modern period is characterized by a growing realization that no field of inquiry exists in isolation. No science or profession is an island.

REFERENCES

1. American Psychiatric Association, Committee on Nomenclature and Statistics. *Diagnostic and Statistical Manual: Mental Disorders.* American Psychiatric Assoc., Washington, D.C., 1952.
2. Buros, O. K. (Ed.). *The Fourth Mental Measurements Yearbook.* Gryphon Press, Highland Park, N.J., 1953.
3. Goodenough, Florence. *Mental Testing, Its History, Principles, and Applications.* Rinehart, New York, 1949.
4. Halliday, J. I. *Principles of Aetiology.* Brit. J. Med. Psychol., 19: 367-380, 1941-1943.
5. Hebb, D. O. *The Role of Neurological Ideas in Personality.* J. Pers., 20: 39-55, 1951.
6. Henry, J. "Anthropology and Orthopsychiatry," in *Orthopsychiatry, 1923-1948: Retrospect and Prospect* (L. G. Lowrey and V. Sloane, Eds.), pp. 263-286. American Orthopsychiatric Assoc., New York, 1948.
7. Hunt, W. A. *The Clinical Psychologist.* Thomas, Springfield, Ill. (in press).
8. Jones, H. E. *Studies in Child Development.* Institute of Child Welfare. Univ. of California. Research Bull. No. 16. Undated.
9. Kluckhohn, C. "The Influence of Psychiatry on Anthropology in America During the Past One Hundred Years," in *One Hundred*

years of American Psychiatry (J. K. Hall, Ed.), pp. 589-616. Columbia Univ. Press, New York, 1944.
10. Krugman, M. "Orthopsychiatry and Education," in *Orthopsychiatry, 1923-1948: Retrospect and Prospect* (L. G. Lowrey and V. Sloane, Eds.), pp. 248-262. American Orthopsychiatric Assoc., New York, 1948.
11. Lippman, H. S. (Pres.). Annual business meeting, American Orthopsychiatric Association, 1954. *Am. J. Orthopsychiatry*, 24: 858-882, 1954.
12. Menninger, K. *Changing Concepts of Disease*. Ann. Int. Med., 29: 318-325, 1948.
13. Saslow, G. *On the Concept of Comprehensive Medicine*. Bull. Menninger Clin., 16: 57-65, 1952.
14. Senn, M. J. E. "Pediatrics in Orthopsychiatry," in *Orthopsychiatry, 1923-1948: Retrospect and Prospect* (L. G. Lowrey and V. Sloane, Eds.), pp. 300-309. American Orthopsychiatric Assoc., New York, 1948.
15. Shakow, D. "Clinical Psychology: An Evaluation," in *Orthopsychiatry, 1923-1948: Retrospect and Prospect* (L. G. Lowrey and V. Sloane, Eds.), pp. 231-247. American Orthopsychiatric Assoc., New York, 1948.
16. Stillman, C. W. *Academic Imperialism*. Am. Scientist, 43: 77-88, 1955.
17. Tulchin, Simon H. *Clinical Studies of Mental Tests*. Am. J. Psychiatry, 13: No. 6, May 1934.
18. United States Children's Bureau. *Research Relating to Children*. U.S. Dept. Educ. and Welf. Bull., No. 2, 1953.
19. Watson, R. I. *Readings in the Clinical Method in Psychology*. Harper, New York, 1949.
20. ——. *The Clinical Method in Psychology*. Harper, New York, 1951.
21. ——. *A Brief History of Clinical Psychology*. Psychol. Bull., 50: 321-346, 1953.
22. ——. *Psychology as a Profession*. Doubleday, New York, 1954.
23. Wyatt, F. "Clinical Psychology and Orthopsychiatry," in *Orthopsychiatry, 1923-1948: Retrospect and Prospect* (L. G. Lowrey and V. Sloane, Eds.), pp. 217-230. American Orthopsychiatric Assoc., New York, 1948.
24. Yarrow, Marion R., and L. J. Yarrow. "Child Psychology," in *Annual Review of Psychology* (C. Stone, Ed.), pp. 1-28. Annual Reviews, Inc., Stanford, Calif., 1955.

16. Historical Review of Objective Personality Testing: The Search for Objectivity

The noted philosopher of science, Herbert Feigl, considers a major standard of science to be intersubjective testability. Concerning intersubjective testability he writes:

> This is only a more adequate formulation of what is generally meant by the "objectivity" of science. What is here involved is not only the freedom from personal or cultural bias or partiality, but—even more fundamentally—the requirement that the knowledge claims of science be in principle capable of test (confirmation or disconfirmation, at least indirectly and to some degree) on the part of any person properly equipped with intelligence and the technical devices of observation or experimentation. The term *intersubjective* stresses the social nature of the scientific enterprise. If there be any "truths" that are accessible only to privileged individuals, such as mystics or visionaries—that is, knowledge-claims which by their very nature cannot independently be checked by anyone else—then such "truths" are not of the kind that we seek in the sciences. The criterion of intersubjective testability thus delimits the scientific from the nonscientific activities of man. (15, p. 11.)

I would add that objectivity is a goal of science, not a prerequisite for scientific endeavors. Objectivity is not absolute, but relative. It is not unusual in science for basic phenomena to be first described in a qualitative way. Objective methods emerge only upon more intensive study. Our efforts are in the direction of increasing objectivity whenever possible, but this does not mean that we can neglect problems simply because they are not yet objective. At least some of us select problems which we feel are capable of being rendered more objective and make our research task this search for increasing objectivity. For example, in Chapter 9 by Hunt, we shall find that a demonstration of the reliability of clinical judgment is a means whereby the clinician himself becomes a more objective instrument. In the present chapter, a major theme is the search for objectivity in personality testing.

Of necessity, my topic must be considered in a somewhat narrower framework than the entire scope of personality theory. A major omission in the consideration of objectivity in personality evaluation is the argument as to why one should go beyond the objective approach, as advanced by philosophical and phenomenological characterologists. This otherwise serious omission is tempered somewhat by the fact that the characterologists have not been particularly interested in psychological testing, despite the fact that many projective tests can be shown to be interpretable on phenomenological principles.

In order to place objective personality testing in historical perspective, it is necessary to say something about objective psychological testing in general. We cannot ignore early mental testing in our search for the beginnings of personality testing, for to do so would be to ignore a truism of historical research—that the beginnings of attention to a topic may not be referred to in the same manner as it is referred to in later years. Personality, as our various conceptions now regard it, was not a systematic rubric in the earlier psychological traditions. Lack of specific reference, however, does not prevent us from seeing in the perspective of the present day some of the aspects of what we now call personality. So we begin with the history of testing, not the history of personality testing, narrowly regarded.

BEGINNINGS OF OBJECTIVE TESTING

At the time the history of objective psychological testing begins, in about 1880-1890, the mind was still the subject matter of psychology. For our purposes, we can turn to a classification of tests adopted by Whipple in his 1910 publication, *Manual of Mental and Physical Tests* (37).[1] Mental tests served the purpose of determining and measuring some phase of mental capacity or trait. I would like to add parenthetically that even in 1910 he could plead that what was needed was not new tests, but an exhaustive investigation

---

1. Numerals in parentheses refer to bibliographical references at the end of each chapter.

of those already available. But to return to his classification of mental tests, the major headings (disregarding the anthropometric) were physical and motor capacity, sensory capacity, attention and perception, description and report, association learning and memory, suggestibility, imagination and invention, and intelligence. Note, there is no mention of personality. However, the tests of suggestibility and imagination and invention could be called personality tests in today's perspective. It would also be possible to include description and report in the scope of personality. Note also that tests for emotion were not mentioned, for measures of emotion came later. Many of the personality questionnaires of the twenties were called measures of emotionality. So, too, were more objective efforts, such as the X-O, or cross-out, tests of Pressey, in which the number of words found to be unpleasant was the affectivity score. With this justification of what is included in the discussion to follow, we may now turn to the history of mental tests.

Sir Francis Galton shares with James McKeen Cattell the founding of psychological testing. As early as 1882, Galton had established a small laboratory in London where, for a small fee, individuals could take a series of physical measurements and tests of reaction time and sensory acuity. (One might ask in passing whether this payment meant that he was the first psychological practitioner). The very fact that he thought people would be interested in their standing on these measures shows their test-orientation.

Galton was primarily interested in no less than an inventory of human abilities. He related these to his evolutionary views and to his studies of inheritance, but the fact remains that he conceived of his various measures as tapping as broad a spectrum of psychological characteristics as was possible. If the term personality had been used as it is now, I believe he would not have hesitated to use it to describe some of his efforts.

In a paper published in 1890, in which he coined the term mental tests, Cattell proposed a standard series of tests to be applied for "discovering the constancy of mental processes, their interdependence, and their variation under different circumstances" (6, p. 373). He offered both a select list of ten tests then being used in the Psychological Laboratory of the University of Pennsylvania and a longer list of 50 others proposed for further consideration. The ten tests were dynamometer pressure, rate of movement, two-point threshold, pain sensitivity, least noticeable difference in weight, reaction time for sound, time for naming colors, bisection of a 50 cm. line, judgment of ten seconds' time, and the number of letters repeated on one hearing. The list of 50 was essentially similar. The fact that Galton (6) contributed a number of comments at the end of his article gives unequivocal evidence of the connection between Galton's interest in individual differences and the mental-test movement.

Earlier, in 1883, with his already formed interests in individual differences and in reaction time as a measure of intelligence, Cattell had gone to Wundt's laboratory. Here he had completed his doctoral dissertation on his own problem of individual differences in reaction times, which Wundt, it might be added, had viewed dubiously as a suitable problem for a psychologist to undertake.

After Cattell's sojourn at the University of Pennsylvania, he moved to Columbia University, where he continued his testing program with essentially the same battery of tests. After several years' data had been collected, a monograph by Clark Wissler (39) appeared in 1901 reporting the findings. Correlation between results from the various tests and academic class standing was negligible. Moreover, the tests were no more intercorrelated among themselves than they were related to class standing. This was in sharp contrast to the substantial correlations found between standings on the various college subjects. These disappointing results, plus another negative trial made in Titchener's laboratory by Sharp (29), probably did much to make psychologists lose interest in the topic. Certainly, other students of Titchener and Cattell did not follow up these matters with laboratory devices. These two men were training the majority of psychologists who did not receive their training in Europe. On the continent Wundt's emphasis upon the generalized human mind, a view which was shared by most other European psychologists, did nothing to encourage further exploration.

The interest in simple sensory and motor tests during this period was theoretical and was laboratory-bound. Interest in individual differences was central. Measuring devices were single tests, not organized into scales. The now usual checks on reliability were missing, and standardization, aside from a certain similarity of instruction, was lacking. The first period of objective testing, then, is that of the laboratory. After these negative findings, the enthusiasm for, and interest in, them was much less.

So we have seen that initial enthusiasm for mental tests in the

United States was met by negative results and this particular line of development lapsed, in what may be, for convenience, referred to as the laboratory period in psychological testing.

EARLY LACK OF CONCERN FOR OBJECTIVE TESTING

It is pertinent to pause to consider psychologists' views in relation to this search for objectivity. It is probable that the question of objectivity did not concern them because of the origins of test materials in the laboratory. Reaction time devices measure reaction time; learning nonsense syllables is learning. The process measured was defined by the material, just as in the laboratory today one does not ask, "Are we really measuring learning?" when serial learning lists are exposed or maze paths are threaded. These measures had what we now would call content validity. Content validity is the degree to which the test samples the universe of content specified, as in an achievement test and in the usual measures for the experiments in learning. The step from measuring reaction time to using it for the measurement of intelligence "because intelligence calls for speedy reaction" seemed plausible but of no great theoretical moment. It was not then seen that it was a great leap from observed behavior to construct.

By and large, the question of objectivity was not verbalized during these years. Psychology, after all, was still the study of mental structures or functions, and introspection the method for advancement of psychological knowledge. For example, Whipple (37), in his 1910 authoritative and widely used test manual, does not mention objectivity. He does, however, speak of standardization of conditions, which is conducive to objectivity. Familiarity with instructions and their clarity were also stressed. General knowledge of the literature and an inspection of some of the textbooks of the period, however, did not reveal discussion of objectivity as a topic. After all, psychologists could not use "objective" in referring to a subjective science. But this does not mean they were unaware of the problem. In fact, the centuries-old question of the personal equation which, years later, Wundt's students and others investigated is a recognition of precisely this point. So, too, is the psychologist's fallacy of James, the confusion of the personal standpoint with the mental facts. Training of introspectors served the same function of increasing what we could call objectivity.

INTELLIGENCE TESTING

It is tempting, but not particularly germane to the major issue, to turn now to the work of Binet, who, after working with similar sensory and motor tests with similarly unproductive results, eventually found in more complex or higher mental functions the means to measure intelligence. But this is part of the history of intelligence testing of 1900–1920. In the United States this history of intelligence testing was not closely bound to personality testing, for various reasons. Interest in and research on intelligence testing were directly related to Binet's efforts, but the others who came after him did not continue his systematic analytic interests. Those who followed Binet were pragmatic and interested in the application of intelligence tests to social matters, such as mental retardation, school placement, and the like. But they were so absorbed with their instruments of measurement that they were not very much interested in problems beyond these instruments.

As the well-known definition would have it, psychologists of that day, and for some years to come, tended to consider the intelligence to be whatever intelligence tests measured. So, in this sense, interest was in intelligence as a global concept. And yet, what Spearman called the anarchic theory of mental structure, a theory of extreme specificity of mental structure and function, was the prevailing view. The studies of William James, Thorndike, and others on transfer of training had fostered the view that abilities were highly specific. The results of sensory-motor testing, described earlier, had much the same effect. Thus, we had the practical pragmatic interests in intelligence testing, on the one hand, and, on the other, even larger segments of the psychological field in which abilities and traits were viewed as highly specific.

This lack of relevance of developments in the specific areas of intelligence testing during these years in the United States, curiously enough, does not seem to have a counterpart in Britain. In a sense, the British psychologists continued more closely the tradition of the laboratory that has been described. In part, this was due to the impetus of Galton and a continued stress on the part of his students on individual difference. In part, it was due to the statistical advances in England, first under Galton and Pearson, and later under Spearman and Burt.

Many of the tests used in Britain at the turn of the century were the logical derivatives of earlier sensory and motor tests, but they also included as measures, association tests, such as retention measures, target aiming, card-sorting, and the like.

In an important paper published in 1904, Spearman (30) criticized the previous methodological efforts on statistical grounds. For example, many earlier workers had failed to use quantitatively precise statements of the degree of correlation between tests, they did not calculate the probable error, and they did not allow for errors of observation. In addition, based upon his correlation between sensory tests and estimates of intelligence, Spearman arrived at the conclusion that "all branches of intellectual activity have in common one fundamental function . . ." (30, p. 284). Thus was launched the beginnings of the thinking from which, a few years later, came factor analysis. The British psychologists saw more clearly than their American contemporaries the reasons why early attempts at testing had failed.

Above all, they had something positive and challenging to work with in factor analysis. Their general associationist background was conducive to continuing this tradition. They continued an interest in these measures, gradually including more and more material relevant to the higher mental processes.

Factor analysis is a tool by the very nature of which you cannot in advance tell what factors will emerge. True, the material was so selected as to get at intellectual function, but the nature of the technique required an analytic attitude. Nor were nonintellectual factors entirely neglected. The pioneering factor analytic study of Webb (36) in 1915 was based on ratings and yielded a factor which seemed to be strength of character or will, called w. Burt (4), the same year, briefly reported on the interrelation of ratings of emotions. But now we must return to developments taking place in the United States in 1910's and 1920's.

BEHAVIORISM AND OBJECTIVITY OF MEASUREMENT

The appearance of Behaviorism, with its militant espousal of an objective approach, had a profound effect on psychological thinking. For our purposes, it may be dated by the appearance of the work of John B. Watson, beginning in 1913 with his articles and culminating in his 1919 publication, *Psychology from the Standpoint of a Behaviorist.* Mentalistic terms, including "subjective," became epithets. The Russian reflexology, which came into being in the immediately preceding years, is sometimes referred to as "Objective Psychology," after the book by that name published in 1910 by Bekhterev.

Psychologists then found in objectivity a standard of science. No longer did they have to struggle with mediate and immediate experience, dependent and independent experience, and the differences between the objective science of physics and the subjective science of psychology. They could then use "objectivity" proudly, as we do to this very day. In the recently received copy of the supplement to the *Psychological Review*, there was a "Glossary of Some Terms Used in the Objective Science of Behavior," by Verplanck (34), who did not even find it necessary to define objective among the many, many terms covered.

The spirit of the times, or the *Zeitgeist*, a term popularized by E. G. Boring, had prepared the way for the appearance of an interest in performance tests. An interesting example is the Will-Temperament Test, a behavior measure, which fitted in with the times. In 1919, June Downey (11) introduced a test for the measurement of what she called will-temperament. Its nature was intriguing, consisting largely as it did of handwriting samples under different conditions and, thus, behavioral in nature. A sample of writing was obtained at "ordinary" speed (for a baseline), as rapidly as possible (to get a comparison with ordinary speed on the theory that those writing much slower than they can are subject to a load or inhibition), in a different style (to measure flexibility), as slowly as possible (to measure motor inhibition or control), and so on. The test appealed to the desire for objectivity; so it was met with enthusiasm. It was given trial after trial until about fifty studies were performed, despite almost uniformly negative results from the beginning. It was as if such a behavioral test as this could not fail to work, just because it was a behavioral approach. The test is also important as the first major performance measure of personality.

Another of the earlier performance measures of personality was that used in 1921 in the study by Voelker (35) of "moral reactions to conduct." This was followed in 1923 by the Character Education Inquiry, with which we associate the names of Hartshorne and May, and which produced well-known performance tests for honesty, trustworthiness, helpfulness, inhibition, and persistence.

The nature of these tests is too well known to pause over them. Their findings of the low correlation between specific measures helped to accentuate an era of considerable skepticism about tests as measures of personality, or what Spearman referred to as the anarchic view.

Behaviorism itself, with its emphasis upon S-R bonds and personality as a bundle of habits, had helped to bring about this skepticism concerning tests on the part of many psychologists. The results of Hartshorne and May, even though behavioral, however, were another invitation akin to that furnished by the earlier results of Wissler and Sharp, to see testing in a skeptical light.

Performance tests are logically and chronologically related to assessment procedures of the miniature life situation sort. They, too, have a long past despite their short history. The earliest statement of the potentials of this method is probably that of Galton (19). In 1884 he wrote:

> Emergencies need not be waited for, they can be extemporized; traps, as it were, can be laid. Thus, a great ruler whose word can make or mar a subject's fortune, wants a secret agent and tests his character during a single invertiew. He contrives by a few minutes' questioning, temptation, and show of displeasure, to turn his character inside out, exciting in turn his hopes, fear, zeal, loyalty, ambition, and so forth. Ordinary observers who stand on a far lower pedestal, cannot hope to excite the same tension and outburst of feeling in those whom they examine, but they can obtain good data in a more leisurely way. If they are unable to note a man's conduct under great trials for want of opportunity, they may do it in small ones, and it is well that those small occasions should be such as are of frequent occurrence, that the statistics of men's conduct under like conditions may be compared. After fixing upon some particular class of persons of similar age, sex, and social conditions, we have to find out what common incidents in their lives are most apt to make them betray their character. We may then take note as often as we can, of what they do on these occasions, so as to arrive at their statistics of conduct in a limited number of well-defined small trials (30, p. 182).

He goes on to offer specific suggestions, such as the following:

> The poetical metaphors of ordinary language suggest many possibilities of measurement. Thus when two persons have an "inclination" to one another, they visibly incline or slope together when sitting side by side, as at a dinner-table, and they then throw the stress of their weights on the near legs of their chairs. It does not require much ingenuity to arrange a pressure gauge with an index and dial to indicate changes in stress, but it is difficult to devise an arrangement that shall fulfill the threefold con-

dition of being effective, not attracting notice, and being applicable to ordinary furniture. I made some rude experiments, but being busy with other matters, have not carried them on, as I had hoped (30, p. 184).

In view of the date in which this was published, 1884, it would be possible to argue that this was the first proposal for an objective personality measure.

MODERN ASSESSMENT METHODS

Modern assessment procedures, as in the stress interview, the OSS procedures, and the Michigan VA trainee study, are apparently moving out of a period in which they were enthusiastically accepted and tried, to a period of skepticism about them. If there is to be a period of synthesis, it is too early to predict its nature.

Personality Questionnaire. I shall now turn to personality questionnaires in this search for objectivity. During World War I, Woodworth's *Personal Data Sheet*, or, as it was later called, the *Psychoneurotic Inventory*, was developed. It contained 116 items derived from descriptions of symptoms of neurotic patients (18). "Yes" or "no" responses were called for and were scored by simple counting to arrive at a total. Because the Armistice intervened, this inventory was not used extensively in the military setting. It became, over the years, the form to which to turn to select and develop items.

We have had since that time a phenomenal growth in the development and application of personality questionnaires. Macfarlane (22), in a critique of projective testing, spoke of the rapidity of appearance of projective instruments as partaking of the nature of a virulent infection. This remark can be applied with equal force to the self-report personality questionnaire. I would roughly estimate from the Buros reviews of mental measurements and other sources that either as single short questionnaires or in multiple capsule form, at least 500 commercially available personality questionnaires have appeared. A tremendous number of psychologists (including the present writer) helped to develop these get-knowledge-quick devices.

There is no question that personality questionnaires had their period of enthusiastic acceptance. Their appeal was to be found in their partial objectivity; a score could be derived on which independent scorers could agree. Scoring did not then, nor does it now, ordinarily involve subjective judgment. Nevertheless, several very important sources of subjectivity were present which, at first, were obscured by scoring objectivity. Customarily, they are not independent of the motivation of the person completing the questionnaire; there is conscious deception, and there is unconscious distortion. It is to another subjective factor, however, to which detailed illustrative attention will be given. These questionnaires are subjective in that they require interpretation of the meanings of the questions asked by the tester.

Interpretive subjectivity for the person taking them is rampant in most personality questionnaires. Consider an early study of Benton (3). He interviewed subjects after completion of questionnaire items, as to what they thought was meant by the items. He found, for example, that the item, "Do you take pride in your physical appearance?" was answered as if the question meant, do you always feel proud, sometimes feel proud, are you always careful, and are you sometimes careful of your physical appearance? Similar results have been found by others.

Instead of dealing with other more detailed and significant findings, let me indulge in an anecdote from personal experience. The psychological interview on the receiving line in a Naval Recruit Training Center during World War II partook of the quality of a verbally administered personality questionnaire, since sheer press of time did not allow using that distinctive characteristic of the interview, the follow-through probing of replies. Enuresis was a rather common and disturbing symptom and, consequently, precious time was taken to inquire about it. An affirmative or a negative reply to the question "Do you wet the bed at night?" had to be checked, since "Yes" might mean, "Yes, because fifteen years ago at the age of six I had an accident," while "No" might mean "No, I haven't for two nights in a row." Wording "When did you last wet the bed?" was found to increase objectivity in that a better understanding of the intent of the question followed. In this pedestrian, minute improvement we can see how objectivity improves.

Sometimes personality questionnaires are criticized as if objectivity were an absolute. In view of Thurstone's work with the personality questionnaire, it is of interest to note that this is not the position he took. He asserts flatly that such questionnaires are not tests in any strict sense since tests are ". . . objective procedures" (321, p. 353) with the implication that questionnaires are not. One may sharply separate tests from questionnaires, as Cattell does, without denying questionnaires some objective status. To Thurstone's position, one may take exception, as I have tried to do in arguing that objectivity is a relative matter.

Most personality questionnaires, in my opinion, have proven to be unsuccessful in their tasks as scientific instruments. The indictments by Ellis (12) and Ellis and Conrad (13) in large measure seem justified. One may, however, argue on certain points, such as classifying all questionnaires together, when a breakdown by the particular instrument may show more encouraging results. The Minnesota Multiphasic Personality Inventory, for example, fared considerably better in its reviews than other instruments.

Certain measures, particularly the MMPI, probably owe their continuing use and expanded value, despite the general failure in part, to the development of specific means of increasing objectivity. The Lie Scale is one such device. In addition to indices of increasing objectivity, there is the intimately related fact that the MMPI is a more complete, complex, and intricate instrument than many of the other personality measures.

Psychology is a broad subject, and other influences, perhaps running counter to the prevailing *Zeitgeist* (perhaps representing still another trend) which appeared in some measure in the late twenties reached a considerably higher peak of visibility in the mid-thirties. I refer, of course, to projective testing.

Projective Techniques. At first, it might seem that the present concern does not call for direct attention to projective techniques. Nevertheless, in our search for objectivity some reminder of the beginning of projective testing is necessary to place its developing influence upon objectivity.

Rorschach worked with his inkblots in Switzerland during the decade 1910-1920. Studies with the Rorschach Test in the United States can be dated from about 1930 with the appearance of Beck's monograph (2). He, in turn, had been trained in *Rorschach* by David Levy. The Rorschach was not deliberately planned to test projection, despite its preeminence today as a projective test.

Inkblots themselves are nothing new or startling. Indeed, Leonardo da Vinci (8) proposed for the training of painters throwing a sponge full of various colors against the wall, for the perceptions one might see and, significantly, he added, provided one wants to. So far as psychological research in the narrow sense is concerned, inkblots were proposed as a measure of visual imagination in 1895 by Binet and Henri (36). Dearborn (9, 10), two years later, published material on the use of inkblots with a small group of Harvard professors and students.

The recognition of projection as a method of testing arose more or less simultaneously and independently. In 1935 Murray (23) published with Morgan his first paper on the Thematic Apperception Test. Sears (28) published the first of his papers on experimental studies of projection in 1936. In Britain, in the same year, Cattell (7) published his *Guide to Mental Testing*, including a description of a projection test. Since it is probably not too well known to American audiences, it will be described briefly. He called it a "projection test," which, I believe, is the first time the term was applied directly to a test. It consists of 74 items in which each item has three alternatives, as in the following instance (33, p. 71):

John strained every nerve to beat the others because:
> he was determined to be top
> his father wished him to succeed
> he needed the scholarship.

The most appropriate of the three endings was to be checked on the assumption that one person will project his own chief impulses onto the ending chosen. If self-assertive, he would be likely to choose the first; if submissive, he would prefer the second. The items were developed so as to give scores on Self-Assertive *versus* Submissive, Cautious *versus* Bold, Acquisitive, Gregarious, Curious, and Dependent tendencies, adapted from McDougall's list of instincts. Standardization was not carried out and not too much use has been made of the test. In today's perspective, it could be called a multiple-choice, sentence-completion test. It is pertinent to my theme to indicate that, if standardized, this could have been an objective test in the sense that scoring was objective. The more detailed and explicit formulation of the projective hypothesis of L. K. Frank (16) appeared in 1939. This was the first major source of knowledge of projection which became well known to psychologists.

Thurstone considered the projective procedures "the nearest approach to personality tests" in revealing personal idiosyncracies. He asked only that it be unstructured for the subject but well structured for the psychologists, since with this structure it could be objectively scored. However, he went on to add, if the interpretation were as unstructured as the test, it would be useless for scientific inquiry. Structure, from the point of view of the examiner, may be equated with objectivity. Rorschach inkblots seem highly subjective, but experts can prepare independent interpretations which agree on essential particulars. This form of objectivity is one of the grounds on which the Rorschach is defended.

The influence of projective techniques upon objective personality testing involves diametrically opposed influences. Undoubtedly, this kind of measurement increased subjective, impressionistic, intuitive trends in psychology. The heady wine of its multidimensional character; its relation to dynamic theory, particularly psychoanalysis; its enthusiastic reception by psychiatric colleagues; and its usefulness in clinical settings all contributed to this antiobjective trend. Yet, without its challenge to objectivity, psychologists would probably not have seen the possibilities of increasing the scope of objectivity to include improving the objectivity of the psychologist himself. In considerable measure, whether viewing the use of projective techniques sympathetically or as irritants, it has forced us to reevaluate and broaden our meaning of objectivity.

The many validity studies of the Rorschach that have produced negative results have given for the third time in the last fifty years an excuse to be skeptical of testing, this time of projective personality testing. Since this is a current skepticism, no one can say "what happened next." But something will happen, and I would suggest that it will be further objectification of projective techniques, but without disregard of the complexity and subtlety these devices permit. Holtzman[1] focuses attention on the problems of objective scoring of projective techniques, while preserving their underlying purpose.

WHAT IS AN OBJECTIVE TEST?

Now that the historical survey has been completed, I would like to consider present-day thinking about objective personality testing.

In order to be able to present a cross-section of present-day conceptions of objective personality testing, the authors of this symposium indicated what they considered to be the meaning of "Objective Approaches to Personality Assessment," with special emphasis upon the qualifying term "Objective."

Bass considered objectivity to be complete independence from

1. In B. M. Bass and I. A. Berg (Eds.). *Objective approaches to personality assessment.* New York: Van Nostrand, 1959, 119-145.

examiner effects, or, as he also put it, zero variance due to the examiner. Berg referred to scorable, fairly clearly structured tests for which scoring would be identical if performed by competent persons. Edwards emphasized the rigorously defined method of scoring. McQuitty considered it to mean the isolation of consistent individual differences in a manner such that numbers can be applied, resulting in a similar classification or measurement of behavior by different users of the approach. Pepinsky, in relating objectivity to an approach to personality testing, disclaimed use of the term but believed what is meant is two-fold: (1) minimization of errors of observing and recording, and (2) minimization of variability in the task conditions on separate occasions (not, he adds, in minimizing stimulus ambiguity or uncertainty for the subject).

In varying degrees and either implicitly or explicitly, many of these statements stressed not the test alone, but objectivity as a matter of *interaction* of test material and examiner. Objectivity is localized not only in the material, but also in the examiner. Objectivity is not the same as numerical scores or impersonal records, although it is the one way objectivity is expressed. Blood-pressure records are numerical and X-ray photographs are objective, but both are open to subjectivity of interpretation.

It must be remembered that these were succinct replies to a question. It does not follow that the respondents would not agree in some instances with expansion of the meanings they specify, or even with other, more extended ways of putting the matter. I will also add that they reserve the right to disagree, violently or otherwise, with later remarks, either of my own, or of the other participants. I shall now proceed to summarize the somewhat more lengthy statements.

Cattell gives a more specific meaning than do the others, drawing upon his glossary to *Personality and Motivation Structure and Measurements*, wherein he defines an objective test as follows: "A test in which the subject's behavior is measured, for inferring personality, without his being aware in what ways his behavior is likely to affect the interpretation." To leave no doubt about their differentiation from questionnaires and the like, he further expands in the text as follows: "It is a portable, exactly reproducible, stimulus situation, with an exactly prescribed mode of scoring the response, *of which the subject is not informed.* All objective tests are also *experimental measurements*, but not all experimental measurements are tests. The difference of T data from Q data resides in the last clause, for "the *response* cannot be deliberately self-evaluative and self-revelatory if the subject is not told how his response is going to be evaluated." Cattell would, thereby, rule out personality questionnaires as tests, but not, of course, as personality measures.

Super goes beyond this discussion, to speak of a test as objective in any one or more of three ways: "(1) its stimulus, (2) the response which it permits, and (3) the scoring method used." He continues:

> The quality of objectivity is one of clarity of structure; in this sense the objectivity-subjectivity continuum is equivalent to the clarity-ambiguity dimension and the structured-unstructured dimension. This means that a truly, completely, objective test is one in which the stimulus has the same significance to all subjects, the responses which he may make are limited in number and clear in meaning, and the scoring leaves no room for judgment by the scorer. By this definition, the tests we actually use are scattered along a continuum, and any judgment as to whether a particular test is objective or otherwise is somewhat arbitrary.

As I see it, Super is saying that objectivity is either clarity or structure, suggesting that these terms are more clear in the present context than is objectivity, though not denying meaning to objectivity. His personal preference, he goes on to state, is the structured-unstructured continuum, so far as classification of tests are concerned.

Hunt, as might be expected from his present interests in objectification of clinical impression, does not limit himself to test settings. He writes:

> I interpret "objective" as pertaining to "public" rather than "private" information. Thus the data of introspection are private until turned into some form of report when they thus become public, since the forms of report, language or behavioral, can be handled as public, verifiable (by others) phenomena. "Objective" has many parameters, loosely the clarity and specificity of definition of the phenomena, its duplicability, its control for experimental observation, its statistical amenability, etc.

This is a still broader definition, and very close in spirit to Feigl's account of intersubjective testability.

Hathaway gives the most detailed analysis, but I am taking the liberty of quoting him verbatim.

I believe I am correct in placing our local emphasis in definition of the word "objective" upon the qualities of reproducibility and most of all upon the absence of an intervening interpretation between behavior of the subject and the material available to a third person. Data are objective when they are transmitted directly from the subject to others who may then interpret them. The verbatim responses to Rorschach cards are objective items, but they become something else (loosely, improperly called subjective) when they are classified or in any other way characterized by the examiner. The MMPI items checked by a subject constitute objective information, and these remain objective when put into scales. Discussion of the meaning of the scales or profiles is no longer objective. A TAT story is an objective item when presented verbatim but loses objectivity as soon as any interpretation or condensation or expansion occurs on the part of the examiner. There are intermediate situations. A series of experiments may establish that certain Rorschach responses occur with a greater frequency than others. Preserving objectivity, one could then classify a given response or set of responses as having a certain degree of frequency. The frequency score becomes, therefore, an objective item. It is to be noted, however, that responses frequently occur in slightly unusual form, although elements of the responses are frequent. The examiner could exercise freedom and call a response either a frequent one or an infrequent one. When such examiner freedom enters the situation, the resulting score loses objectivity. Similarly, an MMPI administered under special deviant conditions that may not be mentioned in presentation of the objective data from the responses also loses objectivity. One ordinarily has the right to expect of an objective test that roughly standard administration was used.

I have not developed the idea of reproducibility, but it is inherent in what I have been saying. One does not require that the objective score be reproducible in exactly the usual sense of reliability but rather, that there be possible a hypothetical construct representing a reproducible element in the subject. This construct is not possible if the product of the situation represents some interaction of the examiner with the subject or some aspect of the examiner's psyche.

Most projective devices (and I tend to use "test" as almost completely implying objectivity) have traditionally been much less objective than devices that permit the patient to make responses that can be treated by clerical means. It is unfortunate that objectivity has been tied to "paper and pencil" and to the idea of formulated items such as in the MMPI. I believe that we would benefit from the attempt to extend objective measurement to include not only the objective aspects of projective devices, which has been partly developed, but also objective ways of treating interview material and free behavior as this may be observed by others.

PROJECTIVE AND OBJECTIVE TESTS ARE NOT DICHOTOMOUS

Interest in searching for objectivity is by no means confined to the authors just cited. A considerable variety of opinion has been expressed by others. One that I consider especially pernicious, when the distinction is made without qualification or explanation, is that between objective and projective tests, treating them as if they were mutually exclusive. One rather widespread systematic error has been to contrast projective tests with all other tests to which, unfortunately, we have sometimes applied the undeserved label of objective tests. For example, in some *Annual Review of Psychology* chapters, two of the major sections on diagnostic testing have been labeled *projective* and *objective*. Many "objective" tests are not objective in any of the senses we find the word to have been used, and projective test materials may be treated objectively. If we must have only projective tests and something else, which I do not believe is the case, the lame category of nonprojective is a shade better, because, at least, it does not make an invidious comparison.

There has been some involvement, spurious in my opinion, in the question of objective *versus* projective, in relation to the nomothetic and idiographic approaches. Beck (2) has asserted that objective tests are limited to the "subpersonality" in the course of discussing the question, or pseudo-question if you will, of the idiographic and nomothetic approaches. It may be that projective tests have more adherents from those with an idiographic approach and objective tests have more from the nomothetic camp, but it does not follow that objective tests cannot be used as measures of personality. To be sure, single objective tests or test items will certainly fail in this task. Factor and pattern analyses, as in the Cattell and McQuitty approaches, are surely approaches to the total personality, although with the inevitable loss of individuality or uniqueness that accompanies any theoretical formulation of personality, *including* that in projective formulations.

WHAT IS TESTED?

White's discussion (38) of what is tested by psychological tests is pertinent. He points out that psychological tests can no longer be regarded as inducing specimens or samples of performance of restricted functions. The samples may be conceived of as inducing, say, problem-solving capacity, but many other characteristics of personality also contribute. He argues that we can never arrange a situation on which one variable alone is tested. For example, the problem-solving measure may also tap frustration tolerance, anxiety control, and level of aspiration. Tests consequently supply overlapping information. In line with this, White goes on to propose we must use test batteries since we can no longer pin our faith on single tests. By use of a test battery, there is an increase in knowledge, not merely in an additive fashion, but in geometric progression. In the same vein he proposes multiple examiners. He speaks, in this connection, of psychological tests not yet being so objective as to dispense with this safeguard. In a sense, then, the whole discussion is a plea for objectivity, but objectivity at a high enough level of complexity so as not to do violence to the complexity of personality.

This point of view can be seen in contrast with the position of factoring psychologists who are interested in purifying their measures so they are free of what could be called contamination. But one man's contamination is another man's extra premium of subtlety. A not inconsiderable group of psychologists accept this position, considering that it is not only futile to try to purify their existing instruments, but also that it is quite valuable, especially in clinical settings, to have these additional premiums of information.

SOME CLASSIFICATIONS

There has been some interest expressed in the classification of tests and personality measures. Rosenzweig (27) has classified personality measures into objective or overt, subjective or covert, and projective or implicit levels of reference. He explicitly indicates, however, that they are not too exclusively associated with one or another of the diagnostic methods. In fact, the same instrument may supply information at all three levels. They are not defined so as to give objectivity to only one level. Campbell (5) has developed a classification of tests based on three dichotomies. In the first dichotomy he contrasts objective tests for which the subjects understand there are correct responses, and voluntary tests in which, in one fashion or another, the subjects are informed that there are no right or wrong answers. The other dichotomies are direct *versus* indirect, having to do with the subject's understanding of the purpose of the test, and free-response *versus* structured, having to do with the usual distinction made between them, but from the point of view of the subject. He would classify tests in terms of these three dimensions simultaneously, as in the voluntary, indirect, free-response type, which would include the *Rorschach* and the TAT, and the voluntary, direct, structured type, which would include the MMPI, and so on. His use of objective runs counter to several of the meanings of objective we have considered. In large measure, this arises from his use of objective in a phenomenological orientation—the phenomenologically objective environment. Accuracy and error, as he says, are in the subject's mind. Rosenzweig, in contrast, refers to the psychologist's orientation, not the subject's. Perhaps some classification uniting both the subject's and the examiner's frames of reference will give us an even more adequate classification than do Campbell's and Rosenzweig's when considered separately. I am reminded in this connection of George Kelly's witty remark that, "When the subject is asked to guess what the examiner is thinking, we call it an objective test; when the examiner tries to guess what the subject is thinking, we call it a projective device" (20).

Space limitation makes impossible an exhaustive survey of the remainder of modern literature relevant to the question of objectivity in personality testing. Certain other selected references might be mentioned. Frank (17) contrasts the psychometric and projective approach. In the context of norms for the TAT, Rosenzweig (26) has offered a discussion of how they help in the process of objectification. Levinson (21) compares and contrasts projective and ability tests. Rapaport (24) discusses the principles underlying nonprojective tests of personality. Allport (1) considers the advantages of straightforward, direct methods over projective techniques. Among his various publications, Eysenck deals more directly with what he means by objective personality tests in a review (14); Stephenson (31) has devoted considerable effort to demonstrating the objectivity of his variety of Q-technique.

REFERENCES

1. Allport, G. W. The trend in motivational theory. *Amer. J. Orthopsychiat.*, 1953, *23*, 107-119.
2. Beck, S. J. The science of personality: nomothetic or idiographic? *Psychol. Rev.*, 1953, *60*, 353-359.
3. Benton, A. L. The interpretation of questionnaire items in a personality schedule. *Arch. Psychol., N.Y.*, 1953, No. 190.
4. Burt, C. L. General and specific factors underlying the primary emotions. Rep. Brit. Assoc., 1915, 694.
5. Campbell, D. T. A typology of tests, projective and otherwise. *J. consult. Psychol.*, 1957, *21*, 207-210.
6. Cattell, J. M. Mental tests and measurements. *Mind*, 1890, *15*, 373-381.
7. Cattell, R. B. *A guide to mental testing*. London: University of London Press, 1936.
8. da Vinci, L. *Treatise on painting*. In L. da Vinci, *Buch von der Malerei*. Nach dem Codex Vaticanus (Urbinas), 1270. Vienna: W. Braumüller, 1882.
9. Dearborn, G. Blots of ink in experimental psychology. *Psychol. Rev.*, 1897, *4*, 390-391.
10. Dearborn, G. A study of imagination. *Amer. J. Psychol.*, 1898, *9*, 183-190.
11. Downey, June E. The Will-Profile. *Univ. Wyoming Dept. Psychol. Bull.*, 1919, No. 3.
12. Ellis, A. The validity of personality questionnaires. *Psychol. Bull.*, 1946, *43*, 385-440.
13. Ellis, A., and Conrad, H. S. The Validity of personality inventories in military practice. *Psychol. Bull.*, 1948, *45*, 385-426.
14. Eysenck, H. Personality tests 1944-49. In G. W. T. H. Fleming (Ed.), *Recent progress in psychiatry*. London: Churchill, 1950.
15. Feigl, H. The scientific outlook: naturalism and humanism. In H. Feigl and May Brodbeck (Eds.), *Readings in the philosophy of science*. New York: Appleton-Century-Crofts, 1953, 8-18.
16. Frank, L. K. Projective methods of the study of personality. *J. Psychol.*, 1939, *8*, 389-413.
17. Frank, L. K. *Projective methods*. Springfield, Ill.: Thomas, 1948.
18. Franz, S. I. *Handbook of mental examination methods*. New York: Macmillan, 1919.
19. Galton, F. Measurements of character. *Fortnightly Rev.*, 1884, *36*, 179-185.
20. Kelly, G. A. The theory and technique of assessment. *Annual Review of Psychology, Vol. 9,* Palo Alto: Annual Reviews, 1958, 323-352.
21. Levinson, D. J. A note on the similarities and differences between projective tests and ability tests. *Psychol. Rev.*, 1946, *53*, 189-194.
22. Macfarlane, Jean W. Problems of validation inherent in projective methods. *Amer. J. Orthopsychiat.*, 1942, *12*, 405-410.
23. Morgan, Christina D., and Murray, H. A. A method for investigating phantasies: the thematic apperception test. *Arch. Neurol. Psychiatr., Chicago*, 1935, *34*, 289-306.
24. Rapaport, D. Principles underlying non-projective tests of per-

sonality. *Ann. N.Y. Acad. Sci.,* 1946, *46*, 643-652.
25. Rorschach, H., and Oberholzer, E. The application of the form interpretation test. In H. Rorschach, *Psychodiagnostics.* Bern, Switzerland: Huber, 1942.
26. Rosenzweig, S. Apperceptive norms for the Thematic Apperception Test. I. The problem of norms in projective methods. *J. Personality,* 1949, *17*, 475-482.
27. Rosenzweig, S. Levels of behavior in psychodiagnosis with special reference to the Picture-Frustration Study. *Amer. J. Orthopsychiat.,* 1950, *20*, 63-72.
28. Sears, R. R. Experimental studies of projection: I. Attribution of traits. *J. soc. Psychol.,* 1936, *7*, 151-163.
29. Sharp, Stella E. Individual psychology: a study in psychological method. *Amer. J. Psychol.,* 1899, *10*, 329-391.
30. Spearman, C. "General intelligence," objectively determined and measured. *Amer. J. Psychol.,* 1904, *15*, 201-293.
31. Stephenson, W. *The study of behavior: Q-technique and its methodology.* Chicago: University of Chicago Press, 1953.
32. Thurstone, L. L. The criterion problem in personality research. *Educ. psychol. Measmt.,* 1955, *15*, 353-361.
33. Vernon, P. E. *The assessment of psychological qualities by verbal methods.* London: HMS Stationery Office, 1938.
34. Verplanck, W. S. A glossary of some terms used in the objective science of behavior. *Psychol., Rev. Suppl.,* 1957, *64*, 1-42.
35. Voelker, P. F. An account of certain methods of testing of normal reactions in conduct. *Relig. Educ.,* 1921, *16*, 81-83.
36. Webb, E. Character and intelligence. *Brit. J. Psychol. Monogr. Suppl.,* 1915, *1*, No. 3.
37. Whipple, G. M. *Manual of mental and physical tests.* Baltimore: Warwick and York, 1910.
38. White, R. W. What is tested by psychological tests? in P. H. Hoch and J. Zubin (Eds.), *Relation of psychological tests to psychiatry.* New York: Grune and Stratton, 1952, 3-14.
39. Wissler, C. The correlation of mental and physical tests. *Psychol. Rev. Monogr. Suppl.,* 1901, *3*, No. 16.

17. Historical Perspectives on the Relationship of Psychologists to Medical Research

The present theme is the contribution of psychologists to medical research. It would be incorrect, as well as ungracious, if one did not acknowledge that a reciprocal relation exists—the physicians' contributions to psychology. As a scientific discipline, psychology owes much to medicine. If one had to summarize the origin of scientific psychology in a sentence, it might be as follows: in rebelling against philosophy, psychology looked for its inspiration to medicine as well as to those parts of physiology and of physics which were medically oriented. It must be remembered that at the time psychology emerged as a science, physiology was not yet entirely a separate science, but still a part of medicine. Physics and chemistry were known to the first psychologists primarily through medical physics and medical chemistry. In this connection it is no accident that Weber, Fechner, Helmholtz, Wundt, and James held medical degrees.

Turning to the topic of sketching the relation of psychology to medicine, it will first be done by making a comment or two on the history of medicine.

SOME RELEVANT ASPECTS OF THE HISTORY OF MEDICINE

In considering the research contributions of psychology and medicine, a little knowledge of the history of medicine is a dangerous thing. It is dangerous because it may give an erroneous conception of the length of time that medicine has had a scientific basis. Having heard of Hippocrates and Galen, one might reach the conclusion that medicine has been firmly rooted in science since the Golden Age of Greece. This is incorrect. Those ancient and medieval figures of which we know are but brilliant stars in a dark sky of superstition. Medicine, even until well into the present century, showed the signs of its youthful, nonscientific disorganization. Medicine continued until relatively recently to be philosophical or theological, as shown by the presence of various systems of practice, e.g. homeopathy, allopathy.

Throughout its history, although it made use of contributions of scientific medicine, nonscientific concepts existed side by side with these advances. To be sure, bits of folklore which later proved scientifically valid, e.g. the use of quinine, were stumbled upon and used because of their pragmatic value. But they were isolated foreign bodies within the mainstream of medical thinking. They worked, but the medical men of those days either did not know why they worked or explained their value erroneously. Their scientific value was not established until much later.

The scientific advance of medicine may be dated in 1543 with the work of Vesalius. His "Seven Books on the Structure of the Human Body" gave medicine a scientific basis in anatomy. In 1628 Harvey described the circulation of the blood. It remained for Morgagni in 1761, who published "Five Books on the Seats and Causes of Diseases Investigated Anatomically," to take the forward step of combining data of the clinical case history and the autopsy report. He came to the conclusion that disease can be localized, and that it has a seat in the organs of the body. Still later Bichat traced disease back to the tissue. But it was not until 1858 that Virchow established the source of disease in the cells.

On the basis of this all-too-brief excursion into the history of medicine, it can be said that a thorough-going scientific basis for medicine is of relatively recent origin. It is hardly surprising that psychology's relation to experimental medicine can be dated from the beginnings of the latter half of the past century. Indeed, by and large, the histories of medicine have disregarded relations between psychological and medical research. Sigerist (7), for example, refers to Wundt only in connection with Helmholtz, where he is referred to as professor of physiology in 1857 at Heidelburg and as someone who ultimately became a professor at Leipzig in an unspecified field. Be that as it may, both medicine and psychology had reached the stage toward the end of the last century where collaboration became a possibility. The beginnings of collaboration will now be sketched.

THE BEGINNINGS OF COLLABORATION

The first form of collaborative research between medicine and psychology was illustrated by the trio who contributed so much to psychology's beginning—Fechner, Helmholtz, and Wundt. Each of these men held the M.D. degree. Each carried out his collaborative research by uniting in his own person the psychologist and the physician. Collectively their backgrounds had much to do with the fact that scientific psychology in the beginning was primarily a physiological psychology.

Wundt, as is well known, founded the first institute of experimental psychology at Leipzig in 1879. One of his first students was Emil Kraepelin, a physician, who saw the possibility of extending the experimental method to the field of psychopathology. As Murphy puts it, "Not only were mental abnormalities to be studied through experiment, and their phenomena stated in quantitative terms, but mental abnormalities of the milder type were to be experimentally *induced*" (6, p. 170). Disturbing influences such as hunger, fatigue, and alcohol were studied by Kraepelin in terms of analysis of associations. He observed that they all had in common an increase in the number of superficial associations, and their similarity to disorders of attention in mania was noted. Kraepelin then went on to his sytematic classificatory work in describing mental diseases. His classification of psychoses and his grasp of the fundamental similarity underlying several types of deteriorating psychoses which led to his use of the concept of dementia praecox are but two of his most important contributions. In Kraepelin we see a pattern of collaborative medical and psychological research—i.e., a physician studying psychology and thereafter working independently.

In this historical sketch, it is appropriate to make the transition to the United States through August Hoch. Hoch, a physician, had been chosen in 1893 by Edward Cowles, superintendent of McLean Hospital in Waverly, Massachusetts, to serve as pathologist *and* psychologist in the newly established laboratory at the hospital. This laboratory "sought to combine neurological studies in the departments of psychiatry and physiological psychology and their relations with anatomical and chemical pathology" (3, p. 358).

Hoch (5) accordingly went through training in psychology, studying under Wundt, Külpe, Marbe, Kiesow, and Kraepelin. On his return he worked for a short time on ergographic problems, publishing in the first volume of the *Psychological Bulletin*. But he very soon turned aside from directly psychological interests and carried on a very successful career in the field of psychiatry, with little or no indications of his psychological training.

Perhaps the history of his career is prophetic of present-day combinations of full, formal medical and psychological training within one person. Such combinations seem to be relatively infrequent in the United States today as compared to physiologists, anatomists, and biochemists, who are trained both in medicine and in their scientific specialty. Not only that, those few who combine formal training in psychology and medicine tend to choose a career in one of these fields with a relative minimization of the other. In no way is this meant to minimize the efforts of those in fields who have combined training in the two fields—a large proportion are distinguished members of their particular field. But they have not been distinguished by contributions to interstitial research. To mention some of those who hold allegiance to psychology, does one find in the work of William McDougall, or, to mention a contemporary, in that of Otto Klineberg, clear indications of their medical background? Combined training in both disciplines, it is clear, is not the usual pattern on which collaboration is based. Encouragement of medical research by combined full formal training in both fields has been neither typical nor outstandingly fruitful. It would seem that there is a commitment to patterns of research involving psychologists trained primarily in psychology and physicians trained primarily in medicine, working either independently or in collaboration on medical problems. It is on the basis of these patterns that the remainder of this paper is written.

INDEPENDENT PSYCHOLOGICAL RESEARCH ON MEDICAL PROBLEMS

In the perspective of history one aspect that may be overlooked is that research of direct medical interest and value may be done by psychologists without directly collaborating with medical men. Time limitation permits reference merely to one illustration.

In the United States it was at McLean Hospital that a

psychological laboratory in connection with a hospital was first founded (2). This was in 1904, with Shepard Ivory Franz as psychologist. He left shortly thereafter for what is now St. Elizabeths Hospital in Washington. At both McLean and St. Elizabeths Hospitals, Franz did much of his research on animal experimental psychophysiology with special reference to cerebral function. By and large, Franz was a solitary worker, working without collaborators, medical or otherwise.

Although other illustrations could be given from the work of Yerkes, Miles, and others, this will suffice to bring home the point that not all psychological research on medical problems is necessarily collaborative in the sense of psychologists and physicians working together on problems of common interest. Sometimes stimulation through research relevant to medicine comes from work in psychology independent of medicine.

Another phase of the stimulation of medical research comes from the participation of the psychologists in the training of physicians. It is to this topic I now turn.

PSYCHOLOGISTS AND THE TRAINING OF PHYSICIANS

So far as training of physicians by psychologists is concerned, it occurs in three settings—pre-medical education; undergraduate medical education; and post-graduate training, particularly in the residencies. I shall first consider pre-medical training. Psychology is not a prerequisite for entrance into medical school. Quite wisely, I think, medical educators discourage attempts to introduce further prerequisites into pre-medical preparation. So, aside from general college requirements, the trio biology, chemistry, and physics has been and will probably continue to be the only subjects required by a majority of medical schools. Nevertheless, in my experience at least, a majority of undergraduate medical students have taken one or more courses in psychology. It is not unusual for some to have taken a psychology major with a pre-medicine minor. However, it is also my impression that, by and large, medical students are *not* impressed by their undergraduate psychology training. Although it might be interesting to follow up this last remark, time limitation forces me to leave it as a mere assertion. The issue of how we might make physicians more psychologically minded during their college training, I am convinced, is a worthwhile question to explore.

The story of medical school teaching by psychologists probably begins with J. E. W. Wallin (8), who taught psychology in the University of Michigan Medical School in 1902. He offered the course in psychology only once because he left the University after one year. It is not certain whether or not his course was continued. There are indications that sporadically over the next 40 years courses were offered in medical schools by psychologists. By and large, however, they were few and far between, and stressed psychological content and not research methodology. Moreover, very few class hours were involved. Quite literally, a medical student could be exposed to a thousand hours of biological teaching for each hour of psychological teaching.

The training in psychology that was offered medical students and specialists tended to be done through departments of psychiatry. This placement of psychologists has continued to this day (4). The great majority of the nearly 300 full-time psychologists on the staffs of our medical schools are attached to departments of psychiatry. There is, of course, a sizable proportion attached to other departments, including pediatrics, internal medicine, surgery, and physiology. Since World War II, the number of teaching hours devoted to psychology has increased and greater stress has been placed upon training in research methodology. However, there is no cause for too self-congratulatory a point of view. If it used to be one hour of psychological to one thousand of biological teaching, it is now one hour to a hundred!

So far as medical specialties are concerned, psychologists have had the closest relation with psychiatry. It is therefore appropriate to conclude by referring to the relation of psychologists to psychiatric research.

THE RELATION OF PSYCHOLOGISTS TO PSYCHIATRIC RESEARCH

The relation of psychologists to psychiatric research is influenced by confusing complicating factors. On one hand, psychologists—or, rather, some psychologists—talk the same language as do psychiatrists, which makes for ease of communication and congeniality in collaborative work. But psychiatry has not developed a firm core of generally accepted scientifically verifiable knowledge of the sort that has contributed to the medical specialties which depend upon the advancement of biology or chemistry. Certainly until relatively recently, psychiatry drew little upon psychology. This is evident in Zilboorg's volume, "The History of Medical Psychology," published in 1941. There is hardly a reference in its 600 pages to psychology as we use the term. To offer another example, W. C. Menninger could write, in 1948, a book entitled "Psychiatry, its Evolution and Present Status" without mentioning a single research contribution of psychology to psychiatry. Indeed, the index does not carry a single entry for research of any sort. Psychiatry as it developed until recent years was in the paradoxical position of being a clinical specialty without a direct basic science on which it was clearly based. This has resulted in a neglect of research.

Psychiatry still shows the effects of the lack of a firm scientific underpinning. This is true whether one takes the position that psychology—our psychology—or that some development indigenous to psychiatry, such as psychoanalysis or psychobiology, is that basic science. Psychiatry is traditionally considered to be a clinical specialty. Some dim recognition that psychiatry and psychology, either together or separately, might provide the basic science is shown by the fact that undergraduate teaching in psychology is apt to be offered in the first two, or basic science, years in the medical school. This is but the barest beginning of a trend, while many forces continue to be active which serve to accentuate the clinical aspects of psychiatry.

The Group for the Advancement of Psychiatry (1) echoes informed opinion that psychiatric research has been neglected. They go on to indicate that this relative absence may be traced to the complexity of the problem and lack of personnel, lack of professional time, lack of funds, lack of training in research methodology, lack of rewards for research, and lack of administrative support.

These lacks are, as they say, obvious. But they do not draw the conclusion, which to me is inescapable, that these lacks are either a consequence or a cause, probably both, of *lack of interest in research* on the part of psychiatrists. In psychiatry, after all, as in all medical specialties, research is a concern of only a minority. Since we come in contact with a segment of that small minority it is sometimes easy for us to forget that the M.D. degree is not primarily a degree signifying training for a scientific career. It signifies training for professional practice. Moreover, there has been a positive attraction for psychiatrists of a substitution of theorizing for research. Encouragement of research in psychiatry means first encouraging interest in research.

REFERENCES

1. Committee on Psychopathology of the Group for the Advancement of Psychiatry. *Report No. 25*. Topeka, Kansas: 1954.
2. Franz, S. I. The present status of psychology in medical education and practice. *J. Amer. Med. Assoc.*, 1912, *58*, 909-911.
3. Hall, G. S. Laboratory of the McLean Hospital. *Amer. J. Insanity*, 1894, *51*, 358-364.
4. Matarazzo, J. D., and Daniel, R. S. The teaching of psychology by psychologists in medical school. *J. med. Educ.*, 1957, *32*, 410-415.
5. Meyer, A. August Hoch, M.D. *Arch. Neurol. Psychiat.*, 1919, *2*, 573-576.
6. Murphy, G. *Historical introduction to modern psychology*. (Rev. ed.) New York: Harcourt Brace, 1949.
7. Sigerist, H. E. *Great doctors: a biographical history of medicine*. London: Allen and Unwin, 1933.
8. Wallin, J. E. W. Vagrant reminiscences of an oligophrenist. *Amer. J. Ment. Def.*, 1953, *58*, 39-55.

18. The Experimental Tradition and Clinical Psychology

A psychologist reading contemporary journal literature is being influenced unknowingly by an editorial decision that took place not too many years ago. The sheer productivity of the increased number of psychologists forced editors to eliminate or drastically curtail what at one time was an essential part of the research report—the historical introduction. Today, the first rule of article writing is to come immediately to the point. The setting for this point is often limited to no more than, "Since Brown (1959) has found that . . . then, . . . ," or the immortal phrase, "In a previous communication . . . ." It is not surprising, then, that readers, especially among younger psychologists, may slip into thinking that this work began with "Brown (1959)" or with the "previous communication," since this is the only work cited. Thus a valuable source of historical perspective has been lost, with no foreseeable chance that the custom will change. In the master's essay and the doctoral dissertation some attempt is still made to place a research problem in its historical context, but the value of these attempts is blunted by the sponsors' injunction to students: "When you prepare for publication, the first thing to eliminate is the historical introduction."

The change of policy about historical introductions may be both an effect of an ahistorical, or even antihistorical, attitude on the part of psychologists and one of the causes of the continued neglect of history.

This foreshortening of historical vision is perhaps one of the reasons that clinical psychologists are, to a considerable degree, blithely oblivious to much of the content of experimental psychology on which their clinical efforts are based. The breach between "experimental" and "clinical" psychologists is obviously widened if no attempt is made to show that they are related. One of the sources of furthering *rapprochement* between these factions is attention to the historical antecedents of clinical work to be found in nonclinical settings.

Looking at historically rooted experimental antecedents of clinical psychology is a process similar to the clinical investigation of the individual. A psychological problem viewed in present context and in historical perspective is like viewing the patient as reflecting both contemporary forces and past experiences. Most clinical psychologists, in attempting to understand a patient's current problem, feel that they need to know the individual's past history; so too should we be sensitive to the need for understanding current research in the light of its historical antecedents.

THE TRADITIONS OF CLINICAL PSYCHOLOGY

The history of psychology shows a cumulative advance by the building up of a body of research findings, theories, procedures, and techniques which are passed on from one generation of psychologists to the next. Because of this passage between generations it is proper to speak of a tradition of psychology. Within this general tradition, it is possible to discern several more specific traditions, not completely separable and tending to blend with each other, but sufficiently distinguishable so that they have come to receive meaningful identifying labels.

As a field, clinical psychology originated in a matrix of older, already existing traditions within psychology. Indeed, no tradition of psychology is so remote from clinical endeavor as to be ruled out completely as one of the foundations of clinical psychology. Discernible among these as particularly relevant to clinical psychology are the psychometric, the dynamic, the social, the biological-medical, and the experimental traditions.

The intent of this book requires that the experimental tradition be made central. Some of the other traditions are peripheral to this emphasis. What is meant by these traditions is already familiar. In a Presidential Address to the American Psychological Association, Cronbach (1957) focused on the contrast between experimental psychology and what he called correlation psychology. He was in fact contrasting the experimental and psychometric traditions.

Bindra and Scheier (1954), who wrote on the relation between what they called psychometric and experimental research, were also considering these two traditions. Omitted from this chapter is the psychiatric tradition as it is reflected, in the immediate past, in the field of the study of individual differences, stemming from Galton and Cattell, and the effect of this study upon psychology in general (Boring, 1957; Murphy, 1949), and upon clinical psychology in particular (Watson, 1953; Watson, 1959). This omission is justified, not because the study of individual differences is unimportant, but because it is sufficiently separable from the experimental tradition in the direction of the psychometric tradition to justify omission. The absence of much material on the human child illustrates this point, since so much research using children is dependent upon the use of already established differences. Some aspects of the psychometric tradition are discussed in the chapter by Berg on measurement and evaluation.

Clinical psychology also draws upon the dynamic tradition, epitomized in the work of Freud, James, Hall, and Janet. In a previous publication the writer (1953) explored historically the psychometric and dynamic tradition of clinical psychology. To write this chapter without further mentioning Freud (and the others in the dynamic tradition) except incidentally shows the selectivity of the point of view of this book. And yet it is fully justified. Despite his fecundity in stimulating research and thinking, Freud contributed nothing relevant to the *experimental* foundations of clinical psychology. It is convenient to refer to the biological-medical tradition in psychology as a more or less coherent, interrelated whole. Not only does this draw attention to the fact that medical research is rooted in biology, making them for present purposes essentially one, but it also serves to distinguish it from medicine's contributions to the dynamic tradition.

The social tradition, drawing unto itself social philosophy, sociology, and social psychology (as well as experimental and clinical psychology), is in itself a hybrid similar in this respect to clinical psychology. Insofar as these traditions draw upon experiment they are relevant to that which follows. Their rich contentual and theoretical heritage as well as their use of other methodologies must be neglected.

Each of these other traditions has a symbiotic relation with clinical psychology. Each tradition supplies content and approaches to the clinical field and receives in return content and procedures, but here attention is centered on the contribution from the experimental field. The reverse relation is another story.

Implicit in the title of this book is the contention that clinical psychological research has as one of its bases the contributions of experimental behavioral study. In this sense the entire history of experimental psychology bears relation to clinical psychology. No attempt has been made in this volume to limit the experimental tradition to a narrow definition. Rather, experimental psychology was interpreted as behavioral study oriented to and derived from the laboratory but not confined to it, providing that the concern in nonlaboratory settings attempted to preserve, insofar as the problem and setting permitted, the controls of the laboratory. Despite the broad context of the entire book, however, it would be absurd to try in the space of a few pages to sketch the history of experimental psychology.

This chapter instead presents selected historical material in settings that will bring out their contemporary significance. The illustrations used are drawn from the experimental tradition particularly relevant to some of the major problems discussed in later chapters. Selection of each topic was guided by its usefulness not only as an illustration of historical relationships as such but also by its capacity to deepen the value of knowledge of the history of psychology. Knowledge, for example, that contemporary investigation of clinical judgment is rooted in the very oldest of problems in the experimental tradition, that of psychophysics, helps us to understand the significance of the research and to gain some understanding of the direction it has taken. Moreover, the possibility of showing that psychophysics—which occupies one of the highest floors in the Ivory Tower—is relevant to clinical psychology is a temptation that could not be resisted.

CLINICAL PSYCHOLOGY AND THE EXPERIMENTAL TRADITION IN THE PAST

Clinical psychology, as a separate discipline, arose some time after the turn of the century (Watson, 1953). This approximate date is used to differentiate its past from its historical period.

This past stretched back in time to the earliest known experimentally controlled research study of the Ancient World. In fact, the earliest psychological experiment known to the writer is relevant to the topic of Chapter 6, which is concerned with the effects of early experience on later behavior. As told by Herodotus, one Psammetichus, ruler of Egypt in the seventh century before Christ, wanted to enhance Egyptian national pride by proving that Egyptian was the oldest of languages. Accordingly, he ordered his herdsman to take two children "of the common sort" and to isolate them from birth onward in a hut, accompanied only by goats from which to draw nourishment; further, he gave strict instructions that no human beings be allowed to approach them. Two years later, when the hut was opened, the children rushed out crying, "becos." To the Pharaoh's chagrin, "becos" proved to be the Phrygian word for bread, forcing him to acknowledge that this, not Egyptian, was the oldest of languages.

To return to the period more than 2500 years later than Psammetichus—a considerable number of psychologists and other research workers can be considered possible early representatives of the experimental tradition in psychology. Some contributed so much to the intellectual climate of their times and influenced our own so forcefully that attention is forced upon them, despite the fact that they did their work before there was a clinical psychology. Representative of these are Darwin and Pavlov, towering above the others, who did not work with clinical problems and were, in fact, not even psychologists. But their contributions were so far-reaching that they must be considered. Others, not so important, did experimental work which had direct relation with clinical problems, both in the past before clinical psychology emerged as a discipline and after the turn of the century, when clinical psychology was beginning to emerge. By definition they were not clinical psychologists. Rather, they were individuals who contributed materially to experimental psychology but did so using clinical problems. Emil Kraepelin is representative of the past; Shepard Ivory Franz is representative of the period of emergence of clinical psychology.

Charles Darwin. Darwin was not the first biologist to concern himself with evolution. During the first half of the nineteenth century and even before, evolutionary theory excited considerable interest and furious discussion (Murphy, 1949). Darwin's genius rested not upon proposing the problem, but upon his long and painstaking collection of the relevant evidence. The period of preparation began in 1831 with the voyage of H.M.S. *Beagle* to the South Seas, lasted through the years of travel, and culminated with his reading of Malthus's *Essay on Population* in 1838. Thereafter he had a biological premise to work with and his own theory of evolution began to take shape in the doctrine of the transmutation of the species. Over the next *twenty* years he collected the necessary mass of relevant data. Only in 1859 did *On the Origin of Species* appear. What happened thereafter, we can assume, is generally familiar. We need be concerned only with Darwin's effect on psychology; there, his *The Expression of the Emotions in Man and Animals* was important.

For the remainder of the century, psychology clearly evidenced the influence of Darwin. His work shaped psychology in the direction of biology and function and away from the model of physics and chemistry and structure of the German psychologists. One facet of the biological orientation, as a matter of fact, was the line of development, from Galton through Baldwin and Hall, in the study of individual differences. Evidences of this biological orientation were manifested in other ways as well. A sign of Darwin's influence was found in the increasing tendency to interpret mental processes in terms of the functions they served. Moreover, the comparative viewpoint of a continuity of mental development became prominent because of his work. It has even been suggested by Beck and Molish (1959) that to Darwin we owe the beginning of "scientific clinical psychology." They reach this conclusion because of his recognition of the importance of the dynamics of behavior. These trends in the work of those influenced by Darwin will be apparent in later discussion.

It was Darwin's work that stimulated the study of comparative psychology immediate prior to the modern era (Warden, 1927; Watson, 1961). For some years after Darwin the anecdotal method, dependent upon casual observation of "clever" and unusual animals, was the dominating technique for collecting data. This inadequate method was accompanied by a tendency to anthropomorphize the lower animals. About 1890 the work of Jacques Loeb and C. Lloyd Morgan introduced the modern era in animal psychology. Loeb's work on tropisms helped to demolish the trend toward anthropomorphism. So too did Morgan's canon, which might be stated briefly as advancing the rule that no action should be interpreted as being due to a higher behavioral function if it is capable of being interpreted as the outcome of a behavioral function lower on the scale.

This adaptation of the law of parsimony served to discourage extravagant interpretation of animal behavior.

Ivan P. Pavlov. In his autobiography, Pavlov (1955) acknowledged that he was enormously influenced by Darwin, first through the intermediary of Pisarev's expositions of Darwin and the theory of evolution (Pisarev was a Russian writer of the sixties and seventies) and later directly by Darwin's works. The second major influence he acknowledged was the writings of Sechenov, whom he called the "father" of Russian physiology.

Through his researches Sechenov had become convinced that spinal reflexes are capable of inhibition by the cerebral cortex. He further argued that thinking and intelligence were dependent upon exercise for their stimulation and that all psychological acts are reflexes. As Pavlov (1927) indicated, Sechenov's view was based on conjecture. Pavlov proceeded to carry out his well-known research studies to demonstrate the validity of this hypothesis.

Pavlov (1927) acknowledged that Thorndike's researches of 1898 were the first experiments in this general area, but he further indicated that at the time he began investigation he was not familiar with this work.

Before embarking on the study of conditioning, a detailed study of the digestive glands had occupied a considerable amount of his research time. While working on these glands, Pavlov (Wells, 1956) noticed that gastric juice was secreted by his experimental dogs not only when food was taken in the mouth but also when they saw it at a distance. Later on he found the same phenomenon with the secretion of saliva. This "mouth watering" he first termed "psychical secretions," to distinguish this action-at-a-distance from direct stimulation of the nerve endings in the mouth. Heretofore, and indeed in his own early work, this and similar phenomena were considered in the then-current setting of introspective interpretation. The animal "judged" that it was food, that it "smelled good," and that he "desired" it. Pavlov's great contribution was to forego this introspective approach and treat the phenomena objectively. In other words, external stimulation and underlying nervous processes were studied experimentally by objective means. Pavlov followed this course by working on conditioned reflexes for his remaining thirty-five years.

His method, it should be noted, is extraordinarily flexible and has had far-reaching consequences. The conditioning referred to in later chapters, although perhaps initiated by problems quite alien to his range of interests, nevertheless all owe a debt to this physiologist. Vladimir Bechterev, too, beginning about 1907, studied the conditioning of motor responses (Bechterev, 1932; Rosenzweig, 1960). Bechterev's work (Rosenzweig, 1960) stimulated John B. Watson's (1916) enthusiastic presidential address in 1915, which was devoted to the topic of conditioning. However, as Hilgard and Marquis (1940) indicate, it was Pavlov's detailed approach to conditioning, not Bechterev's, which was accepted in the United States.

Emil Kraepelin. Born in 1856, Emil Kraepelin took a medical degree and subsequently was Professor of Psychiatry, first at Heidelberg and then at Munich. He is quite properly judged one of the founders of modern psychiatry—and sometimes described as the "father of descriptive psychiatry." This, in some circles, is dangerously close to condemnation. What such critics forget is that his work on the classification and description of mental disorders made it possible for his successors to go further. Kraepelin himself seems to have been aware that it was too early to attempt more than description, for one of his papers (Kahn, 1956) ends expressly on the note that, once we have more knowledge, one can proceed to the main task—understanding the disorder.

He opened the first issue of his journal, *Psychologische Arbeiten* (1895), with an account of his own previous researches. He then proceeded to write eloquently that the psychological experiment is not merely useful but indispensable. He indicated that every psychiatrist seemed to judge it his right, or perhaps even his obligation, to construct his own psychological system and went on to ask what internist would dare to proclaim a new system of physiology without basing it on laboriously acquired laboratory facts? All of this has a modern ring; it was written more than sixty-five years ago but might still be pertinent today as comment and question.

Nevertheless, because his contributions to descriptive psychiatry were so immense, other facets of his work which are of more direct concern to psychiatry are often neglected, and it is seldom pointed out that experimental laboratory research was a major interest to Kraepelin.

Wundt had taken over the word association technique from Galton, and several of his students, including Kraepelin, worked in this area. On the heels of Cattell's first work on reaction time, Kraepelin showed that characteristic alterations in association occurred when experimentally induced abnormal conditions, such as fatigue, hunger, and alcoholic intoxication, were introduced. Another area in which Kraepelin was a pioneer was the study of continuous work, such as adding. He was able to show the classic phenomena—the shape of the curve, the mutually opposing influence of fatigue and learning, warming-up, spurts, and so on—which were nearly always found in subsequent investigations.

Shepard Ivory Franz. A physician, Edward Cowles, founded at McLean Hospital the first psychological laboratory for the investigation of psychotic patients (Franz, 1919). A charter member of the American Psychological Association in 1892 (Dennis and Boring, 1952), Cowles became director of the McLean Hospital some years before the turn of the century (Hall, 1894).

In 1903 Cowles invited psychologist Shepard Ivory Franz to come to the hospital laboratory to carry out some research that earlier he had asked Franz to outline (Franz, 1932). This work had to do with relating the nerve physiology that Sherrington was then developing to problems of excitement and depression as formulated by Kraepelin. In 1907, after carrying out this research, Franz went to what is now St. Elizabeths Hospital in Washington, D.C., the federal mental hospital. He also had an appointment at George Washington University. His first task was to prepare a standard clinical psychological examination, adopted for use in the hospital in 1907 and expanded into a book, first published in 1912 (1919). This was almost certainly the first routine psychological examination program in the world. However, his work in the experimental tradition is more relevant to the present interest.

Before going to McLean Hospital, Franz, a Cattell Ph.D. from Columbia, had published his first paper in the field with which he was to become identified. This was the study entitled "On the function of the cerebrum: the frontal lobes in relation to the production and retention of simple sensory-motor habits" (1902). His years at St. Elizabeths were productive in various fields. He studied, for example, the knee jerk in paretics. However, probably his most important work continued to have to do with cerebral function, especially in subjects in which brain areas were destroyed, and he published a considerable number of studies. Associated with him was Karl S. Lashley, and in 1917 they published together on the effects of cerebral destruction on habit formation in the white rat. From this point on the distinguished research work of Lashley continued along the lines thus laid down. Among his other younger associates was E. G. Boring, who spent the summer of 1913 with him, working in learning (and introspection) in dementia praecox (Boring, 1923, a,b).

Franz was by no means the only psychologist concerned with the abnormal person during these years. In a review of the experimental literature on psychotics through 1923, J. McV. Hunt (1936) reported on a considerable number of studies. After eliminating those irrelevant to present interests, such as psychometric and statistical studies, there were still about fifty experimental studies published before 1920. Among the other workers cited who used experimental methods with the psychotics before 1920 were J. W. Baird, A. Hoch, Grace H. Kent, T. V. Moore, E. W. Scripture, E. K. Strong, D. Wechsler, and F. L. Wells. Even this brief summary disproves the notion sometimes expressed that experimental study of the abnormal person was not taken seriously until more recent years.

CLINICAL PROBLEMS AND THE EXPERIMENTAL TRADITION

At this point, the approach of this chapter shifts to consider historically some of the major themes of the topics to follow. It is manifestly impossible in short compass to trace, one by one, the historical backgrounds for the topics of the chapters that follow. Instead, the general headings of the sections, each including several chapters, supply the remaining topics; the first of these is divided into two parts. The topic of *psychophysiology* is not discussed specifically since in considerable measure it draws upon the biological-medical tradition. Insofar as psychophysiology draws upon learning, that section is relevant. The topics, then, are *learning, communication*, and *behavior modification*. The next chapter, concerned with clinical judgment, gives us the first topic of *psychophysics*. Each topic is examined in a different way in order to bring out its value in illustrating historically important issues.

Psychophysics. In Chapter 2 Hunt and Jones describe the experimental bases of clinical judgment. This discussion of its historical antecedents will center on the work of Hunt partly because of considerable familiarity with his work. So far as his contributions are concerned, research clinical selection procedures during and following World War II form the content. In the course of his duties as a clinical psychologist in the United States Navy, Hunt was faced with a practical clinical problem: psychologists' and psychiatrists' established practice of using clinical judgment in selecting, rejecting, and placing naval personnel. In his research, Hunt has applied a psychophysical analogue to this problem.

A short digression is necessary here; it also illustrates the value of knowledge of the experimental tradition. The history of psychology is replete with appeals to analogy. When the appeal stopped with the drawing of the analogy it was futile and essentially self-defeating. For example, the gigantic analogy between the individual —the microcosm—and the world—the macrocosm—plagued the history of intellectual development from the time of the pre-Socratic Greeks (Watson, 1961). The Platonic tripartite division of the individual soul as having the functions of reason, spirit, and sense corresponding to the ruling, warrior, and worker classes in the state is a specific instance of this analogy.

Hunt and his associates took the crucial and imperative step of going beyond analogy and testing it experimentally. Hunt, drawing on his knowledge of the history of psychology in general and the experimental tradition in particular, was able to see the experimental procedures of psychophysics as relevant to the problem.

The history of psychophysics (and the actuarial trend in the field of judgment) began with Weber's (1834–1846) and Fechner's (1860) classical work on the measurement of sensory mechanisms (Boring, 1950a). Weber's statement that the just noticeable difference in a stimulus bears a constant ratio to that stimulus was expanded by Fechner into the formula $S = K \log R$. Without going into the stormy history over the intervening years, let us move forward to the late twenties. One of the problems exciting considerable interest at this time was that of relative, as opposed to absolute, judgment in psychophysics as expressed, for example, by Wever and Zener (1928). As Hunt (1960) pointed out:

> The orientation in psychophysics at that time, and particularly so at Harvard, was a peripheral, end-organ one. More and more of us, however, and I remember particularly Volkmann, Chapman, Cantril, and Sherif who were fellow graduate students at the time, were becoming convinced of the importance of "central" as opposed to "peripheral" processes.

If the processes producing psychophysical phenomena were central, and not confined to peripheral processes, then, it followed that they might appear in areas other than that of classical psychophysics. Volkmann and Hunt (1937) found anchoring effects in affective judgment; Hunt (1941) found them in aesthetic judgment. In these two areas, far removed from that of classical psychophysics, they found that subjective standards are built up which in turn provide a standard against which other stimuli are judged.

With the demonstration of lawful predictable phenomena in judgment in different types of stimulus material, Hunt was encouraged to draw the analogy between psychophysical and clinical judgment.* An insightful transfer of knowledge and methodology derived from the experimental tradition to a clinical problem was effected.

Learning. In the nineteenth century some of the previously mentioned animal research of Morgan and Loeb, as well as that of Fabre, Lubbock, and Verworn, was experimental in intent, but it was Edward L. Thorndike who introduced the modern laboratory type of experiment into animal psychology (Warden, 1927). Beginning in 1898, his pioneer studies of learning and imitation in chicks, dogs, cats, and monkeys began to appear. Work similar in spirit immediately became popular among psychologists. The animal work of Yerkes, Carr, and Hunter during the first twenty-five years of this century is illustrative. However, it was John B. Watson who made the most far-reaching innovations in his popularization of behaviorism.

Before dealing with his work, it is necessary to say something about functional psychology, which was a characteristic expression of psychology in the United States during the early years of the century. Many factors were at work in its development. There was, for example, the influence of James from the United States and Höffding and Külpe from Europe (Murphy, 1949). Another important factor was certainly the Darwinian influence. At the risk of some oversimplification, it will be this influence that will be sketched.

It was through functional psychology that the Darwinian view extended beyond animal psychology to psychology in general. The philosopher of social change, John Dewey, was influential

---

*The same general context that led to these studies was one of the elements entering into Sherif's studies (1936) of the assimilation of social norms in frames of reference as expressed in the autokinetic phenomenon.

in developing the functional point of view. As Boring (1950) demonstrates, he had been influenced by Darwinian thinking. The paper by Dewey (1896) published in 1896 with the self-explanatory title "The reflex arc concept in psychology" had considerable influence. After Dewey's simultaneous departure from the University of Chicago (for Columbia University) and from psychology (for philosophy), his work was carried on by Angell. Angell (1907), too, acknowledged a direct debt to Darwin (Boring, 1950), arguing that functional psychology was not new but had its modern impetus from the views of Darwin and Spencer (who also wrote in an evolutionary vein). As a "school," functionalism was relatively short-lived, and need not concern us further.

To return to Watson, who was trained at Chicago: much of the emphasis of functionalism lived on in behaviorism and in the neobehavioristic tendency, so prevalent today, to stress activity as contrasted with conscious states. Nevertheless, in one way functionalism strengthened Watson's rebellion—in this respect he was reacting as much against functionalism as against structuralism—in that functionalism, too, made no "clean break" with consciousness (Watson, 1929), and it was this break for which Watson argued. Watson himself stated that his debt was to C. Lloyd Morgan and Thorndike (Watson, 1929). The influence of Bechterev and Pavlov on Watson has already been mentioned. Watson began to formulate his views conversationally in 1903, gave them first public expression in 1905 to 1912, and first published them in 1913. Human behavior, learned and unlearned, with vigorous exclusion of introspective material, became a dominating force in American psychology under the enthusiastic sponsorship of Watson from about 1913 onward.

As behaviorism broadened, in the 1930's, from a school to a point of view without a school's in-group manifestations, the next important figure to appear on the psychological scene was Clark L. Hull. In his autobiography (1952) Hull indicates how he came to his study of the quantitative laws of human behavior. He attributed his interest to his early training in the physical sciences; to being influenced favorably by Watson, although repelled by his dogmatism; and to reading Pavlov's *Conditioned Reflexes*, which had been translated in the late twenties. He goes on to indicate that about 1930 (after a considerable number of years of research endeavor on other problems) he came to the conclusion that the task of psychology as a natural science was the development of a "moderate" number of primary laws expressible quantitatively by means of ordinary equations, with the complex behavior of individuals to be derivable as secondary laws. His seminar became popular at the Institute of Human Relations at Yale University. Students, notably Kenneth W. Spence and Neal E. Miller, discussed this point of view with him, shared the general view, and conducted research along the lines laid down by Hull. It was to this program that he addressed the rest of the life work expressed in his three books (1940, 1943, 1951).

Of Hull's students, Spence continued his work most directly; in a recent series of books surveying the present situation in psychology as a science, a chapter is entitled "The Hull-Spence Approach" (Logan, 1959). The work of Spence is highly systematic and detailed. He insists, more than did Hull, upon holding his theorizing more closely to the research data, extending his views only as new data become available (Logan, 1959). His general attitude, his techniques, and his methods are summarized in an article which shows by its title his allegiance to a modified behaviorism (Spence, 1948).

Spence's collaborative studies with Janet A. Taylor serve to illustrate another historical point: sometimes the experimental foundations of clinical psychology are to be found in contemporary research which precedes the clinically significant research by only a few years. For example, Taylor and Spence, initiating their studies on the relation of manifest anxiety and learning, first reported on them in 1952 and 1953 (Taylor, 1953; Taylor and Spence, 1952). Taylor (1960) estimated that papers using the Manifest Anxiety Scale, published from 1952 through 1960, numbered about 300. Of these, 90 to 100 are quite directly concerned with the drive theory as proposed by Taylor and Spence. Their interest is and has been primarily in the role of drive in certain learning situations. Nevertheless, the extension of their work to the study of the phenomena of anxiety has also stimulated clinically oriented research—for example, that on the relationship of anxiety to stress.

Neal E. Miller, too, played an extensive role in the S-R reinforcement interpretation of learning. He has taken leadership in extending Hull's general point of view to approach-avoidance conflict behavior to psychotherapy and to social behavior. A recent account (Miller, 1959) covers his work on these problems.

B. F. Skinner is, of course, extremely important for much of the research reported in many chapters to follow. In 1959 he published a personal account of the development of his research approach. In his college days, although he had no courses in psychology, he had read about John B. Watson and studied Loeb and Pavlov. In his book he recounted these readings briefly, and next reported that he was at Harvard as a graduate student. It is plausible to infer, from this, that these men most influenced Skinner to follow a career in psychology. In another book (1953), which mentions remarkably few psychologists by name, Skinner refers only to Darwin, Freud, Pavlov, and Thorndike more than twice. All four men were cast in historical perspective and as initiating major developments in psychology. His dependence upon the work of Pavlov may be inferred from his early work, *The Behavior of Organisms* (1938). By 1938 he had some conception of his research plans for the future but had had only a few years to carry them out. As a consequence he had to depend upon the work of other men in his presentation. It would be no great exaggeration to say that in this work he referred to Pavlov as often as all other men combined.

Nevertheless, Skinner (1938, 1953) insists that the physiological activity which Pavlov thought he was studying was inferential. The processes being studied by Pavlov had not been reduced to neural events. No direct observations of the cortex are reported. In his view, Pavlov's achievement consisted not in describing neural processes, but in formulating quantitative relations in behavior. It was in espousing the study of the behavior of the empty organism that he parted company with Pavlov. In short, it is unnecessary to concern oneself with physiological data in order to understand psychological phenomena. As Greenspoon put it, in introducing his chapter on verbal conditioning, Skinner made it possible to see verbal behavior as a response in its own right. Hefferline, in his statement of learning theory, speaks of work in the area less clogged with surplus meaning. Nevertheless, it should be noted in passing that this attempt to eliminate "physiologizing" has been criticized sharply by Pratt (1939), Köhler (1940), and Hebb (1949). The chapters in the section in this volume on psychophysiology show that there is still vigor to this approach. Moreover, the chapter by Hefferline attempts to demonstrate that Skinner's general approach is not vitiated by dealing with the internal environment.

It would appear that Pavlov's influence on relatively recent work in learning has been sufficiently demonstrated, but Darwin's more general influence has been neglected to this point. Before closing this discussion of learning some comment seems indicated.

As to the implications for later chapters of the work stimulated by Darwin, it is perhaps directly most pertinent to Levine's chapter on the effects of early experience upon adult behavior and to Wolpe's chapter on experimental approaches to neuroses. What began with the work following Darwin in the study of the continuity of mind in animals and man has reached such a degree of acceptance that these chapters are written without any except incidental reference to human subjects. Presumably only poorly controlled research exists with our species. Moreover, the feasibility of using much more radical experimental conditions than would be possible with humans is a compelling reason for the use of lower animals.

In his chapter Levine states that recent interest in his topic comes from Hebb's emphasis upon perceptual learning and the observations of European ethologists on early social stimulation and its later effect on various species of birds. This historical introduction should be significant to the clinician, who is apt to interpret present research in the perspective of his own interests. Hearing of the work on the effect of deprivation of animals and lacking historical information, the clinician might plausibly assume that the historical sequence was from Freud's theory of psychosexual stages to the work of Spitz, and thence to the animal work. He would thus be misled by what he thinks *should* have happened. The work on animal deprivation does indeed have clinical implications, but its historical roots are elsewhere. If the clinician does not appreciate the possibility that a problem with clinical significance may have a nonclinical origin, he would find much current work difficult to comprehend.

Communication. The chapter on small group research, by Petrullo, best illustrates the relation of communication research to clinical psychology. Clearly, in this area we are dealing simultaneously with a limited aspect of social psychology and with a special problem in learning. It is the social psychological aspect that will be stressed.

Murphy, Murphy, and Newcomb (1937) state that the first systematic studies of suggestion performed by Braid between 1841 and 1860 represent the inception of experimentation in social psychology. Braid (1899) rejected the concept of Mesmerism as magical in nature and invented the term "hypnotism" to describe the experimentally obtained phenomena. At one and the same time there occurred the beginning of experimentation in social psychology and the opening up of experimental research on a clinical problem. Following the work of Braid, there was a long procession of investigations concerned with related phenomena, including those by Ambroise-Auguste Liébeault, Hippolyte Bernheim, Jean Charcot, Pierre Janet, Boris Sidis, and Morton Prince. The work initiated by Bernheim had repercussions in other areas of psychology also. For example, Charcot's pupil, Gustave Le Bon, stimulated by his teacher's doctrine of dissociation, found in it the explanation of crowd phenomena as a consequence of the splitting of personality (1895).

A slight trickle of experimental reports concerning group or communication problems appeared throughout the years until World War I. After the war, W. Moede and F. H. Allport independently advanced pleas that social psychology could and should be placed upon an experimental basis. Moede's work, beginning in 1913 with research on co-acting groups (as distinguished from face-to-face groups), had priority over that of Allport (Allport, 1954). Moede studied the introduction of the social variable into standard experiments, such as the threshold of audibility. He did this by comparing the results obtained with subjects working alone with those found when subjects were working in groups of two or more. Using a similar experimental design, he studied imitation, fixation of attention, and learning. His work was not widely known in the United States, partly because the book that gives his major findings was not translated. Münsterberg, at Harvard, being familiar with his results, encouraged F. H. Allport to carry on studies in this area; these launched a whole series of studies (Allport, 1924).

Face-to-face studies were slower to appear than those on co-acting groups. In connection with priorities in this field, Allport (1954) states that the earliest experimental studies were performed by the Russians. They had been stimulated to this work by their concern for individual, as contrasted with collective, behavior—for example, the study of Bechterev and DeLange (1924). These studies, however, did not make much impression upon psychology in the United States.

Lewin's studies bring us almost to the present. His work, probably arrived at independently of the Russian work, stems directly from Gestalt tradition and to some extent from the work of Moreno (Moreno, 1952). Lewin and his coworkers introduced the concept of *social climate or group atmosphere* in a research setting. Thereafter this work was to have a pronounced effect on research in social psychology. Variation in productivity of subjects was studied under so-called "authoritarian," "democratic," and "laissez faire" working conditions (Lewin, Lippitt, and White, 1939). Despite the fact that unwarranted generalizations were derived from them, the studies have demonstrated that face-to-face groups could be studied under reasonably well controlled conditions.

Research expanded rapidly after the work of Lewin. Interest in research study spread to community, industrial, and therapeutic research settings. Group dynamics, group cohesion, group decision, and group conflict became intensively studied issues. In 1945 the Massachusetts Institute of Technology Research Center for Group Dynamics was established. In 1948, after the death of Lewin, the Center was moved to the University of Michigan. The Tavistock Institute, located in London, follows in some respects the Lewinian tradition. Under the joint sponsorship of the Center and the Institute a periodical, *Human Relations*, has appeared, which is devoted to research in this area. Deutsch (1954) has written a very useful review of Lewin's work and that inspired by him in the setting of field theory as a way of thinking. These comments about small group research are extended in a later chapter in this volume by Petrullo. Because the "small group" includes within its rubric the face-to-face interaction of two individuals, this historical discussion is also relevant to the chapters by Matarazzo and by Strupp.

Behavior modification. "Behavior modification," as used as a section heading in this book, covers a multitude of approaches. It includes behavior modification as shown in the structured interview, in verbal conditioning, in the production of experimental neuroses, and in patient-doctor relationships. In a broader sense, the topic of behavior modification is related to the whole field of learning. Studies of behavior modification are studies of learning with a particular intent—the clinical goal of treatment. For example, Wolpe in his consideration of experimental approaches to the neuroses defines them as learned habits acquired in anxiety-generating situations. In his chapter he discusses experimental neuroses and behavior therapy, including his own work in psychotherapy through reciprocal inhibition. In his book (1958) devoted to the topic Wolpe acknowledged his debt especially to Pavlov and to Hull, although Thorndike, Watson, Tolman, and Skinner are also specifically mentioned. The topic of behavior modification also has a close relation with communication of face-to-face pairs. It is, in fact, correct to say that the psychological study of behavioral modification began with the studies of Bernheim in the middle of the last century. Since his particular technique was that of hypnotic suggestion, a psychotherapeutic technique, his pioneer study is directly relevant.

The study of the behavioral effects of nonpsychological agents, such as drugs or operations, is an obscure and unwritten phase of the history of psychology. Although it is somewhat more peripheral in nature than the other matters considered here, it is fair to make at least one comment—in this area, the earliest work in the modern tradition was that of Kraepelin.

In a more specific way, recent research on behavioral modification is separable into two phases—the formal and the contentual. This is a distinction that we make in conversational behavior between *what* is said and *how* the speaker says it (Goldmann-Eissler, 1951). Formal analysis is concerned with how it is said and includes measurement of speed of talking, length of pauses, rate of talking, expressive movements, gestures, and facial expressions. Although studies of movements, gestures, and facial expressions are not unknown, in later chapters more attention is paid to the temporal relations in speaking.

Studies in the formal phase of behavioral modification were initiated by the work of Chapple (1939, 1940), an anthropologist, who published what he called the quantitative analysis of the interaction of individuals. At that time he was concerned neither with the interview nor with behavior modification. He saw the method of study he developed in the broader perspective of methodology for anthropological and social psychological study. Chapple (1939) saw as a weakness the fact that with the original primitive apparatus only two individuals could be studied simultaneously. The original studies (Chapple, 1939, 1940) were designed to give the durations of "actions" and "inactions" for calculation of the cumulative plot and the subsequent study and interpretation of the slope of the curves obtained. Later this interaction method was applied to the interview and behavior modification. By 1946 (Chapple, 1946) they were referring to the period of time with the subjects as an "interview." This interaction method in the interview forms the basis for the studies reported in a later chapter by Matarazzo. Since this chapter contains a thorough review, attention hereafter will now be directed to the contentual phases of research on behavior modification.

The research study of the contentual phase of behavior modification by psychotherapy is a relatively new development. Its recent appearance cannot be attributed to a lack of an earlier literature on psychotherapy. Psychotherapy had been recognized as a specialized technique at least as early as the temple medicine of the Greeks in about the fifth century before Christ. Its rich history is attested to in various detailed accounts (e.g., Bromberg, 1954; Zilboorg and Henry, 1941). Nor was an extensive modern professional literature lacking. Individual psychotherapy has been a concern for a large number of clinical workers for a considerable number of years. A vast literature was already developing before 1940. Moreover, psychologists, as distinguished from other clinicians, had been engaging in psychotherapy and recounting their experiences with it since before 1910, as witness the work of Boris Sidis and Walter Dill Scott (Watson, 1953). Material was available on many issues and problems, even for as specialized a problem as group psychotherapy, for Slavson (1950) was able to cite forty articles published from 1905 to 1939. Nevertheless, until quite recently the published work relied on anecdotal methods supplemented by gross statistical findings. In evaluating psychoanalytic therapy as late as 1941, Knight (1941) reported an evaluation in which he had to fall back upon brochures of various institutes and a count of the number "cured," "better," and the like for his sources of information. Pleas for a research approach to the contentual phase of behavior modification had been made directly or indirectly in the twenties and thirties by Lasswell (1929, 1933, 1936, 1938), Rosenzweig (1937), Saul (1939), and Symonds (1939). In fact, Lasswell (1933, 1936) went beyond this appeal to report some data on electrically recorded psychoanalytic sessions.

It was a psychologist, Carl Rogers, who in 1942, through a book (1942a) and an article (1942b), launched the research approach in behavioral modification through psychotherapy.*

---

*Five years earlier (1937) Rogers had reported on three statistical surveys he had performed preparatory, he said, to the study of the treatment of child guidance clinic cases "as it is actually carried out" (1937, p. 48). The unpublished doctoral dissertation dated 1941 by E. H. Porter, Jr., carried out under Rogers' direction, developed and evaluated a measure of counselor responses (Rogers, 1942b).

Rogers' work needs no review here; we will move, instead, to a brief evaluation of early workers who influenced him. It is fashionable when speaking of Rogers to allege his debt to Otto Rank, to Jessie Taft, and possibly to Frederick Allen. All of these are non-psychologists. To my inquiry concerning his indebtedness to psychology, Rogers (1960) replied, in a personal communication:

> So far as psychology goes, I guess I would say that Goodwin Watson and Leta Hollingworth of Teachers College, Columbia, both had real impact on me. E. K. Wickman of the Institute for Child Guidance was another psychologist whose thinking had some effect on me. Watson was very independent in his thinking and gave his students a great deal of freedom. Leta Hollingworth was an excellent clinician. Wickman was the careful, thoughtful, cautious researcher, though not a research man in a laboratory sense.

These three psychologists shared the tendency, which Rogers attributes to Wickman, to carry their research beyond the laboratory. None of them would be called an experimental psychologist in the narrow sense. Yet all three shared in that laboratory tradition through the training they themselves had received, and all three maintained familiarity with experimental work. It is as if Rogers had grandparents who were from among the experimentalists. Directly relevant to the issue at hand is a thoughtful article by Rogers (1955) written to describe the conflict and resulting gap that he felt existed between his work as a psychotherapist and his work as a researcher. His personal reconciliation, recounted therein, is an exercise in the reconciliation of the clinical and experimental traditions.

Rogers' work typifies still another way that the experimental tradition in psychology operates. He brought to the problem of psychotherapy neither a particular approach nor a problem analogous to an early experimental one, but a tendency to transfer his research training. He and his students, challenged by the problem of quantification of the process of psychotherapy, used ingeniously a variety of psychological tools—recording devices, rating scales, and so on—to attack the problem. They approached it with an internalized experimental tradition and, basing their methods on this tradition, proceeded to work with the materials of clinical psychology.

Rogers' influence upon his own students and others is direct and obvious in many instances. It probably influenced many other psychologists who by no stretch of the imagination could be called

"Rogerian." Many research studies bearing no direct obligation to his particular work but stimulated by it came about once it was realized that Rogers had made a "breakthrough" in this area of research, although these studies were quite different in nature.

By definition this chapter has been concerned with the past. The experimental researches significant to the extended present are yet to come in the remainder of the book. Nevertheless, if we are to go beyond antiquarian interests, even this chapter has had to be concerned with the significance of the past for the present, and concerned with this in a variety of ways. Throughout, the author has tried to keep in the forefront the men and the issues to which they addressed themselves—the two major aspects of any historical account in psychology.

REFERENCES

Allport, F. H. *Social psychology.* Boston: Houghton Mifflin, 1924.

Allport, G. W. The historical background of modern social psychology. In G. Lindzey (Ed.), *Handbook of social psychology.* Vol. 1. Reading, Mass.: Addison Wesley, 1954, 3-56.

Angell, J. R. The province of functional psychology. *Psychol. Rev.*, 1907, *14*, 61-91.

Bechterev, V. M. *General principles of human reflexology.* (Trans. 4th Russian ed.), New York: International Publishers, 1932.

Bechterev, V. M., and De Lange, M. Die Erbegnisse des experiments auf dem Gebiete der kollektiven Reflexologie. *Z. angew. Psychol.*, 1924, *24*, 305-344.

Beck, S. J., and Molish, H. B. *Reflexes to intelligence: a reader in clinical psychology.* Glencoe, Ill.: Free Press, 1959.

Bindra, D., and Scheier, I. H. The relation between psychometric and experimental research in psychology. *Amer. Psychologist*, 1954, *9*, 69-71.

Boring, E. G. Introspection in dementia praecox. *Amer. J. Psychol.*, 1913a, *26*, 145.

Boring, E. G. Learning in dementia praecox. *Psychol. Monogr.*, 1913b, *5*, No. 63.

Boring, E. G. The influence of evolutionary theory upon American psychological thought. In S. Persons (Ed.), *Evolutionary thought in America.* New Haven, Conn.: Yale Univ. Press, 1950, 268-298.

Boring, E. G. *A history of experimental psychology.* (2nd ed.) New York: Appleton-Century-Crofts, 1950a.

Braid, J. *Neurypnology.* (Rev. ed.), London: Redway, 1899. (Originally published 1843.)

Bromberg, W. *Man above humanity: a history of psychotherapy.* New York: Lippincott, 1954.

Chapple, E. D. Quantitative analysis of the interaction of individuals.

Proc. Nat. Acad. Sci., 1939, *25*, 58-67.

Chapple, E. D. "Personality" differences as described by invariant properties of individuals in interaction. *Proc. Nat. Acad. Sci.*, 1940, *26*, 10-16.

Chapple, E. D., and Donald, G., Jr. A method for evaluating supervisory personnel. *Harvard Bus. Rev.*, 1946, *24*, 197-214.

Cronbach, L. J. The two disciplines of scientific psychology. *Amer. Psychologist*, 1957, *12*, 671-684.

Dennis, W., and Boring E. G. The founding of the APA. *Amer. Psychologist*, 1952, *7*, 95-97.

Deutsch, M. Field theory in social psychology. In G. Lindzey (Ed.), *Handbook of social psychology*. Vol. 1. Reading, Mass.: Addison Wesley, 1954, 181-222.

Dewey, J. The reflex arc concept in psychology. *Psychol. Rev.*, 1896, *3*, 357-370.

Franz, S. I. On the functions of the cerebrum: the frontal lobes in relation to the production and retention of simple sensory-motor habits. *Amer. J.Physiol.*, 1902, *8*, 1-22.

Franz, S. I. *Handbook of mental examination methods*. (2nd ed.) New York: Macmillan, 1919.

Franz, S. I. Shepard Ivory Franz. In C. Murchison (Ed.), *A history of psychology in autobiography*. Vol. II. Worcester: Clark Univ. Press, 1932, 89-113.

Goldman-Eissler, Frieda. The measurement of time sequences in conversational behavior. *Brit. J. Psychol.*, 1951, *42*, 355-362.

Hall, G. S. Laboratory of the McLean Hospital. *Amer. J. Insanity*, 1894, *51*, 358-364.

Hebb, D. O. *The organization of behavior*. New York: Wiley, 1949.

Herodotus. History (Trans. by G. Rawlinson). In R. M. Hutchins (Ed.), *Great books of the western world*. Chicago: Encyclopaedia Britannica, 1952.

Hilgard, E. R., and Marquis, D. G. *Conditioning and learning*. New York: Appleton-Century-Crofts, 1940.

Hull, C. L. *Principles of behavior*. New York: Appleton-Century-Crofts, 1943.

Hull, C. L. *Essentials of behavior*. New Haven, Conn.: Yale Univ. Press, 1951.

Hull, C. L. Clark L. Hull. In Boring, E. G., et al. (Eds.), *A history of psychology in autobiography*. Vol. IV. Worcester, Mass.: Clark Univ. Press, 1952, 143-162.

Hull, C. L., et al., *Mathematicodeductive theory of rote learning*. New Haven, Conn.: Yale Univ. Press, 1940.

Hunt, J. McV. Psychological experiments with disordered persons. *Psychol. Bull.*, 1936, *33*, 1-58.

Hunt, W. A. Anchoring effects in esthetic judgment. *Amer. J. Psychol.*, 1941, *44*, 395-403.

Hunt, W. A. Personal communication, 1960.

Hunt, W. A., and Volkmann, J. The anchoring of an affective scale. *Amer. J. Psychol.*, 1937, *49*, 88-92.

Kahn, E. Emil Kraepelin, February 15, 1856-October 7, 1926-February 15, 1956. *Amer. J. Psychiat.*, 1956, *113*, 289-294.

Knight, R. P. Evaluation of the results of psychoanalytic therapy. *Amer. J. Psychiat.*, 1941, *98*, 434-446.

Köhler, W. *Dynamics in psychology*. New York: Liveright, 1940.

Kraepelin, E. Der psychologische Versuch in der Psychiatrie.

Psychol. Arb., Leipzig, 1895, *1*, 1-91.

Lasswell, H. D. The problem of adequate personality records: a proposal. *Amer. J. Psychiat.*, 1929, *85*, 1057-1066.

Lasswell, H. D. Verbal references and psychological changes during the psychoanalytic interview: a preliminary communication. *Psychoanal. Rev.*, 1935, *22*, 10-24.

Lasswell, H. D. Certain prognostic changes during trial (psychoanalytic) interviews. *Psychoanal. Rev.*, 1936, *23*, 229-293.

Lasswell, H. D. A provisional classification of symbol data. *Psychiatry*, 1938, *1*, 197-204.

Le Bon, G. *Psychologie des foules.* Paris: Alcan, 1895.

Lewin, K., Lippitt, R., and White, R. Patterns of aggressive behavior in experimentally created "social climates." *J. soc. Psychol.*, 1939, *10*, 271-299.

Logan, F. A. The Hull-Spence approach. In S. Koch (Ed.), *Psychology: a study of a science, Study 1, conceptual and systematic:* Vol. 2, *general systematic formulations, learning and special prlcesses.* New York: McGraw-Hill, 1959, 293-358.

Miller, N. E. Liberalization of basic S-R concepts: extensions to conflict behavior, motivation and social learning. In S. Koch (Ed.), *Psychology: a study of a science, Study 1, conceptual and systematic:* Vol. 2, *general systematic formulation, learning and special processes.* New York: McGraw-Hill, 1959, 196-292.

Moede, W. *Experimentelle Massenpsychologie.* Leipzig: Hirzel, 1920.

Moreno, J. L. How Kurt Lewin's "Research Center for Group Dynamics" started and the question of paternity. *Group Psychotherapy*, 1952, *5*, 1-6.

Murphy, G. *Historical introduction to modern psychology.* (Rev. ed.) New York: Harcourt, Brace, 1949.

Murphy, G., Murphy, Lois B., and Newcomb, T. M. *Experimental social psychology.* (Rev. ed.) New York: Harper, 1937.

Pavlov, I. P. *Conditioned reflexes.* London: Oxford Univ. Press, 1927.

Pavlov, I. P. *Selected works.* (K. S. Koshtoyants, Ed.) Moscow: Foreign Languages Publishing House, 1955.

Pratt, C. C. *The logic of modern psychology.* New York: Macmillan, 1939.

Rogers, C. R. Three surveys of treatment measures used with children. *Amer. J. Orthopsychiat.*, 1937, *7*, 48-57.

Rogers, C. R. *Counseling and psychotherapy: newer concepts in practice.* Boston: Houghton Mifflin, 1942a.

Rogers, C. R. The use of electrically recorded interviews in improving psychotherapeutic technique. *Amer. J. Orhopsychiat.*, 1942b, *12*, 429-435.

Rogers, C. R. Persons or science? A philosophical question. *Amer. Psychologist*, 1955, *10*, 267-278.

Rogers, C. R. Personal communication, 1960.

Rosenzweig, M. R. Pavlov, Bechterev, and Twitmyer on conditioning. *Amer. J. Psychol.*, 1960, *73*, 312-316.

Rosenzweig, S. The experimental study of psychoanalytic concepts. *Char. & Person.*, 1937, *6*, 61-71.

Saul, L. J. Psychoanalytic case records. *Psychoanal. Quart.*, 1939, *8*, 186-190.

Sherif, M. *The psychology of social norms.* New York: Harper, 1936.

Skinner, B. F. *The behavior of organisms: an experimental analysis.* New York: Appleton-Century, 1938.

Skinner, B. F. *Science and human behavior.* New York: Macmillan, 1953.

Skinner, B. F. A case history in scientific method. In S. Koch (Ed.), *Psychology: a study of a science, Study 1, conceptual and systematic:* vol. 2. *general systematic formulations, learning and special processes.* New York: McGraw-Hill, 1959, 359-379.

Slavson, S. R. Bibliography of group psychotherapy. *Group Ther. Brochure,* 1950, No. 32.

Spence, K. W. The postulates and methods of behaviorism. *Psychol. Rev.,* 1948, *55,* 67-78.

Symonds, P. M. Research in the interviewing process. *J. educ. Psychol.,* 1939, *30,* 346-353.

Taylor, Janet A. A personality scale of manifest anxiety. *J. abnorm. soc. Psychol.,* 1953, *48,* 285-290.

Taylor, Janet A. Personal communication, 1960.

Taylor, Janet A., and Spence, K. W. The relationship of anxiety level to performance in serial learning. *J. exp. Psychol.,* 1952, *44,* 61-64.

Warden, C. J. *A short outline of comparative psychology.* New York: Norton, 1927.

Watson, J. B. The place of the conditioned-reflex in psychology. *Psychol. Rev.,* 1916, *23,* 89-116.

Watson, J. B. *Psychology from the standpoint of a behaviorist.* (3rd ed. rev.) Philadelphia: Lippincott, 1929.

Watson, R. I. A brief history of clinical psychology. *Psychol. Bull.,* 1953, *50,* 321-346.

Watson, R. I. Historical review of objective personality testing: the search for objectivity. In B. M. Bass and I. A. Berg (Eds.), *Objective approaches to personality assessment.* Princeton, N.J.: Van Nostrand, 1959a, 1-23.

Watson, R. I. *The psychology of the child: personal, social and disturbed child development.* New York: Wiley, 1959b.

Watson, R. I. *The great psychologists: from Aristotle to Freud.* New York: Lippincott, 1963.

Wells, H. K. *Ivan P. Pavlov: toward a scientific psychology and psychiatry.* New York: International Publishers, 1956.

Wever, E. G., and Zener, K. E. Method of absolute judgment in psychophysics. *Psychol. Rev.,* 1928, *35,* 466-493.

Wolpe, J. *Psychotherapy by reciprocal inhibition.* Stanford, Calif.: Stanford Univ. Press, 1958.

Zilboorg, G., and Henry, G. W. *A history of medical psychology.* New York: Norton, 1941.

19. The Individual, Social-Educational, Economic, and Political Conditions for the Original Practices of Detection and Utilization of Individual Aptitude Differences

In order to set the stage for consideration of the problem at hand, a word about my orientation to the methodological problem seems indicated. "Externalist" explanations in historiography calling for interpreting of history in general cultural, economic, and social terms ran strongly in the twenties and thirties (1). These views were influenced by Marx's contentions that the character of a society is largely determined by its economy and the closely related but independent contention of the anthropologists that a culture is a unity. As Hall stated recently:

> Adding these two ideas together, one is led to conclude that a man's thoughts on any topic—say, celestial mechanics—are not independent of his thoughts on all other topics, nor of the economic state of the society in which he lives. So far, if we allow that "not independent of" is by no means equivalent to "causally determined by," we have a historiographical notion that is, today, hardly open to dispute. Some thirty years ago, however, historians were more apt to regard the case as one of causal determinism and to suppose that any correlation between an intellectual event A and a social event B could be understood as justifying the view that B in some sense "caused" A, or at least was a necessary condition for the occurrence of A (2).

Generally speaking, historians have moved away from this approach, not by denying its limited value, but because they have come to a sobering realization that the evidence must show more than compatibility, or, to refer back to the quotation just made, must go beyond "not independent of" to "causally determined by." It is considered that this externalist view has not been conspicuously successful as an explanatory principle in recent historiography of science. I am wary of using an externalist interpretation of general cultural, economic, and social factors as influencing the rise of the psychological study of individual differences.

A better case for the influence of broader socioeconomic factors might be made after the pioneering phase of research when development and application takes over. That is to say, after the initial research is carried out, utilitarian, educational, and social influences may well supply additional incentives for further investigations. In other words, it is contended that society does not knock at the scientist's doorstep until he knows what at least in a general way has already been done. Only then does society know what it is looking for. The Binet Test and its relative popularity in the United States and lack of it in France in the period just *after* its development will serve as a by no means fully developed example.

What happened in France? In the 1960's Théodore Simon, Binet's faithful collaborator (3), insisted that in these early years the Binet Scale gained no fame in France and that it was not until early in the twenties that it was used in France by more than Simon himself and one other of Binet's supporters, Rémy, a directress of a school. The Binet Test was rediscovered by a French social worker who visited clinics in the United States, found Terman's revision in wide use, and on returning to France and with Simon as chief consultant, organized a public service whose clientele were delinquent children. During World War II, the Binet Tests became à la mode—in an adaptation of the Terman-Merrill revision, not of the original Binet Tests.

This situation stands in sharp contrast with that prevailing in the United States. The Binet Scale was first introduced in 1908 by Henry H. Goddard at the Vineland Training School. Its rapid and extensive development has been the subject of many accounts (4). Suffice it to say that by 1917, an almost exclusively American bibliography (5) of 344 separate papers and books had appeared.

American research at this period in time was pragmatic in character and directed toward application of intelligence measurements in dealing with mental retardation, school placement, and similar problems. Characteristically, interest centered in the instrument as such. The mass testing that immediately preceded the entry of the United States into World War I was inspired in large measure by developments traceable back to work with the Binet when the adaptation for group testing was made. Without trying to trace its precise nature, I am convinced that these and similar national differences are attributable to these broad external influences. I do hold the reservation that such an analysis might yield only rather vague references to increased demand for education for larger segments of society, occupational mobility, increased immigration, increased industrialization, and the like.

The pioneering phase of the conditions which led to the study of individual differences will hereafter receive consideration. A more intimate and therefore more precise level of influence will be considered—the distinctive personal and academic interests that are found to characterize the pioneers in the study of individual differences. This distinctiveness will be demonstrated by comparison with characteristics exhibited by the majority of their colleagues interested in nomothetic problems. Out of this comparison, it is held that it is possible to isolate with some assurance the conditions which led to the study of individual differences.

For reasons made clear in a moment, the temporal period under direct scrutiny will begin in the seventies. For psychology in general the event that immediately comes to mind is the founding of the Leipzig Laboratory by Wilhelm Wundt.

Founded in 1875 (6), this laboratory did not have available to it techniques for the investigation of individual differences. The designation of physiological psychology Wundt applied to its activities is still sometimes misunderstood. He did not refer to physiological psychology as we conceive the field today. His title was intended to signalize the inspiration the methods of physiology were to the opening up of his new experimental psychology. It is small wonder, then, that it asked and answered questions that it could by the techniques it borrowed from physiology.

True, Wundt did propose the establishment of "a practical psychology, namely a characterology which should investigate the basic and typical forms of individual character with the aid of principles from a general theoretical psychology" (7). Aside from this, he did nothing about it. Why did this and similar proposals from J. S. Mill, Samuel Bailey, and others come to nothing? In part, at least, it may have been because either implicitly or explicitly they conceived the problem of human individuality to lie outside the domain of psychology and to be the work of someone else besides the one making the proposition.

Historians of the period aided and abetted in this determination to make psychology the study of the immutable, the unchanging about human nature, reserving for history that which is variable, his beliefs, his range of ideas and the things which are transformed when these are transformed. This was the position, for example, called for in the inaugural lecture at Strasbourg in 1862 by Fusstel de Coulanges (8), author of the monumental *History of the Political Institutions of Medieval France*. Indeed, it was not uncommon practice to differentiate psychology and history on precisely this point. It was against a dominant nomothetic trend that the psychology of individual differences was initiated.

Research on individual differences in psychology had its decisive beginnings in the period from about 1870 to 1910. A mere mention of the men whose major work was initiated during this period will suffice for preliminary demonstration of this contention. In France, this was the period of Pierre Janet (1859-1947) and Alfred Binet (1857-1911); in England, that of Francis Galton (1822-1911) and Charles Spearman (1863-1945); in Germany, that of William Stern (1871-1938); and in the United States, that of James McKeen Cattell (1860-1944) and James Mark Baldwin (1861-1934). Their accomplishments in the area under scrutiny are so well known that it is unnecessary to devote direct attention to specification of the nature of their specific research and theories. Instead, the origin of their psychological interests in general and individual differences in particular will be examined. One source is what the men themselves have to say, and another what their biographers say about these matters.

In his autobiography (9), Pierre Janet argued that the influences which led him to combine philosophical-psychological and medical studies were his fondness for scientific rigor and yet a strong religious bent. Specifically, he said it was his uncle, Paul Janet, a follower of Victor Cousin, attempting to combine religious, scientific, and political interests, who originally wakened his particular pattern of interests. In the forties and fifties, Victor Cousin (1791-1867) had dominated French philosophy and psychology in his teachings of an "eclectic" spiritualism, meant to serve essentially as a secular religion to take the place of what he was convinced was the outmoded Catholic orthodoxy. Through "his academic regiments" Cousin, a key figure in the centralized educational system of France, controlled the academic scene (10). While he held that psychology was observational and experimental, in reality this meant exclusive dependence upon introspection and not the disciplined Germanic blend of introspection and experiment. Antagonist and bitter enemy of Cousin was Auguste Comte. A fledgling academic psychology, if I may be permitted to play on words, could hardly find positive inspiration from a man who insisted that in his vision of the sciences, psychology had no place at all! But Pierre Janet, of a later generation than Paul Janet and Cousin, lived in a time when the stirrings of modern academic nonpsychopathological psychology were being brought to France. It was Théodule Ribot (1839–1916) who served as its interpreter through his books on English associationism and German experimentalism. Many years later, in Ribot's centennial celebration of 1939 (11), Janet was to acknowledge specifically his debt to him. But an even stronger influence was at work: when Janet started his productive career, medical neurology in the characteristic French tradition had already been launched.

At the age of twenty-two, Janet taught at a lycée in Havre (12). It was suggested to him that for his medical dissertation he study a subject already noted for hypnotic phenomena. He did so, and became acquainted with Charcot and Ribot. It may be judged from the preface that Charcot (13) wrote for a book of Janet, that he saw in him a kindred spirit, who united somatic and psychological strains both already present upon the Parisian psychopathological scene. Characteristically, thereafter, Janet's approach was to center upon particular cases and to combine this with careful quantified research. In 1890, Charcot chose him to direct the psychological laboratory at the Salpêtrière, and in 1895, Ribot nominated him to teach experimental psychology for him at the Collège de France. Janet succeeded to Ribot's chair in 1902. Throughout his writings, he insisted that it was essential that psychology be concerned with the study of individuals. His clearest plea for attention to the individual in the psychological investigation was a methodological paper, *L'Analyse Psychologique* (14), published in 1930, which he defined as "that method by which we distinguish an individual from others."

Alfred Binet found his career in psychology without having studied under anyone in the field (15). After attending Lycée in Nice and Paris, he entered a school of law, took his "license" and began to study for the doctorate. Reading psychology in the *Bibliothèque Nationale* decided him on a shift of vocation with the British Associationist School, particularly Mill, his first guide. Having met Féré, and Charcot, he began to utilize patients at Salpêtrière and to work in Charcot's tradition on problems of hypnosis. He saw this problem however as being set in the major psychopathological, not neurological, tradition. On describing the state of psychology in France, circa 1890, he argued for an overwhelming centering on mental pathological psychology (16). In 1891, he sought out Beaunis, asked permission to work in the newly founded Laboratory at the Sorbonne, and left behind hypnosis to turn to his work in individual differences. Best known for his work in individual differences in intelligence, he also worked on the issue as demonstrated in responses to suggestion and in abnormalities in handwriting.

Especially important at this time (1890) were his studies of his two young daughters (17). What became apparent to him was the significant differences between them, not in simple motor and sensory tasks, but in complex functions: for example, one was cautious, the other was impulsive. It was during this and subsequent years that he was groping toward his mature definition of intelligence; for example, it was at this time that he came to appreciate the utilitarian quality of children's thinking with their stress in definitions on the use of objects.

What was perhaps in the earliest formulated definitions of a mental test, Binet and his collaborator Victor Henri in 1895 said that the method "consists in the selection of a number of tasks designed to give detailed information on individual differences" (18).

In this work, he was relatively independent of the academic world. He had an independent income, held no professorship, and the direction of the Laboratory of the Physiological Psychology at the Sorbonne carried with it no specific requirements (19). Much of his energies were channeled through a society for the psychological study of children, of which he was co-founder, the *Société Libre pour l'Etude de l'Enfant*. Its membership was composed primarily of teachers.

One bit of the folklore of psychology centers on the incident of the Paris Commission of 1904, which commonly was supposed to have invited him to develop examinations so as to identify those subnormal children that needed special instruction. Almost needless to say, this has been widely interpreted as an excellent illustration of how a social need influenced psychology.

Binet (20) sometimes gave the impression that it was a high placed commission and that the government sought him out. Actually, it was a group from his own society, mentioned earlier, that urged it upon the government (21). So, it was Binet who maneuvered the situation and not the government's recognition of the social need that brought about the development of the first Binet-Simon Scale.

The outlook of Francis Galton very directly represents the tradition established by his older cousin, Charles Darwin. Man is an animal and the study of man and his variability is a branch of biological science. His whole outlook rested upon a belief in the continuity of evolution from animals to man and the biological origin of all man's highest human characteristics.

Born into an eminent family, he never had to worry about money. He remained an amateur in the best sense of the term, without academic professional connections through his life. From earliest age, he was in touch with eminent men and women of his day (22). In his memoirs, he introduced their names with casual references to their accomplishments, as, for example, his description of his father-in-law as Dean of Peterborough and Headmaster of Harrow. His friends and acquaintances were so highly placed that for his memoirs he could find their birth and death years by the simple expedient of turning to the *Dictionary of National Biography*.

He was characterized by a roving insatiable curiosity, constantly attracted to new problems on which he brought to bear his considerable originality while leaving details either to be filled in by others or never to be followed up (23). Pearson, his biographer, considered another salient trait to be his search for social utility as "an instinct almost amounting to a moral sense" (24).

Galton himself singled out the *Origin of Species* as marking an "epoch in . . . [his] mental development" (25). Already interested in heredity, he selected the Cambridge men of his own time who had received "firsts" in Classics and proceeded to identify their relatives. He found a remarkable number of these relatives had also achieved scholastic eminence. As early as 1885, a paper of his contained the germs of many subsequent books. One of these, *Hereditary Genius* (26), drew from Charles Darwin an enthusiastic statement of his conversion to the view, hitherto not accepted, that men do show pronounced differences in intelligence (27).

Although in some of his work he compared nature and nurture, there seems little doubt his stress was on the former. That eminence followed along family lines was clear evidence to him that hereditary influences were overwhelming. His incapacity to assess properly environmental influences presumably arose from his own position in the "establishment," and this, in turn, was congruent with the social, economic, and political influences brought to bear upon him.

In establishing, as he did, a psychometric laboratory in London in 1882, where for a fee members of the public could obtain their test scores, he was marked as the first psychological practitioner outside of psychopathology.

His contributions to statistical method worked hand in hand with investigation of individual differences. Under the head of "The Claims of Statistics," Galton (28) complained that he could not understand why research workers commonly limited inquiries to averages when attention to variability added so much comprehensiveness. "An average is but a solitary fact," and a measure of variability, if added, contributed so much more to the comprehensiveness of one's view.

The continuity between Galton and later developments in psychology is clear. One chain extends through McDougall to the work on tests by Sir Cyril Burt. Another chain is his recognition of the correlation coefficient, which was refined by Karl Pearson, his student, and then utilized by Charles Spearman in his studies of factor analysis.

As a result of vocational indecision, Spearman tells us, he first turned to military service as a career, but both before and during this period he read avidly in philosophy (29). Ethical considerations, he held, were paramount. He found in psychology the means to an advance of philosophy. From the beginning he rejected the concept of association and the English school of Hartley, Hume, the Mills, and Bain. He left the army at the age of 37 and for many years became a student of psychology, first going to Leipzig and Wundt and then on to work in physiology, considerable experience in mental hospitals, a period under Külpe, another under G. E. Müller, and the courses of Husserl. He expressed admiration for Wundt as a man, but not for his system of psychology, which, as he saw it, centered upon sensation, with other matters only added as afterthoughts.

After accepting appointment at the University of London, in 1906, his work first turned to imageless thought as a means of combatting the sensationalistic doctrinal emphasis. During World War I, as a result of a suggestion by a submarine officer whose consultant he was, to the effect that mere reproduction is not enough for intelligence decisions to be made, he turned to his well-known work on the education of correlates. At this point, earlier work (30) dating back to 1904 and inspired by work of Galton, in which he had found that mental abilities in school children correlated appreciably, assumed greater significance to him. By his paper, he was led to his conclusion that all intellectual tasks are aspects of a single factor, general intelligence, or "G"—and thereby launched factor analysis and his two-factor theory. In this work Spearman depended upon intercorrelations of test scores of school children. With the basic theoretical framework provided by this much later emphasis upon education of correlates, he proceeded to his well-known work on two-factor theory.

In his autobiography (31), William Stern reports that his undergraduate work was in philosophy but that he also studied experimental psychology with Ebbinghaus. They both appealed to him, he says, because equally strong were his love of speculation and direct empirical contact with the concreteness of fact.

His philosophical motives, he says, determined his psychological investigations, when he turned to the study of individual differences, including a book of 1900 (32) in which he argued that the problem of the twentieth century was that of individuality. In 1912, he suggested the use of what later came to be called the intelligence quotient (33). His contribution to the applied psychology of testimony was, from his point of view, conceived as studies of differential psychology. Studies of children reinforced this position.

Both at Breslau, where he succeeded Ebbinghaus, and at Berlin, through the Institute of Applied Psychology, of which he was co-founder, he did much to further educational and applied psychology (34). In 1916, he accepted a professorship at Hamburg, which, it is significant to note, was not at that time a university but the Colonial Institute, and when organized as one, was essentially designed as a city college.

As a term for this field of interest it was Stern in 1900 who first proposed "differential psychology" (35). Differential psychology, he held, occupies a special halfway position between classical psychology and individual diagnosis and description. He realized that this could not depend upon differential psychology alone and that for a rounded approach it must be integrated with general psychology.

In the years to follow, he devoted himself to implementing and articulating his own particular views. His goal was to widen the behavioral scope of experimental psychology and to increase the number of subjects used in experiments so as to more directly study the differential characteristics of individuals. In his *General Psychology from the Personalistic Standpoint* (36), published after the time limitation imposed in the paper, Stern made his entire account of psychology rest on the assumption that everything that is mental is at the same time personal.

Although a year younger than Cattell, James Mark Baldwin not only left from the psychological scene much before him, since his last psychological publication was in 1911 (37); but also much more closely resembled the speculative, nonexperimental generation of psychologists immediately preceding his own. It is therefore appropriate to turn to him before Cattell.

Baldwin (38) states his interest was directed toward psychology from an intention to go into the ministry and from the courses in mental philosophy, taught by McCosh, president of Princeton, which contained a perhaps surprising amount of attention devoted to the empirical aspects of psychology.

He remained on at Princeton to take his Ph.D. and then taught at Lake Forest and Toronto before returning to Princeton and then to Johns Hopkins before leaving for the University of Mexico for a few years. He then settled in France, where he was a Professor in the School of Higher Social Studies until retirement in 1924. He lived in France until his death in 1934. Over these years, he was so active in developing cordial relationships between France and the United States as to be decorated several times.

He was led by his early work on motor functioning using principles of dynamogenesis to abandon the older associationistic structural psychology for a functional and developmental view. These interests brought about a visit to France to become acquainted with the works of Charcot, Janet, and Bernheim.

In 1895, he published *Mental Development of Child and Race* (39). As the title indicates, he was trying to do for the mental development of the child what Darwin did for the animal in *Origin of Species*. It was, as were his later works, devoted almost entirely to speculative theorizing and very little observation. What he did carry out was guided by a conviction that the psychologist must be so saturated with his theories "that the conduct of the child becomes instinct with meaning for these theories of mind and body."

Later publications centered on social psychology (40). Perhaps for the first time, and certainly for the first time stated so explicitly, imitation is made the means of the integrated process of personal and social development (41). One of these books published in 1911 was his last contribution to psychology. Thereafter, as his entries in *American Men of Science* show, he held that his fields of interest were logic and aesthetics.

In contrast to the somewhat old-fashioned Baldwin, James McKeen Cattell was a psychologist whose outlook is practically that of a contemporary. His interests centered on introducing quantitative methods and using these methods for the measurement of individual differences, and in furthering the significance and dignity of psychology both as a science and as a profession.

After graduation from Lafayette, where his major interest was in literature, he visited European universities, Göttingen, Leipzig, Paris, and Geneva, and then studied at Hopkins with G. Stanley Hall, afterward returning to Leipzig, where he took his Ph.D. in 1886 (42). He brought his own research problems to Wundt, who, contrary to his practice of doling out research topics to his students, allowed him to work on variability of reaction time. In 1885, his very first year of publication, he ended a paper, "The Inertia of Eye and Brain," with a discussion of "individual differences," using this particular expression (43). The characteristic difference he discovered stimulated his interest in mental tests. He worked with Galton, the older man, *after* he developed his interest in individual differences. He was later to refer to him as the "greatest man I have known" (44).

In a paper published in 1890, he coined the expression "mental tests." He also reported on a variety of tests that he urged be given a trial by psychologists (45). Collection of these data, he held, would have both theoretical and practical value in discovering constancy and variability of mental processes.

His career thereafter was dramatic. In 1888 he was appointed to the first professorship of psychology in America at the University of Pennsylvania at the age of twenty-eight, and in 1891, to a professorship at Columbia University at thirty-one. He was elected to the presidency of the American Psychological Association at thirty-five, and the first psychologist elected to the National Academy of Sciences at forty.

He occupied himself with research on testing of college students and studies of the nature and origin of scientific ability. In 1895, he purchased and began editing *Science*, a weekly journal, which in 1900 was made the official organ of the American Association for the Advancement of Science. He was co-founder of the *Psychological Review* and helped to found the American Association of University Professors. At the same time, he helped to train more graduate students at Columbia than was the case with any other American university.

His direct connection with the academic world came to an abrupt end in 1917, when he was dismissed from Columbia University because of advocacy of conscientious objection for those who had scruples about combatant service during World War I. On the larger psychological scene, outside of the University, he continued much as before.

He vigorously defended the growth of applied psychology and predicted as early as 1904 that there would be a profession as well as a science of psychology (46). In 1921, he organized the Psychological Corporation to promote application of psychology.

As did Galton before him, Cattell turned to statistics and found thereby a methodological tool for reconciling the predominant emphasis of experimental psychology upon general lawfulness with his own more idiosyncratic concern with the problem of individual differences. This use of the probable error to reconcile these competing claims was possible for Cattell and the rest who found their interest to lie in the degree to which individuals differ along continua. In so doing, Cattell placed the quantitative study of individual differences into the matrix of general experimental psychology.

That these eminent pioneers in the study of individual differences ran counter to the dominant nomothetic character of the psychology of their day is evident. It is not so obvious perhaps that they showed divergences in other respects. Examination of these other factors may help us to understand how they are related to the problem posed by this paper. What are some of these dominant characteristics against which we can examine the men under consideration? The university settings dominated the training of the fledgling psychologists. Their thinking was shaped within their walls. Their careers, too, were in most instances carried on exclusively within the settings of the universities. In the continental universities, their livelihood and their chance of professional advancement rested with the professor in whose institute they worked, while in England they were uneasily housed in philosophy departments. In the United States, because of independent departments of psychology and more than one professor in a department, there was perhaps more personal autonomy. The dominant psychology of the day was not only nomothetic, it was statically nondevelopmental and concerned almost exclusively with adult mind. Attention to child psychology was almost nonexistent among academic men. Moreover, most psychologists, meaning academic psychologists of the day, viewed askance the applications of psychology to the problems of everyday life—perhaps in part because application was viewed as endangering its newly won and somewhat precarious scientific dignity. The use of statistics was at its barest beginnings. Simple counting practices so much sufficed for their procedures (except in psychophysics) that not a single textbook of statistics was available until toward the end of the period in question.

In all of these respects, these seven pioneers showed significant divergences from this typical pattern. In both their training and their later locus of activity, there was considerable freedom from academic influences. Only two of the seven, Baldwin and Cattell, had more or less typical academic careers; and even here, each in his own way left the academic setting long before his career ended. Five of them were characterized by a freedom from narrowly academic interest and activities.

The interests that led these men to psychology were varied but distinctly not an interest in the psychology of the time that they entered the field. At best, the fields and individuals who served as inspiration were peripheral to psychology. Only Stern mentioned psychology as among his original strong interests and only he derived part of the original inspiration from a psychologist, Ebbinghaus. Moreover, Binet, Galton, Spearman, and Baldwin first were engaged, for an appreciable period of time, in some other intellectual activity before they turned to psychology.

Among these men, an interest in child psychology was quite strong. Binet, Stern, and Baldwin were as much leading pioneers in child psychology as they were in the study of individual differences. Even Spearman used children as subjects in his historic 1904 study. Only Janet, Galton, and Cattell were not particularly concerned with research on childhood.

Living in an age for which there was hardly any precedent (except the French psychopathological tradition) they showed strong utilitarian interests and drew inspiration from practical matters. In the group Baldwin was the only exception where perhaps the social motif served instead.

Galton, Spearman, and Cattell were clearly outstanding for their contributions to statistical procedures. Binet and Stern both made already noted statistical contributions in intelligence testing, although of lesser moment. Only Janet and Baldwin were exceptions.

Aside from their concern with individual differences, what characterized these men? They were freed from the current academic atmosphere both in their training period and in their later professional responsibilities. Did they seek this freedom to pursue their interest in the study of individual differences, or did this freedom make it easier to find a research outlet in this area? A strong current of interest in the developmental aspects of psychology was present. Did this interest precede the central interest, or did it follow in its wake? They were interested in the applications of psychological principles to daily affairs. Was it because it was hard to escape an interest in practical matters when concerned with individual differences, or did the interest in practical matters lead them to the study of individual differences? They not only made use of statistical procedures, they significantly contributed to their advance as a tool of research. Was their pre-eminence in statistics a consequence of an interest in individual difference, or did it come about because they found a statistical challenge in the study of individual differences?

We could probably find some bits of evidence that would show that in a particular individual, prior interest in individual differences seemed to lead to one or another of these interests and other lines of evidence of the opposite relationship. It is most plausible to believe that what we are dealing with is an intricately intertwined network of configuration of influences in the sense that these interests affected one another reciprocally. Such, then, seem to be the conditions which led to the pioneer studies of individual differences.

REFERENCES

1. A. R. Hall, Merton revisited, or science and society in the Seventeenth Century. *Hist. Sci.*, 1963, *2*, 1-16.
2. *Ibid.*, p. 2.
3. Theta H. Wolf, An individual who made a difference. *Amer. Psychologist*, 1961, *16*, 245-248.
4. J. Peterson, *Early Conceptions and Test of Intelligence*. Yonkers: World Book, 1925.
5. Helen Boardman, *Psychological Tests: A bibliography*. New York: Bureau of Educational Experiments, 1917.
6. R. I. Watson, *The Great Psychologists: From Aristotle to Freud*. (2nd ed.) Philadelphia, Pa., Lippincott, 1968.
7. W. Wundt, *Logik*, Band 2 (2 au fl.) Stuttgart: Enke, 1895, p. 64.
8. F. de Coulanges, The ethos of a scientific historian. In F. Stern (Ed.), *The Varieties of History from Voltaire to the Present*. New York: Meridian, 1956, pp. 178-190.
9. P. Janet, Pierre Janet. In C. Murchison (Ed.), *History of Psychology in Autobiography*, Vol. 1, Worcester, Mass.: Clark University Press, 1930, pp. 123-133.
10. W. M. Simon, The "two cultures" in nineteenth century France: Victor Cousin and Auguste Comte. *J. Hist. Ideas*, 1965, *26*, 45-58.
11. (Various) *Centenaire de Th. Ribot. Jubilé de la psychologie scientifique française*. Paris: Imprimerie Moderne, 1939.
12. W. S. Taylor, Pierre Janet, 1859-1947, *Amer. J. Psychol.*, 1947, *60*, 637-645.
13. J. M. Charcot, Préface. In P. Janet, *L'état mental des hystériques*. Paris: Rueff et Cie., 1892.
14. P. Janet, L'analyse psychologique. In C. Murchison (Ed.), *Psychologies of 1930*. Worcester, Mass.: Clark University Press, 1930, pp. 369-373, p. 369.
15. Theta H. Wolf, Alfred Binet: A time of crisis. *Amer. Psychologist*, 1964, *19*, 762-771.
16. A. Binet, Experimental psychology in France. *Open Court*, 1889, *2*, 1427-1429; *On Double Consciousness: Experimental Psychological Studies*. Chicago: Open Court, 1896.
17. Theta H. Wolf, Intuition and experiment. Alfred Binet's first efforts in child psychology. *J. Hist. Behav. Sci.*, 1966, *2*, 233-239.
18. A. Binet and V. Henri, Psychologie individuelle. *L'Année Psychologique*, 1895, 411-465, p. 464.
19. Wolf, *Amer. Psychologist*, 1961, *op. cit.*
20. A. Binet and T. Simon, Upon the necessity of establishing a scientific diagnosis of inferior states of intelligence. In W. Dennis (Ed.), *Readings in the History of Psychology*. New York: Appleton-Century-Crofts, 1948, pp. 407-411.
21. A. Binet, Sommaire des travaux en cours à la Société de Psychologie de l'enfant. *L'Année Psychologique*, 1903, *10*, 116-130.
22. F. Galton, *Memories of My Life*. London: Methuen, 1908.
23. F. Galton, *Inquiries into Human Faculty and its Development*. (2nd ed.) New York: Dutton, undated.
24. K. Pearson, *The Life, Letters and*

Labours of Francis Galton. (3 vols. in 4) Cambridge, England: University of Cambridge Press, 1914-1924, Vol. 1, p. 56.
25. Galton, *Memories, op. cit.*, p. 287.
26. F. Galton, *Hereditary Genius: An Inquiry into its Laws and Consequences.* New York: Meridian, 1962.
27. Galton, *Memories, op. cit.*, p. 290.
28. F. Galton, *Natural Inheritance.* New York: Macmillan, 1894. (1889), p. 62.
29. C. Spearman, C. Spearman. In C. Murchison (Ed.), *A History of Psychology in Autobiography.* (Vol. 1) Worcester, Mass.: Clark University Press, 1930, pp. 299-333.
30. C. E. Spearman, "General intelligence," objectively determined and measured. *Amer. J. Psychol.*, 1904, *15*, 201-293.
31. W. Stern, William Stern. In C. Murchison (Ed.), *A History of Psychology in Autobiography.* (Vol. 1) Worcester, Mass.: Clark University Press, 1930, pp. 335-388.
32. W. Stern, *Ueber Psychologie der individuellen Differenzen.* Leipzig: Barth, 1900.
33. W. Stern, *Die psychologischen Methoden der Intelligenz-Prüfung.* Leipzig: Barth, 1912: G. M. Whipple (Trans.) *The Psychological Method of Testing Intelligence.* Baltimore, Md.: Warwick and York, 1914.
34. *Autobiography, op. cit.*
35. V. C. Jarl, Historical note on the term differential psychology. *Nord Psychol.*, 1958, *10*, 114-116.
36. W. Stern, *General Psychology from the Personalistic Standpoint.* New York: Macmillan, 1938.
37. Margaret F. Washburn, James Clark Baldwin 1961-1934, *Amer. J. Psychol.*, 1935, *47*, 168-169.
38. J. M. Baldwin, James Mark Baldwin. In C. Murchison (Ed.), *A History of Psychology in Autobiography.* (Vol. 1) Worcester, Mass.: Clark University Press, 1930, pp. 1-30.
39. J. M. Baldwin, *Mental Development in the Child and the Race: Methods and Processes.* New York: Macmillan, 1895, p. 37.
40. J. M. Baldwin, *Individual and Society, or Psychology and Sociology.* New York: Doubleday, 1911; *Social and Ethical Interpretations in Mental Development: A Study in Social Psychology.* New York: Macmillan, 1897.
41. *Ibid.*, p. 15; *Mental Development, op. cit.*, p. 339.
42. R. S. Woodworth, James McKeen Cattell, 1860-1944. *Psychol. Rev.*, 1944, *51*, 201-209.
43. J. McK. Cattell, The inertia of the eye and brain. *Brain*, 1885, *8*, 295-312.
44. J. McK. Cattell, Psychology in America. *Scient. Mo.*, 1930, *30*, 114-126, p. 116.
45. J. McK. Cattell, Mental tests and measurements. *Mind*, 1890, *15*, 373-381.
46. A. T. Poffenberger (Ed.), *James McKeen Cattell: Man of Science.* (Vol. 1) *Psychological Research.* Lancaster, Pa.: Science Press, 1947, p. 498.

IV. Eminent Psychologists

20. Important Psychologists, 1600-1967

Psychologists' interest in the history of psychology has been growing rapidly in recent years, and the individual interests converge and overlap in this field as in any other. No sooner had one author of this article (Boring) conceived the idea of getting up a biographical dictionary of perhaps 500 psychologists and persons important in the history of psychology than another author (Watson) sent him a list of more than 800 names of psychologists gleaned in his historical research and writing.* Subsequently two other similar projects of somewhat smaller scope—a picture-dictionary and a list, each of perhaps 200 psychologists—have come to our attention, and there may be others in the works. Thus does the current of interest produce multiples in discoveries and projects.

We think a list of this sort will find uses. Again and again a psychologist looks for a sample list of distinguished or at least important psychologists—the past presidents of the APA or its Council or its Directors, or the starred names in the older issues of *American Men of Science* or the psychological members of the National Academy of Sciences or the American Philosophical Society or some other list of selected members who may be taken adequately to represent some special kind of psychologist.

In a way one such list is as valid as any other, for every such list represents only an expression of opinion by the judges who made the selection, but many of the selections made on the basis of membership are already the result of a careful application of criteria of election. When prestige is the quality under consideration, there is

---

*On July 1, 1968, Edwin G. Boring died with this paper still in galley form.

apt to be pretty good agreement at the top among competent judges; nevertheless, since any such list is an expression of opinion by the jury who selected it, the reader must be told whose opinions this list embodies and how the selections and the rankings were made.

To the original Watson list of 800-odd names, further investigation added approximately another 300. We then agreed to exclude those who were living in 1966, when this project was undertaken,[1] and to obtain as far as possible full names and dates of birth and death for all the persons retained on the list, procedures which after considerable research left us with a "working" list of 1040 psychologists, including a few uncertainties as to whether persons were living and as to names and dates.[2]

One thousand forty psychologists! The list seemed potentially useful, but unwieldy. The problem was how to boil it down and, perhaps, make it broader and less arbitrary as an expression of opinion. An unselected poll—of every 50th Fellow of the APA, for example—seemed likely to produce overabundant data of little usefulness, for what was needed was not numbers, but interest, background, and sophistication in the history of psychology. Nor would persons without those attributes be willing to undertake so onerous a task as rating 1040 names.

We therefore asked four other American psychologists, of different ages and geographical locations but of recognized competence in the field, to join in as jurors, making six Americans in all: Edwin G. Boring (Harvard), Richard J. Herrnstein (Harvard), Ernest R. Hilgard (Stanford), Robert B. MacLeod (Cornell), Robert I. Watson (New Hampshire), and Michael Wertheimer (Colorado). To broaden the scope still further and to reduce provincialism, Megumi Imada (Kyoto), Paul Fraisse (Sorbonne), and Joseph R. Nuttin (Louvain) were approached and agreed to participate. (A British representative was sought, but found himself unable to carry through.) We are enormously grateful to the jurors but hope that they found the task fun.

Each member of this jury of nine was then asked to take the basic list of 1040 psychologists and to rate each name according to the following scale:

> *1 check mark* if he recognized the name in the history of psychology, even if he could not specify the person's contribution;

---

1. The names of 5 persons who died in 1967 were later added to the list.
2. A few data are still lacking, as indicated by the 6 asterisks in Table IV.

2 check marks if he could identify the person's contribution to psychology, even if not very precisely;

3 check marks if he considered the person of such distinction that his name should surely be included in a list of the 500 most important psychologists since 1600 and not living.

No group of jurors, surely, could have been more careful and conscientious. Two, in fact, doubled their labors: Wertheimer went through the entire list twice, once according to a lenient criterion and again according to a strict criterion; Nuttin, operating on a rather strict criterion, distinguished between important psychologists and important others—scientists or philosophers.[3] (In the following tables, Nuttin's and Wertheimer's more lenient criteria have been used.)

With the nine returns in hand, we translated the check marks into scores, counting a triple check as 3, a double check as 2, a single check as 1, and a blank as 0. Thus the highest score obtainable was 27—nine triple checks—and so on down, 26-25-24 . . . 1, according to the different combinations of check marks. Actually it turns out that there are 219 possible combinations (excluding zero) in this series. For example, there are four possible combinations of check marks that result in a score of 23: $(7 \times 3) + (1 \times 2) + (0 \times 0)$; $(7 \times 3) + (0 \times 0) + (2 \times 1)$; $(6 \times 3) + (2 \times 2) + (1 \times 1)$; $(5 \times 3) + (4 \times 2) + (0 \times 0)$. For a score of 14, there are fifteen possible combinations.

Below are listed the top-rated 538 psychologists,[4] first in groups

---

3. Professor Imada furnishes the following list of 16 persons important in the development of psychology in Japan, some of whom are included in the main list.

Hayami, Hiroshi, 1876-1943   Nogami, Toshio, 1882-1963
Kawata, Teijiro, 1879-1959   Onojima, Usao, 1893-1944
Kubo, Ryoei, 1883-1942   Takashima, Heizaburo, 1865-1946
Kuroda, Ryo, 1890-1947   Tanaka, Kanichi, 1882-1962
Masuda, Koreshige, 1883-1933   Tsukahara, Seiji, 1872-1946
Nakajima, Taizo, 1866-1918   Ueno, Yoicki, 1883-1957
Nishi, Amane, 1826-1894   Watanabe, Toru, 1883-1957
Nishimura, Shigeki, 1828-1902   Yatabe, Tatsuo, 1893-1958

4. The full list was reduced from 1040 to 1027 by the exclusion of the living and of those who received no jurors' votes. A list of the 489 names for whom scores of ten or below were obtained and not reported in this article has been deposited as Document number *10006* with the ADI Auxiliary Publications Project, Photoduplication Service, Library of Congress, Washington, D.C. 20540. A copy may be secured by citing the Document number and by remitting $1.25 for photoprints and $1.25 for 35 mm microfilm. Advance payment is required.

Table 1. *Number and Percentage of Score-Checks Given by Each Member of the Jury*

	Watson	MacLeod	Imada	Hilgard	Boring	Wertheimer	Nuttin	Herrnstein	Fraisse	Mean
					N u m b e r					
Triple check	384	353	287	280	277	234	137	131	115	244
Double check	479	203	138	244	144	194	254	347	210	246
Single check	115	191	84	150	300	232	161	135	128	166
No check	62	293	531	366	319	380	488	427	587	384
	1040	1040	1040	1040	1040	1040	1040	1040	1040	1040
					P e r c e n t					
Triple check	37	34	27	27	26	22	13	13	11	23
Double check	46	20	13	23	14	19	24	33	20	24
Single check	11	18	9	15	30	22	16	13	12	16
No check	6	28	51	35	30	37	47	41	57	37
	100	100	100	100	100	100	100	100	100	100

according to scoring categories from 27 down through 11, and then alphabetically with full names, dates of birth and death, and scores. The lower score groups (13, 12, and 11) undoubtedly are affected by an American emphasis, which we regard as legitimate in view of psychology's recent American proliferation and the impossibility of avoiding this bias completely. Analysis of the six American returns separately, with a consequent top score for any name of 18, showed that almost exactly half the names—521, or approximately the original goal of 500—achieved the median score of 9 or above, whereas on the basis of all nine returns, only 408 names reached or exceeded the median score of 14. Only two names were carried above the median by the votes of the non-Americans: Victor Cousin and Ludwig Klages each received an American score of only 8, but a non-American score of 7, giving a total of 15. Readers who are more interested in a high degree of consensus than in the authors' arbitrary goal of approximately 500 may, therefore, stop reading at the median score of 14.

Table 2.
Number of Persons Out of the Total of 538 in Each Score Group From the Highest Score, 27, Down Through 11

Score	N		
27	53	18	29
26	23	17	24
25	27	16	33
24	23	15	30
23	31	14	27
22	24	13	34
21	20	12	39
20	34	11	58
19	29		
			538

Table II gives the number of persons falling into each score group from the highest score, 27, down through 11. Table III lists the 538 names individually according to score groups, and Table IV presents them alphabetically, with full names, dates of birth and death, and scores (in parentheses).

Table 3

Names of 538 Deceased Important Persons Contributing in 1600-1967, Arranged in Ranked Groups for Their Importance to Psychology as Judged by a Jury of Nine Psychologists

The score for greatest importance is 27 points, for the next highest group it is 26, and so on down to a score of zero when no juror recognized the name, but the table omits from the total of 1027 names the 489 scoring 10 or lower, since there must be hundreds of these less important psychologists who are unknown to any of the jurors. See above, *page 329, note 3.*

Score: 27 (53 persons)

Adler, Alfred
Allport, G. W.
Angell, J. R.
Bekhterev, V. M.
Binet, Alfred
Brentano, Franz
Cannon, W. B.
Charcot, J. M.
Darwin, Charles
Descartes, René
Dewey, John
Ebbinghaus, Hermann
Fechner, G. T.
Freud, Sigmund
Galton, Francis
Hall, G. S.
Helmholtz, H. L. F. v.
Herbart, J. F.
Hering, Ewald
Hull, C. L.
Hume, David
James, William
Janet, Pierre
Jung, C. G.
Köhler, Wolfgang
Koffka, Kurt
Kraepelin, Emil
Külpe, Oswald
Lashley, K. S.

Locke, John
McDougall, William
Mill, James
Mill, J. S.
Morgan, C. L.
Pavlov, I. P.
Pearson, Karl
Piéron, Henri
Rubin, E. J.
Sherrington, C. S.
Spearman, C. E.
Spencer, Herbert
Stumpf, Carl
Terman, L. M.
Thorndike, E. L.
Thurstone, L. L.
Titchener, E. B.
Tolman, E. C.
Watson, J. B.
Weber, E. H.
Wertheimer, Max
Woodworth, R. S.
Wundt, Wilhelm
Yerkes, R. M.

Score: 26 (23 persons)

Ach, N. K.
Bain, Alexander
Brunswik, Egon
Buhler, Karl
Cattell, J. McK.
Claparéde, Edouard
Ehrenfels, C. v.
Goldstein, Kurt
Guthrie, E. R.
Husserl, Edmund
Kretschmer, Ernst
La Mettrie, J. O. de
Leibnitz, G. W. v.
Lewin, Kurt
Loeb, Jacques
Michotte, A. E.
Müller, G. E.
Newton, Isaac
Ribot, T. A.
Rorschach, Hermann
Sechenov, I. M.
Stern, William
Stout, G. F.

Score: 25 (27 persons)

Baldwin, J. M.
Berkeley, George
Bernhard, Claude
Bleuler, E.
Cajal, S. R y
Comte, Auguste
Condillac, E. B. de
Gesell, Arnold
Goethe, J. W. v.

Head, Henry
Hunter, W. S.
Jaensch, E. R.
Jennings, H. S.
Kant, Immanuel
Katz, David
Kries, J. v.
Lotze, R. H.
Mach, Ernst
Magendie, François
Mesmer, F. A.
Müller, Johannes
Pinel, Philippe
Reid, Thomas
Romanes, G. J.
Spence, K. W.
Spranger, Eduard
Wolff, C. v.

Score: 24 (23 persons)

Bell, Charles
Bridgman, P. W.
Broca, Paul
Delboeuf, J. R. L.
Flourens, P. J. M.
Gall, F. J.
Hartley, David
Hobbes, Thomas
Höffding, Harald
Ladd, G. T.
Le Bon, Gustave
Maine de Biran
Marbe, Karl
Meinong, A. v.
Münsterberg, Hugo
Purkinje, J. E.
Quételet, Adolphe
Rousseau, J. J.
Seashore, C. E.

Spinoza, Benedict
Tarde, Gabriel
Ward, James
Werner, Heinz

Score: 23 (31 persons)

Avenarius, R. H. L.
Bacon, Francis
Bernheim, Hippolyte
Bessel, F. W.
Bingham, W. F.
Breuer, Josef
Carr, H. A.
Dalton, John
Drever, James
Du Bois-Reymond, Emil
Durkheim, Emile
Ellis, Havelock
Frey, M. v.
Horney, Karen
Hovland, C. I.
Itard, Jean
Lamarck, J. B. P. A. de M.
Lévy-Bruhl, Lucien
Lipps, Theodor
Meumann, Ernst
Prince, Morton
Rank, Otto
Révész, Géza
Scripture, E. W.
Stewart, Dugald
Sullivan, H. S.
Thomson, Godfrey
Warren, H. C.
Washburn, M. F.
Young, Thomas
Zwaardemaker, Hendrik

Score: 22 (24 persons)

Bentham, Jeremy
Bergson, Henri
Brown, Thomas
Cabanis, P. J. G.
Dilthey, Wilhelm
Dunlap, Knight
Elliotson, John
Galilei, Galileo
Gauss, Christian
Gemelli, Agostino
Hecht, Selig
Holt, E. B.
Jastrow, Joseph
Jones, Ernest
Judd, C. H.
Ladd-Franklin, Christine
Malinowski, B. K.
Mariotte, Edmé
Pestalozzi, J. H.
Preyer, W. T.
Schopenhauer, Arthur
Stratton, G. M.
Sully, James
Weiss, A. P.

Score: 21 (20 persons)

Bentley, Madison
Braid, James
Dumas, Georges
Hall, Marshall
Hamilton, William
Jackson, J. H.
Kelley, T. L.
Kinsey, A. C.
Liébeault, A. A.
Malabranche, N. de
Mendel, G. J.

Meyer, Adolf
Montessori, Maria
Myers, C. S.
Pillsbury, W. B.
Rapaport, David
Simon, Théodore
Spurzheim, J. K.
Taine, H. A.
Troland, L. T.

Score: 20 (34 persons)

Abraham, Karl
Aubert, Hermann
Babinski, J. F. F.
Benussi, Vittorio
Bonnet, Charles
Brücke, E. W. v.
Calkins, M. W.
Coghill, G. E.
Condorcet, M. J. A.
Dodge, Raymond
Esdaile, James
Fabre, J. H.
Fisher, R. A.
Franz, S. I.
Galvani, Luigi
Goodenough, F. L.
Harvey, William
Henning, Hans
Hollingworth, H. L.
Klemm, G. O.
Krueger, Felix
Langfeld, H. S.
Lombroso, Cesare
McGeoch, J. A.
Meyer, M. F.
Murchison, Carl
Nietzsche, F. W.

Ogden, R. M.
Sanford, E. C.
Schlosberg, Harold
Strong, E. K.
Vygotsky, L. S.
Whipple, G. M.
Yule, G. U.

Score: 19 (29 persons)

Beebe-Center, J. G.
Binswanger, Ludwig
Boas, Franz
Diderot, Denis
Donders, F. C.
Ferenczi, Sándor
Frenkel-Brunswik, Else
Goddard, H. H.
Hobhouse, L. T.
Kepler, Johannes
Kiesow, Federico
Linnaeus, Carolus
Linton, Ralph
Maxwell, J. C.
Mead, G. H.
Müller-Lyer, Franz
Pascal, Blaise
Peirce, C. S. S.
Rivers, W. H.
Sapir, Edward
Schumann, Friedrich
Uexküll, J. J. v.
Voltaire
Warden, C. J.
Watt, H. J.
Weber, Max
Wheeler, R. H.
Witasek, Stephan
Witmer, Lightner

Score: 18 (29 persons)

Alexander, Franz
Beaunis, H. E.
Brett, G. S.
Brill, A. A.
Coué, Emile
Crozier, W. J.
Dessoir, Max
Dreisch, H. A. E.
Duncker, Karl
Esquirol, J. E.
Exner, Sigmund
Féré, Charles
Fernberger, S. W.
Fritsch, Gustav
Goldscheider, Alfred
Hegel, G. W. F.
Hitzig, Eduard
Huxley, T. H.
Kluckhohn, C. K. M.
Lapicque, Louis
Messer, August
Pflüger, E. F. W.
Pintner, Rudolf
Plateau, J. A. F.
Rayleigh, Lord
Seguin, Edouard
Small, W. S.
Wiener, Norbert
Ziehen, Theodor

Score: 17 (24 persons)

Baird, J. W.
Beers, C. W.
Beneke, F. E.
Bichat, M. F. X.
Emmert, Emil

Ewald, J. R.
Haller, A. v.
Healy, William
Heymans, Gerardus
Humboldt, W. v.
Humphrey, George
Kelly, G. A.
Klein, Melanie
Laplace, P. S. de
Malthus, T. R.
Montesquieu, C. de S.
Richet, Charles
Roback, A. A.
Ruckmick, C. A.
Selz, Otto
Sidis, Boris
Smith, Adam
Vierordt, K. v.
Zilboorg, Gregory

Score: 16 (33 persons)

Ames, Adelbert
Angell, Frank
Benedict, Ruth
Bethe, Albrecht
Bryan, W. L.
Darwin, Erasmus
de Vries, Hugo
Fichte, J. G.
Fitts, P. M.
Flugel, J. C.
Fröbes, Joseph
Groos, Karl
Guillaume, Paul
Henri, Victor
Herrick, C. J.
Hornbostel, E. v.
Jost, Adolph

König, Arthur
Landis, Carney
Lavoisier, A. L.
Leeuwenhoek, A. v.
Lehmann, A. G. L.
Lubbock, John
Marx, Karl
Maudsley, Henry
Merleau-Ponty, Maurice
Muenzinger, K. F.
Poppelreuter, Walther
Robinson, E. S.
Royce, Josiah
Sanford, F. H.
Stekel, Wilhelm
Stone, C. P.

Score: 15 (30 persons)

Boole, George
Comenius, J. A.
Cousin, Victor
Croce, Benedetto
D'Alembert, J. L.
Delacroix, Henri
Donaldson, H. H.
Faraday, Michael
Fenichel, Otto
Gelb, Adhémar
Haeckel, E. H.
Hartmann, E. v.
Helvétius, C. A.
Klages, Ludwig
Leuba, J. H.
Lindworsky, Johannes
Müller-Freinenfels, Richard
Paterson, D. G.
Pilzecker, Alfons
Ponzo, Mario

Rignano, Eugenio
Rolando, Luigi
Rosanoff, A. J.
Rush, Benjamin
Schelling, F. W. J. v.
Shand, A. F.
Störring, Gustav
Wallace, A. R.
Whytt, Robert
Zener, K. E.

Score: 14 (27 persons)

Blix, Magnus
Brown-Séquard, C. E.
Carpenter, W. B.
Downey, J. E.
English, H. B.
Feuerbach, P. J. A. v.
Fourier, Charles
Fullerton, G. S.
Fulton, J. F.
Golgi, Camillo
Huygens, Christian
Kafka, Gustav
Lange, C. G.
Lorge, Irving
Ludwig, C. F. W.
Nissen, H. W.
Pfungst, Oskar
Reymert, M. L.
Scheerer, Martin
Twitmyer, E. B.
Urban, F. M.
Verworn, Max
Wheatstone, Charles
White, W. A.
Whitehead, A. N.
Wirth, Wilhelm

Wissler, Clark

Score: 13 (34 persons)

Agassiz, Louis
Angyal, Andras
Bourdon, B. B.
Buffon, G. L. L. de
Burnham, W. H.
Cooley, C. H.
De Sanctis, Sante
Dusser de Barenne, J. G.
Flechsig, P. E.
Franklin, Benjamin
Fröbel, Friedrich
Gosset, W. S.
Herskovits, M. J.
Kolzinger, K. J.
Kellogg, C. E.
Kornilov, K. N.
Lazarus, Moritz
Louttit, C. McK.
McCosh, James
Mercier, D. J.
Mira y Lopez, Emilio
Moll, Albert
Molyneux, William
Orth, Johannes
Parsons, J. H.
Priestley, Joseph
Sachs, Hanns
Schiller, Friedrich
Schiller, P. H.
Smuts, J. C.
Stouffer, S. A.
Tylor, E. B.
Valentine, C. W.
Valentine, W. L.

Score: 12 (39 persons)

Angier, R. P.
Bernstein, Julius
Book, W. F.
Bosditch, H. P.
Carlson, A. J.
Cuvier, G. L. C. F. D.
Dearborn, W. F.
Delabarre, E. B.
Erdmann, Benno
Euler, Leonhard
Farnsworth, Dean
Fearing, Franklin
Forel, August
Fromm-Reichmann, Frieda
Goltz, F. L.
Gruhle, W. H.
Hellpach, Willy
Hollingworth, L. S.
Johnson, Samuel
Kroh, Oswald
Lange, Ludwig
MacCurdy, J. T.
McGregor, Douglas
Meynert, T. H.
Moede, Walther
Monakow, C. v.
Nagel, Wilibald
Ogden, C. K.
Peckham, G. W.
Polyak, Stephen
Ranschburg, Paul
Rubinstein, S. L.
Spalding, D. A.
Starbuck, E. D.
Steinthal, Heymann

Stoelting, C. H.
Volkmann, A. W.
Wallon, H. P. H.
Wiersma, E. D.

Score: 11 (58 persons)

Aveling, Francis
Ballard, P. B.
Banister, Harry
Bernoulli, Daniel
Bird, Charles
Blondel, Charles
Bronner, A. F.
Brown, Warner
Brown, William
Brunschvicg, Léon
Cason, Hulsey
Coleridge, S. T.
Davenport, C. B.
Decroly, O. J.
Destutt de Tracy, A. L. C.
Dix, D. L.
Edwards, Jonathan
Farrand, Livingston
Ferree, C. E.
Flourney, Théodore
Freeman, F. N.
Gassendi, Pierre
Geulinex, Arnold
Henmon, V. A. C.
Herder, J. G. v.
Jaensch, Walter
Jevons, W. S.
Jodl, Friedrich
Karwoski, Theodore
Kirkpatrick, E. A.
Kris, Ernst

Kuhlmann, Frederick	Prochaska, George	Swedenborg, Emanuel
Lessing, G. E.	Róheim, Géza	Symonds, P. M.
Lewes, G. H.	Ross, E. A.	Tetens, J. N.
Matsumoto, Matataro	Saudek, Robert	Tiedemann, Dietrich
Mayo, Elton	Scott, W. D.	Vaihinger, Hans
Meissner, Georg	Seashore, H. G.	Wallas, Graham
Mersenne, Marin	Shepard, J. F.	Warner, L. H.
Paulhan, Frédéric	Snoddy, G. S.	Wells, F. L.
Porter, Noah	Southard, E. E.	Wheeler, W. M.

Editors' Note. Material originally found in Table IV has been separately published in this volume as "Classification of Eminent Contributors to Psychology, 1600–1967." This paper includes corrections.

21. Characteristics of Individuals Eminent in Psychology in Temporal Perspective

Present concern is with the nationality, the major field of endeavor, and the particular temporal period of contribution for 538 individuals eminent in the history of psychology.

This study is conducted against a larger pattern of investigations that began with a study published in 1968 by Annin, Boring, and Watson (1), and supplemented and corrected by Merrifield and Watson (2). This paper reported the 538 individuals who had been selected by an international panel of nine psychologist judges from four countries. A rating technique had been used. Each judge applied a checkpoint system to the names of 1040 deceased contributors to psychology who lived during the period 1600 to 1967. One checkmark indicated that the name was recognized even though his contribution to psychology could not be specified, two check-marks indicated not only recognition but also that contributions to psychology could be specified, and three check-marks indicated that his contributions were judged to be of such distinction that his name would, in our judgment, be included in a list of the 500 most important psychologists of the past. The ratings of the judges were summed for each individual on the list. Consequently, the highest

---

This and the succeeding part are a modification and expansion of an invited address given at the fourth annual meeting of Cheiron, the International Society for the History of the Behavioral and Social Sciences, at the University of Calgary, Alberta, Canada, June 27, 1972.

Marilyn Merrifield, who collected the information to make possible the various classifications and made a preliminary classification in each category, was the recipient of a scholarship from the Undergraduate Research Participation Program sponsored by the Graduate School of the University of New Hampshire for the summer of 1969. Its help is gratefully acknowledged.

cumulative rating was 27, indicating that all judges maximally rated this individual. Fifty-three persons received this score. To illustrate, the fifteen American contributors to psychology who received this unanimous maximum rating were Gordon Allport, J. R. Angell, W. B. Cannon, John Dewey, G. Stanley Hall, Clark Hull, William James, Karl Lashley, L. M. Terman, E. L. Thorndike, L. L. Thurstone, E. B. Titchener, E. C. Tolman, J. B. Watson, R. S. Woodworth, and R. M. Yerkes. Other contributors received scores from 26 to 0. To arrive at a list of about 500, a cut-off score of 11 was used, with those individuals scoring less being eliminated from further consideration. Although this lowest rating of those included in the population could be arrived at in various ways, often it was obtained by seven judges rating one and two others giving a rating of two, with none giving a rating of zero or of three check-marks. Representative Americans falling in this group were Augusta Bronner, W. D. Scott, Elton Mayo, Percival Symonds, and F..L. Wells.

The population sample of contributors lent itself to a variety of investigations. Two reference volumes are under way: one, entitled *Eminent Contributors to Psychology: Primary Sources*, is in press; the other, a companion volume, *Secondary Sources*, is to be published later. Aided immeasurably by the advice of specialists, over 12,000 primary references, verified as to accuracy of citation, have been selected and are to be reported in the first volume. This works out to an average of 24 references per person, although the range is from one to about a hundred. (In case one wonders how a contributor can be confined to one publication, C. H. Stoelting, the instrument maker, has a modest place in this company and his catalogue is his sole publication.) Although research and theoretical contributions are stressed, collected works are cited, and autobiographies and personally prepared bibliographies are included whenever available. The book will be published by Springer within a year.

The other volume, *Secondary Sources*, will include about 55,000 citations to one or another of the 538 eminent contributors. Variability in number of citations per person is greater than for the primary references, since it ranges from something over 500 for a Freud or a James down to three or four for Mr. Stoelting. A special effort was made to indicate available bibliographies and biographies as leads for investigation at greater depth than the volume can supply.

Some recent historiographic developments in psychology give

point to why it is worthwhile to examine certain of the characteristics of these eminent contributors to psychology.

The history of psychology as a field of scholarly investigation is a very youthful one. During the last ten years a number of events have taken place which show a sharp increase in interest. In psychology as a discipline, a Division of the History of Psychology has been organized within the American Psychological Association; Cheiron, The International Society for the History of the Behavioral and Social Sciences has been meeting; the *Journal* has been founded; a Ph.D. degree program in the history of psychology has been operative; and two institutes on the teaching of the history of psychology have been held.

One consequence of this recent growth has been an increase in the number of graduate students and younger professionals who have turned to history as a field of specialization. The intellectual milieu which we provide for the student and young professional is important. One aspect of this scholarly background expressed in teaching and research comes from the impression conveyed about just who in our past has been considered important. In varying degrees practitioners, too, have a need to block out the structure in what they are going. That I belong to the structured wing is obvious from the very task with which this paper concerns itself. I, too, have need for a rough map to help in moving within an area.

The availability of information about these contributors to psychology may help subsequent generations of historians of psychology to avoid playing that somewhat stultifying game of following the leader, that is to say, the structuring of a subfield of historical study by the fact that some individual has been singled out for initial study by historians—students who have been exposed to this received opinion then proceeding to follow the same course while tending to neglect other persons and times. To illustrate this point, the writer must confess to feeling a certain impatience with what appears to him to be a disproportionate emphasis by American historians of psychiatry on Benjamin Rush and by historians of philosophy-theology on Jonathan Edwards.

The results of this project, then, may help to open up a structure of relatively wide scope against which the fledgling historian of psychology can more properly see some of the potentials for scholarly investigations. So far as selection of the particular problems to be investigated is concerned, the project quite properly is silent. But once selection of man or area in relation to a problem is made, the reference volumes become a presumably useful tool conveniently spreading out before him some of the relevant publications available.

The nationality of these contributors will be first considered, then their particular fields of endeavor, and, lastly, an examination of the temporal periods of their contributions.

At first glance, to classify 538 eminent individuals according to nationality seemed a straightforward task. However, preliminary scrutiny revealed that the facts about the individuals did not allow them to fall neatly into national categories.

At the onset of the study it was decided to consult the categorizations made by a dozen or so presumably authoritative sources, such as the *Dictionary of National Biography, The International Encyclopedia of the Social Sciences*, and *The Encyclopedia of Philosophy*. But we found that the information they supplied about nationality could not always be relied upon to provide the information necessary for clear-cut decision. Contradictions and use of national groupings of narrower scope than are current were not infrequent. Judgment on our part was still necessary and no claim is made that our specification of nationality is identical with those given elsewhere.

Aside from the vicissitudes created by shifting boundaries, individuals who remained in one country throughout their lifetimes generally gave no trouble. Nor were problems experienced concerning individuals who migrated to another country in the course of their higher education and remained there. A considerable number of persons, however, seemed to resist easy classification in that place of birth, education, and professional activity (all of which were taken into consideration) crossed national boundaries in an intricate and often bewildering fashion. It was those persons who received their training in more than one country; those who were trained in one country and carried on their teaching and research in one, two, three, or even four other countries who required decision about relative weights to be given in reaching an assignment of nationality.[1]

---

1. For each person about whom there was some perplexity, more detailed biographical data were sought and all countries that might enter into the decision were specified before a decision was reached.

Difficulty in assigning some persons to even a dual nationality resulted in a temporary consideration of a triple nationality classification, but the temptation was not great enough to overcome the disadvantages of employment of such

Table 1 includes the classification arrived at according to single or dual nationalities. [*Editor's Note*. Material originally appearing in Table 1 has been published separately in this volume as "Classification of Eminent Contributors to Psychology, 1600–1967."] Since

unwieldy categories. Allowing a certain amount of latitude, we found it possible to contain all of the 538 eminent psychologists within the framework of either single or dual nationality classifications. Since the basis for the classification of individuals with debatable nationality is probably not yet very explicit, we will attempt to clarify the rationale behind the decisions with a few illustrations.

An example of straightforward dual classification is that of Kurt Lewin, who was both in Germany, studied at German universities, and spent quite a few productive years in Germany. When he was 42, he emigrated to the United States, where he spent the remainder of his years, most of which were very productive. He was classified as a German-American, both countries being considered as deserving the right to claim him.

Along with the length of stay in a given country, productivity during these years was also taken into consideration in arriving at either a dual or single categorization. Heinz Werner illustrates the problem of more than two countries with a legitimate claim upon him. Born in Vienna and educated at its university, he emigrated to Germany in 1915 at the age of 24 or 25. Thereafter he was at German universities for twenty or more years before coming to the United States. If we permitted a threefold classification he would surely have been called Austro-German-American. It was decided that German-American reflected more of this than would the alternative Austro-American. An argument could also be made for the inclusion of Otto Rank in a triple nationality category of Austro-French-American, on the basis of his study and work in Austria, his eight years of practice in Paris, and his final productive years at a Philadelphia school for social work. However, the decision was to classify him as an Austro-American and to ignore the French claims, as he did not publish significant work in French. Because Spurzheim traveled quite extensively, there was great difficulty in placing him in only two nationality groups. Since his lengthy visits to England and America were for the purpose of recruiting converts to the school of phrenology, he was classified, along with Gall, as Austro-French.

Cogent reasons were also found to make exceptions to the application of dual classification even though the parts of national residence seemed to justify it. Although Karl Bühler emigrated to the United States in 1939, where he remained until his death in 1963, he always remained a German, publishing almost exclusively in German even during his years in the United States. In his case, a dual classification was not used. Similarly, there is one individual classified as American only who spent many years abroad without affecting his classification. James Mark Baldwin spent his last years in France, not working in psychology, but in advancing Franco-American relationships, and, to a lesser extent, in continuing his philosophical interests. Edward Bradford Titchener, who was born in England, retained his citizenship there and trained in Germany in the tradition of Wundt; he has been classified as an American because of his profound influ-

the contents of this table are useful primarily when information about an individual is sought, a summary table, Table 2, seemed indicated. A collapse into German, French, British, American, and "other" nationality-language categories was used. Individuals of dual nationality as reported in Table 1 were included now only once and classified by the country or language where they first did their work. The German category included not only Germans and Austrians but also those Swiss, Czechs, Hungarians, Scandinavians, and Dutch who published in German. The French included Swiss and Belgians writing in French. The Scots and the two Irishmen were somewhat shamefacedly classed as British. The N reported is reduced to 506 by elimination of other nationality-language groupings, particularly Italian and Russian, and of a few representatives of fields not reducible to the broad categories to be discussed shortly.

Table 2
Eminent Contributors to Psychology by General Field and Language-National Grouping

	German	British	French	American	Total
Psychologists	60	26	18	117	221
Physiologists	45	16	18	15	94
Philosophers	33	21	25	9	88
Psychiatrists-Psychoanalysts	30	5	8	11	54
Physical Scientists	8	14	6	2	30
Social Scientists	2	4	4	9	19
Total	178	86	79	163	506

ence upon the development of structural psychology in America. I admit a certain irony here. Of the three nationalities this would probably have been his third choice! Adolf Meyer has likewise been classified as an American, even though he was born in Switzerland and received his training in Germany. His emigration to the United States shortly after attainment of his degree and his powerful influence upon American psychiatry are factors which induced us to dispense with the dual classification in his case. Because of Zilboorg's introduction to psychoanalysis occurring in the United States, he was classified as an American, even though he had received his M.D. degree in Russia. Similarly, Rudolf Pintner was an exception. He was classified as an American, disregarding his birthplace in England and his years of study in Scotland and Germany, since the years most important for his contributions to psychology occurred after his arrival in the United States in 1912. Elton Mayo born in Australia, Martin

We might first concern ourselves with the totals in the bottom row of Table 2. Inspection shows that a summary statement could be made that one-third of the eminent contributors to psychological science were German, one-third American, and one-sixth each French and British. It should be remembered that other nationals were excluded; but even inclusion of the Russian (N = 6) and the Italian (N = 11) representatives would not have changed this picture in any appreciable fashion. Despite psychology today having its representatives in all countries as a science, it can be said that it is a product of German-American-British-French science.

To what extent did scholars cross these language nationality boundaries? From data not given in the table in the years under consideration, American psychology gained 37 and lost only one eminent contributor. The gain for the American was mostly from the German grouping and from the British. To anticipate discussion of fields of endeavor for a moment, the gains of the Americans were relatively heavier in what will be called the psychiatric-psychoanalytic category—12 out of a total of the 37 dual nationals who moved from the French-British-German groupings. The United States, in contrast, supplied but nine native born for this category. In absolute terms, however, more psychologists in the narrower sense were gained, since there were Germans who migrated to the United States. Since these two categories account for 28 of the total of 37, other linguistic-national groupings and fields of endeavor had relatively few dual nationals. Twenty-eight shifts within the German linguistic grouping took place. Inspection of the data shows that Austria was particularly

---

Reymert born in Norway, and David Rapaport born in Hungary were classified as Americans because all of their significant work was done in the United States.

Around the end of the nineteenth century and the beginning of the twentieth, graduate work in Germany attracted a considerable number of foreigners, particularly from the United States. Upon return to their native countries they proceeded to utilize this training. Since these individuals did not make this German-acquired knowledge the sole foundation for their later contributions, but included it as a part of their entire outlook, these persons were classified in the category of the country to which they returned. Martin Scheerer could have been considered as falling in this category and classified as American alone. He was born in New York and returned to America after his studies at several German universities and a three-year teaching stint at Hamburg. His orientation was primarily German, and like those psychologists who were European refugees, he taught at the New School for Social Research so he was classified as German-American.

open to change. In all, twenty-four individuals spent a substantial part of their scientific careers in Austria, but only seven remained there throughout. Six came from Germany; none went on to Germany. Ultimately, eight worked in the United States. The very few British who did move were apt to migrate to the United States; but there was reverse trend. The French were relatively stable. Confining attention to French nationals, 64 out of 68 spent their entire careers in France. In French-speaking Switzerland, there was somewhat more movement, since five did cross national boundaries, while 14 remained throughout their lifetimes. Most of the other smaller countries, e.g. the Scandinavian countries and Belgium and Holland, tended to be stable in the sense that they neither lost nor gained through individuals crossing national boundaries. Brain drain, it would appear, is but a new phrase for an old phenomenon.

Further comments about nationality will be foregone until some aspects of the findings concerning fields of specialization are considered.

The panel members made their evaluations of eminent contributions to psychology without regard to the fields of specialization. Their task was to identify major contributors to psychology, irrespective of field. It will prove instructive to examine the fields from which these individuals came. While all of them have contributed to psychology, the group may be broken down into separate field categories, only one of which is psychology in a narrower sense.

Even more than was the case with classification by nationality, that for major field of endeavor required exercise of judgment. The various reference sources that were consulted to help arrive at specific classifications were under no obligation to limit themselves to a few clear-cut categories. Quite commendably they used idiosyncratic categorizations whenever it was thought that to do so would capture the *raison d'être* of an individual scientist's work. We were moved by a different intent. We wished to use as few categories as possible commensurate with at least some attention to the complexity of the data and their relevance for psychology.

Many problems were encountered in placement. Accurate placement in a specific field was difficult, especially for certain individuals like Cabanis, Condorcet, Benjamin Franklin, Goethe, Galton, James, Leibniz, Pascal, Royce, and others. Criteria which entered into our choice were the field upon which most authoritative sources consulted agreed upon, his self-estimate, and that which was most relevant to psychology. Difficulties arose when application of these criteria did not yield the same results, particularly when authority and self-estimate were in agreement but relevance to psychology was discrepant.[2] Suffice it here to illustrate very briefly

---

2. Classification into fields of endeavor was neither merely by the particular degree taken nor even professional post held. Also taken into consideration was how the individual in question accepted his work as a legitimate expression in a particular field. Arthur König *was* a physicist despite his intimate connection with physiological optics, his editorship for psychology on the *Zeitschrift für Psychologie*, and editorship of a handbook of physiology. Hendrik Zwaardemaker was a physiologist, as he put it succinctly, "with psychological aspirations."

Relevance as a criterion for classification may be illustrated from the fact that, when in doubt about Americans of the last 80 years or so, it was decided that membership in the APA was evidence for acceptance of classification as a psychologist. It must be stressed that this criterion was used only in cases of doubt. If we had applied this membership rule by rote, we would have classified John Dewey, William James, and Josiah Royce (who were not only members but even presidents of the APA) as psychologists. To have done so would have been to be guilty of academic imperialism of the rankest sort. Instead, we classified each of them as philosopher. Even within these three instances there is a gradation of judgment of certainty. Probably no one will disagree with our contention that Josiah Royce was primarily a philosopher. Indeed, the problem might be to convince many that he made contributions to psychology! If one examines a list of his publications it will be seen that a considerable number are on psychological topics no matter how narrowly interpreted. Greater general familiarity with the work of John Dewey, we would hazard, would produce less argument, based on knowledge that he was a psychologist at the Universities of Michigan and Chicago and a philosopher-educator for a much longer length of time at Columbia University. Surrendering William James to the philosophers might be the source of the greatest disagreement of all. Our major argument for this abnegation was his own self-image—he was a philosopher all of the time, a psychologist only some of the time.

Pierre Janet is an instance where the evidence was interpreted as showing that he most properly was designated as psychologist rather than as psychiatrist despite his M.D. degree. This degree was taken after other forms of graduate study, and it was as much as seven years before that degree that he published on topics essentially similar to his later ones. Later he organized more than one psychological society, suggesting that his self-image was not of a psychiatrist; his title was Professor of Experimental Psychology at the College of France, and he published his autobiography as a psychologist. For these reasons he was claimed as a psychologist.

For men like Kepler, Galileo, and Newton, at first astronomer seemed the most appropriate title; but because the sources consulted classified these men as mathematicians as well as astronomers and because the field of mathematics had more relevancy to psychology, the formation of a dual classification was decided

by mentioning some of the more difficult to place. William James was reluctantly surrendered to the philosophers; Josef Breuer, despite work as a general practitioner and otologist and never strictly speaking a psychoanalyst, nevertheless was so designated; Coleridge (much more the poet) and Goethe and Schiller (much more dramatists) are philosophers insofar as they concern us.

As reported in Table 3, the specific fields of endeavor of these 538 eminent contributors to psychology, as finally eventuated, number 23. One is immediately struck by their diversity. Only a moment's reflection by anyone familiar with psychology's history would have led to the conclusion that contributions to psychology

---

upon—that of astronomer-mathematician. Considerable difficulty in specifying an individual as primarily a neurologist, as differentiated from either a physiologist or an anatomist, was experienced in distinguishing between representatives of the latter two fields.

Particularly important in classifying some individuals was the nature of the relation they later had to psychology. There is no doubt that Goethe was a poet-dramatist, Schiller a dramatist, and Coleridge a poet. But if selected as making a contribution to psychology, as they were, it was not in their dramatic or poetical roles. A clue is supplied in later edited collections of their works, where what are included are referred to as *Philosophical Works*. With noticeable regularity the secondary literature contains articles and books with such titles as "Coleridge as Philosopher." Consequently, it was decided to classify them as philosophers so far as their relation with psychology was concerned.

Some other specific problems might be mentioned. Is Josef Breuer an internist, a general practitioner, an otologist, or, because of Anna O., a psychoanalyst? He might possibly have appeared in this list without his association with Freud because of his work on the semi-circular canals; but clearly his major claim to recognition today is his findings with Anna O., that neurotic symptoms disappear when the unconscious processes become conscious. Hence the man who gave up his association with psychoanalysis is a forerunner of it and is so labeled.

What to label Alfred Adler and Carl Jung? Psychoanalytic pioneers they certainly were. Nevertheless it would be just as inappropriate to classify them as psychoanalysts or even as Neo-Freudians as to refer to Spinoza and Leibniz as Cartesians, and for the same reason. These two were considerably influenced by Descartes, but they showed enough originality and independence to demand that they not be classed as followers. So, too, the work of Jung and Adler was influenced by Freud, but its independent originality demanded some other designations of their views respectively as analytical and individual psychology. Here was still another problem, since it was felt that they should not be classified among the psychologists, at least not in the way we were delimiting the field. The upshot was that they were classed somewhat lamely among the psychiatrists.

Table 3
Specific Fields of Endeavor of the Eminent Contributors

	N	%
Psychologists	228	42
Philosophers	92	17
Physiologists	56	10
Psychiatrists	31	6
Biologists	22	4
Psychoanalysts	17	3
Sociologists	11	2
Physicists	11	2
Anatomists	9	2
Anthropologists	9	2
Neurologists	9	2
Hypnotists	7	1
Astronomer-Mathematicians	6	1
Mathematicians	6	1
Statisticians	5	1
Ophthalmologists	4	1
Educators	4	1
Chemists	3	1
Geneticists	3	1
Laymen	3	1
Theologian	1	—
Logician	1	—

would have been made by philosophers, by physiologists, by psychiatrists, and by psychoanalysts. After some consideration it can be hazarded that general biologists, anatomists, sociologists, anthropologists, neurologists, and statisticians would have been predicted as well. But could it have been anticipated that a substantial ten percent of the most eminent contributors to psychology would turn out to be physicists, hypnotists, astronomer-mathematicians, mathematicians in a narrower sense, ophthalmologists, educators, chemists, geneticists, laymen, a theologian and a logician?

Since almost sixty percent of these contributors were not psychologists in the narrower sense, it is evident that psychology is much indebted to workers in other fields.

If number is any criterion, the influence of philosophers is very strong, since they numbered ninety-two, or seventeen percent. I cannot forbear from commenting that I hope that this finding gives a touch of disquiet to my colleagues who persist in denying psychology's philosophical heritage.

For purposes of further comparison, certain groups may be combined in the manner reported earlier for Table 2. The physiologist-biologist-anatomist-geneticist combination supply an even larger percentage (sixteen percent) than do the philosophers, demonstrating another source of our heritage. The psychiatrists-psychoanalysts total fifty-five, or ten percent.

When we turn to the group of individuals representing socially oriented influences—the sociologists and anthropologists—there is a dramatic drop. There are but twenty, or less than four percent. To be sure, included among the philosophers were those with definite social leanings, such as Adam Smith and Comte, but so too were there biologically and medically oriented philosophers, such as Lotze and Rignano, who are numerous enough to form a sufficiently strong counterbalance so that a systematic bias probably is avoided. Actually, representatives of the physical sciences—physicists, astronomer-mathematicians, mathematicians, and chemists—outnumber the social scientists, since here there are 25, or five percent, in this category.

In psychology today probably the strongest emphasis is upon social aspects. Not only is social psychology a most viable field, but also work in clinical, counseling, industrial, and educational psychology is embedded in a social matrix. A case can be made that more than a majority of current American psychologists are socially oriented. This is in sharp contrast to the situation which obtained during the temporal period in which our eminent contributors carried out their work, since the social scientists were so few in number. I hope I may be forgiven a bit of speculation. The historical background for current social psychological work, it seems to me, must be embedded in general psychology or owes a great deal to relatively more recent developments than that carried out by these eminent contributors. Unraveling this paradox of the most flourishing field in psychology today having relatively little in the way of obvious progenitors does seem to deserve investigation in depth.

Only eleven of the eminent contributors, or about two percent, were women. From what fields did they come? Augusta

Bronner, Mary W. Calkins, June Downey, Else Frenkel-Brunswik, Leta S. Hollingworth, Christine Ladd-Franklin, and Margaret Floy Washburn were psychologists; Ruth Benedict was an anthropologist, Frieda Fromm-Reichmann a psychiatrist, Melanie Klein a psychoanalyst, and Maria Montessori an educator. The absence from among them of physiologists and of philosophers, unless we so designate some of the contributions of Calkins, is evident. Also worth noting is that they came from the relatively recent past, since all contributed during this century. Three had husbands who were also on the list—Bronner, married to the psychiatrist William Healy, and Hollingworth and Frenkel-Brunswik, married to psychologists.

Information about field of contribution in relation to nationality has been given in Table 2, to which attention is again directed. More than fifty percent of the Americans were psychologists. Next in productivity of psychologists were the Germans, providing more than twenty-five percent. Among physiologists, Germany predominates, supplying three times as many as either the American, the English, or the French groups. Germany dominates among the philosophers, although not to the extent they did for physiologists, since the British and the French are also prominent, together supplying about fifty percent. American philosophers, in contrast, make up only about ten percent of the total. Among psychiatrists-psychoanalysts Germans clearly dominate, supplying fifty-five percent. Americans supply about twenty percent, but this is only slightly more than the British. The British come into major prominence for their physical scientists-mathematicians, supplying almost fifty percent, with the Germans and the French providing practically all of the rest. There were but two Americans (Bridgman and Wiener). There were only twenty social scientists, of whom not quite fifty percent were Americans. The remainder were distributed among the other three nationality-language groupings in a more or less equal manner.

For eminent contributors from fields other than psychology in the narrower sense, the Germans clearly are dominant. In Table 2, subtracting the number of psychologists from the totals for each nationality-language grouping shows that of the remainder the Germans supplied 118, or forty-two percent, the British 60, or twenty-two percent, the French 61, or twenty-one percent, and the Americans 46, or sixteen percent.

Many of these findings are influenced by the temporal period of the contribution under consideration. For example, the predominance of American psychologists, its lack of philosophers, and even its relative dominance with social scientists are related to the recency of its contribution to these fields. The temporal characteristics of the group will be considered in Part 2.

REFERENCES

1. Annin, Edith L., Boring, E. G., and Watson, R. I. Important psychologists, 1600-1967. *J. hist. Behav. Sci.*, 1968, *4*, 303-315.

2. Merrifield, Marilyn, and Watson, R. I. Eminent psychologists: Corrections and additions. *J. hist. Behav. Sci.*, 1970, *6*, 261-262.

22. Classification of Eminent Contributors to Psychology, 1600-1967, According to Nationality, Field, Date of Birth, and Eminence Score

Abraham, Karl. German Psychoanalyst. 1877-1925 (20)
Ach, Narziss Kaspar. German Psychologist. 1871-1946 (26)
Adler, Alfred. Austrian-American Psychiatrist. 1870-1937 (27)
Agassiz, (Jean) Louis (Rodolphe). Swiss-American Biologist. 1807-1873. (13)
Alembert, Jean LeRond de. French Philosopher. 1717-1783 (15)
Alexander, Franz. German-American Psychoanalyst. 1891-1964 (18)
Allport, Gordon Willard. American Psychologist. 1897-1967 (27)
Ames, Adelbert, Jr. American Ophthalmologist. 1880-1955 (16)
Angell, Frank. American Psychologist. 1857-1939 (16)
Angell, James Rowland. American Psychologist. 1869-1949 (27)
Angier, Roswell Parker. American Psychologist. 1874-1946 (12)
Angyal, Andras. Austrian-American Psychiatrist. 1902-1960 (13)
Aubert, Hermann. German Physiologist. 1826-1892 (20)
Aveling, Francis. English Psychologist. 1875-1941 (11)
Avenarius, Richard Heinrich Ludwig. Swiss Philosopher. 1843-1896 (23)
Babinski, Joseph François Félix. French Neurologist. 1857-1932 (20)
Bacon, Francis. English Philosopher. 1561-1626 (23)

*This paper combines the sources of data reported in Annin, Edith L., Boring, E. G., and Watson, R. I., Important psychologists, 1600-1967 (*J. Hist. Behav. Sci.*, 1968, *4*, 303-315); Watson, R. I., and Merrifield, Marilyn, Eminent psychologists: Corrections and additions (*J. Hist. Behav. Sci.*, 1970, *6*, 261-262); and Watson, R. I., and Merrifield, Marilyn, Characteristics of individuals eminent in psychology in temporal perspective: Part I (*J. Hist. Behav. Sci.*, 1973, *9*, 339-359.

Bain, Alexander. Scottish Psychologist. 1818-1903 (26)
Baird, John Wallace. American Psychologist. 1869-1919 (17)
Baldwin, James Mark. American Psychologist. 1861-1934 (25)
Ballard, Philip Boswood. English Psychologist. 1865-1950 (11)
Banister, Harry. English Psychologist. 1882-1963 (11)
Beaunis, Henri Etienne. French Physiologist. 1830-1921 (18)
Beebe-Center, John Gilbert. American Psychologist. 1897-1958 (19)
Beers, Clifford Whittingham. American Layman. 1876-1943 (17)
Bekhterev, Vladimir Mikhailovich. Russian Physiologist. 1857-1927 (27)
Bell, Charles. English Anatomist. 1774-1842 (24)
Benedict, Ruth (Fulton). American Anthropologist. 1887-1948 (16)
Beneke, Friedrich Eduard. German Philosopher. 1798-1854 (17)
Bentham, Jeremy. English Philosopher. 1748-1832 (22)
Bentley, (Isaac) Madison. American Psychologist. 1870-1955 (21)
Benussi, Vittorio. Italian-Austrian Psychologist. 1878-1927 (20)
Bergson, Henri. French Philosopher. 1859-1941 (22)
Berkeley, George. English Philosopher. 1685-1753 (25)
Bernard, Claude. French Physiologist. 1813-1878 (25)
Bernheim, Hippolyte. French Hypnotist. 1840-1919 (23)
Bernoulli, Daniel. Swiss Mathematician. 1700-1782 (11)
Bernstein, Julius. German Physiologist. 1839-1917 (12)
Bessel, Friedrich Wilhelm. German Astronomer-Mathematician. 1784-1846 (23)
Bethe, Albrecht. German Physiologist. 1872-1954 (16)
Bichat, Marie François Xavier. French Physiologist. 1771-1802 (17)
Binet, Alfred. French Psychologist. 1857-1911 (27)
Bingham, Walter Van Dyke. American Psychologist. 1880-1952 (23)
Binswanger, Ludwig. Swiss Psychiatrist. 1881-1966 (19)
Bird, Charles. American Psychologist. 1893-1957 (11)
Bleuler, (Paul) Eugen. Swiss Psychiatrist. 1857-1939 (25)
Blix, Magnus (Gustav). Swedish Physiologist. 1849-1904 (14)
Blondel, Charles. French Psychologist. 1876-1939 (11)
Boas, Franz. German-American Anthropologist. 1858-1942 (19)
Bonnet, Charles. Swiss Biologist. 1720-1793 (20)
Book, William Frederick. American Psychologist. 1873-1940 (12)
Boole, George. Irish Mathematician. 1815-1864 (15)
Bourdon, Benjamin Bienaimé. French Psychologist. 1860-1943 (13)
Bowditch, Henry Pickering. American Physiologist. 1840-1911 (12)
Braid, James. English Hypnotist. 1795?-1860 (21)

Brentano, Franz. German-Austrian Philosopher. 1838-1917 (27)
Brett, George Sidney. English-Canadian Psychologist. 1879-1944 (18)
Breuer, Josef. Austrian Psychoanalyst. 1842-1925 (23)
Bridgman, Percy Williams. American Physicist. 1882-1961 (24)
Brill, Abraham Arden. American Psychoanalyst. 1874-1948 (18)
Broca, Paul. French Neurologist. 1824-1880 (24)
Bronner (Healy), Augusta Fox. American Psychologist. 1881-1966 (11)
Brown, Thomas. Scottish Philosopher. 1778-1820 (22)
Brown, Warner. American Psychologist. 1882-1956 (11)
Brown, William. English Psychologist. 1881-1952 (11)
Brown-Séquard, Charles Edouard. French Physiologist. 1817?-1894 (14)
Brücke, Ernst Wilhelm von. German-Austrian Physiologist. 1819-1892 (20)
Brunschvicg, Léon. French Philosopher. 1869-1944 (11)
Brunswik, Egon. Austrian-American Psychologist. 1903-1955 (26)
Bryan, William Lowe. American Psychologist. 1860-1955 (16)
Buffon, Georges Louis Leclerc de. French Biologist. 1704-1788 (13)
Bühler, Karl. German-Austrian Psychologist. 1879-1963 (26)
Burnham, William Henry. American Psychologist. 1855-1941 (13)
Cabanis, Pierre Jean Georges. French Philosopher. 1757-1808 (22)
Calkins, Mary Whiton. American Psychologist. 1863-1930 (20)
Cannon, Walter Bradford. American Physiologist. 1871-1945 (27)
Carlson, Anton Julius. American Physiologist. 1875-1956 (12)
Carpenter, William Benjamin. English Physiologist. 1813-1885 (14)
Carr, Harvey A. American Psychologist. 1873-1954 (23)
Cason, Hulsey. American Psychologist. 1893-1951 (11)
Cattell, James McKeen. American Psychologist. 1860-1944 (26)
Charcot, Jean-Martin. French Neurologist. 1825-1893 (27)
Claparède, Edouard. Swiss Psychologist. 1873-1940 (26)
Coghill, George Ellett. American Anatomist. 1872-1941 (20)
Coleridge, Samuel Taylor. English Philosopher. 1772-1834 (11)
Comenius, Joann Amos. Czechoslovakian Educator. 1592-1670 (15)
Comte, (Isadore) Auguste (Marie François). French Philosopher. 1798-1857 (25)
Condillac, Etienne Bonnot de. French Philosopher. 1715-1780 (25)

Condorcet, Marie Jean Antoine (Marie Jean Antoine Nicholas de Caritat, Marquis de Condorcet). French Philosopher. 1743-1794 (20)
Cooley, Charles Horton. American Sociologist. 1864-1929 (13)
Coué, Emile. French Hypnotist. 1857-1926 (18)
Cousin, Victor. French Philosopher. 1792-1867 (15)
Croce, Benedetto. Italian Philosopher. 1866-1952 (15)
Crozier, William John. American Physiologist. 1892-1955 (18)
Cuvier, (Baron) Georges Léopold Chrétien Frédéric Dagobert. French Biologist. 1769-1832 (12)
Dalton, John. English Chemist. 1766-1844 (23)
Darwin, Charles (Robert). English Biologist. 1809-1882 (27)
Darwin, Erasmus. English Biologist. 1731-1802 (16)
Davenport, Charles Benedict. American Geneticist. 1866-1944 (11)
Dearborn, Walter Fenno. American Psychologist. 1878-1955 (12)
Decroly, Ovide Jean. Belgian Psychologist. 1871-1932 (11)
Delabarre, Edmund Burke. American Psychologist. 1863-1945 (12)
Delacroix, Henri. French Psychologist. 1873-1937 (15)
Delboeuf, Joseph Rémy Léopold. Belgian Psychologist. 1831-1896 (24)
DeSanctis, Sante. Italian Psychologist. 1862-1935 (13)
Descartes, René. French Philosopher. 1596-1650 (27)
Dessoir, Max. German Psychologist. 1867-1947 (18)
Destutt de Tracy, Antoine Louis Claude. French Philosopher. 1754-1836 (11)
de Vries, Hugo. Dutch Geneticist. 1848-1935 (16)
Dewey, John. American Philosopher, 1859-1952 (27)
Diderot, Denis. French Philosopher. 1713-1784 (19)
Dilthey, Wilhelm. German Philosopher. 1833-1911 (22)
Dix, Dorothea (orig. Dorothy) Lynde. American Layman. 1802-1887 (11)
Dodge, Raymond. American Psychologist. 1871-1942 (20)
Donaldson, Henry Herbert. American Neurologist. 1857-1938 (15)
Donders, F(ranciscus) C(ornelis). Dutch Ophthalmologist. 1818-1889 (19)
Downey, June Etta. American Psychologist, 1875-1932 (14)
Drever, James. Scottish Psychologist. 1873-1950 (23)
Driesch, Hans Adolf Eduard. German Biologist. 1867-1941 (18)

Du Bois-Reymond, Emil. German Physiologist. 1818–1896 (23)
Dumas, Georges. French Psychologist. 1866–1946 (21)
Duncker, Karl. German Psychologist. 1903–1940 (18)
Dunlap, Knight. American Psychologist. 1875–1949 (22)
Durkheim, Emile. French Sociologist. 1858–1917 (23)
Dusser de Barenne, Johannes Gregorius. Dutch-American Physiologist. 1885–1940 (13)
Ebbinghaus, Hermann. German Psychologist. 1850–1909 (27)
Edwards, Jonathan. American Philosopher. 1703–1758 (11)
Ehrenfels, Christian von. Austrian Philosopher. 1859–1932 (26)
Elliotson, John. English Hypnotist. 1791–1868 (22)
Ellis, (Henry) Havelock. English Psychologist. 1859–1939 (23)
Emmert, Emil. Swiss Ophthalmologist. 1844–1911 (17)
English, Horace Bidwell. American Psychologist. 1892–1961 (14)
Erdmann, Benno. German Psychologist. 1851–1921 (12)
Esdaile, James. English Hypnotist. 1808–1859 (20)
Esquirol, Jean Etienne. French Psychiatrist. 1772–1840 (18)
Euler, Leonhard. Swiss-Russian Mathematician. 1707–1783 (12)
Ewald, Julius Richard. German Physiologist. 1855–1921 (17)
Exner, Sigmund. Austrian Physiologist. 1846–1926 (18)
Fabre, Jean Henri. French Biologist. 1823–1915 (20)
Faraday, Michael. English Physicist. 1791–1867 (15)
Farnsworth, Dean. American Psychologist. 1902–1959 (12)
Farrand, Livingston. American Psychologist. 1867–1939 (11)
Fearing, Franklin. American Psychologist. 1892–1962 (12)
Fechner, Gustav Theodor. German Philosopher. 1801–1887 (27)
Fenichel, Otto. Austrian-American Psychoanalyst. 1898–1946 (15)
Féré, Charles. French Psychiatrist. 1852–1907 (18)
Ferenczi, Sándor. Hungarian Psychoanalyst. 1873–1933 (19)
Fernberger, Samuel Weiller. American Psychologist. 1887–1956 (18)
Ferree, Clarence Errol. American Psychologist. 1877–1942 (11)
Feuerbach, Paul Johann Anselm von. German Philosopher. 1775–1833 (14)
Fichte, Johann Gottlieb. German Philosopher. 1762–1814 (16)
Fisher, (Sir) Ronald Aylmer. English Statistician. 1890–1962 (20)
Fitts, Paul Morris. American Psychologist. 1912–1965 (16)
Flechsig, Paul Emil. German Physicist. 1847–1929 (13)
Flourens, Pierre Jean Marie. French Physiologist. 1794–1867 (24)
Flournoy, Théodore. Swiss Psychologist. 1854–1920 (11)
Flugel, John Carl. English Psychologist. 1884–1955 (16)

Forel, August. Swiss Anatomist. 1848-1931 (12)
Fourier, (François Marie) Charles. French Philosopher. 1772-1837 (14)
Franklin, Benjamin. American Philosopher. 1706-1790 (13)
Franz, Shepherd Ivory. American Psychologist. 1874-1933 (20)
Freeman, Frank Nugent. American Psychologist. 1880-1961 (11)
Frenkel-Brunswik, Else. Austrian-American Psychologist. 1908-1958 (19)
Freud, Sigmund. Austrian Psychoanalyst. 1856-1939 (27)
Frey, Max von. German Physiologist. 1852-1932 (23)
Fritsch, Gustav. German Anatomist. 1838-1927 (18)
Fröbel, Friedrich. German Educator. 1782-1852 (13)
Fröbes, Joseph. German-Dutch Psychologist. 1866-1947 (16)
Fromm-Reichmann, Frieda. German-American Psychoanalyst. 1889-1957 (12)
Fullerton, George Stuart. American Psychologist. 1859-1925 (14)
Fulton, John Farquhar. American Physiologist. 1899-1960 (14)
Galilei, Galileo. Italian Astronomer-Mathematician. 1564-1642 (22)
Gall, Franz Joseph. Austrian-French Physiologist. 1758-1828 (24)
Galton, Francis. English Psychologist. 1822-1911 (27)
Galvani, Luigi (or Aloisio). Italian Physiologist. 1737-1798 (20)
Gassendi, Pierre. French Philosopher. 1592-1655 (11)
Gauss, Carl (Friedrich). German Mathematician. 1777-1855 (22)
Gelb, Adhémar. German Psychologist. 1887-1936 (15)
Gemelli, Agostino (Edoardo). Italian Psychologist. 1878-1959 (22)
Gesell, Arnold (Lucius). American Psychologist. 1880-1961 (25)
Geulincx, Arnold. Flemish Philosopher. 1624-1669 (11)
Goddard, Henry Herbert. American Psychologist. 1866-1957 (19)
Goethe, Johann Wolfgang von. German Philosopher. 1749-1832 (25)
Goldscheider, Alfred. German Physiologist. 1858-1935 (18)
Goldstein, Kurt. German-American Neurologist. 1878-1965 (26)
Golgi, Camillo. Italian Anatomist. 1843-1926 (14)
Goltz, Friedrich Leopold. German Physiologist. 1834-1902 (12)
Goodenough, Florence Laura. American Psychologist. 1886-1959 (20)
Gosset, William Sealy ("Student"). English Statistician. 1876-1937 (13)
Groos, Karl. German Psychologist. 1861-1946 (16)
Gruhle, Hans Walter. German Psychiatrist. 1880-1958 (12)

Guillaume, Paul. French Psychologist. 1878-1962 (16)
Guthrie, Edwin Ray. American Psychologist. 1886-1959 (26)
Haeckel, Ernst Heinrich. German Biologist. 1834-1919 (15)
Hall, G(ranville) Stanley. American Psychologist. 1844-1924 (27)
Hall, Marshall. English Physiologist. 1790-1857 (21)
Haller, Albrecht von. Swiss Physiologist. 1708-1777 (17)
Hamilton, (Sir) William. Scottish Philosopher. 1788-1856 (21)
Hartley, David. English Philosopher. 1705-1757 (24)
Hartmann, Karl Robert Eduard von. German Philosopher. 1842-1905 (15)
Harvey, William. English Physiologist. 1578-1657 (20)
Head, Henry. English Neurologist. 1861-1940 (25)
Healy, William. American Psychiatrist. 1869-1963 (17)
Hecht, Selig. American Physiologist. 1892-1947 (22)
Hegel, Georg Wilhelm Friedrich. German Philosopher. 1770-1831 (18)
Hellpach, Willy. German Psychologist. 1877-1955 (12)
Helmholtz, Hermann Ludwig Ferdinand von. German Physiologist. 1821-1894 (27)
Helvétius, Claude Adrien. French Philosopher. 1715-1771 (15)
Henmon, Vivian Allen Charles. American Psychologist. 1877-1950 (11)
Henning, Hans. German Psychologist, 1885-1946 (20)
Henri, Victor. French Psychologist. 1872-1940 (16)
Herbart, Johann Friedrich. German Philosopher. 1776-1841 (27)
Herder, Johann Gottfried von. German Philosopher. 1744-1803 (11)
Hering, Ewald. German Physiologist. 1834-1918 (27)
Herrick, Charles Judson. American Physiologist. 1868-1960 (16)
Herskovits, Melville Jean. American Anthropologist. 1895-1963 (13)
Heymans, Gerardus. Dutch Psychologist. 1857-1930 (17)
Hitzig, Eduard. German Psychiatrist. 1838-1907 (18)
Hobbes, Thomas. English Philosopher. 1588-1679 (24)
Hobhouse, Leonard Trelawney. English Sociologist. 1864-1929 (19)
Höffding, Harald. Danish Philosopher. 1843-1931 (24)
Hollingworth, Harry Levi. American Psychologist. 1880-1956 (20)
Hollingworth, Leta Stetter. American Psychologist. 1886-1939 (12)
Holt, Edwin Bissell. American Psychologist. 1873-1946 (22)
Holzinger, Karl John. American Psychologist. 1892-1954 (13)
Hornbostel, Erich von. German Psychologist. 1877-1935 (16)

Horney, Karen. German-American Psychoanalyst. 1885-1952 (23)
Hovland, Carl Iver. American Psychologist. 1912-1961 (23)
Hull, Clark Leonard. American Psychologist. 1884-1952 (27)
Humboldt, Wilhelm von. German Philosopher. 1767-1835 (17)
Hume, David. Scottish Philosopher. 1711-1776 (27)
Humphrey, George. English Psychologist. 1889-1966 (17)
Hunter, Walter Samuel. American Psychologist. 1889-1954 (25)
Husserl, Edmund. German Philosopher. 1859-1938 (26)
Huxley, Thomas Henry. English Biologist. 1825-1895 (18)
Huygens, Christian. Dutch Astronomer-Mathematician. 1629-1695 (14)
Itard, Jean (Marc Gaspard). French Psychiatrist, 1775-1838 (23)
Jackson, John Hughlings. English Neurologist. 1835-1911 (21)
Jaensch, Erich Rudolf. German Psychologist, 1883-1940 (25)
Jaensch, Walter. German Psychiatrist. 1889- (11)
James, William. American Philosopher, 1842-1910 (27)
Janet, Pierre. French Psychologist. 1859-1947 (27)
Jastrow, Joseph. American Psychologist. 1863-1944 (22)
Jennings, Herbert Spencer. American Biologist. 1868-1947 (25)
Jevons, William Stanley. English Logician. 1835-1882 (11)
Jodl, Friedrich. German-Austrian Philosopher. 1849-1914 (11)
Johnson, Samuel. American Philosopher. 1696-1772 (12)
Jones, (Alfred) Ernest. English Psychoanalyst. 1879-1958 (22)
Jost, Adolph. German Psychologist. Ca. 1874-ca. 1930 (16)
Judd, Charles Hubbard. American Psychologist. 1873-1946 (22)
Jung, Carl Gustav. Swiss Psychiatrist. 1875-1961 (27)
Kafka, Gustav. German Psychologist. 1883-1953 (14)
Kant, Immanuel. German Philosopher. 1724-1804 (25)
Karwoski, Theodore Francis. American Psychologist. 1896-1957 (11)
Katz, David. German Psychologist. 1884-1953 (25)
Kelley, Truman Lee. American Psychologist. 1884-1961 (21)
Kellogg, Chester Elijah. American Psychologist. 1888-1948 (13)
Kelly, George Alexander. American Psychologist. 1905-1967 (17)
Kepler, Johannes. German Astronomer-Mathematician. 1571-1630 (19)
Kiesow, Federico. German-Italian Psychologist. 1858-1940 (19)
Kinsey, Alfred Charles. American Biologist. 1894-1956 (21)
Kirkpatrick, Edwin Asbury. American Psychologist. 1862-1937 (11)
Klages, Ludwig. German-Swiss Psychologist. 1872-1956 (15)

Klein, Melanie. German-English Psychoanalyst. 1882-1960 (17)
Klemm, Gustav Otto. German Psychologist. 1884-1939 (20)
Kluckhohn, Clyde Kay Maben. American Anthropologist. 1905-1960 (18)
Köhler, Wolfgang. German-American Psychologist. 1887-1967 (27)
König, Arthur. German Physicist. 1856-1901 (16)
Koffka, Kurt. German-American Psychologist. 1886-1941 (27)
Kornilov, Konstantin (N.). Russian Psychologist. 1879-1957 (13)
Kraepelin, Emil. German Psychiatrist. 1856-1926 (27)
Kretschmer, Ernst. German Psychiatrist. 1888-1964 (26)
Kries, Johannes von. German Physiologist. 1853-1928 (25)
Kris, Ernst. Austrian-American Psychoanalyst. 1900-1957 (11)
Kroh, Oswald. German Psychologist. 1887-1955 (12)
Krueger, Felix (E.). German Psychologist. 1874-1948 (20)
Kuhlmann, Frederick. American Psychologist. 1876-1941 (11)
Külpe, Oswald. German Psychologist. 1862-1915 (27)
Ladd, George Trumbull. American Psychologist. 1842-1921 (24)
Ladd-Franklin, Christine. American Psychologist. 1847-1930 (22)
Lamarck, Jean Baptiste Pierre Antoine de Monet. French Biologist. 1744-1829 (23)
La Mettrie, Julien Offray de. French Philosopher. 1709-1751 (26)
Landis, Carney. American Psychologist. 1897-1962 (16)
Lange, Carl Georg. Danish Physiologist. 1834-1900 (14)
Lange, Ludwig. German Psychologist. 1863-1936 (12)
Langfeld, Herbert Sidney. American Psychologist. 1879-1958 (20)
Lapicque, Louis. French Physiologist. 1866-1952 (18)
Laplace, Pierre Simon de. French Astronomer-Mathematician. 1749-1827 (17)
Lashley, Karl Spencer. American Psychologist. 1890-1958 (27)
Lavoisier, Antoine Laurent. French Chemist. 1743-1794 (16)
Lazarus, Moritz. German Philosopher. 1824-1903 (13)
Le Bon, Gustave. French Sociologist. 1841-1931 (24)
Leeuwenhoek, Anton van. Dutch Biologist. 1632-1723 (16)
Lehmann, Alfred Georg Ludwig. Danish Psychologist. 1858-1921 (16)
Leibnitz, Gottfried Wilhelm von. German Philosopher. 1646-1716 (26)
Lessing, Gotthold Ephraim. German Philosopher. 1729-1781 (11)
Leuba, James Henry. American Psychologist. 1868-1946 (15)
Lévy-Bruhl, Lucien. French Anthropologist. 1857-1939 (23)

Lewes, George Henry. English Philosopher. 1817-1878 (11)
Lewin, Kurt. German-American Psychologist. 1890-1947 (26)
Liébeault, Ambroise Auguste. French Hypnotist. 1823-1904 (21)
Lindworsky, Johannes. German-Czechoslovakian Psychologist. 1875-1939 (15)
Linnaeus, Carolus. Swedish Biologist. 1707-1778 (19)
Linton, Ralph. American Anthropologist. 1893-1953 (19)
Lipps, Theodor. German Psychologist. 1851-1914 (23)
Locke, John. English Philosopher. 1632-1704 (27)
Loeb, Jacques. German-American Physiologist. 1859-1924 (26)
Lombroso, Cesare. Italian Sociologist. 1835-1909 (20)
Lorge, Irving. American Psychologist. 1905-1960 (14)
Lotze, Rudolf Hermann. German Philosopher. 1817-1881 (25)
Louttit, Chauncey McKinley. American Psychologist. 1901-1956 (13)
Lubbock, John (Baron Avebury). English Biologist. 1834-1913 (16)
Ludwig, Carl Friedrich Wilhelm. German-Austrian Physiologist. 1816-1895 (14)
McCosh, James. Scottish-American Philosopher. 1811-1894 (13)
MacCurdy, John Thomson. English Psychologist. 1886-1947 (12)
McDougall, William. English-American Psychologist. 1871-1938 (27)
McGeoch, John Alexander. American Psychologist. 1897-1942 (20)
McGregor, Douglas (Murray). American Psychologist. 1906-1964 (12)
Mach, Ernst. Austrian Physicist. 1838-1916 (25)
Magendie, François. French Physiologist. 1783-1855 (25)
Maine de Biran (Marie François Pierre Gonthier de Biran). French Philosopher. 1766-1824 (24)
Malebranche, Nicolas de. French Philosopher. 1638-1715 (21)
Malinowski, Bronislaw Kaspar. English Anthropologist. 1884-1942 (22)
Malthus, Thomas Robert. English Philosopher. 1766-1834 (17)
Marbe, Karl. German Psychologist. 1869-1953 (24)
Mariotte, Edmé. French Physicist. 1620?-1684 (22)
Marx, Karl. German Philosopher. 1818-1883 (16)
Matsumoto, Matataro. Japanese Psychologist. 1865-1943 (11)
Maudsley, Henry. English Psychiatrist. 1835-1918 (16)
Maxwell, James Clerk. English Physicist. 1831-1879 (19)
Mayo, (George) Elton. Australian-American Psychologist. 1880-1949 (11)

Mead, George Herbert. American Philosopher. 1863-1931 (19)
Meinong, Alexius von. Austrian Philosopher. 1853-1920 (24)
Meissner, Georg. German Physiologist. 1829-1905 (11)
Mendel, Gregor Johann. Austrian Geneticist. 1822-1884 (21)
Mercier, Désiré Joseph. Belgian Philosopher. 1851-1926 (13)
Merleau-Ponty, Maurice. French Philosopher. 1908-1961 (16)
Mersenne, Marin. French Philosopher. 1588-1648 (11)
Mesmer, Franz (or Friedrich) Anton. Austrian-French Hypnotist. 1734-1815 (25)
Messer, August. German Psychologist. 1867-1937 (18)
Meumann, Ernst. German Psychologist. 1862-1915 (23)
Meyer, Adolf. Swiss-American Psychiatrist. 1866-1950 (21)
Meyer, Max Frederick. German-American Psychologist. 1873-1967 (20)
Meynert, Theodor Hermann. German-Austrian Neurologist. 1833-1892 (12)
Michotte (van den Berck), (Baron) Albert Edward. Belgian Psychologist. 1881-1965 (26)
Mill, James. English Philosopher. 1773-1836 (27)
Mill, John Stuart. English Philosopher. 1806-1873 (27)
Mira y Lopez, Emilio. Spanish-Brazilian Psychiatrist. 1896-1964 (13)
Moede, Walther. German Psychologist. 1888-1958 (12)
Moll, Albert. German Psychiatrist. 1862-1939 (13)
Molyneux, William. Irish Astronomer. 1656-1698 (13)
Monakow, Constantin von. Swiss Neurologist. 1853-1930 (12)
Montesquieu, Charles de Secondat (Charles de Secondat, Baron de La Brède et de Montesquieu). French Philosopher. 1689-1755 (17)
Montessori, Maria. Italian Educator. 1870-1952 (21)
Morgan, Conwy Lloyd. English Psychologist. 1852-1936 (27)
Muenzinger, Karl Friedrich. American Psychologist. 1885-1958 (16)
Müller, Georg Elias. German Psychologist. 1850-1934 (26)
Müller, Johannes. German Physiologist. 1801-1858 (25)
Müller-Freienfels, Richard. German Psychologist. 1882-1949 (15)
Müller-Lyer, Franz (Carl). German Psychiatrist. 1857-1916 (19)
Münsterberg, Hugo. German-American Psychologist. 1863-1916 (24)
Murchison, Carl. American Psychologist. 1887-1961 (20)
Myers, Charles Samuel. English Psychologist. 1873-1946 (21)
Nagel, Wilibald (A.). German Physiologist. 1870-1911 (12)
Newton, Isaac. English Astronomer-Mathematician. 1642-1727 (26)

Nietzsche, Friedrich Wilhelm. German Philosopher. 1844-1900 (20)
Nissen, Henry Wieghorst. American Psychologist. 1901-1958 (14)
Ogden, C(harles) K(ay). English Psychologist. 1889-1957 (12)
Ogden, Robert Morris. American Psychologist. 1877-1959 (20)
Orth, Johannes. German Psychologist. 1847-1923 (13)
Parsons, (Sir) John Herbert. English Ophthalmologist. 1868-1957 (13)
Pascal, Blaise. French Philosopher. 1623-1662 (19)
Paterson, Donald Gildersleeve. American Psychologist. 1892-1961 (15)
Paulhan, Frédéric (M.). French Psychologist. 1856-1931 (11)
Pavlov, Ivan Petrovitch. Russian Physiologist. 1849-1936 (27)
Pearson, Karl. English Statistician. 1857-1936 (27)
Peckham, George Williams. American Biologist. 1845-1914 (12)
Peirce, Charles Santiago Sanders. American Philosopher. 1839-1914 (19)
Pestalozzi, Johann Heinrich. Swiss Educator. 1746-1827 (22)
Pflüger, Eduard Friedrich Wilhelm. German Physiologist. 1829-1910 (18)
Pfungst, Oskar. German Psychiatrist. 1874-1932 (14)
Piéron, Henri. French Psychologist. 1881-1964 (27)
Pillsbury, Walter Bowers. American Psychologist. 1872-1960 (21)
Pilzecker, Alfons. German Psychologist. 1865-ca. 1920 (15)
Pinel, Philippe. French Psychiatrist. 1745-1826 (25)
Pintner, Rudolf. American Psychologist. 1884-1942 (18)
Plateau, Joseph Antoine Ferdinand. Belgian Physicist. 1801-1883 (18)
Polyak, Stephan. Jugoslavian-American Anatomist. 1889-1955 (12)
Ponzo, Mario. Italian Psychologist. 1882-1960 (15)
Poppelreuter, Walther. German Psychologist. 1886-1939 (16)
Porter, Noah. American Philosopher. 1811-1892 (11)
Preyer, Wilhelm Thierry. German Physiologist. 1841-1897 (22)
Priestley, Joseph. English-American Chemist. 1733-1804 (13)
Prince, Morton. American Psychiatrist. 1854-1929 (23)
Prochaska, George. Czechoslovakian Physiologist. 1749-1820 (11)
Purkinje, Johannes Evangelista. Czechoslovakian Physiologist. 1787-1869 (24)
Quételet, (Lambert) Adolphe (Jacques). Belgian Statistician. 1796-1874 (24)
Ramon y Cajal, Santiago. Spanish Anatomist. 1852-1934 (25)

Rank, Otto. Austrian-American Psychoanalyst. 1884–1939 (23)
Ranschburg, Paul. Hungarian Psychologist. 1870–1945 (12)
Rapaport, David. Hungarian-American Psychologist, 1911–1960 (21)
Rayleigh, Lord (John William Strutt, 3rd Baron). English Physicist. 1842–1919 (18)
Reid, Thomas. Scottish Philosopher. 1710–1796 (25)
Révész, Géza. Dutch Psychologist. 1878–1955 (23)
Reymert, Martin Luther. Norwegian-American Psychologist. 1883–1953 (14)
Ribot, Théodule Armand. French Psychologist. 1839–1916 (26)
Richet, Charles. French Physiologist. 1850–1935 (17)
Rignano, Eugenio. Italian Philosopher. 1870–1930 (15)
Rivers, (Baron) William Halse. English Psychologist. 1864–1922 (19)
Roback, A(braham) A(aron). American Psychologist, 1890–1965 (17)
Robinson, Edward Stevens. American Psychologist, 1893–1937 (16)
Róheim, Géza. Hungarian-American Psychoanalyst. 1891–1953 (11)
Rolando, Luigi. Italian Anatomist. 1773–1831 (15)
Romanes, George John. English Biologist. 1848–1894 (25)
Rorschach, Hermann. Swiss Psychiatrist. 1884–1922 (26)
Rosanoff, Aaron Joshua. American Psychiatrist. 1878–1943 (15)
Ross, Edward Alsworth. American Sociologist. 1866–1951 (11)
Rousseau, Jean-Jacques. Swiss-French Philosopher. 1712–1778 (24)
Royce, Josiah. American Philosopher. 1855–1916 (16)
Rubin, Edgar John. Danish Psychologist. 1886–1951 (27)
Rubinstein, Sergei (L.). Russian Psychologist. 1889–1960 (12)
Ruckmick, Christian Alban. American Psychologist. 1886–1961 (17)
Rush, Benjamin. American Psychiatrist. 1745–1813 (15)
Sachs, Hanns. Austrian-American Psychoanalyst. 1881–1947 (13)
Sanford, Edmund Clark. American Psychologist. 1859–1924 (20)
Sanford, Fillmore Hargrave. American Psychologist. 1914–1967 (16)
Sapir, Edward. American Anthropologist. 1884–1939 (19)
Saudek, Robert. English Psychologist. 1881–1935 (11)
Scheerer, Martin. German-American Psychologist. 1900–1961 (14)
Schelling, Friedrich Wilhelm Joseph von. German Philosopher. 1775–1854 (15)
Schiller, Friedrich. German Philosopher. 1759–1805 (13)
Schiller, Paul Harkai. Hungarian-German Psychologist. 1908–1949 (13)
Schlosberg, Harold. American Psychologist. 1904–1964 (20)

Schopenhauer, Arthur. German Philosopher. 1788-1860 (22)
Schumann, Friedrich. German Psychologist. 1863-1940 (19)
Scott, Walter Dill. American Psychologist. 1869-1955 (11)
Scripture, Edward Wheeler. American-Austrian Psychologist. 1864-1945 (23)
Seashore, Carl Emil. American Psychologist. 1866-1949 (24)
Seashore, Harold Gustav. American Psychologist. 1906-1965 (11)
Sechenov, Ivan Michailovich. Russian Physiologist. 1829-1905 (26)
Seguin, Edouard. French-American Psychiatrist. 1812-1880 (18)
Selz, Otto. German Psychologist. 1881-1944 (17)
Shand, Alexander Faulkner. English Psychologist. 1858-1936 (15)
Shepard, John Frederick. American Psychologist. 1881-1965 (11)
Sherrington, Charles Scott. English Physiologist. 1857-1952 (27)
Sidis, Boris. American Psychologist. 1867-1923 (17)
Simon, Théodore. French Psychologist, 1873-1961 (21)
Small, Willard Stanton. American Psychologist. 1870-1943 (18)
Smith, Adam. Scottish Philosopher. 1723-1790 (17)
Smuts, Jan Christiaan. South African Philosopher. 1870-1950 (13)
Snoddy, George Samuel. American Psychologist. 1882-1947 (11)
Southard, Elmer Ernest. American Psychiatrist. 1876-1920 (11)
Spalding, Douglas Alexander. English Biologist. 1840?-1877 (12)
Spearman, Charles Edward. English Psychologist. 1863-1945 (27)
Spence, Kenneth Wartenbe. American Psychologist. 1907-1967 (25)
Spencer, Herbert. English Philosopher. 1820-1903 (27)
Spinoza, Benedict (or Baruch). Dutch Philosopher. 1632-1677 (24)
Spranger, Eduard. German Psychologist, 1882-1963 (25)
Spurzheim, Johann Kaspar. Austrian-French Physiologist. 1776-1832 (21)
Starbuck, Edwin Diller. American Psychologist. 1866-1947 (12)
Steinthal, Heyman. German Philosopher. 1823-1899 (12)
Stekel, Wilhelm. Austrian Psychoanalyst. 1868-1940 (16)
Stern, (Louis) William. German Psychologist. 1871-1938 (26)
Stewart, Dugald. Scottish Philosopher. 1753-1828 (23)
Stoelting, Christian (H.). American Layman. 1864-1943 (12)
Stone, Calvin Perry. American Psychologist. 1892-1954 (16)
Störring, Gustav. German Psychologist. 1860-1946 (15)
Stouffer, Samuel Andrew. American Sociologist. 1900-1960 (13)
Stout, George Frederick. English Psychologist. 1860-1944 (26)
Stratton, George Malcolm. American Psychologist. 1865-1957 (22)
Strong, Edward Kellogg. American Psychologist. 1884-1963 (20)

Stumpf, Carl. German Psychologist. 1848–1936 (27)
Sullivan, Harry Stack. American Psychiatrist. 1892–1949 (23)
Sully, James. English Psychologist. 1842–1923 (22)
Swedenborg, Emanuel. Swedish Theologian. 1688–1772 (11)
Symonds, Percival Mallon. American Psychologist. 1893–1960 (11)
Taine, Hippolyte Adolphe. French Philosopher. 1828–1893 (21)
Tarde, Gabriel. French Sociologist. 1843–1904 (24)
Terman, Lewis Madison. American Psychologist. 1877–1956 (27)
Tetens, Johann Nicholas. German Philosopher. 1736–1807 (11)
Thomson, (Sir) Godfrey (Hilton). English Psychologist. 1881–1955 (23)
Thorndike, Edward Lee. American Psychologist. 1874–1949 (27)
Thurstone, Louis Leon. American Psychologist. 1887–1955 (27)
Tiedemann, Dietrich. German Philosopher. 1748–1803 (11)
Titchener, Edward Bradford. American Psychologist. 1867–1927 (27)
Tolman, Edward Chace. American Psychologist. 1886–1959 (27)
Troland, Leonard Thompson. American Psychologist. 1889–1932 (21)
Twitmyer, Edwin Burket. American Psychologist. 1873–1943 (14)
Tylor, (Sir) Edward Burnett. English Anthropologist. 1832–1917 (13)
Uexküll, (Baron) Jakob Johann von. German Biologist. 1864–1944 (19)
Urban, Francis M. American Psychologist. Ca. 1883–ca. 1950 (14)
Vaihinger, Hans. German Philosopher. 1852–1933 (11)
Valentine, Charles Wilfrid. English Psychologist. 1879–1964 (13)
Valentine, Willard Lee. American Psychologist. 1904–1947 (13)
Verworn, Max. German Physiologist. 1863–1921 (14)
Vierordt, Karl von. German Physiologist. 1818–1884 (17)
Volkmann, Alfred Wilhelm. German Physiologist. 1800–1877 (12)
Voltaire (assumed name of François Marie Arouet). French Philosopher. 1694–1778 (19)
Vygotsky, Leo Semenovich. Russian Psychologist. 1896–1934 (20)
Wallace, Alfred Russel. English Biologist. 1823–1913 (15)
Wallas, Graham. English Sociologist. 1858–1932 (11)
Wallon, Henri Paul Hyacinthe. French Psychologist. 1879–1962 (12)
Ward, James. English Psychologist. 1843–1925 (24)
Warden, Carl John. American Psychologist. 1890–1961 (19)
Warner, Lucien Hynes. American Psychologist. 1900–1963 (11)

Warren, Howard Crosby. American Psychologist. 1867-1934 (23)
Washburn, Margaret Floy. American Psychologist. 1871-1939 (23)
Watson, John Broadus. American Psychologist. 1878-1958 (27)
Watt, Henry Jackson. English Psychologist. 1879-1925 (19)
Weber, Ernst Heinrich. German Physiologist. 1795-1878 (27)
Weber, Max. German Sociologist. 1864-1920 (19)
Weiss, Albert Paul. American Psychologist. 1879-1931 (22)
Wells, Frederick Lyman. American Psychologist. 1884-1964 (11)
Werner, Heinz. German-American Psychologist. 1890-1964 (24)
Wertheimer, Max. German-American Psychologist. 1880-1943 (27)
Wheatstone, Charles. English Physicist. 1802-1875 (14)
Wheeler, Raymond Holder. American Psychologist. 1892-1961 (19)
Wheeler, William Morton. American Biologist. 1865-1937 (11)
Whipple, Guy Montrose. American Psychologist. 1876-1941 (20)
White, William Alanson. American Psychiatrist. 1870-1937 (14)
Whitehead, Alfred North. English-American Philosopher. 1861-1947 (14)
Whytt, Robert. Scottish Physiologist. 1714-1766 (15)
Wiener, Norbert. American Mathematician. 1894-1964 (18)
Wiersma, Enno Dirk. Dutch Psychiatrist. 1858-1940 (12)
Wirth, Wilhelm. German Psychologist. 1876-1952 (14)
Wissler, Clark. American Anthropologist. 1870-1947 (14)
Witasek, Stephan. German Psychologist. 1870-1915 (19)
Witmer, Lightner. American Psychologist. 1867-1956 (19)
Wolff, (Baron) Christian von. German Philosopher. 1679-1754 (25)
Woodworth, Robert Sessions. American Psychologist. 1869-1962 (27)
Wundt, Wilhelm (Max or Maximilian). German Psychologist. 1832-1920 (27)
Yerkes, Robert Mearns. American Psychologist. 1876-1956 (27)
Young, Thomas. English Physicist. 1773-1829 (23)
Yule, George Udny. English Statistician. 1871-1951 (20)
Zener, Karl Edward. American Psychologist. 1903-1964 (15)
Ziehen, Theodor. German Psychiatrist. 1862-1950 (18)
Zilboorg, Gregory. American Psychoanalyst. 1890-1959 (17)
Zwaardemaker, Hendrik. Dutch Physiologist. 1857-1930 (23)

Bibliography of the Writings of Robert I. Watson

BOOKS

A Manual of Standard Experiments in Psychology. Ann Arbor, Mich.: Edwards, 1939.

(Editor) *Readings in the Clinical Method in Psychology.* New York: Harper, 1949.

The Clinical Method in Psychology. New York: Harper, 1952. (Reprinted in paperback, Wiley Science Editions, 1963.)

Psychology as a Profession. New York: Doubleday, 1954.

Psychology of the Child. New York: Wiley, 1959. (Oriental and Spanish editions in later years) (2nd ed. 1965)

The Great Psychologists: From Aristotle to Freud. Philadelphia: Lippincott, 1963. (Trade and Text Editions) (2nd ed. 1968, 3rd ed. 1971)

(Edited with Donald T. Campbell) *History, Psychology and Science: The Collected Papers of Edwin G. Boring.* New York: Wiley, 1963.

(With H. C. Lindgren) *Psychology of the Child.* (3rd ed.) New York: Wiley, 1972.

Eminent Contributors to Psychology. Vol. 1. *Primary Bibliographic References.* New York: Springer, 1974.

ARTICLES AND CHAPTERS IN BOOKS

(With F. J. Gaudet) The relation between insanity and marital conditions. *Journal of Abnormal and Social Psychology*, 1935, *30*, 366–370.

An experimental study of the permanence of course material in introductory psychology. *Archives of Psychology*, 1938, *64*, No. 225.

The relationship between intelligence and the retention of course material in introductory psychology after lengthy delay periods. *Journal of Educational Psychology*, 1939, *30*, 265-279.

The content of experimental manuals in psychology. *Journal of General Psychology*, 1941, *24*, 183-194.

(With V. E. Fisher) An inventory of affective tolerance. *Journal of Psychology*, 1941, *12*, 139-148.

(With V. E. Fisher) An inventory of affective tolerance. *Journal of Psychology*, 1941, *12*, 149-157.

(With V. E. Fisher) *Inventory of Affective Tolerance.* Sheridan Supply Co., Beverly Hills, California, 1942.

The relationship of the Affective Tolerance Inventory to other personality inventories. *Educational and Psychological Measurement*, 1942, *2*, 83-90.

School and sex differences in affective tolerance. *Educational and Psychological Measurement*, 1943, *3*, 43-48.

Clinical validity of the Inventory of Affective Tolerance. *Journal of Social Psychology*, 1945, *22*, 3-15.

(With H. Weinstock) The usefulness of the Cornell Selectee Index at a neuropsychiatric unit of a naval training center. *Naval Medical Bulletin*, 1946, *46*, 1583-1588.

The use of a Wechsler-Bellevue Scales with normal and abnormal persons: A supplement. *Psychological Bulletin.* 1946, *43*, 61-68.

The Wechsler-Bellevue Intelligence Scale. In O. K. Buros (Ed.), *The Third Mental Measurements Yearbook.* New Brunswick, N.J.: Rutgers University Press, 1948, pp. 386-387.

Aptitude testing. In O. J. Kaplan (Ed.), *Encyclopedia of Vocational Guidance.* New York: Philosophical Library, 1948, pp. 31-39.

Interviewing. In O. J. Kaplan (Ed.), *Encyclopedia of Vocational Guidance.* New York: Philosophical Library, 1948, pp. 627-638.

The professional status of the clinical psychologist. In R. I. Watson (Ed.), *Readings in the Clinical Method in Psychology*, pp. 29-48.

Functions of other clinical psychologists. In R. I. Watson (Ed.), *Readings in the Clinical Method in Psychology*, pp. 166-175.

Diagnosis as an aspect of the clinical method: A review. In R. I. Watson (Ed.), *Readings in the Clinical Method in Psychology*, pp. 405-427.

Treatment as an aspect of the clinical method: A review. In R. I. Watson (Ed.), *Readings in the Clinical Method in Psychology*, pp. 674-718.

Clinical psychology. In J. P. Guilford (Ed.), *Fields of Psychology*. New York: Van Nostrand, 1950, pp. 413-449.

(With I. N. Mensh) Psychiatric opinions on personality factors in psychotherapy. *Journal of Clinical Psychology*, 1950, 6, 237-242.

(With P. H. Dubois) The selection of patrolmen. *Journal of Applied Psychology*, 1950, 34, 90-95.

(With I. N. Mensh) The evaluation of the effects of psychotherapy. I. Sources of material. *Journal of Psychology*, 1951, 32, 259-273.

(With I. N. Mensh) The evaluation of the effects of psychotherapy. II. A case study. *Journal of Psychology*, 1951, 32, 275-291.

(With I. N. Mensh and E. F. Gildae) The evaluation of the effects of psychotherapy. III. Research design. *Journal of Psychology*, 1951, 32, 293-308.

(With B. M. Caldwell) An evaluation of psychologic effects of female sex hormone replacement in aged women. I. Results of therapy after six months. *Journal of Gerontology*, 1952, 7, 228-244.

Training in clinical psychology from the perspective of the internship. *American Journal of Orthopsychiatry*, 1952, 22, 140-152.

Research design and methodology in evaluating the results of psychotherapy. *Journal of Clinical Psychology*, 1952, 8, 29-33.

Measuring the effectiveness of psychotherapy: Problems for investigation. *Journal of Clinical Psychology*, 1952, 8, 60-64.

(With R. G. Matarazzo and G. A. Ulett) Relationship of Rorschach scoring categories to modes of perception induced by intermittent photic stimulation—a methodological study of perception. *Journal of Clinical Psychology*, 1952, 8, 368-374.

(With M. F. Zemlick) Maternal attitudes of acceptance and rejection during and after pregnancy. *American Journal of Orthopsychiatry*, 1953, 23, 570-584.

Counseling activities in a medical school setting. *Journal of Medical Education*, 1953, 28, 23-30.

A brief history of clinical psychology. *Psychological Bulletin*, 1953, 50, 321-346. (Reprinted five times in various sources.)

Tests of intelligence. D. Wechsler-Bellevue Intelligence Scale for adolescents and adults. In A. Weider, *Contributions toward medical psychology: Theory and psychodiagnostic methods.* New York: Ronald Press, 1953, pp. 530-544.

(With B. M. Caldwell) An evaluation of sex hormone replacement in aged women. *Journal of Genetic Psychology*, 1954, *85*, 181-200.

The personality of the aged: A review. *Journal of Gerontology*, 1954, *9*, 309-315.

Training the psychologist for work with the chronically ill. *Texas Reports on Biology and Medicine*, 1954, *12*, 659-661; also in Molly Harrower (Ed.), *Medical and Psychological Teamwork in the Care of the Chronically Ill.* Springfield, Ill.: Thomas, 1954, pp. 92-94.

Predicting academic success through achievement and aptitude tests. *Medical Education*, 1955, *30*, 383-390.

Progress in orthopsychiatry: Psychology. *American Journal of Orthopsychiatry*, 1955, *25*, 491-510; also in *Progress in Orthopsychiatry: Selected papers.* New York: American Orthopsychiatric Association, 1955.

Necrology–Lightner Witmer. *American Journal of Psychology*, 1957, *60*, 680-682.

(With B. M. Caldwell) An evaluation of sex hormone replacement in aged women. Reprinted, after adaptation, in *Current Studies in Psychology.* Ed. F. J. McGuigan and A. Calvin. New York: Appleton-Century-Crofts, 1958, pp. 91-95.

Historical review of objective personality testing. In B. M. Bass and I. A. Berg (Eds.), *Objective Approaches to Personality Assessment.* New York: Van Nostrand, 1959.

The first distance-controlled telepathic test. *Americal Journal of Psychology*, 1959, *72*, 463-464.

Coriolanus: An exercise in psychoanalysis. *Northwestern University Quarterly*, 1960, *2*, 41-43.

Historical perspectives on the relationship of psychologists to medical research. *Neuropsychiatry*, 1960, *6*, 51-59.

The history of psychology: A neglected area. *American Psychologist*, 1960, *15*, 251-255.

Child guidance clinics. In C. W. Harris (Ed.), *Encyclopedia of Educational Research.* (3rd ed.) New York: Macmillan, 1960, pp. 192-194.

A brief history of educational psychology. *Psychological Record*, 1961, *11*, 209-242. Reprinted in H. C. Lindgren and Frederica Lindgren (Eds.), *Current Readings in Educational Psychology*. (2nd ed.) New York: Wiley, 1971, pp. 5-33. (1968)

The experimental tradition and clinical psychology. In A. J. Bachrach (Ed.), *Experimental Foundations of Clinical Psychology*. New York: Basic Books, 1962, pp. 3-25.

Psychology. In C. M. White and Associates. *Sources of Information in the Social Sciences*. Totawa, N.J.: Bedminster Press, pp. 273-398.

(Co-author) Research prevention and scientific manpower. In *Patterns for Planning: The Illinois Approach to Mental Retardation*. Harrisburg, Ill.: State of Illinois, 1965, pp. 9-21.

(With D. Holmes) Early recollections and vocational choice. *Journal of Consulting Psychology*, 1965, *29*, 486-488.

The historical background for national trends in psychology: United States. *Journal of the History of the Behavioral Sciences*, 1965, *1*, 130-137.

Editorial: The birth of a journal. *Journal of the History of the Behavioral Sciences*, 1965, *1*, 3-4.

Editorial: Policy and its implementation. *Journal of the History of the Behavioral Sciences*, 1965, *1*, 107-108.

The role and use of history in the psychology curriculum. *Journal of the History of the Behavioral Sciences*, 1966, *2*, 64-69.

(With N. Reingold) The organization and preservation of private papers. *American Psychologist*, 1966, *21*, 971-973.

(With H. C. Quay) Clinical psychology. In J. P. Guilford (Ed.), *Fields of Psychology*. (3rd ed.) Princeton: Van Nostrand, 1967, pp. 245-263.

Psychology: A prescriptive science. *American Psychologist*, 1967, *22*, 435-443. (Reprinted five times to date.)

A note on the history of psychology as a specialization. *Journal of the History of the Behavioral Sciences*, 1967, *3*, 192-193.

Recent developments in the historiography of American psychology. *Isis*, 1968, *59*, 199-205.

The individual, social, educational, economic and political conditions for the original practices of detection and utilization of individual aptitude differences. *Colloques: Textes des Rapports XIIe Congrès International d'Histoire des Sciences*. Paris: Michel, 1968, pp. 355-368.

(With Edith L. Annin and Edwin G. Boring) Important psychologists, 1600-1967. *Journal of the History of the Behavioral Sciences*, 1968, *4*, 303-315.

G. Stanley Hall. In D. L. Sills (Ed.), *International Encyclopedia of Social Science*. Vol. 6. New York: Macmillan, 1968, pp. 310-313.

Jean Charcot. In D. L. Sills (Ed.), *International Encyclopedia of Social Science*. Vol. 2. New York: Macmillan, 1968, pp. 384-386.

Pierre Janet. In D. L. Sills (Ed.), *International Encyclopedia of Social Science*. Vol. 8. New York: Macmillan, 1968, pp. 234-236.

(With J. Brožek and Barbara Ross) A summer institute on the history of psychology. I, II. *Journal of the History of the Behavioral Sciences*, 1969, *5*, 307-319; 1970. *6*, 25-35.

(With Marilyn Merrifield) Eminent psychologists: Corrections and additions. *Journal of the History of the Behavioral Sciences*, 1970, *6*, 261-262.

Orientation to psychology. In G. Sjule, *Contemporary Psychology: A Book of Readings*. Belmont, Calif.: Dickenson, 1970, pp. 17-26. (Excerpt reprinted from *Psychology as a Profession*. New York: Random House, 1954.)

A prescriptive analysis of Descartes' psychological views. *Journal of the History of the Behavioral Sciences*, 1971, *7*, 223-248.

Prescriptions as operative in the history of psychology. *Journal of the History of the Behavioral Sciences*, 1971, *7*, 311-322.

Discussion. L'élaboration des concepts et des méthodes de la psychologie differentielle au XIXe siècle et au début du XXe. In *Discours et conférences, colloques, discussion des rapports. XIIe Congrès International d'Histoire des Sciences, Paris, 1969*. Vol. 1B. Paris: Blanchard, 1971, pp. 238-240, 248-249, 263-264.

The history of psychology: A neglected area; The role and use of history in the psychology curriculum; Psychology: A prescriptive science; The historical background for national trends in psychology: United States. Reprinted in Virginia S. Sexton and H. Misiak (Eds.), *Historical Perspectives in Psychology: Readings*. Belmont, Calif.: Brooks/Cole, 1971, pp. 30-39, 40-49, 183-200, 287-298.

Working paper (Autobiography). In T. S. Krawiec (Ed.), *The Psychologists*. New York: Oxford University Press, 1972, pp. 275-297.

Psychology section. In C. White (Ed.), *Sources of Information in the Social Sciences.* (2nd ed.) Chicago: American Library Association, 1973, pp. 375-398.

(With Marilyn Merrifield) Characteristics of individuals eminent in psychology in temporal perspective: Part I. *Journal of the History of the Behavioral Sciences*, 1973, *9*, 339-359.

ADDENDUM

Eminent Contributors to Psychology. Vol. 2. *Secondary Bibliographic References.* New York: Springer, 1975.

The history of psychology as a specialty: A personal view of its first fifteen years. *Journal of the History of the Behavioral Sciences*, 1975, *11*.

Prescriptive theory and the social sciences. In H. Strasser *et al.* (Eds.), *Determinants and Controls of Scientific Development.* Dordrecht, Holland: Reidel, 1975.

IN PREPARATION

The Search for Man: A History of Personality Theories. Chicago: Aldine.

PLANNED

The Great Psychologists. (4th ed.)
Psychology of the Child. (4th ed.)

Index of Names

Abraham, K., 334, 352
Ach, N. K., 332, 352
Acton, J., 34, 42 ref., 49
Adler, A., 107, 332, 347, 352
Adler, M. H., 224 ref.
Agassiz, J., 71, 116-117, 129 ref.
Agassiz, L., 116-117, 336, 352
Albrecht, F. M., 83, 93 ref.
Alembert, J. L. d., 335, 352, 355
Alexander, F., 334, 352
Allen, F., 304
Allport, F. H., 305 ref.
Allport, G. W., 4, 91, 101, 112 refs., 212, 273, 274 ref., 300, 305 ref., 332, 339, 352
Ames, A., Jr., 335, 352
Anderson, H., 242
Andresen, M. A., 55, 65
Andrews, T. G., 221-222, 225 ref.
Angell, F., 335, 352
Angell, J. R., 88, 296, 305 ref., 332, 339, 352
Angier, R. P., 336, 352
Angyal, A., 336, 352
Annin, E. L., 21 ref., 338, 351 ref., 352 ref.
Aristotle, 31, 37, 100, 109, 158, 175
Aubert, H., 335, 352
Augustine, 187-188
Aveling, F., 336, 352
Avenarius, R. H. L., 333, 352

Babinski, J. F. F., 334, 352
Bacon, F., 102, 116, 121, 156, 157, 168, 173, 175, 333, 352
Bagg, R. A., 69
Bailey, S., 311

Bain, A., 316, 332, 353
Baird, J. W., 293, 334, 353
Baldwin, J. M., 70, 146-147, 209-210, 312, 318-319, 321, 324 refs., 332, 342, 353
Ballard, P. B., 336, 353
Banister, H., 336, 353
Baruch, D., 237
Beach, F., 86
Beauchamps, Miss, 203
Beaunis, H. E., 314, 334, 353
Beck, S. J., 214, 215, 225 ref., 235, 265, 271, 274 ref., 289, 305 ref.
Beebe-Center, J. G., 52 ref., 334, 353
Beers, C. W., 201, 225 ref., 334, 353
Bekhterev, V. M., 261, 291, 296, 300, 305 refs., 332, 353
Bell, C., 333, 353
Ben-David, J., 139, 154 ref.
Benedict, R., 6, 335, 350, 353
Beneke, F. E., 334, 353
Bentham, J., 151, 333, 353
Bentley, M., 333, 353
Benton, A. L., 264, 274 ref.
Benussi, V., 334, 353
Bergson, H., 333, 353
Berkeley, G., 242, 332, 353
Bernard, C., 332, 353
Bernheim, H., 300, 302, 318, 333, 353
Bernoulli, D., 336, 353
Bernstein, J., 336, 353
Bessel, F. W., 333, 353
Bethe, A., 335, 353
Bichat, M. F. X., 277, 334, 353
Bindra, D., 286, 305 ref.
Binet, A., 115, 196ff, 233-234, 236-328, 259, 266, 310, 312-315, 321-322, 323 refs., 332, 353

376 : NAME INDEX

Bingham, W. V. D., 333, 353
Binswanger, L., 334, 353 ·
Bird, C., 336, 353
Black, J. D., 225 ref.
Blanchard, P., 202, 220, 237
Bleuler, E., 332, 353
Blight, J., 69, 70
Blix, M., 335, 353
Blondel, C., 336, 353
Boas, F., 6, 334, 353
Boas, M., 160 ref.
Bobbitt, J. M., 225 ref.
Bohannan, P., 55, 65
Bonnet, C., 334, 353
Book, W. F., 336, 353
Boole, G., 335, 353
Boring, E. G., 15, 20, 21 ref., 40, 42 ref., 52, 52 ref., 53, 53 ref., 54, 54 ref., 55, 63–64, 65, 68, 85, 89, 93 ref., 115, 129 ref., 208, 225 ref., 226 ref., 261, 286, 292ff, 296, 305 refs., 306 ref., 327ff, 338, 351 ref., 352
Bourdon, B. B., 198, 336, 353
Bowditch, H. P., 336, 353
Boyle, R., 176
Braid, J., 299–300, 305 ref., 333, 353
Brand, J., 68
Brazier, M., 55, 65
Brentano, F., 44, 332, 354
Brett, G. S., 28, 37, 53, 53 ref., 334, 354
Breuer, J., 333, 347, 354
Bridgman, P. W., 89, 93 ref., 333, 350, 354
Brill, A. A., 203–204, 225 ref., 334, 354
Britt, S. H., 221, 225 ref.
Broca, P., 333, 354
Brodbeck, M., 130, 154 ref.
Bromberg, W., 303, 305 ref.
Bronner, A. F., 206, 215, 218, 225 ref., 227 ref., 236, 336, 339, 350, 354
Brotemarkle, R. A., 225 refs.
Brown, T., 333, 354
Brown, W(arner), 336, 354
Brown, W(illiam), 336, 354
Brown-Séquard, C. E., 335, 354
Brožek, J., 16, 22 ref., 57, 59, 60, 66, 67, 68, 69, 72, 73
Brücke, E. W. v., 334, 354
Bruner, J. S., 101, 112 ref.
Brunschvicg, L., 336, 354
Brunswik, E., 100, 103, 112 ref., 332, 354
Bryan, W. L., 335, 354
Buck, J. N., 217, 225 ref.

Buffon, G. L. L. d., 336, 354
Bühler, K., 332, 342, 354
Burnham, J. C., 13, 45, 47, 54, 62, 64, 263
Burnham, W. H., 198, 336, 354
Buros, O. K., 252 ref., 263
Burt, C., 259–260, 274 ref., 316
Buytendijk, F. J. J., 137, 154 ref.

Cabanis, P. J. G., 333, 345, 354
Cajal, S. R. y., 332, 354, 363
Caldwell, B. M., 10
Calkins, M. W., 334, 350, 354
Campbell, D. T., 21 ref., 272–273, 274 ref.
Cannon, W. B., 332, 339, 354
Cardno, J. A., 69, 70, 83, 93 ref.
Carlson, A. J., 336, 354
Carlson, E. T., 46ff, 55 ref., 62, 65, 68
Carmichael, L., 56, 57, 66
Carpenter, W. B., 335, 354
Carr, H. A., 88, 295, 333, 354
Cason, H., 336, 354
Cattell, J. McK., 71, 84, 88, 115, 197, 209, 210, 225 refs., 256-258, 266, 268, 271, 274 ref., 286, 291, 312, 318, 319–322, 324 refs., 332, 354
Chaplin, J. P., 97, 112 ref.
Chapple, E. D., 302, 305–306 refs.
Charcot, J.-M., 200, 300, 313, 318, 323 ref., 332, 354
Claparède, E., 332, 354
Clark, T. N., 152–153, 154 ref.
Clarke, E., 56, 65
Coghill, G. E., 334, 354
Coleridge, S. T., 336, 347, 354
Collingwood, R. G., 34, 42 ref.
Combs, A. W., 225 ref.
Comenius, J. A., 335, 354
Comte, A., 89, 93 ref., 312, 332, 349, 354
Conant, J. B., 39, 42 ref.
Condillac, E. B. d., 332, 354
Condorcet, M. J. A., 334, 345, 355
Conklin, ––, 202
Conrad, H. S., 265, 274 ref.
Cooley, C. H., 336, 355
Copernicus, 96
Coriat, I. H., 203, 225 ref.
Coué, E., 334, 355
Coulanges, F. d., 312, 323 ref.
Cousin, V., 100, 112 ref., 312–313, 331, 335, 355
Cowan, E. A., 225 ref.
Cowles, E., 207, 208, 225 ref., 278, 292

Crawford, M., 7
Croce, B., 32, 36, 335, 355
Cronbach, L. J., 90, 285, 306 ref.
Crozier, W. J., 334, 355
Cuvier, G. L., 336, 355

Dain, N., 56, 65
Dallenbach, K., 68
Dalton, J., 333, 355
Dana, C. L., 202
Daniel, R. S., 26, 33 ref., 283 ref.
Darley, J. G., 225-226 ref.
Darwin, C., 36-37, 288-290, 295-296, 298-299, 315, 318, 332, 355
Darwin, E., 335, 355
Davenport, C. B., 336, 355
daVinci, L., 265, 274 ref.
Davis, A., 62
Davis, K., 131
Davis, R. C., 43, 57, 66ff, 71
Dearborn, G., 266, 274 refs.
Dearborn, W. F., 336, 355
Decroly, O. J., 198, 336, 355
Delabarre, E. B., 336, 355
Delacroix, H., 335, 355
DeLange, M., 300, 305 ref.
Delboeuf, J. R. L., 333, 355
Democritus, 159
Dennis, W., 53 ref., 57, 63, 226 ref., 292, 306 ref.
DeSanctis, S., 336, 355
Descartes, R., 20, 102, 121-122, 134, 144, 156-192, 158ff refs., 332, 347, 355
Dessoir, M., 334, 355
Destutt de Tracy, A. L. C., 336, 355
Deutsch, M., 301, 306 ref.
de Vries, H., 335, 355
Dewey, J., 88, 238, 295-296, 306 ref., 332, 339, 346, 355
Diamond, S., 57, 67
Diderot, D., 334, 355
Diethelm, O., 47, 56, 65
Dilthey, W., 42 ref., 333, 355
Dix, D. L., 336, 355
Dodge, R., 334, 355
Doll, E. A., 215, 226 ref., 237
Donaldson, H. H., 335, 355
Donale, G., Jr., 306 ref.
Donders, F. C., 334, 355
Downey, J. E., 261, 274 ref., 335, 350, 355

Dreese, M., 221, 225 ref.
Drever, J., 333, 355
Driesch, H. A. E., 334, 355
DuBois, P., 10
Du Bois-Reymond, E., 333, 356
Dumas, G., 333, 356
Duncan, C., 11
Duncker, K., 334, 356
Dunlap, K., 333, 356
Durkheim, E., 152, 333, 356
Dusser de Barenne, J. G., 336, 356

Ebbinghaus, H., 122, 198, 317, 321, 332, 356
Edwards, J., 71, 336, 340, 356
Ehrenfels, C. v., 332, 356
Elliotson, J., 332, 356
Elliott, R. M., 225-226 ref.
Ellis, A., 226 refs., 265, 274 refs.
Ellis, H., 333, 356
Emmert, E., 337, 356
English, H. B., 212, 226 ref., 335, 356
Erdmann, B., 336, 356
Esdaile, J., 334, 356
Esquirol, J. E., 334, 356
Estes, W. K., 91
Euler, L., 336, 356
Evans, R., 67, 70, 72
Ewald, J. R., 335, 356
Exner, S., 334, 356
Eysenck, H. J., 223, 226 ref., 273, 274 ref.

Fabre, J. H., 295, 334, 356
Faraday, M., 335, 356
Farnsworth, D., 336, 356
Farrand, L., 336, 356
Fearing, F., 52 ref., 63, 165 ref., 336, 356
Fechner, G. T., 200, 276, 277, 278, 294, 332, 356
Feigl, H., 254, 269, 274 ref.
Fenichel, O., 335, 356
Féré, C., 313, 334, 356
Ferenczi, S., 334, 356
Ferguson, L. W., 47
Fernald, G. M., 205-206, 218
Fernberger, S. W., 209-210, 226 refs., 334, 356
Ferree, C. E., 336, 356
Feuerbach, P. J. A. v., 335, 356
Fichte, J. G., 335, 356
Finch, F. H., 211, 226 ref.
Fisher, R. A., 334, 356

378 : NAME INDEX

Fisher, V. E., 8
Fitts, P. M., 335, 356
Flechsig, P. E., 336, 356
Flourens, P. J. M., 333, 356
Flournoy, T., 336, 356
Flugel, J. C., 335, 356
Forel, A., 336, 357
Fourier, C., 335, 357
Fowerbaugh, C. C., 226 ref.
Fraisse, P., 328ff
Frank, L. K., 214, 226 ref., 266, 273, 274 refs.
Franklin, B., 336, 345, 357
Franz, S. I., 202, 208, 226 refs., 274 ref., 280, 283 ref., 288, 292–293, 306 refs., 334, 357
Freeman, F. N., 336, 357
Frenkel-Brunswik, E., 334, 350, 357
Freud, S., 41, 201, 202–204, 206, 213, 226 ref., 235, 242, 286, 298, 299, 332, 339, 347, 357
Frey, M. v., 333, 357
Fritsch, G., 334, 357
Fröbel, F., 336, 357
Fröbes, J., 335, 357
Fromm-Reichmann, F., 336, 350, 357
Fryer, D., 226 ref.
Fuchs, A. H., 141ff, 154 ref.
Fullerton, G. S., 335, 357
Fulton, J. F., 335, 357
Futterman, S., 224 ref.

Galen, 276
Galilei, G., 96, 100, 156, 158–159, 174ff, 176 ref., 177–178, 333, 346, 357
Gall, F. J., 71, 333, 342, 357
Galton, F., 196–197, 198, 226 ref., 256–258, 259, 262–263, 274 ref., 286, 289, 312, 315ff, 319–322, 323–324 refs., 332, 345, 357
Galvani, L., 334, 357
Gardiner, H. M., 52, 52 ref., 63
Gassendi, P., 159–160, 160 ref., 336, 357
Gaudet, F. J., 5
Gauss, C. See Gauss, K.
Gauss, K., 333, 357
Gelb, A., 335, 357
Gemelli, A., 333, 357
Gengerelli, J. A., 57
Gesell, A., 237–238, 332, 357
Geulincx, A., 336, 357
Gibson, J. J., 89

Gibson, K. R., 70, 127, 147–148, 154 ref.
Gildae, E. F., 10
Gillespie, C., 45
Goddard, H. H., 198, 202, 209ff, 217, 310, 334, 357
Goethe, J. W. v., 332, 345, 347, 357
Goldman-Eissler, F., 302, 306 ref.
Goldscheider, A., 334, 357
Goldstein, K., 212, 332, 357
Golgi, C., 335, 357
Goltz, F. L., 336, 357
Goodenough, F. L., 233, 252 ref., 334, 357
Goodman, E., 70, 71, 73
Gosset, W. S., 336, 357
Gouldner, A., 56, 65
Graham, C. H., 86
Granick, S., 10
Graumann, C.-F., 132, 154 ref.
Greenbaum, J. J., 57
Gregg, A., 226 ref.
Groos, K., 335, 357
Gruhle, H. W., 336, 357
Guerlac, H., 44, 62, 71
Guillaume, P., 335, 358
Guthrie, E. R., 90, 91, 332, 358

Hackbusch, F., 217, 226 ref.
Haeckel, E. H., 335, 358
Haldane, E., 174 ref., 186 ref.
Hall, A. R., 309, 323 ref.
Hall, G. S., 63, 84, 198–199, 201–204, 207, 227 ref., 232, 234, 238, 283 ref., 286, 289, 306 ref., 319, 332, 339, 358
Hall, J. K., 229 ref.
Hall, M., 333, 358
Haller, A. v., 335, 358
Halliday, J. I., 249, 252 ref.
Hamer, P. M., 77, 79 ref.
Hamilton, W., 333, 358
Harlow, H. F., 86
Harms, E., 69
Harper, R., 38, 42 refs., 68
Hartley, D., 316, 333, 358
Hartmann, K. R. E. v., 335, 358
Hartson, L. D., 227 ref.
Harvey, W., 122, 156, 158, 158 ref., 162, 174, 277, 334, 358
Hathaway, S. R., 225–226 ref., 269–270
Hawley, P. R., 227 ref.
Hayami, H., 329
Head, H., 333, 358
Healy, W., 199, 205–206, 215, 218, 225

ref., 227 ref., 242, 335, 350, 358
Hearnshaw, L. S., 69
Hebb, D. O., 90, 231-232, 252 ref., 298, 299, 306 ref.
Hecht, S., 333, 358
Hegel, G. W. F., 334, 358
Heidbredder, E., 53, 53 ref., 63
Heiser, K. F., 227 ref.
Hellpach, W., 336, 358
Helmholtz, H. L. F. v., 116, 178, 200, 276, 277, 332, 358
Helson, H., 63
Helvétius, C. A., 335, 358
Hempel, C., 45
Henle, M., 68, 69, 71, 72, 73
Henmon, V. A. C., 336, 358
Henning, H., 334, 358
Henri, V., 266, 314, 335, 358
Henry, G. W., 308 ref.
Henry, J., 230, 252 ref.
Herbart, J. F., 332, 358
Herder, J. G. v., 336, 358
Hering, E., 332, 358
Herodotus, 288, 306 ref.
Herrick, C. J., 335, 358
Herrnstein, R. J., 328ff
Herskovits, M. J., 336, 358
Hertz, M., 214
Heymans, G., 335, 358
Hilgard, E. R., 57, 83, 91, 291, 306 ref., 328ff
Hillix, W. A., 70, 107, 112
Hinkle, G., 62
Hinkle, R., 62
Hippocrates, 276
Hitzig, E., 334, 358
Hobbes, T., 102, 109, 121, 156, 168, 333, 358
Hobbs, N., 227 ref.
Hobhouse, L. T., 334, 358
Hoch, A., 202, 208, 227 refs., 278ff, 293
Höffding, H., 295, 333, 358
Hollingworth, H. L., 334, 358
Hollingworth, L. S., 218, 304, 336, 350, 358
Holt, E. B., 333, 358
Holzinger, K. J., 336, 358
Homer, 37
Hornbostel, E. v., 335, 358
Horney, K., 333, 359
Hovland, C. I., 333, 359
Hughes, E., 131

Hull, C. L., 63, 89, 91, 93 ref., 98, 296-297, 301, 306 refs., 332, 339, 359
Humboldt, W. v., 335, 359
Hume, D., 75, 109, 134, 316, 332, 359
Humphrey, G., 335, 359
Hunt, J. McV., 90, 293-295, 306 ref.
Hunt, W. A., 12, 227 ref., 236, 248, 252 ref., 254-255, 293ff, 306 refs.
Hunter, W. S., 5, 333, 359
Husserl, E., 121, 191, 191 ref., 316, 332, 359
Huxley, T. H., 334, 359
Huygens, C., 335, 359
Hymes, D., 56, 65

Ierardi, G., 15
Imada, M., 328ff
Isaac of Stella, 29
Itard, J., 333, 359

Jackson, J. H., 333, 359
Jacobson, C., 10
Jaeger, W., 37
Jaensch, E. R., 333, 359
Jaensch, W., 336, 359
James, H., 201, 227 ref.
James, W., 38, 84, 88, 92, 199, 200-201, 203, 206, 227 refs., 258, 259, 276, 286, 295, 332, 339, 345, 346, 347, 359
Janet, P., 200, 202, 286, 300, 312-313, 318, 321, 323 refs., 332, 346, 359
Jarl, V. C., 324 ref.
Jastrow, J., 198, 333, 359
Jaynes, J., 16, 17, 59, 59 ref., 63, 69, 71, 72, 73
Jenkinson, H., 78
Jennings, H. S., 333, 359
Jevons, W. S., 336, 359
Jodl, F., 336, 359
Johnson, S., 336, 359
Johnson, W., 211
Jones, E., 203, 333, 359
Jones, H. E., 242, 252 ref.
Jones, V., 5
Jones, W. T., 103, 112 ref.
Jost, A., 335, 359
Jourdain, M., 88, 105
Judd, C. H., 333, 359
Jung, C. G., 203, 332, 347, 359

Kafka, G., 335, 359
Kahn, E., 291, 306 ref.

Kant, I., 144, 152, 172, 333, 359
Kantor, J. R., 118, 129 ref.
Karwoski, T. F., 336, 359
Katz, D., 131, 333, 359
Kawash, G., 141ff, 154 ref.
Kawata, T., 329
Kelley, T. L., 333, 359
Kellogg, C. E., 336, 359
Kelly, E. L., 90
Kelly, G. A., 227 ref., 273, 274 ref., 335, 359
Kent, G. H., 208-209, 293
Kepler, J., 166, 166 ref., 334, 346, 359
Kiesow, F., 208, 279, 334, 359
Kinsey, A. C., 333, 359
Kirkpatrick, E. A., 336, 359
Klages, L., 331, 335, 359
Klein, M., 335, 350, 360
Klemm, G. O., 334, 360
Klineberg, O., 279
Klopfer, B., 214
Kluckhohn, C. K. M., 252 ref., 334, 360
Knight, R. P., 303, 306 ref.
Koch, S., 87, 90, 93 ref., 97, 112 ref.
Koffka, K., 92, 332, 360
Köhler, W., 89, 92, 298, 306 ref., 332, 360
König, A., 335, 346, 360
Kornilov, K., 336, 360
Kraepelin, E., 198, 200, 227 ref., 288, **291-**292, 302, 306 ref., 332, 360
Krantz, D. L., 45
Krawiec, T. S., 97, 112 ref.
Kretschmer, E., 332, 360
Kries, J. v., 333, 360
Kris, E., 336, 360
Kroh, O., 336, 360
Krueger, F., 334, 360
Krugman, M., 215, 238-239, 253 ref.
Kubo, R., 329
Kuhlmann, F., 198, 202, 218, 337, 360
Kuhn, T. S., 18, 45, 87, 94 ref., 95-98, 112 refs., 114, 131, 132, 140, 154 ref.
Külpe, O., 208, 279, 295, 316, 332, 360
Kult, M. L., 43, 57 ref.
Kuroda, R., 329

Ladd, G. T., 70, 333, 360
Ladd-Franklin, C., 333, 350, 360
Lamarck, J. B. P. A. d. M., 333, 360
La Mettrie, J. O. d., 332, 360
Landis, C., 6, 212, 335, 360
Lange, C. G., 335, 360

Lange, L., 336, 360
Langfeld, H. S., 225 ref., 334, 360
Lapicque, L., 334, 360
Laplace, P. S. d., 335, 360
Larson, C., 64
Larzarsfeld, P. F., 131
Lashley, K. S., 85, 292-293, 332, 339, 360
Lasswell, H. D., 303, 307 refs.
Laver, A. B., 71
Lavoisier, A. L., 96, 335, 360
Lazarus, M., 336, 360
Le Bon, G., 300, 307 refs., **333**, 360
Leeuwenhoek, A. v., 335, 360
Lehmann, A. G. L., 335, 360
Leibnitz, G. W. v., 100, 102, 112 ref., 121, 134, 332, 345, 347, 360
Lessing, G. E., 337, 360
Leuba, J. H., 335, 360
Levinson, D. J., 273, 274 ref.
Levy, D. M., 214, 215, 265
Lévy-Bruhl, L., 333, 360
Lewes, G. H., 337, 361
Lewin, K., 67, 100, 112 ref., 244, 300-302, 307 ref., 332, 342, 361
Liddell, E. G. T., 165 ref.
Liébeault, A. A., 300, 333, 361
Lindsay, D., 86
Lindworsky, J., 335, 361
Linnaeus, C., 334, 361
Linton, R., 334, 361
Lippitt, R., 301, 307 ref.
Lippman, H. S., 253 ref.
Lipps, T., 333, 361
Lipsit, S., 131
Locke, J., 19, 102, 104, 120-121, 134, 140, 150, 169, 176, 332, 361
Lockman, R. F., 86, 94 ref.
Loeb, J., 289, 294, 298, 332, 361
Logan, F. A., 297, 307 ref.
Lombroso, C., 334, 361
Longstaff, H. P., 227 ref.
Lorge, I., 335, 361
Lotze, R. H., 333, 349, 361
Louttit, C. M., 9, 26, 33 ref., 227 ref., 336, 361
Lovejoy, A. O., 104, 112 ref.
Lowe, G. M., 225 ref.
Lowrey, L. G., 225 ref., 227 ref., 228 ref., 229 ref.
Lubbock, J., 295, 335, 361
Ludwig, C. F. W., 335, 361

MacCorquodale, K., 90, 94 ref.

NAME INDEX : 381

McCosh, J., 318, 336, 361
MacCurdy, J. T., 336, 361
McDougall, W., 266, 279, 316, 332, 361
Macfarlane, J. W., 242, 263, 273, 274 ref.
McGeoch, J. A., 334, 361
McGregor, D., 336, 361
Mach, E., 89, 94 ref., 361
MacLeod, R. B., 44, 56, 57, 59, 65, 66, 68, 71, 93, 94 ref., 192, 192 ref., 328ff
McPherson, M. W., 67
McReynolds, P., 69
McTeer, W., 227 ref.
Maimonides, M., 30
Magendie, F., 333, 361
Maine de Biran, M., 333, 361
Malebranche, N. d., 333, 361
Malinowski, B. K., 333, 361
Malthus, T. R., 289, 335, 361
Mandler, G., 57
Marbe, K., 208, 279, 333, 361
Mariotte, E., 333, 361
Marquis, D. G., 91, 291
Marshall, M., 71, 72
Marx, K., 334, 361
Marx, M. H., 107, 112 ref.
Marx, O., 62, 68
Mason, E., 11
Masuda, K., 329
Matarazzo, J. D., 10, 30, 283 ref., 301, 302
Mateer, ––, 202
Matsumoto, M., 337, 361
Maudsley, H., 334, 361
Maxwell, J. C., 334, 361
May, R., 93, 94 ref.
Mayer, R., 58, 58 ref., 64
Mayo, E., 337, 339, 343, 361
Mead, G. H., 334, 362
Mead, M., 240
Meehl, P. E., 90, 92, 94 ref.
Meenes, M., 47, 57 ref., 66
Meinong, A. v., 333, 362
Meissner, G., 337, 362
Meltzer, H., 237
Mendel, G. J., 333, 362
Menninger, K., 215, 227 ref., 249, 253 ref., 282
Menninger, W. C., 227 ref.
Mensh, I., 10
Mercier, D. J., 336, 362
Merleau-Ponty, M., 335, 362
Merrifield, M., 338, 351 ref., 352
Merrill, M. A., 212, 214, 227 ref.

Mersenne, M., 337, 362
Merton, R. K., 56, 65
Merzbach, U., 62
Mesmer, F., 333, 362
Messer, A., 334, 362
Metcalf, R. C., 52 ref.
Meumann, E., 333, 362
Meyer, A., 199, 202, 208, 227 refs., 283 ref., 334, 343, 362
Meyer, M. F., 334, 362
Meynert, T. H., 336, 362
Michotte, A. E., 332, 362
Miles, W. R., 212, 280
Mill, J., 316, 332, 362
Mill, J. S., 311, 313, 316, 332, 362
Miller, G. A., 103, 112 ref.
Miller, N. E., **91**, **297**, 307 ref.
Mills, E., 16, 70, 71
Mira y Lopez, E., 336, 362
Mirabito, J., 127
Mischel, T., 68
Misiak, H., 92, 94 ref.
Moede, W., 300, 307 ref., 336, 362
Molish, H. B., 289, 305 ref.
Moll, A., 336, 362
Molyneux, W., 336, 362
Monakow, C. v., 336, 362
Montesquieu, C. d. S., 335, 362
Montessori, M., 334, 350, 362
Moore, T. V., 293
Mora, G., 56, 59, 62, 65, 68, 71
Morell, J. D., 100, 112 ref.
Moreno, J. L., 300, 307 ref.
Morgan, C. D., 266, 274 ref.
Morgan, C. L., 289, 295, 296, 332, 362
Morgan, J. D., 221, 225 ref.
Morris, L., 200–201, 227 ref.
Morrow, W. R., 210, 227 ref.
Mowrer, O., 90
Mueller, R., 69, 70, 146–147, 155 ref.
Muenzinger, K. F., 335, 362
Müller, G. E., 316, 362
Müller, J., 333, 362
Müller-Freienfels, R., 335, 362
Müller-Lyer, F., 334, 362
Münsterberg, H., 202, 300, 333, 362
Murchison, C., 5, 53, 53 ref., 54, 54 ref., 63, 209, 226 ref., 227 ref., 228 ref., 334, 362
Murphy, G., 53, 53 ref., 56, 63, 68, 71, 98, 101, 112 ref., 200, 212, 227 ref., 286, 288, 295, 307 ref.
Murphy, L. B., 299, 307 ref.

NAME INDEX

Murray, H. A., 91, 101, 112 ref., 215, 228 ref., 266, 274 ref.
Myers, C. S., 334, 362

Nafe, J. P., 5
Nagel, W., 336, 362
Nakajima, K., 329
Newcomb, T. M., 90, 299, 307 ref.
Newton, I., 102, 160, 332, 346, 362
Nietzsche, F. W., 334, 363
Nishi, A., 329
Nishimura, S., 329
Nissen, H. W., 335, 363
Nogami, T., 329
Norsworthy, N., 197, 228 ref.
Noyes, William, 208
Nuttin, J. R., 328ff

Oberholzer, E., 214, 275 ref.
Odoroff, M. E., 211, 226 ref.
Ogden, C. K., 336, 363
Ogden, R. M., 334, 363
O'Neil, W., 69
Onojima, U., 329
Orth, J., 336, 363
Orton, S., 211

Palmer, J., 10
Parsons, J. H., 336, 363
Parsons, T., 131, 139, 152, 155 ref.
Pascal, B., 334, 345, 363
Paterson, D. G., 199, 225–226 ref., 228 ref., 335, 363
Paulhan, F., 337, 363
Pavlov, I. P., 288, 290–291, 296, 298, 301, 307 refs., 332, 363
Pearson, K., 259, 315, 316, 323 ref., 332, 363
Peckham, G. W., 336, 363
Peirce, C. S. S., 334, 363
Pestalozzi, J. H., 333, 363
Peter of Spain, 29–30
Peters, R. S., 53, 53 ref.
Peterson, J., 52, 52 ref., 63, 197, 228 ref., 323 ref.
Pfaffman, C., 86
Pflüger, E. F. W., 334, 363
Pfungst, O., 335, 363
Piaget, J., 100
Piéron, H., 332, 363
Pillsbury, W. B., 334, 363
Pilzecker, A., 335, 363

Pinel, P., 333, 363
Pintner, R., 7, 8, 199, 218, 228 refs., 334, 343, 363
Piotrowski, Z., 214
Plateau, J. A. F., 334, 363
Plato, 37, 109, 118, 144
Poffenberger, A. T., 6, 212, 324 ref.
Polyak, S., 336, 363
Ponzo, M., 334, 363
Popovich, M., 131, 133, 155 ref.
Poppelreuter, W., 335, 363
Popplestone, J. A., 43, 57, 57 ref., 66, 67, 68, 72
Porter, E. H., Jr., 303
Porter, N., 337, 363
Porteus, S. D., 217
Pratt, C. C., 298, 307 ref.
Preyer, W. T., 234, 238, 333, 363
Price, D. J. d. S., 30 ref., 58, 58 ref.
Priestley, J., 336, 363
Prince, M., 200, 202, 203, 208, 214–215, 300, 333, 363
Prochaska, G., 337, 363
Psammethicus, 288
Purkinje, J. E., 333, 363
Putnam, J., 202, 203

Quen, J., 62, 65, 69, 72
Quételet, A., 333, 363

Rabin, A., 237
Rahmani, L., 71
Ramon y Cajal. *See* Cajal
Rancurello, A., 44
Rand, B., 53, 53 ref.
Randall, J. H., Jr., 191 ref.
Rank, O., 304, 333, 342, 364
Ranschburg, P., 336, 364
Rapaport, D., 237, 273, 274 ref., 334, 343, 364
Rayleigh, Lord, 334, 364
Reichenbach, H., 169 ref.
Reid, T., 333, 364
Reingold, N., 57 ref., 66
Reisman, D., 131
Reiss, T., 7
Reuchlin, M., 132, 155 ref.
Révész, G., 333, 364
Reymert, M. L., 335, 343, 364
Ribot, T. A., 313, 332, 364
Richet, C., 165, 335, 364
Rignano, E., 335, 349, 364

NAME INDEX : 383

Rivers, W. H., 334, 364
Roback, A. A., 228 ref., 335, 364
Robinson, E. S., 335, 364
Rogers, C. R., 89, 220, 228 ref., 303-305, 307 refs.
Róheim, G., 337, 364
Rolando, L., 335, 364
Romanes, G. J., 333, 364
Rorschach, H., 213-214, 235, 275 ref., 332, 364
Rosanoff, A. J., 335, 364
Rosenzweig, M. R., 291, 307 ref.
Rosenzweig, S., 10, 68, 228 refs., 237, 272-273, 275 refs., 303, 307 ref.
Ross, B., 18, 61, 65-66, 69-73, 124-127, 129 ref., 148-150, 155 ref.
Ross, E. A., 337, 364
Rousseau, J.-J., 109, 333, 364
Royce, J., 92, 94 ref., 335, 345, 346, 364
Rubin, E. J., 332, 364
Rubinstein, S., 336, 364
Ruckmick, C. A., 335, 364
Rush, B., 335, 340, 364
Russell, W. A., 57, 66, 67

Sachs, H., 336, 364
St. John, C. W., 5
Sanford, E. C., 198, 334, 364
Sanford, F. H., 16, 335, 364
Santayana, G., 37, 42 ref.
Sapir, E., 334, 364
Sargent, S. S., 47
Sarton, G., 28-31, 40, 42 ref., 54
Saslow, G., 249, 253 ref.
Saudek, R., 337, 364
Saul, L. J., 303, 307 ref.
Scheerer, M., 335, 343, 364
Scheier, I. H., 286, 305 ref.
Schellenberg, T. R., 78
Schelling, F. W. J. v., 335, 364
Schiller, F., 336, 347, 364
Schiller, P. H., 336, 364
Schlosberg, H., 334, 364
Schopenhauer, A., 333, 365
Schrickel, H. G., 47
Schumann, F., 334, 365
Scott, W. D., 203, 220, 228 ref., 303, 337, 339, 365
Scripture, E. W., 333, 365
Sears, R. R., 71, 90, 242, 266, 275 ref.
Seashore, C. E., 205, 211, 228 ref., 365
Seashore, H. G., 337, 365

Sechenov, I. M., 290, 332, 365
Seguin, E., 334, 365
Seidenfeld, M. A., 47
Sells, S., 7, 57
Selz, O., 335, 365
Senn, M. J. E., 237, 253 ref.
Sexton, V. S., 57, 67, 72
Shaffer, L. F., 10, 90
Shaffer, P. A., 207
Shakow, D., 201-202, 206, 217, 228 refs., 230, 237, 253 ref.
Shand, A. F., 335, 365
Sharp, S. E., 197, 198, 228 ref., 257, 262, 275 ref.
Shepard, J. F., 337, 365
Sherif, M., 294, 295, 307 ref.
Sherrington, C. S., 292, 332, 365
Shils, E. A., 139, 155 ref.
Shimberg, M. E., 225 ref.
Sidis, B., 202, 203, 208, 220, 228 ref., 300, 303, 335, 365
Sigerist, H. E., 42 ref., 277, 283 ref.
Simon, T., 310, 323 ref., 334, 365
Simon, W. M., 323 ref.
Simpson, M., 65, 66
Singer, C., 42 ref.
Skinner, B. F., 90, 91, 121, 130, 136, 155 ref., 297-298, 301, 308 refs.
Skodak, M., 57
Slavson, S. R., 303, 308 ref.
Small, W. S., 334, 365
Smelzer, N., 131
Smith, A., 41, 335, 349, 365
Smith, G., 228 ref.
Smith, N., 72
Smith, T. L., 228 ref.
Smuts, J. C., 336, 365
Snoddy, G. S., 337, 365
Sokal, M., 69, 71, 73
Solomon, R., 71
Southard, E. E., 337, 365
Spalding, D. A., 336, 365
Spearman, C. E., 198, 259ff, 275 ref., 312, 316-317, 321-322, 324 ref., 332, 365
Speer, G. S., 227 ref., 228 ref.
Spence, K. W., 91, 297, 308 refs., 333, 365
Spencer, H., 296, 332, 365
Spinoza, B., 102, 109, 333, 347, 365
Spranger, E., 333, 365
Spurzheim, J. K., 71, 334, 342, 365
Starbuck, E. D., 336, 365
Steinthal, H., 336, 365
Stekel, W., 335, 365

NAME INDEX

Stephenson, W., 273, 275 ref.
Stern, L. B., 65
Stern, W., 115, 198, 312, 317-318, 324 refs., 332, 365
Stevens, S. S., 86, 89, 90, 94 ref.
Stevenson, G. S., 228 ref.
Stewart, D., 333, 365
Stillman, C. W., 251-252, 253 ref.
Stocking, G. W., Jr., 56, 65, 116, 129 ref.
Stoelting, C., 336, 339, 365
Stone, C. P., 335, 365
Stone, L. J., 7, 242
Störring, G., 335, 365
Stouffer, S. A., 336, 365
Stout, G. F., 332, 365
Stratton, G. M., 52, 52 ref., 63, 333, 365
Strong, E. K., 293, 334, 365
Stumpf, C., 332, 366
Sullivan, H. S., 333, 366
Sullivan, J. J., 69, 73
Sully, J., 333, 366
Swedenborg, E., 337, 366
Swift, S., 66
Symonds, J. P., 218, 228 ref., 308 ref.
Symonds, P. M., 237, 337, 339, 366

Taine, H. A., 334, 366
Takashima, H., 329
Tanaka, K., 329
Tarde, G., 333, 366
Taylor, J. A., 297, 308 refs.
Taylor, W. S., 323 ref.
Terman, L. M., 85, 196ff, 202, 215, 218, 228 ref., 233, 234, 237, 310, 332, 339, 366
Tetens, J. N., 337, 366
Theman, V., 229 ref.
Thomas, N., 6
Thomson, G., 333, 366
Thorndike, E. L., 85, 197, 198, 238, 259, 290, 295-296, 298, 301, 332, 339, 366
Thorndike, R., 7
Thorne, F. C., 14
Thurstone, L. L., 85, 264ff, 275 ref., 332, 339, 366
Tiedemann, D., 337, 366
Titchener, E. B., 5, 63, 67, 84, 100, 200, 257, 332, 339, 342, 366
Toft, J., 304
Tolman, E. C., 63, 89, 90, 91, 94 ref., 301, 332, 339, 366
Travis, E. L., 7

Troland, L. T., 334, 366
Trow, W. C., 56, 66
Tsukahara, S., 329
Tulchin, S., 237, 253 ref.
Twitmyer, E. B., 335, 366
Tylor, E. B., 336, 366

Ueno, Y., 329
Uexküll, J. J. v., 334, 366
Underwood, B. J., 11
Urban, F. M., 335, 366

Vaihinger, H., 337, 366
Valentine, C. W., 336, 366
Valentine, W. L., 336, 366
Van Hoorn, W., 65, 70, 73
Verhave, T., 69, 71
Vernon, P. E., 275 ref.
Verplanck, W. S., 261, 275 ref.
Verworn, M., 295, 335, 366
Vesalius, 277
Vestermark, S. D., 229 ref.
Vierordt, K. v., 335, 366
Voelker, P. F., 261, 275 ref.
Volkmann, A. W., 294-295, 306 ref., 336, 366
Voltaire, 334, 366
Vygotsky, L. S., 334, 366

Wallace, A. R., 335, 366
Wallas, G., 337, 366
Wallin, J. E. W., 205, 215, 229 ref., 281, 283 ref.
Wallon, H. P. H., 336, 366
Walsh, A., 69, 70, 71
Walsh, W. H., 41, 42 ref.
Ward, J., 333, 366
Warden, C. J., 6, 7, 289, 295, 308 ref., 334, 366
Warner, L. H., 337, 366
Warren, H. C., 52, 52 ref., 63, 333, 367
Washburn, M. F., 324 ref., 333, 350, 367
Watanabe, T., 329
Watkins, J. W. N., 131, 155 ref.
Watson, G., 212, 304
Watson, J. B., 138, 140, 147, 234, 238, 260, 291, 295-296, 298, 301, 308 refs., 332, 339, 367
Watson, R. I., refs.: 21-23, 45-55, 57, 61, 74, 93, 94, 112, 129, 130, 155ff, 229, 253, 308, 351, 368-374
Watt, H. J., 5, 334, 367

Webb, E., 260, 275 ref.
Webb, R., 224 ref.
Weber, E. H., 276, 294, 332, 367
Weber, M., 334, 367
Wechsler, D., 237, 293
Weiss, A. P., 333, 367
Wells, F. L., 202, 208, 212-213, 216, 218, 229 ref., 237, 293, 337, 339, 367
Wells, H. K., 290, 308 ref.
Wendt, G. R., 229 ref.
Werner, H., 225 ref., 333, 342, 367
Wertheimer, Max, 67, 92, 332, 367
Wertheimer, Michael, 57, 66ff, 328ff
Wesley, F., 65
Wever, E. G., 86, 294, 308 ref.
Weyant, R., 65, 66, 69, 72, 73
Wheatstone, C., 335, 367
Wheeler, R. H., 334, 367
Wheeler, W. M., 337, 367
Whipple, G. M., 199, 210, 218, 229 ref., 255, 258, 275 ref., 334, 367
White, R. W., 271, 275 ref., 301, 307 ref.
White, W. A., 335, 367
Whitehead, A. N., 104, 112 ref., 146, 155 ref., 335, 367
Whitehorn, J. C., 229 ref.
Whytt, R., 335, 367
Wickman, E. K., 304
Wiener, D. N., 229 ref.
Wiener, N., 334, 350, 367
Wiersma, E. D., 336, 367
Wiley, B., 176 ref.
Wirth, W., 335, 367
Wissler, C., 197-198, 229 ref., 257, 262, 275 ref., 336, 367

Witasek, S., 334, 367
Witmer, L., 204ff, 210, 229 ref., 236, 334, 367
Witty, P. S., 215, 229 ref.
Wolf, T. H., 323 refs.
Wolff, C. v., 333, 367
Wolfle, D., 229 refs.
Wolpe, J., 299, 301, 308 ref.
Woodger, J. H., 102, 112 ref.
Woodword, W., 71
Woodworth, R. S., 6, 7, 53, 53 ref., 88, 197, 199, 229 ref., 324 refs., 332, 339, 367
Wundt, W., 38, 84, 106, 117, 197, 200, 208, 257, 258, 277ff, 291, 311, 316, 319, 323 ref., 332, 342, 367
Wyatt, F., 229 ref., 230, 253 ref.

Yarrow, L. J., 243-244, 253 ref.
Yarrow, M., 243-244, 253 ref.
Yatabe, T., 329
Yerkes, R. M., 199, 211, 212, 218, 225 ref., 229 ref., 280, 295, 332, 339, 367
Young, K., 195, 229 ref.
Young, R. M., 44, 58, 59-60, 69
Young, T., 333, 367
Yule, G. U., 334, 367

Zangwill, O., 44, 58
Zener, K. E., 294, 308 ref., 335, 367
Ziehen, T., 334, 367
Zilboorg, G., 282, 303, 308 ref., 335, 343, 367
Zwaardemaker, H., 333, 346, 367

Index of Subjects

AAAP. *See* American Association for Applied Psychology
AACP. *See* American Association of Clinical Psychologists
Abnormal psychology, at Columbia University, 6
Adolescent Growth Study, 242
Affective tolerance, 8
Alpha scale, 199. *See also* Quantification in psychology, Testing
American Archivist, 77
American Association for Applied Psychology (AAAP), 218
American Association of Clinical Psychologists (AACP), supplanted by APA's clinical section, 218
American Association of Psychiatric Social Workers, 250
American Board of Examiners in Professional Psychology, 223, 245
American Historical Association, 74
American Institute of Physics, 74
American Journal of Insanity, no reviews of psychoanalysis until 1914, 203
American Journal of Psychology, historical articles in, 25-26
American Orthopsychiatric Association, 230ff, 240; aims, 246; and children, 215, 231; and psychoanalysis, 213; interdisciplinary collaboration, 250
American Psychiatric Association: lack of interdisciplinary collaboration, 248ff; reference on, 252
American Psychological Association (APA), and growth of psychology as a profession, 218; archives of, 56f, 66; budget of, 86; clinical division of, 210, 218; directory, 26, 43, 85; founding, 209; history division, 43, 67, 340; references to, 224-225
Anatomy, seventeenth century, 157
Animal psychology, 290-291, 295
Annual Review of Psychology, 243
Anomaly, as catalyst in scientific revolution, 95
Anthropology, 239-240
Anthropomorphism, 289
Anxiety, study of, 297
APA. *See* American Psychological Association
Apperception. *See* Thematic Apperception Test
Appetites, natural (Descartes), 167
Archives, 43, 56-57, 66, 77f
Archives of the History of American Psychology, 43
Armed services, and psychology, 220ff
Assessment, modern methods of, 263ff
Association of Consulting Psychologists, 218
Associationism, British school, 313-314, 316
Associations, analysis of (Kraepelin), 278
Attention, function of, 300
Attitude study, 90
Audition, 86
Automota, 163
Awareness, as a form of consciousness, 186-187

Beagle, H. M. S., 288
Beast-Machine, as antiquated concept, 117
Behavior modification, 301ff

Behaviorism, 85, 88; and objectivity of measurement, 260ff
Berkeley Growth Study, 242
Beta scale, 199
Binet test: as early tool, 202; introduction to United States, 198, 209, 310; revision of, 198, 233, 310
Binet-Simon Scale, 206, 315
Biographical dictionary, 327ff
Body and mind, 179ff
Boston group, 199
Boston Psychopathic Hospital, 216
Brain: function, 90; physiology, 85. *See also* Cerebral function
British Psychological Society, 74

Cartesian: dualism, 176; meditation, 184
Catholic Church: influence on Descartes, 189; legitimate prejudgments of, 100
Causality: determinism, 40; in historiography, 309
Cerebral function, 292-293. *See also* Brain
Cheiron (International Society for the History of the Behavioral and Social Sciences), 340; charter meeting, 122; founding, 17, 72; sixth annual meeting, 72
Child guidance: and psychologists, 205-206; clinics, 205-206, 216, 235-236; study by Rogers, 303
Child psychology: and Piagetian literature, 12; book by R. I. Watson, 11; development of, 230ff; early interest in, 321-322; guide to progress in orthopsychiatry, 231; testing, 197, 236
Children, intellectual classification of, 198
Clark University, host of Freud and Jung, 203
Clinical Method in Psychology, The, 11-12
Clinical psychology: advent marked by opening of Psychological Clinic at University of Pennsylvania, 236; and behavior modification, 295-296; and functionalism, 295ff; and growth of mental hospitals, 217; and learning, 295ff; and psychophysics, 287, 293ff; and R. I. Watson, 8ff; as separate discipline, 287ff; Boston group, 199; current, 222ff; diagnostic functions in, 223, 237, 248; from 1920-1940, 211ff; history of, 195ff; origins of, 196ff; relation to experimental tradition, 293; section of at APA, 210; testing, 195; traditions of, 285ff. *See also* Orthopsychiatry, Personality, Psychiatry, Psychoanalysis
Clincial psychologists, certification of, 210
Clinics in psychology, 204ff, 214ff; first one at University of Pennsylvania, 236
Cognitive psychology, at University of New Hampshire, 16
Columbia University, number of graduate students trained at, 320
Committee on Physical and Mental Tests, 210
Committee on the History of Psychiatry, 46
Communication, relation to clinical psychology, 299ff
Comparative psychology, 6, 289
Conditioning (Pavlovian), 290-291
Configurations, as part of Gestalt psychology, 92
Conscious mentalism, 186-187
Contentual objectivity and subjectivity, 191-192
Cornell University: history of psychology program, 59. *See also* New York Hospital
Corpuscular theory, 122, 160
Correlational analysis, 285, 316
Counseling, 248
Counter-prescriptions. *See* Prescriptions

Dana College, and R. I. Watson, 6
Dark Ages, and transmission of science, 31
Darwinian theory: and learning, 295ff; evolution of ideas, 36-37; natural selection, 287-288
Deductive rationalism, 169ff
Dementia praecox, learning and introspection, 293
Developmental psychology, 318. *See also* Child psychology
Differential psychology, 317-318
Digestive glands, research by Pavlov, 290
Dispositions, natural (Descartes), 167
Dissertation, first doctoral on history of psychology, 18
Dissociation, Charcot's doctrine of, 300
Dogmatic methodism, of Bacon, Descartes, and Hobbes, 168
Drive, role in learning, 297
Dualism: as a prescription, 88; Cartesian, 175ff

SUBJECT INDEX : 389

Dynamic tradition, 199ff, 213ff; related to clinical, 285-286
Dynamogenesis, Baldwin's principles of, 318

Eminent psychologists: list of names, 332ff, 352ff; major fields of, 345ff; nationalities of, 341ff; primary and secondary references, 22; scoring results, 330ff, 339; system of selection, 328-329, 338-339; women among, 349-350
Empiricism, 119ff, 169
Environmentalism, championed by J. B. Watson, 90
Epicureans, fostered atomic philosphy, 159
Equipotentiality, in Gestalt psychology, 92
Examination, first psychological, 292
Existential psychology, as a philosphical counter-prescription, 92
Experiential positivism, 88
Experiment, earliest psychological, 288
Experimental psychology: as inter-related discipline, 41; at University of New Hampshire, 16; first institute of at Leipzig, 278; traditions of, 285-286. *See also* Laboratories
Externalist explanations in psychology, 309-310

Factor analysis, 85, 271, 316
Faculties of the mind (Descartes), 187ff
France: educational system of, 312; lack of contentual model in, 132; psychopathological school of, 202
Freedom of will, 189
Functionalism, 88, 295, 318

Genius: study by Galton, 315
Gestalt psychology: and Lewin, 300; and molecular constancy hypothesis, 136; counter to dominant prescriptions, 91; relation to American psychology, 85, 92
God: and freedom of will, 189; as functional promoter of thought processes, 173; as purveyor of understanding, 190
Great Man: approach to history of psychology, 114-115, 123; R. I. Watson paper on, 153
Great Psychologists, 15, 18, 115-116
Group for the Advancement of Psychiatry, 282
Groups: atmosphere of, 301; research on small, 301; testing, 212. *See also* Social climate
Guidance Study, The, 242
Guide for the Perplexed, 30

Harvard Psychological Clinic, 213; founding, 214-215
Healy form board test, 199
Heart, Descartes' faulty ideas on, 174
Heredity, study by Galton, 315
Historiography: and American psychology, 43, 51ff; externalist view, 309-310; inductive methods in, 117; interdisciplinary cooperation, 49; need for, 33; specialization in, 43
History of psychology: as a specialization, 43ff, 61ff; basic works of, 28, 53; development of, 51; first dissertation in, 18; graduate programs in, 45, 70-71; medieval period, 28ff; neglect of, 25ff; pre-specialization in, 51; source material in, 28ff. *See also* Great Man, Historiography, Prescriptions, *Zeitgeist*
History of science, 36-37
History of Science Society, number of psychologists in, 26
History of the Behavioral Sciences Newsletter, 47, 55, 62
Hormonal behavior, work of F. Beach, 86
Hospitals, mental, psychologists in, 206ff
Human Relations, founding of, 301
Hypnosis: and Binet, 314; clinical use of, 299ff
Hypnotic suggestion, 302
Hypothetical entities (Hull), 89
Hypothetico-deductivism, 88, 90

Ideas: and perception, 171; origin of, 167, 171, 184
Idiographic theory (Allport), 91
Imageless thought: antiquated concept, 117; work in by C. Spearman, 316
Imagination (Descartes), 180-181
Imitation (W. Moede), 300
Individual differences, 286, 311ff. *See also* Testing
Inkblot test, 266
Innateness: and ideas, 167, 171, 184; and rationalism, 170
Institute for Experimental Psychology (Wundt), date of origin, 38
Institute of Applied Psychology, 317

390 : SUBJECT INDEX

Institute of Child Welfare, University of California, 242
Institutes for the mentally defective, and psychologists, 209
Intelligence: general factor, 317; testing, 85, 259ff. *See also* Binet test, Binet-Simon Scale
Interdisciplinary activity, 243ff
International Society for the History of the Behavioral and Social Sciences. *See* Cheiron
Internship training, 210-211
Intervening variables (Hull), 89, 90
Interview, role in therapy, 302
Introduction to the History of Science, and medieval period, 28
Introspection, and French psychologist Cousin, 313
IQ. *See* Binet test, Intelligence

JHBS. See *Journal of the History of the Behavioral Sciences*
Journal of Abnormal (and Social) Psychology, founding of, 202
Journal of Consulting Psychology, 219
Journal of General Psychology, historical articles in, 25-26
Journal of the History of the Behavioral Sciences (JHBS), 55; and sociology, 50, 65; effect on specialization in history of psychology, 43; first editorial by R. I. Watson, 49-50; founding of, 46ff
Judge Baker Guidance Center (Boston), 206
Judgment, aesthetic and affective, 295
Juvenile delinquency, prominence of, as social problem, 233
Juvenile Psychopathic Institute (Chicago), 211, 235

Laboratories of psychology: Harvard (William James), 84; Leipzig (Wundt), 38, 311; McLean Hospital, 208; University of Pennsylvania, 256ff
Latitudinarian ideal, 90
Learning: and behaviorism, 91; and clinical psychology, 293ff; perceptual, 91, 291; relation to behavior modification, 301; social influence on, 300
Learning theory: D. O. Hebb, 90; E. L. Thorndike, 85
Leipzig Laboratory, 38, 311

Library of Congress, psychological papers at, 57, 66
Linguistics, 50

McLean Hospital, 206-208
McLean Psychological Laboratory, 201-202, 207, 279-280, 292
Manifest Anxiety Scale, 297
Manual of Standard Experiments in Psychology, book by R. I. Watson, 8
Massachusetts Institute of Technology Research Center for Group Dynamics, establishment of, 301
Materialism, early trend toward, 158
Matter: extension as essential part of, 160; relation to thought, 175-176
Mechanism: approach to physical sciences, 158; vs. vitalism, 162
Mechanisms, molar (Descartes), 160ff
Medicine: and psychology, 278ff; history of, 276ff. *See also* Psychiatry
Medieval period, in history of psychology, 28ff
Meditation (Descartes), 183-184
Memory (Descartes), 167
Mental deficiency, 209, 217-218
Mental hospitals and psychology, 206ff, 216-217
Mental processes, interpretation in terms of functions, 289
Mental psychology, 318
Mental tests: classification of, 206, 256. *See also* Testing
Mesmerism, 299
Methodological objectivity and subjectivity, 191-192
Methodology in history. *See* Historiography
Middle ages, psychology in, 28ff
Military psychology, 220ff. *See also* World War I, World War II
Mind: and ideas, 185-186; and meditation, 183-184; and self-consciousness, 187; and thought, 184-185, 188; interaction with body, 179ff; structure of, 184; will as faculty of, 189
Minnesota Multiphasic Personality Inventory (MMPI), 265, 270
MMPI. *See* **Minnesota Multiphasic Personality Inventory**
Molar mechanisms (Descartes), 160ff
Molecular constancy hypothesis, 136

Monism, as psychological prescription, 88
Morgan's canon, 289-290
Motion (Descartes), 179-180

National Academy of Sciences, and biologically-oriented psychologists, 86
National Committee for Mental Hygiene, 216
National Science Foundation, history of psychological grants, 45
Nativism: outgrowth of rationalism, 140. See also Innateness
Natural accumulation (Hume), 75
Naturalism, as a prescription, 88
Nerve physiology, 292
Neural behavior, work of F. Beach, 86
Neurology, 50, 65
Neurophysiology, 50
New Hampshire, University of, doctoral program in psychology, 59
New York Hospital: role in founding *Newsletter* of behavioral sciences, 47. See also Cornell University
New York Psychoanalytic Society, 204
Nomotheticism, 91
Non-atomic theory (Descartes), 122

Objective method (Pavlov), 290-291
Objective testing: beginning of, 255; lack of concern with, 258. See also Testing
Objectivity: methodological and contentual (Descartes), 191-192; search for, 254ff
Oneirology, 28
Operationalism, 89-90
Orthopsychiatry, 230ff

Paradigm: and science, 95ff; contrasted with prescriptions, 88; effect of anomalies on, 95; Kuhn's definition of, 18; Kuhn's use of, 87; lack of in American psychology, 97-98; lack of in American sociology, 131-132; lack of in seventeenth century, 168
Paris Commission (Binet), 314-315
Pattern analysis, approach to personality, 271. See also Quantification in psychology
Patterns, as part of Gestalt psychology, 92
Payne Whitney Clinic, program in history of psychology, 65. See also Cornell University, New York Hospital
Pennsylvania, University of: first psychology professorship, 319; psychology clinic at, 236; psychology laboratory at, 256ff; Wundt and Cattell at, 197
Perception: and Boring, 52; and Descartes, 160-161, 180-181; and Galileo, 177; bringing innate ideas to the conscious, 171; sense (Aristotle and later), 176; visual, 166-167
Performance tests: measure used in personality (Voelker), 261; Pintner-Paterson, 199
Personality: as separate discipline, 13; development, as a tool in orthopsychiatry, 240-241; Maimonides on, 30; research, 17
Personality testing: definition of, 267ff; early, 256; projective method (L. K. Frank), 214; questionnaires, 212, 263ff. See also Performance tests, Testing
Personality theory: and Buytendijk, 137; early development, 260ff; history of, 21, 123; quantification in, 90
Phenomenology: as a philosophical counter-prescription, 92; Buytendijk, 137; method for securing psychological knowledge, 121
Philosophy: as early basis of psychological thought, 105-106; eclectic spiritualism, 312
Phrenology, 83
Physicalism, as a psychological prescription, 88
Physicians, training of by psychologists, 280
Physiological psychology: inter-related discipline, 41; Wundtian, 106, 311
Physiology: and Descartes, 164ff; and Harvey, 122, 156, 158, 162
Pineal gland, as intermediary between body and mind, 167
Practical psychology, 311, 322
Prescriptions, 19, 87, 95ff, 113ff, 130ff; and Descartes, 157ff; as mnemonic device, 111; lists of, 98-99, 119-120, 135; non-random clustering of, 110; partial definition of, 157. See also specific prescriptions (e.g. Functionalism)
Presentism, attacked by Agassiz, 116
Pre-specialization period, 52
Primatology, 86
Princeton University, doctoral program in history of psychology, 59
Projective techniques, 213-214, 263, 266, 271
Protestant Church, legitimate prejudgments of, 100

Provincialism, in American psychology, 25, 97-98
Psychiatric research, relation to psychology, 281ff
Psychiatry: and Kraepelin, 200; child (Levy), 214; descriptive, 291; early development of, 200; represented on board of *JHBS*, 50, 65
Psychoanalysis: counter to dominant prescriptions, 91; first article in English, 203; history of, as studied at Ohio State University, 45; influence on projective techniques, 213; non-Freudian (Murray), 91; represented on board of *JHBS*, 50
Psychoanalytic Review, founding of, 202
Psychological Bulletin, first volume, 229; lack of historical articles in, 25-26
Psychological Clinic, 204, 236
Psychological Corporation, 320
Psychological Review: co-founded by Cattell, 320; glossary of terms in, 260
Psychologische Arbeiter, first issue of, 291
Psychology: and Descartes, 156ff; and philosophy, 105; and psychiatry, 219-220, 281 ff; and psychometrics, 196ff; as a profession, 11, 209ff, 217ff; breach between experimental and clinical, 284-285; collaboration with medicine, 278; convergent trends in, 87; dynamic traditions in, 199ff; in mental hospitals, 206ff; lack of unity in, 97; prescriptions in, 19, 50, 87-88, 95ff, 113ff; professionalization of, 223; quantitative foundations of, 200; sensory, 86. *See* History of psychology and various subdisciplines (e.g. Physiological)
Psychology Laboratory, at University of Pennsylvania, 256
Psychology as a Profession, 11
Psychology of the Child, 11-12
Psychology Press, Inc., sponsored *JHBS*, 47-48
Psychometric testing. *See* Testing
Psychometric tradition, 212-213; related to clinical, 285-286
Psychopathology, 202. *See also* Clinical psychology, Psychiatry
Psychophysics: and vision (Stevens), 86; related to clinical, 287, 293ff
Psychoses: classification of, 278; experimental literature on, 293

Psychotherapy: and behavior modification, 303; broadening of, 237; quantification of, 304

Q-technique (Stephenson), 273
Quantification in psychology, 17, 90, 147-148
Questionnaires: in child psychology, 232; in personality, 263ff. *See also* Testing

Rating scales, 304
Rationalism (Descartes), 157, 168ff
Reaction time: influence on speed, 117; studies by Cattell, 319
Readings in the Clinical Methods in Psychology, 11
Reciprocal inhibition, 301
References, role and use in history of psychology, 42
Reflex response (Descartes), 165-166
Reinforcement, in learning theory, 297
Rorschach test, 136, 237, 265, 273; defense of, 267

St. Elizabeths Hospital, 280
Schools of psychology: 1910-1930, 85; prescriptive analysis of, 141ff; volumes on, edited by Murchison, 63. *See also* specific schools (e.g. Gestalt)
Science, purchased by Cattell, 320
Science. *See* History of science
Seguin form board test, 199
Self-consciousness (Descartes), 187
Sensation: as a psychological topic, 28; Boring on, 52; Descartes on, 180ff; Graham on, 86
Sense perception, 176-177
Sensorimotor function, early testing of, 197
Social climate, concept introduced by Lewin (also "group atmosphere"), 301. *See also* Groups
Social psychology, 299ff, 349; and prescriptive theory, 19
Social sciences, and prescriptive theory, 130ff
Social tradition, related to clinical psychology, 285
Sociology, and *JHBS*, 50, 65
Spiritual mind, 175-176
Spiritualism, Cousin's eclectic, 312
Stanford-Binet Intelligence Scale, 233, 236
Statistical methods; Cattell, 320; Galton, 316

Stimulus-response psychology, 297. *See also* Behaviorism
Subjectivity, methodological and contentual (Descartes), 191-192
Symbolic constructs, 89

TAT. *See* Thematic Apperception Test
Tavistock Institute (London), 301
Terman-Merrill revision (of Binet test), 310
Testing, 197, 212, 217, 254ff; *Alpha* and *Beta* scales, 199; and World War I, 212; beginnings of, 90, 255ff, 292; classification of, 272-273; form boards (Seguin, Healy, and Witmer), 199; group, 212; intelligence, 259, 310-311; mental, 195, 206, 314, 319; objective, definition of, 267ff; personality, 212, 214, 256, 263ff; Pintner-Paterson Performance, 199; projective, 214, 266, 271; Thematic Apperception Test (TAT), 241, 266, 270; Will-Temperament Test, 261; Woodworth-Wells Association Tests, 210. *See also* Binet, Inkblot test, MMPI, Performance, Rorschach, Stanford-Binet Intelligence Scale
Thematic Apperception Test (TAT), 214, 266, 270

Thought (Descartes), 172, 175, 184ff

United States Public Health Service, 45, 223

Verbal behavior (Skinner), 298
Vision: and Descartes, 166; psychophysics of, 86
Vitalism, 162

Weber-Fechner law, 294
Will: and passion, 190; freedom of, 188ff
Will-Temperament Test, 261
Witmer form board test, 199
Women, among eminent contributors, 349-350
Woodworth-Wells Association Tests, 210
Work, continuous, experimental study of, 292
World War I, testing during and after, 212
World War II: and Binet tests, 236; and psychology, 85, 220-221; importance to clinical psychology, 223

Zeitgeist: and Boring, 261; definition of, 115; prescriptions and, 109, 111, 115-116, 153